Conference of the North American Chapter of the Association for Computational Linguistics: Human Language Technologies (NAACL HLT 2015)

Student Workshop

Denver, Colorado, USA
31 May – 5 June 2015

ISBN: 978-1-5108-0447-0

Printed from e-media with permission by:

Curran Associates, Inc.
57 Morehouse Lane
Red Hook, NY 12571

Some format issues inherent in the e-media version may also appear in this print version.

Printed by Curran Associates, Inc. (2015)

For permission requests, please contact the Association for Computational Linguistics at the address below.

Association for Computational Linguistics
209 N. Eighth Street
Stroudsburg, Pennsylvania 18360

Phone: 1-570-476-8006
Fax: 1-570-476-0860

acl@aclweb.org

Additional copies of this publication are available from:

Curran Associates, Inc.
57 Morehouse Lane
Red Hook, NY 12571 USA
Phone: 845-758-0400
Fax: 845-758-2634
Email: curran@proceedings.com
Web: www.proceedings.com

Introduction

Welcome to the NAACL-HLT 2015 Student Research Workshop.

This year, we have three different kinds of papers: research papers, thesis proposals, and undergraduate research papers. Thesis proposals were intended for advanced students who have decided on a thesis topic and wish to get feedback on their proposal and broader ideas for their continuing work, while research papers describe completed work or work in progress with preliminary results. In order to encourage undergraduate research, we offered a special track for research papers where the first author is an undergraduate student.

We received a record number of submissions this year – 36 research papers, 16 thesis proposals, and 7 undergraduate research papers – making the total number of submissions 59. Out of these, we accepted 9 research papers, 11 thesis proposals, and 3 undergraduate research papers (23 accepted in total). This translates to an acceptance rate of 25% for research papers, 69% for thesis proposals, and 43% for undergraduate research papers (39% overall).

This year, all the SRW papers will be presented at the main conference poster session. In addition, each SRW paper is assigned a dedicated mentor. The mentor is an experienced researcher from academia or industry who will prepare in-depth comments and questions in advance for the poster session and will provide feedback to the student author.

Thanks to our funding sources, this year's SRW covers registration expenses and provides partial travel and/or lodging support to all student authors of the SRW papers. We gratefully acknowledge the support from the NSF, Google, Baobab and Fusemachines.

We thank our dedicated program committee members who gave constructive and detailed feedback for the student papers. We also would like to thank the NAACL-HLT 2015 organizers and local arrangement chairs – Rada Mihalcea, Joyce Chai, Anoop Sarkar, Priscilla Rasmussen, Matt Post, Adam Lopez, Annie Louis, Kevin B. Cohen, Saif M. Mohammad and Peter Ljunglöf.

Organizers

Student Chairs:

Shibamouli Lahiri, University of Michigan
Karen Mazidi, University of North Texas
Alisa Zhila, Instituto Politécnico Nacional

Faculty Advisors:

Diana Inkpen, University of Ottawa
Smaranda Muresan, Columbia University

Program Committee:

Amjad Abu-Jbara, Microsoft
Gabor Angeli, Stanford University
Yoav Artzi, University of Washington
Beata Beigman Klebanov, Educational Testing Service
Chris Biemann, TU Darmstadt
Arianna Bisazza, University of Amsterdam
Yonatan Bisk, University of Illinois Urbana-Champaign
Jordan Boyd-Graber, University of Colorado
Shu Cai, University of Southern California
Hiram Calvo, Instituto Politécnico Nacional
Asli Celikyilmaz, Microsoft
Monojit Choudhury, Microsoft Research India
Trevor Cohn, University of Melbourne
Hal Daumé III, University of Maryland
Leon Derczynski, University of Sheffield
Kevin Duh, Nara Institute of Science and Technology
Jacob Eisenstein, Georgia Institute of Technology
Aciel Eshky, University of Edinburgh
Kilian Evang, University of Groningen
Paul Felt, Brigham Young University
Michael Flor, Educational Testing Service
Thomas François, UC Louvain
Annemarie Friedrich, Saarland University
Michael Gamon, Microsoft
Qin Gao, Microsoft
Alexander Gelbukh, Instituto Politécnico Nacional
Debanjan Ghosh, Rutgers University
Amit Goyal, Yahoo Labs
Liane Guillou, University of Edinburgh
Eva Hasler, University of Edinburgh

John Henderson, MITRE Corporation
Derrick Higgins, Civis Analytics
Yuening Hu, Yahoo
Ruihong Huang, Stanford University
Héctor Jiménez-Salazar, Universidad Autónoma Metropolitana
Philipp Koehn, University of Edinburgh
Varada Kolhatkar, University of Toronto
Jonathan Kummerfeld, University of California Berkeley
Angeliki Lazaridou, University of Trento
Fei Liu, Carnegie Mellon University
Yang Liu, University of Texas Dallas
Nitin Madnani, Educational Testing Service
Mitch Marcus, University of Pennsylvania
Nisarga Markandaiah, IBM Watson
Thomas Meyer, Google Zurich
Courtney Napoles, Johns Hopkins University
Martha Palmer, University of Colorado
Ted Pedersen, University of Minnesota Duluth
Christopher Potts, Stanford University
Vinodkumar Prabhakaran, Columbia University
Rashmi Prasad, University of Wisconsin Milwaukee
Preethi Raghavan, IBM TJ Watson Research Center, Yorktown Heights NY
Owen Rambow, Columbia University
Sravana Reddy, Dartmouth College
Roi Reichart, Technion
Philip Resnik, University of Maryland
Eduardo Rodriguez, Instituto Politécnico Nacional
Kairit Sirts, Tallinn University of Technology
Thamar Solorio, University of Houston
Swapna Somasundaran, Educational Testing Service
Kapil Thadani, Columbia University
Eva Maria Vecchi, University of Cambridge
Nina Wacholder, Rutgers University
Jason Williams, Microsoft
Travis Wolfe, Johns Hopkins University
Xuchen Yao, Johns Hopkins University
Luke Zettlemoyer, University of Washington
Qiuye Zhao, University of Pennsylvania

Table of Contents

Student Research Workshop Program

Monday, June 1, 2015
18:00–21:00 Poster Session

Thesis Proposals

Reliable Lexical Simplification for Non-Native Speakers
Gustavo Paetzold

Relation extraction pattern ranking using word similarity
Konstantinos Lambrou-Latreille

Exploring Relational Features and Learning under Distant Supervision for Information Extraction Tasks
Ajay Nagesh

Entity/Event-Level Sentiment Detection and Inference
Lingjia Deng

Learning Kernels for Semantic Clustering: A Deep Approach
Ignacio Arroyo-Fernández

Narrowing the Loop: Integration of Resources and Linguistic Dataset Development with Interactive Machine Learning
Seid Muhie Yimam

Improving the Translation of Discourse Markers for Chinese into English
David Steele

Discourse and Document-level Information for Evaluating Language Output Tasks
Carolina Scarton

Lifelong Machine Learning for Topic Modeling and Beyond
Zhiyuan Chen

Bilingual lexicon extraction for a distant language pair using a small parallel corpus
Ximena Gutierrez-Vasques

Morphological Paradigms: Computational Structure and Unsupervised Learning
Jackson Lee

Cache-Augmented Latent Topic Language Models for Speech Retrieval

Jonathan Wintrode
Center for Language and Speech Processing
Johns Hopkins University
Baltimore, MD
jcwintr@cs.jhu.edu

Abstract

We aim to improve speech retrieval performance by augmenting traditional N-gram language models with different types of topic context. We present a latent topic model framework that treats documents as arising from an underlying topic sequence combined with a cache-based repetition model. We analyze our proposed model *both* for its ability to capture word repetition via the cache and for its suitability as a language model for speech recognition and retrieval. We show this model, augmented with the cache, captures intuitive repetition behavior across languages and exhibits lower perplexity than regular LDA on held out data in multiple languages. Lastly, we show that our joint model improves speech retrieval performance beyond N-grams or latent topics alone, when applied to a term detection task in all languages considered.

1 Introduction

The availability of spoken digital media continues to expand at an astounding pace. According to YouTube's publicly released statistics, between August 2013 and February 2015 content upload rates have tripled from 100 to 300 hours of video per minute (YouTube, 2015). Yet the *information* content therein, while accessible via links, tags, or other user-supplied metadata, is largely inaccessible via content search within the speech.

Speech retrieval systems typically rely on Large Vocabulary Continuous Speech Recognition (LVSCR) to generate a lattice of word hypotheses for each document, indexed for fast search (Miller and others, 2007). However, for sites like YouTube, localized in over 60 languages (YouTube, 2015), the likelihood of high accuracy speech recognition in most languages is quite low.

Our proposed solution is to focus on *topic information* in spoken language as a means of dealing with errorful speech recognition output in many languages. It has been repeatedly shown that a task like topic classification is robust to high (40-60%) word error rate systems (Peskin, 1996; Wintrode, 2014b). We would leverage the topic signal's strength for retrieval in a high volume, multilingual digital media processing environment.

The English word *topic*, defined as a particular 'subject of discourse' (Houghton-Mifflin, 1997), arises from the Greek root, $\tau o \pi o \varsigma$, meaning a physical 'place' or 'location'. However, the semantic concepts of a particular subject are not disjoint from the physical location of the words themselves.

The goal of this particular work is to jointly model two aspects of topic information, *local context* (repetition) and *broad context* (subject matter), which we previously treated in an ad hoc manner (Wintrode and Sanjeev, 2014) in a latent topic framework. We show that in doing so we can achieve better word retrieval performance than language models with only N-gram context on a diverse set of spoken languages.

2 Related Work

The use of both repetition and broad topic context have been exploited in a variety of ways by the speech recognition and retrieval communities. Cache-based or adaptive language models were

Proceedings of NAACL-HLT 2015 Student Research Workshop (SRW), pages 1–8,
Denver, Colorado, June 1, 2015.

some of the first approaches to incorporate information beyond a short N-gram history (where N is typically 3-4 words).

Cache-based models assume the probability of a word in a document d is influenced both by the global frequency of that word and N-gram context as well as by the N-gram frequencies of d (or preceding *cache* of K words). Although most words are rare at the corpus level, when they do occur, they occur in bursts. Thus a local estimate, from the *cache*, may be more reliable than the global estimate. Jelinek (1991) and Kuhn (1990) both successfully applied these types of models for speech recognition, and Rosenfeld (1994), using what he referred to as 'trigger pairs', also realized significant gains in WER. More recently, recurrent neural network language models (RNNLMs) have been introduced to capture more of these "long-term dependencies" (Mikolov et al., 2010). In terms of speech retrieval, recent efforts have looked at exploiting repeated keywords at search time, without directly modifying the recognizer (Chiu and Rudnicky, 2013; Wintrode, 2014a).

Work within the information retrieval (IR) community connects topicality with retrieval. Hearst and Plaunt (1993) reported that the "subtopic structuring" of documents can improve full-document retrieval. Topic models such as Latent Dirichlet Allocation (LDA) (Blei et al., 2003) or Probabilistic Latent Semantic Analysis (PLSA) (Hofmann, 2001) are used to the augment the document-specific language model in probabilistic, language-model based IR (Wei and Croft, 2006; Chen, 2009; Liu and Croft, 2004; Chemudugunta et al., 2007). In all these cases, topic information was helpful in boosting retrieval performance above baseline vector space or N-gram models.

Our proposed model closely resembles that from Chemudugunta et al. (2007), with our notions of broad and local context corresponding to their "general and specific" aspects. The unigram cache case of our model should correspond to their "special words" model, however we do not constrain our cache component to only unigrams.

With respect to speech recognition, Florian and Yarowsky (Florian and Yarowsky, 1999) and Khudanpur and Wu (Khudanpur and Wu, 1999) use vector-space clustering techniques to approximate the topic content of documents and augment a baseline N-gram model with topic-specific N-gram counts. Clarkson and Robinson (1997) proposed a similar application of cache and mixture models, but only demonstrate small perplexity improvements. Similar approaches use latent topic models to infer a topic mixture of the test document (soft clustering) with significant recognition error reductions (Heidel et al., 2007; Hsu and Glass, 2006; Liu and Liu, 2008; Huang and Renals, 2008). Instead of interpolating with a traditional backoff model, Chien and Chueh (2011) use topic models with and without a dynamic cache to good effect as a class-based language model.

We build on the cluster-oriented results, particularly Khudanpur and Wu (1997) and Wintrode and Khudanpur (2014), but within an explicit framework, jointly capturing both types of topic information that many have leveraged individually.

Algorithm 1 Cache-augmented generative process

```
for all t ∈ T do
  draw φ^(t) ~ Dirichlet(β)
for all d ∈ D do
  draw θ^(d) ~ Dirichlet(α)
  draw κ^(d) ~ Beta(ν_0, ν_1)
  for w_{d,i}, 1 ≤ i ≤ |d| do
    draw k_{d,i} ~ Bernoulli(κ^(d))
    if k_{d,i} = 0 then
      draw z_{d,i} ~ θ^(d)
      draw w_{d,i} ~ φ^(t=z_{d,i})
    else
      draw w_{d,i} ~ Cache(d, W_{-i})
    end if
```

3 Cache-augmented Topic Model

We propose a straightforward extension of the LDA topic model (Blei et al., 2003; Steyvers and Griffiths, 2007), allowing words to be generated *either* from a latent topic or from a document-level cache. At each word position we flip a biased coin. Based on the outcome we either generate a latent topic and then the observed word, or we pick a new word directly from the cache of already observed words. Thus we would jointly learn the underlying topics and the tendency towards repetition.

As with LDA, we assume each corpus is drawn from $\mathcal{T}$ latent topics. Each topic is denoted $\phi^{(t)}$, a multinomial random variable in the size of the vocabulary where $\phi_v^{(t)}$ is the probability $P(w_v|t)$. For each document we draw $\theta^{(d)}$, where $\theta_t^{(d)}$ is the probability $P(t|d)$.

We introduce two additional sets of variables, $\kappa^{(d)}$ and $k_{d,i}$. The state $k_{d,i}$ is a Bernoulli variable indicating whether a word $w_{d,i}$ is drawn from the cache or from the latent topic state. $\kappa^{(d)}$ is the document specific prior on the cache state $k_{d,i}$.

Algorithm 1 gives the generative process explicitly. We choose a Beta prior $\kappa^{(d)}$ for the Bernoulli variables $k_{d,i}$. As with the Dirichlet priors, this allows for a straightforward formulation of the joint probability $P(W, Z, K, \Phi, \Theta, \kappa)$, from which we derive densities for Gibbs sampling. A plate diagram is provided in Figure 1, illustrating the dependence both on latent variables and the cache of previous observations.

We implement our model as a collapsed Gibbs sampler extending Java classes from the Mallet topic modeling toolkit (McCallum, 2002). We use the Gibbs sampler for parameter estimation (training data) and inference (held-out data). We also leverage Mallet's hyperparameter re-estimation (Wallach et al., 2009), which we apply to α, β, and ν.

4 Language Modeling

Our primary goal in constructing this model is to apply it to language models for speech recognition and retrieval. Given an LVCSR system with a standard N-gram language model (LM), we now describe how we incorporate the inferred topic and cache model parameters of a new document into the base LM for subsequent recognition tasks *on that specific document.*

We begin by estimating model parameters on a training corpus: topics $\phi^{(t)}$, cache proportions $\kappa^{(d)}$, and hyperparameters, α, β, and ν (the Beta hyperparameter). In our experiments we restrict the training set to the LVCSR acoustic and language model training. This restriction is required by the Babel task, not the model. Using other corpora or text resources certainly should be considered for other tasks.

To apply the model during KWS, we first decode a new audio document d with the base LM, P_L and extract the most likely observed word sequence W for inference. The inference process gives us the estimates for $\theta^{(d)}$ and $\kappa^{(d)}$, which we then use to compute *document-specific* and cache-augmented language models.

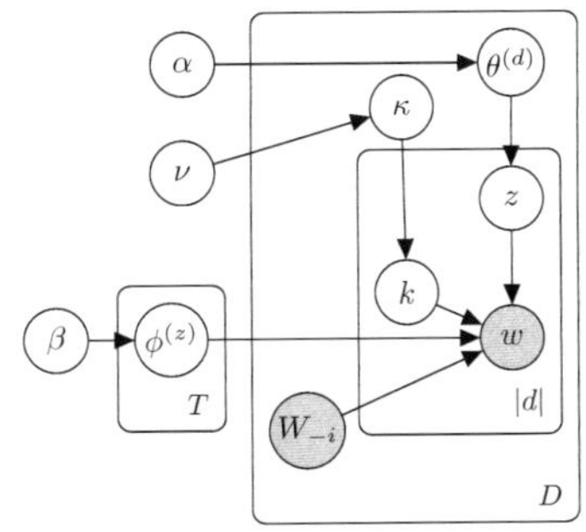

Figure 1: Cache-augmented model plate diagram.

From a language modeling perspective we treat the multinomials $\phi^{(t)}$ as unigram LM's and use the inferred topic proportions $\theta^{(d)}$ as a set of mixture weights. From these we compute the document-specific unigram model for d (Eqn. 1). This serves to capture what we have referred to as the *broad* topic context.

We incorporate both P_d as well as the cache P_c (local context) into the base model P_L using linear interpolation of probabilities. Word histories are denoted h_i for brevity. For our experiments we first combine P_d with the N-gram model (Eqn. 2). We then interpolate with the cache model to get a joint topic and cache language model (Eqn. 4).

$$P_d(w_i) = \sum_{t=1}^{T} \theta_t^{(d)} \cdot \phi_i^{(t)} \quad (1)$$

$$P_{Ld}(w_i) = \lambda P_d(w_i) + (1-\lambda) \cdot P_L(w_i) \quad (2)$$

$$P_{dc}(w_i) = \kappa^{(d)} P_c(w_i) + (1-\kappa^{(d)}) \cdot P_d(w_i) \quad (3)$$

$$P_{Ldc}(w_i|h_i) = \kappa^{(d)} P_c(w_i|h_i) + (1-\kappa^{(d)}) \cdot P_{Ld}(w_i|h_i) \quad (4)$$

We expect the inferred document cache probability $\kappa^{(d)}$ to serve as a natural interpolation weight when combining document-specific unigram model P_{dc} and cache. We consider alternatives to per-document $\kappa^{(d)}$ as part of the speech retrieval evaluation (Section 6) and can show that our model's estimate is indeed effective.

Language	50t	100t	150t	200t
Tagalog	0.41	0.29	0.22	0.16
Vietnamese	0.51	0.39	0.29	0.22
Zulu	0.33	0.26	0.21	0.16
Tamil	0.36	027	0.18	0.14

Table 1: Mean $\kappa^{(d)}$ inferred from 10 hour development data, by number of latent topics

5 Model Analysis

Before looking at the model in terms of retrieval performance (Section 6), here we aim to examine how our model captures the repetition of each corpus and how well it functions as a language model (cf. Equation 3) in terms of perplexity.

To focus on language models for speech retrieval in the limited resource setting, we build and evaluate our model under the IARPA Babel Limited Language Pack (LP), No Target Audio Reuse (NTAR) condition (Harper, 2011). We selected the Tagalog, Vietnamese, Zulu, and Tamil corpora[1] to expose our model to as diverse a set of languages as possible (in terms of morphology, phonology, language family, etc., in line with the Babel program goals).

The Limited LP includes a 10 hour training set (audio and transcripts) which we use for building acoustic and language models. We also estimate the parameters for our topic model from the same training data. The Babel corpora contain spontaneous conversational telephone speech, but without the constrained topic prompts of LDC's Fisher collections we would expect a sparse collection of topics. Yet for retrieval we are nonetheless able to leverage the information.

We estimate parameters $\phi^{(t)}$, $\kappa^{(d)}$, α, β, and ν on the training transcripts in each language, then use these parameters to infer $\theta^{(d)}$ (topic proportions) and $\kappa^{(d)}$ (cache usage) for each document in the held-out set. We use the inferred $\kappa^{(d)}$ and $\theta^{(d)}$ to perform the language model interpolation (Eqns. 3, 4). But also, the mean of the inferred $\kappa^{(d)}$ values for a corpus ought to provide a snapshot of the amount of repetition within.

Two trends emerge when we examine the mean over $\kappa^{(d)}$ by language. First, as shown in Table 1, the more latent topics are used, the lower the inferred κ values. Regardless of the absolute value, we see that κ for Vietnamese is consistently higher than the other languages. This fits our intuition about the languages given that the Vietnamese transcripts had syllable-level word units and we would expect to see more repetition.

Secondly we consider *which* words are drawn from the cache versus the topics during the inference process. Examining the final sampling state, we count how often each word in the vocabulary is drawn from the cache (where $k_{d,i} = 1$). Intuitively, this count is highly correlated ($\rho > 0.95$) with the corpus frequency of each word (cf. Figure 2). That is, cache states are assigned to word types most likely to repeat.

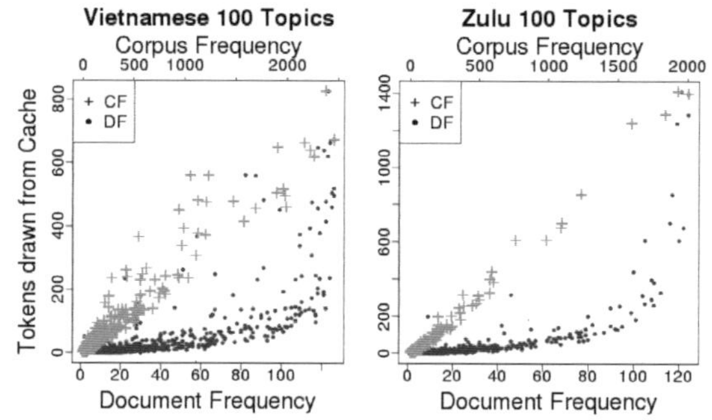

Figure 2: Cache and corpus frequencies for each word type in Vietnamese and Zulu training corpora.

5.1 Perplexity

While our measurements of cache usage corresponds to intuition, our primary goal is to construct useful language models. After estimating parameters on the training corpora, we infer $\kappa^{(d)}$ and $\theta^{(d)}$ then measure perplexity using document-specific language models on the development set.

We compute perplexity on the topic unigram mixtures according to P_d and P_{dc} (Eqns.1 & 3). Here we do not interpolate with the base N-gram LM, so as to compare only unigram mixtures. Table 2 gives the perplexity for standard LDA (P_d only) and for our model with and without the cache added (κLDA$'$ and κLDA respectively).

With respect to perplexity, interpolating with the cache (κLDA) provides a significant boost in perplexity for all languages and values of $\mathcal{T}$. In general,

[1]Releases babel106b-v0.2g, babel107b-v0.7, babel206b-v0.1e, and babel204b-v1.1b, respectively

Language	T	LDA	κLDA$'$	κLDA
Tagalog	50	142.90	163.30	**134.43**
	100	136.63	153.99	**132.35**
	150	139.76	146.08	**130.47**
	200	128.05	141.12	**129.94**
Vietnamese	50	257.94	283.52	**217.30**
	100	243.51	263.03	**210.05**
	150	232.60	245.75	**205.59**
	200	223.82	234.44	**204.25**
Zulu	50	**183.53**	251.52	203.56
	100	**179.44**	267.42	217.11
	150	**174.79**	269.01	223.90
	200	**175.65**	252.03	217.89
Tamil	50	**273.08**	356.40	283.82
	100	**265.02**	369.18	297.68
	150	**259.42**	361.79	301.92
	200	**236.30**	341.32	298.26

Table 2: Perplexities of topic unigram mixtures on held-out data, with and without cache.

perplexity decreases as the number of latent topics increases, excepting certain Zulu and Tamil models. For Tagalog and Vietnamese our cache-augmented model outperforms standard LDA model in terms of perplexity. However, as we will see in the next section, the lowest perplexity models are not necessarily the best in terms of retrieval performance.

6 Speech Retrieval

We evaluate the utility of our topic language model for speech retrieval via the term detection, or keyword search (KWS) task. Term detection accuracy is the primary evaluation metric for the Babel program. We use the topic and cache-augmented language models (Eqn. 4) to improve the speech recognition stage of the term detection pipeline, increasing overall search accuracy by 0.5 to 1.7% absolute over a typical N-gram language model.

The term detection task is this: given a corpus of audio documents and a list of terms (words or phrases), locate all occurrences of the key terms in the audio. The resulting list of detections is scored using Term Weighted Value (TWV) metric. TWV is a cost-value trade-off between the miss probability, $P(miss)$, and false alarm probability, $P(FA)$, averaged over all keywords (NIST, 2006). For comparison with previously published results, we score against the IARPA-supplied evaluation keywords.

We train acoustic and language models (LMs) on the 10 hour training set using the Kaldi toolkit (Povey and others, 2011), according to the training recipe described in detail by Trmal et al. (2014). While Kaldi produces different flavors of acoustic models, we report results using the hybrid HMM-DNN (deep neural net) acoustic models, trained with a minimum phone error (MPE) criterion, and based on PLP (perceptual linear prediction) features augmented with pitch. All results use 3-gram LMs with Good-Turing (Tagalog, Zulu, Tamil) or Modified Kneser-Ney (Vietnamese) smoothing. This AM/LM combination (our baseline) has consistently demonstrated state-of-the art performance for a single system on the Babel task.

As described, we estimate our model parameters $\phi^{(t)}$, $\kappa^{(d)}$, α, β, and ν from the training transcripts. We decode the development corpus with the baseline models, then infer $\theta^{(d)}$ and $\kappa^{(d)}$ from the first pass output. In principle we simply compute P_{Ldc} for each document and re-score the first pass output, then search for keywords.

Practical considerations for cache language models are, for example, just how big should the cache be, or should it decay, where words further away from the current word are discounted proportionally. In the Kaldi framework, speech is processed in segments (i.e. conversation turns). Current tools do not allow one to vary the language model within a particular segment (dynamically). With that in mind, our KWS experiments construct a different language model (P_{Ldc}) for each segment, where P_c is computed from all other segments in the current document except that being processed.

6.1 Results

We can show, by re-scoring LCVSR output with a cache-augmented topic LM, that both the document-specific topic (P_d) and cache (P_c) information together improve our overall KWS performance in each language, up to 1.7% absolute.

Figure 3 illustrates search accuracy (TWV) for each language under various settings for T. It also captures alternatives to using $\kappa^{(d)}$ as an interpolation weight for the cached unigrams. To illustrate this contrast we substituted the training mean κ_{train} instead of $\kappa^{(d)}$ as the interpolation weight when computing P_{Ldc} (Eqn 4). Except for Zulu, the inferred

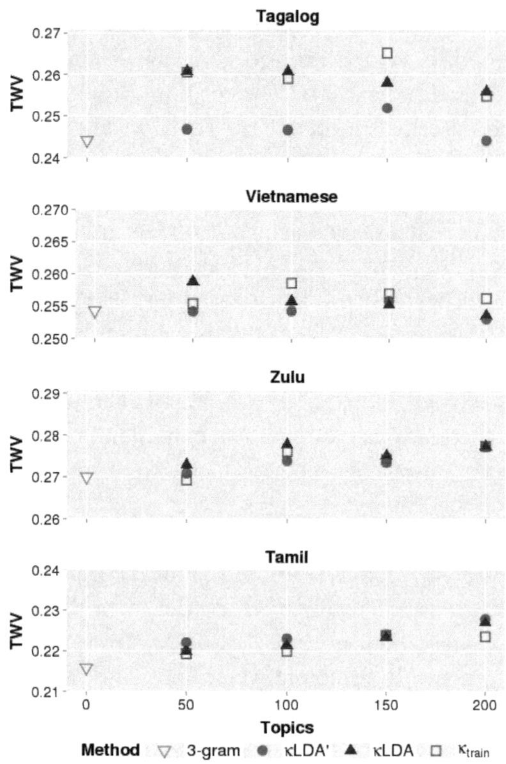

Figure 3: KWS accuracy for different choices of $\mathcal{T}$

$\kappa^{(d)}$ were more effective, but not hugely so.

The effect of latent topics $\mathcal{T}$ on search accuracy also varies depending on language, as does the overall effect of incorporating the cache in addition to latent topics (κLDA$'$ vs. κLDA). For example, in Tagalog, we observe most of the improvement over N-grams from the cache information, whereas in Tamil, the cache provided no additional information over latent topics.

The search accuracy for the best systems from Figure 3 are shown in Table 3 with corresponding choice of $\mathcal{T}$. Effects on WER was mixed under the cache model, improving Zulu from 67.8 to 67.6% and degrading Tagalog from 60.8 to 61.1%, with Vietnamese and Tamil unchanged.

7 Conclusions and Future Work

With our initial effort in formulating model combining latent topics with a cache-based language model, we believe we have presented a model that estimates both informative and useful parameters from the data and supports improved speech retrieval performance. The results presented here reinforce the conclusion that topics and repetition, *broad* and *local* context, are complementary sources of information for speech language modeling tasks.

Language	$\mathcal{T}$	3-gram	κLDA$'$	κLDA
Tagalog	50	0.244	0.247	**0.261**
Vietnamese	50	0.254	0.254	**0.259**
Zulu	100	0.270	0.274	**0.278**
Tamil	200	0.216	**0.228**	0.227

Table 3: Best KWS accuracy (TWV) is each language.

We hope to address two particular limitations of our model in the near future. First, all of our improvements are obtained adding unigram probabilities to a 3-gram language model. We would naturally want to extend our model to explicitly capture the cache and topic behavior of N-grams.

Secondly, our models are restricted by the first pass output of the LVCSR system. Keywords not present in the first pass cannot be recalled by a rescoring only approach. An alternative would be to use our model to re-decode the audio and realize subsequently larger gains. Given that our re-scoring model worked sufficiently well across four fundamentally different languages, we are optimistic this would be the case.

Acknowledgements

This work was partially supported by the Intelligence Advanced Research Projects Activity (IARPA) via Department of Defense U.S. Army Research Laboratory (DoD / ARL) contract number W911NF-12-C-0015. The U.S. Government is authorized to reproduce and distribute reprints for Governmental purposes notwithstanding any copyright annotation thereon. Disclaimer: The views and conclusions contained herein are those of the authors and should not be interpreted as necessarily representing the official policies or endorsements, either expressed or implied, of IARPA, DoD/ARL, or the U.S. Government.

We would also like to thank all of the reviewers for their insightful and helpful comments, and above all their time.

References

David M Blei, Andrew Y Ng, and Michael I Jordan. 2003. Latent Dirichlet Allocation. In *JMLR*, volume 3, pages 993–1022. JMLR.org.

Chaitanya Chemudugunta, Padhraic Smyth, and Steyvers Mark. 2007. Modeling General and Specific Aspects of Documents with a Probabilistic Topic Model. In *Advances in Neural Information Processing Systems 19: Proceedings of the 2006 Conference*, volume 19, page 241. Mit Press.

Berlin Chen. 2009. Latent Topic Modelling of Word Co-occurence Information for Spoken Document Retrieval. In *Proc. of ICASSP*, pages 3961–3964. IEEE.

Jen-Tzung Chien and Chuang-Hua Chueh. 2011. Dirichlet Class Language Models for Speech Recognition. *Audio, Speech, and Language Processing, IEEE Transactions on*, 19(3):482–495.

Justin Chiu and Alexander Rudnicky. 2013. Using conversational word bursts in spoken term detection. In *Proc. of Interspeech*, pages 2247–2251. ISCA.

Kenneth Ward Church and William A Gale. 1995. Poisson Mixtures. *Natural Language Engineering*, 1(2):163–190.

Philip R Clarkson and Anthony J Robinson. 1997. Language Model Adaptation Using Mixtures and an Exponentially Decaying Cache. In *Proc. of ICASSP*, volume 2, pages 799–802. IEEE.

Radu Florian and David Yarowsky. 1999. Dynamic Nonlocal Language Modeling via Hierarchical Topic-based Adaptation. In *Proc. of ACL*, pages 167–174. ACL.

Mary Harper. 2011. Babel BAA. `http://www.iarpa.gov/index.php/research-programs/babel/baa`.

Marti A Hearst and Christian Plaunt. 1993. Subtopic Structuring for Full-length Document Access. In *Proc. of SIGIR*, pages 59–68. ACM.

Aaron Heidel, Hung-an Chang, and Lin-shan Lee. 2007. Language Model Adaptation Using Latent Dirichlet Allocation and an Efficient Topic Inference Algorithm. In *Proc. of Interspeech*. ICSA.

Thomas Hofmann. 2001. Unsupervised Learning by Probabilistic Latent Semantic Analysis. *Machine Learning*, 42(1):177–196.

Houghton-Mifflin. 1997. *The American Heritage College Dictionary*. Houghton Mifflin.

Bo-June Paul Hsu and James Glass. 2006. Style & Topic Language Model Adaptation Using HMM-LDA. In *Proc. of EMNLP*, pages 373–381. ACL.

Songfang Huang and Steve Renals. 2008. Unsupervised Language Model Adaptation Based on Topic and Role Information in Multiparty Meetings. In *Proc. of Interspeech*. ICSA.

Frederick Jelinek, Bernard Merialdo, Salim Roukos, and Martin Strauss. 1991. A Dynamic Language Model for Speech Recognition. *HLT*, 91:293–295.

Sanjeev Khudanpur and Jun Wu. 1999. A Maximum Entropy Language Model Integrating N-grams and Topic Dependencies for Conversational Speech Recognition. In *Proc. of ICASSP*, volume 1, pages 553–556. IEEE.

Roland Kuhn and Renato De Mori. 1990. A Cache-based Natural Language Model for Speech Recognition. *Transactions on Pattern Analysis and Machine Intelligence*, 12(6):570–583.

Xiaoyong Liu and W Bruce Croft. 2004. Cluster-based Retrieval Using Language Models. In *Proc. of SIGIR*, pages 186–193. ACM.

Yang Liu and Feifan Liu. 2008. Unsupervised Language Model Adaptation via Topic Modeling Based on Named Entity Hypotheses. In *Proc. of ICASSP*, pages 4921–4924. IEEE.

Andrew Kachites McCallum. 2002. MALLET: A Machine Learning for Language Toolkit. `http://mallet.cs.umass.edu`.

Tomas Mikolov, Martin Karafiát, Lukas Burget, Jan Cernockỳ, and Sanjeev Khudanpur. 2010. Recurrent Neural Network Based Language Model. In *Proc. of Interspeech*. ICSA.

David Miller et al. 2007. Rapid and Accurate Spoken Term Detection. In *Proc. of Interspeech*. ICSA.

NIST. 2006. The Spoken Term Detection (STD) 2006 Evaluation Plan. `http://www.itl.nist.gov/iad/mig/tests/std/2006/docs/std06-evalplan-v10.pdf`. [Online; accessed 28-Feb-2013].

Barbara et al. Peskin. 1996. Improvements in Switchboard Recognition and Topic Identification. In *Proc. of ICASSP*, volume 1, pages 303–306. IEEE.

Daniel Povey et al. 2011. The Kaldi Speech Recognition Toolkit. In *Proc. of ASRU Workshop*. IEEE.

Ronald Rosenfeld. 1994. *Adaptive Statistical Language Modeling: a Maximum Entropy Approach*. Ph.D. thesis, CMU.

Mark Steyvers and Tom Griffiths. 2007. Probabilistic Topic Models. *Handbook of Latent Semantic Analysis*, 427(7):424–440.

Jan et al. Trmal. 2014. A Keyword Search System Using Open Source Software. In *Proc. of Spoken Language Technoloty Workshop*. IEEE.

Hanna M Wallach, David M Mimno, and Andrew McCallum. 2009. Rethinking LDA: Why Priors Matter. In *Proc. of NIPS*, volume 22, pages 1973–1981. NIPS.

Xing Wei and W Bruce Croft. 2006. LDA-based Document Models for Ad-hoc Retrieval. In *Proc. of SIGIR*, pages 178–185. ACM.

Jonathan Wintrode and Khudanpur Sanjeev. 2014. Combining Local and Broad Topic Context to Improve Term Detection. In *Proc. of Spoken Language Technoloty Workshop*. IEEE.

Jonathan Wintrode. 2014a. Can you Repeat that? Using Word Repetition to Improve Spoken Term Detection. In *Proc. of ACL*. ACL.

Jonathan Wintrode. 2014b. Limited Resource Term Detection For Effective Topic Identification of Speech. In *Proc. of ICASSP*. IEEE.

YouTube. 2015. Statistics - YouTube. `http://www.youtube.com/yt/press/statistics.html`, February.

Reliable Lexical Simplification for Non-Native Speakers

Gustavo Henrique Paetzold
Department of Computer Science
University of Sheffield
Sheffield, United Kingdom
ghpaetzold1@sheffield.ac.uk

Abstract

Lexical Simplification is the task of modifying the lexical content of complex sentences in order to make them simpler. Due to the lack of reliable resources available for the task, most existing approaches have difficulties producing simplifications which are grammatical and that preserve the meaning of the original text. In order to improve on the state-of-the-art of this task, we propose user studies with non-native speakers, which will result in new, sizeable datasets, as well as novel ways of performing Lexical Simplification. The results of our first experiments show that new types of classifiers, along with the use of additional resources such as spoken text language models, produce the state-of-the-art results for the Lexical Simplification task of SemEval-2012.

1 Introduction

Lexical Simplification (LS) is often perceived as the simplest of all Text Simplification sub-tasks. Its goal is to replace the complex words and expressions of a given sentence with simpler alternatives of equivalent meaning. However, this is a very challenging task as the substitution must preserve both original meaning and grammaticality of the sentence being simplified.

However, this is a very challenging task as the substitution needs to ensure grammaticality and meaning preservation. Most LS strategies in the literature are structured according to the pipeline illustrated in Figure 1, which is an adaptation of the one proposed by (Shardlow, 2014).

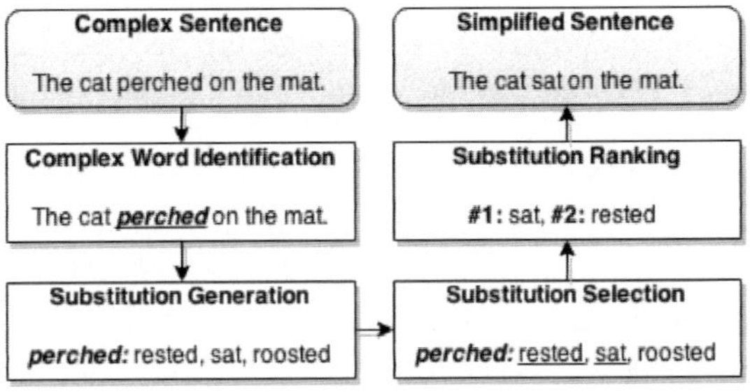

Figure 1: Lexical Simplification pipeline

In this thesis, we intend to identify and address the major limitations of the approaches in the literature with respect to each step of the LS pipeline of Figure 1. In an effort to create new reliable datasets for LS and to unveil information about the needs of those who can most benefit from Text Simplification, we propose new user studies with non-native speakers. We also present novel modelling strategies for each step of the LS pipeline with respect to the limitations of the approaches in the literature.

2 Lexical Simplification: A Survey

To our knowledge, there are no examples of studies which compare the performance of LS approaches in their entirety. For this reason, we choose instead to discuss the merits and limitations of strategies used by authors to address each step of the LS pipeline.

2.1 Complex Word Identification

The goal of Complex Word Identification (CWI) is to identify which words in a given sentence need to be simplified. Some authors, such as (Devlin and Tait, 1998), (Carroll et al., 1998) and (Carroll et al.,

Proceedings of NAACL-HLT 2015 Student Research Workshop (SRW), pages 9–16,
Denver, Colorado, June 1, 2015.

1999) choose to not address this task, but as shown in (Paetzold and Specia, 2013), this can lead to the production of incoherent and/or ungrammatical sentences. Several categories of CWI strategies can be found in literature:

Lexicon-Based Explore the hypothesis that, if a word w is part of a lexicon L of complex/simple words, then it does/does not need to be simplified. While (Watanabe and Junior, 2009) and (Aluisio and Gasperin, 2010) use as lexicons books for children, (Elhadad and Sutaria, 2007), (Deléger and Zweigenbaum, 2009) and (Elhadad, 2006) use a database of complex medical terms. Acquiring lexicons can be easy, but they must correlate with the needs of the target audience in question.

Threshold-Based Explore the hypothesis that a threshold t over a word metric $M(w)$ can separate complex from simple words. The most frequently used metrics are word frequency (Bott et al., 2012), (Leroy et al., 2013) and word length (Keskisärkkä, 2012). However, the corpus evaluation of (Bott et al., 2012) shows that determining such threshold t is impractical.

User-Driven Such approaches allow the users themselves to select which words are complex, and simplify them on demand. Although the results obtained by (Devlin and Unthank, 2006) and (Rello et al., 2013) show that this is a very effective strategy, it might be difficult for it to be used in smaller devices, such as phones.

Classification Methods Train classifiers which discriminate between complex and simple words. For English, the SVM approach of (Shardlow, 2013a) is the only example in literature. Although their study shows that their SVM is not able to outperform neither a threshold-based approach or a "simplify everything" method, we believe the results obtained are controversial.

In another study conducted by the same author (Shardlow, 2014) it was found that replacing words which do not need simplification is one of the most frequent mistakes made by naive LS approaches, and hence we believe the results obtained by (Shardlow, 2013a) do not reveal the potential of classification methods in CWI. Also, the dataset used the experiments of (Shardlow, 2013a) was created automatically and did not attempt to model the needs of any particular target audience. A more substantial comparative study between multiple distinct machine learning methods over a more carefully crafted corpus could be a major milestone in the development of more efficient CWI approaches.

2.2 Substitution Generation

The Substitution Generation (SG) task consists in acquiring candidate substitutions for the complex words in a sentence. This task have been approached by authors in two different ways:

Querying Linguistic Databases Resources such as WordNet (Fellbaum, 1998) and UMLS (Bodenreider, 2004) provide large word ontologies, and have been largely used even in modern contributions. The approaches of (Devlin and Tait, 1998), (Sinha, 2012), (Leroy et al., 2013), (Chen et al., 2012), (Elhadad, 2006) and (Nunes et al., 2013) are some examples. The study of (Shardlow, 2014), however, shows that over 42% of the mistakes made by the approach of (Carroll et al., 1998) are caused by WordNet not having simpler synonyms for complex words. Using such resources also limits the cross-lingual capabilities of the approach, since most of those resources are restricted to one or very few languages.

Automatic Generation Consists in automatically generating pairs of related words and paraphrases. The works of (Elhadad and Sutaria, 2007), (Kauchak and Barzilay, 2006) and (Deléger and Zweigenbaum, 2009) focus on extracting paraphrases from comparable documents. The methods of (Paetzold and Specia, 2013), (Feblowitz and Kauchak, 2013), and(Horn et al., 2014) extract pairs of similar expressions from a aligned sentences from Wikipedia and Simple Wikipedia. But although such approaches do not need linguistic databases, they require for other resources, such as parallel corpora, which are also scarce. They can also suffer for extracting too many meaningless substitutions, such as observed in (Paetzold and Specia, 2013).

In order to solve the cross-lingual problem, an SG approach would have to be able to find substitutions by exploiting only resources which are either abundant in most languages or easy to produce. In Section 3 we discuss how we attempt to address this problem.

2.3 Substitution Selection

Substitution Selection (SS) is the task of determining which substitutions fit the context in which a complex word appears, and hence ensuring meaning preservation. SS have been addressed by authors in three ways:

Word Sense Disambiguation Determine the sense of a complex word in a target sentence, and then filter substitutions which do not share such sense. The approaches of (Sedding and Kazakov, 2004) and (Nunes et al., 2013) have proven to be successful in SS alone, but have not been evaluated in practice. The main limitation of this strategy is that it relies on manually constructed sense databases, which are scarce.

Adapted Disambiguation Use surrogate classes to discriminate between the meanings of an ambiguous word. The words' POS tags are used in the works of (Aluisio and Gasperin, 2010), (Yamamoto, 2013) and (Paetzold and Specia, 2013). While using POS tags may help with words of more than one grammatical type, it does not solve the problem of highly ambiguous words.

Semantic Similarity Estimate the semantic similarity between words and verify if they are replaceable. In (Keskisärkkä, 2012) is employed a simple approach: if a pair of words has a synonymy coefficient higher than a threshold, they are replaceable. This approach, however, requires for a database of synonymy levels. The approach of (Biran et al., 2011) solves that by representing the semantic context of words with word vectors estimated over large corpora, then using the cosine distance between vectors as its semantic dissimilarity.

We did not find mentions of Machine Learning methods being applied to SS. Such methods have been used to produce state-of-the-art results in many classification tasks, and hence modelling SS as a classification problem can be a promising strategy.

2.4 Substitution Ranking

Consists in deciding which substitution is the simplest of the ones available. The LS task of SemEval 2012 brought a lot of visibility to the task, and many authors still visit this subject to this day. The three most efficient strategies found in literature are:

Frequency-based Explore the intuition that the more frequently a word is used, the simpler it is. Most authors use raw frequencies from large corpora (Keskisärkkä, 2012), (Leroy et al., 2013), (Aluisio and Gasperin, 2010), (Nunes et al., 2013) or the Kucera-Francis coefficient (Rudell, 1993), (Devlin and Tait, 1998), (Carroll et al., 1998). Although (Brysbaert and New, 2009) points out several issues with the Kucera-Francis coefficient, the results of SemEval 2012 (Specia et al., 2012) show that raw frequencies from the Google 1T corpus outperform almost all other approaches.

Measuring Simplicity Elaborate metrics to represent the simplicity of a word. The metric of (Sinha, 2012) considers the word's length, number of senses and frequency, and have tied in 2nd place in SemEval 2012 with the Google 1T baseline. The other examples in literature, (Biran et al., 2011) and (Bott et al., 2012), were published before SemEval 2012, and hence have not yet been compared to other approaches.

Linear Scoring Functions Rank candidates based on a linear scoring function over various metrics, such as frequency and word length. This strategy is used by the approach that placed 1st in SemEval 2012 (Jauhar and Specia, 2012).

In (Shardlow, 2014) it is shown that word frequencies from spoken text corpora have great potential in SR. In Section 3.4 we describe an experiment which reveals the potential of such resources.

3 Planning and Preliminary Results

In the following Sections, we discuss which challenges we aim to address in the near future, and briefly describe the solutions we intend explore.

3.1 User Studies and Datasets

As pointed out in Section 2, the scarcity of user studies about audiences that may benefit from LS compel authors to treat simplification as a generalised process, forcing them to use datasets such as the Simple Wikipedia, which can be edited by anyone.

Since we do not believe this ideal, we intend to conduct an array of user studies with non-native speakers. We chose such audience because of three main reasons:

Demand Unfamiliarity with a language is not a medical condition that can be cured, and hence such audience is not likely to disappear in the near future.

Convenience Conducting studies with ill or young subjects needs to be done within various ethical constraints, and can be both expensive and time consuming. Although the needs of these audiences should also be addressed, hiring non-native speakers is much easier, and we believe they fit best our time and resource constraints.

Diversity Statistics show that there is a lot of age, nationality and education level diversity among the non-native speakers (Austin et al., 2006). Such diversity allows for us to investigate several interesting hypothesis regarding possible correlations between the subjects' characteristics and difficulty with certain types of words.

We propose two initial user studies:

Identifying Complex Words In this user study, subjects select which words from a given sentence they do not understand the meaning of. From this study we hope to better understand what types of words are challenging for non-native speakers.

It is very important for a reliable Complex Word Identification dataset to be made available in literature. To our knowledge, there is only one contribution in literature that compares different CWI approaches (Shardlow, 2013a), and since the dataset used was not created with respect to the needs of a specific target audience, the results obtained are not very informative.

This study is already being conducted. Several volunteers of various nationalities were asked to select which words they find complex in 40 English sentences each, of which 10 are part of a set which overlaps between 5 volunteers and 30 are unique. The sentences vary between 20 and 40 words in length, and were extracted from 3 distinct sources: the CW corpus (Shardlow, 2013b), the LexMturk corpus (Horn et al., 2014) and Wikipedia (Kauchak, 2013). From the CW and LexMturk corpora were extracted 231 and 269 non-spurious sentences, respectively, of which exactly 1 word is deemed complex by an anonymous annotator (more specifically, a Wikipedia editor). From Wikipedia were extracted 11945 sentences which were aligned to an identical sentence from Simple Wikipedia. By selecting such sentences, we hope to be able to judge whether or not those resources can be reliably used for the training of Lexical Simplification approaches for non-native speakers.

So far, 51 volunteers participated, who annotated a total of $2,040$ sentences. A total of $1,261$ distinct complex words ($1,597$ total) were identified, 12% of $10,650$ distinct words ($53,125$ total). The volunteers have distinct education levels (8% High School, 57% Undergraduate and 35% Postgraduate), English proficiency levels (11% Advanced, 18% Pre-Advanced, 18% Upper-Intermediate, 37% Intermediate, 14% Pre-Intermediate, 2% Elementary), and have ages varying between 17 and 38 years old (averaging 24 years old).

Selecting the Simplest Candidate We intend to find out what are the key features taken into consideration by non-native speakers on determining which is the simplest word that fits a given context. Just like in the case of Complex Word Identification, we believe that the creation of a reliable dataset for Substitution Ranking is very important.

The only dataset developed specifically for this purpose is the one presented in SemEval 2012. But since the rankings were produced by only 5 non-native annotators, there are a various examples of ties between two candidate substitutions. Also, all subjects were skilled speakers of the English language, which means that, at best, the dataset captures the LS needs of an audience which may not need LS at all. With a larger dataset annotated by more subjects of the same target audience, we will be able to have a more reliable resource to create novel Substitution Ranking approaches.

3.2 Complex Word Identification Methods

We intend to, based on the new datasets produced in our user studies, propose and evaluate the efficiency of multiple different methods of Complex Word Identification. The methods we intend to evaluate are:

Lexicon-Based Approaches We will compile a selection of corpora and see whether or not we can build lexicons from them which separate complex from simple words. The Simple Wikipedia (Horn et al., 2014) and the SUBTLEX corpus (Brysbaert and New, 2009) are some examples.

Threshold-Based Approaches There are multiple metrics which we plan to use in order to train a threshold-based complex word identifier, some of them are: word frequency in a given corpus, word length, number of syllables, familiarity and age of acquisition.

Machine Learning Assisted By combining metrics and lexicons, we can train many different classification systems by using Machine Learning methods. Support Vector Machines, Gaussian Processes and Decision Trees are some Machine Learning methods which we intend to test on Complex Word Identification.

3.3 Substitution Generation and Selection

We propose an entirely new setup for joint modelling Substitution Generation and Selection. Our approach consists in training classifiers capable of deciding which words w_s of a vocabulary V can replace a target word w_c in a sentence s.

Although this seems like a very challenging task, such an approach could be a very powerful tool for LS. It could possibly dismiss entirely the need of using parallel corpora or linguistic databases for such tasks, and hence provide a cost-effective strategy for LS approaches to be ported to multiple languages. We suggest a two-step solution for this task:

1. Define a set $G \subseteq V$ composed by all words w_s from vocabulary V that can replace a word w_c in sentence s without compromising its grammaticality.

2. Define a set $M \subseteq V$ composed by all words w_s from set G that express the same meaning of w_c in sentence s.

Once set M is determined, one can then use a Substitution Ranking method to select which one of them is the simplest. To create a dataset for this task, we plan to hire volunteer native speakers of the English language to manually judge which words can be part of G and M for a large array of different contexts. The user study data will be composed by several automatically generated substitutions for a set of 50 complex words manually selected from the ones produced in the Complex Word Identification study.

3.4 Substitution Ranking

The findings of the Lexical Simplification Task of SemEval 2012 (Specia et al., 2012) have shown that ranking substitution candidates with respect to their simplicity is not an easy task. In order to improve on the state-of-the-art of Substitution Ranking, we intend to explore the usage of spoken textual content. As discussed in (Brysbaert and New, 2009), frequencies extracted from corpora of spoken text, such as subtitles, tend to correlate better with word familiarity than frequencies of other sources, given that the text in subtitles is mostly composed of speech excerpts from character interactions similar to the ones that frequently occur in real life. In order to evaluate their potential, we conducted a preliminary experiment.

Goal In this experiment, we aim to answer the following question: *Can a language model of spoken text be used to outperform state-of-the-art Substitution Ranking approaches?*

Datasets To build a corpus of spoken text, we have parsed 13 HTML lists of movies and series for children created by IMDB[1] users. A total of $1,793$ IMDB IDs of distinct movies and series were gathered. We then used such IDs to query the OpenSubtitles[2] API in search of subtitles for them. Since their API imposes a limit of 100 downloads per day, so far we were only able to collect subtitles of 163 movies and series. By removing the annotations from the files downloaded, we compiled a corpus of $2,103,237$ sentences. For testing, we chose the SemEval $2,012$ corpus, which contains 300 training instances and $1,710$ test instances. Each instance is composed of a sentence, a target word to be simplified, and a list of candidate substitutions.

Approach To rank the candidate substitutions, we propose a novel binary classification setup for the task. For each training instance, we assign the label

[1] http://www.imdb.com

[2] http://www.opensubtitles.org

1 to the highest ranked candidate, and 0 to the remaining ones. We then train a linear classifier over the data to learn ranking weights for the selected features. In testing, we rank substitution candidates according to their distance to the decision boundary: the furthest they are from the "negative" region, the simpler they are.

Our feature set is composed by 9 different collocational features. Each collocational feature of a candidate substitution c in context s is the log probability produced by KenLM (Heafield et al., 2013), given the language model of a certain corpus, of an n-gram $s_{i-l}^{i-1}\ c\ s_{i+1}^{i+r}$, where i is the position of the target complex word in s, and both l and r are token windows in the interval $[0:2]$. If l and r are 0, then the collocational feature says respect to the probability of candidate c independent of context s.

Evaluation Metrics We have chosen the TRnk and *recall-at-n* measures proposed by (Specia et al., 2012) to estimate the performance of our approach. The TRnk calculates the ratio with which a given approach has correctly ranked at least one of the highest ranked substitutions on the gold-standard, while *recall-at-n* measures the coverage of correctly ranked candidates until position $1 \leq n \leq 3$. The reason for using such metrics instead of a ranking score is that we believe they best represent the goal of the task in practice, which is selecting the simplest substitution possible for a complex word.

Results Table 1 shows a performance comparison between the highest ranking approach of SemEval 2012 and our novel strategy trained with 10-fold cross validation over the training set. We extract collocational features from 4 distinct corpora: our corpus of IMDB subtitles (SubIMDB), the Simple Wikipedia corpus (Horn et al., 2014), composed of $505,254$ sentences, the SUBTLEX corpus (Brysbaert and New, 2009), composed of $6,043,188$ sentences taken from assorted subtitles, and the concatenation of SubIMDB and SUBTLEX.

The results show that our strategy outperforms the former state-of-the-art approach of SemEval 2012 by around 5% in TRank and 3% in *recall-at-*1. The *recall-at-*2 and 3 results, although lower than SemEval's best, showcase not a limitation, but rather an advantage of our binary classification setup: by focusing on the task's goal in practice, we are able

Table 1: TRank and *recall-at-n* results obtained

Corpus	TRnk	n=1	n=2	n=3
Best SemEval	0.602	0.575	**0.689**	**0.769**
IMDB+LEX	**0.654**	**0.607**	0.594	0.658
SUBTLEX	0.638	0.592	0.584	0.658
SubIMDB	0.628	0.583	0.578	0.637
Simple Wiki	0.601	0.558	0.571	0.645

to optimize not the correlation between the learned rankings and the gold-standard, but instead the likelihood of the best candidate substitution to be ranked first. We can also notice from the results that, when trained with features extracted from the SubIMDB corpus, our approach performs similarly than when trained with the SUBTLEX corpus, which is 3 times larger. This phenomena suggests that restricting the domain of the subtitles selected to that of movies targeting younger audiences may help ranking approaches in capturing word simplicity.

In the future, we want to experiment with other types of language models, and also explore the potential of other types of spoken content, such as song lyrics and online conversations.

4 Final Remarks and Future work

In this paper we described a thesis proposal which focuses in providing studies on the needs of non-native speakers in terms of LS, producing more reliable datasets for various tasks of the LS pipeline, and devising novel solutions to the limitations of modern LS approaches. We have provided a thorough discussion on the state-of-the-art of LS, a detailed plan of the activities to be conducted throughout the doctorate program and the results of our first experiment, in which we managed to achieve state-of-the-art results for the task of Substitution Ranking.

In the future, we intend to study the simplification needs of other target audiences and explore LS strategies that go beyond replacing complex words and expressions for simpler equivalents, such as by removing unimportant information and learning deep simplification rules from parallel corpora by combining constituency and dependency parses.

References

Aluisio, S. and Gasperin, C. (2010). *Proceedings of the NAACL HLT 2010 Young Investigators Workshop on Computational Approaches to Languages of the Americas*, chapter Fostering Digital Inclusion and Accessibility: The PorSimples project for Simplification of Portuguese Texts, pages 46–53. Association for Computational Linguistics.

Austin, M., Paul, B., and Phil, B. (2006). Current state of english-language learners in the u.s. k-12 student population.

Biran, O., Brody, S., and Elhadad, N. (2011). Putting it Simply: a Context-Aware Approach to Lexical Simplification. *Proceedings of the 49th Annual Meeting of the Association for Computaional Linguistics*, pages 496–501.

Bodenreider, O. (2004). The unified medical language system (umls): integrating biomedical terminology. *Nucleic acids research.*

Bott, S., Rello, L., Drndarevic, B., and Saggion, H. (2012). Can Spanish Be Simpler ? LexSiS : Lexical Simplification for Spanish Puede ser el Español más simple ? LexSiS : Simplificación Léxica en Español.

Brysbaert, M. and New, B. (2009). Moving beyond Kucera and Francis: a critical evaluation of current word frequency norms and the introduction of a new and improved word frequency measure for American English. *Behavior research methods.*

Carroll, J., Minnen, G., Canning, Y., Devlin, S., and Tait, J. (1998). Practical simplification of english newspaper text to assist aphasic readers. In *In Proc. of AAAI-98 Workshop on Integrating Artificial Intelligence and Assistive Technology*, pages 7–10.

Carroll, J., Minnen, G., Pearce, D., Canning, Y., Devlin, S., and Tait, J. (1999). Simplifying Text for Language Impaired Readers. *Proceedings of the 9th Conference of the European Chapter of the ACL (EACL '99).*

Chen, H.-b., Huang, H.-h., Chen, H.-h., and Tan, C.-t. (2012). A Simplification-Translation-Restoration Framework for Cross-Domain SMT Applications.

Deléger, L. and Zweigenbaum, P. (2009). Extracting lay paraphrases of specialized expressions from monolingual comparable medical corpora. *Proceedings of the 2nd Workshop on Building and Using Comparable Corpora: from Parallel to Non-parallel Corpora (BUCC).*

Devlin, S. and Tait, J. (1998). The use of a psycholinguistic database in the simplification of text for aphasic readers. *Linguistic Databases*, pages 161–173.

Devlin, S. and Unthank, G. (2006). Helping aphasic people process online information. *Proceedings of the 8th international ACM SIGACCESS conference on Computers and accessibility.*

Elhadad, N. (2006). Comprehending Technical Texts : Predicting and Defining Unfamiliar Terms. pages 239–243.

Elhadad, N. and Sutaria, K. (2007). Mining a lexicon of technical terms and lay equivalents. *Proceedings of the Workshop on BioNLP 2007: Biological, Translational, and Clinical Language Processing.*

Feblowitz, D. and Kauchak, D. (2013). Sentence simplification as tree transduction. *Proc. of the Second Workshop on Predicting and Improving Text Readability for Target Reader Populations*, pages 1–10.

Fellbaum, C. (1998). *WordNet: An Electronic Lexical Database.* Bradford Books.

Heafield, K., Pouzyrevsky, I., Clark, J. H., and Koehn, P. (2013). Scalable modified Kneser-Ney language model estimation. In *Proceedings of the 51st Annual Meeting of the Association for Computational Linguistics*, pages 690–696, Sofia, Bulgaria.

Horn, C., Manduca, C., and Kauchak, D. (2014). Learning a Lexical Simplifier Using Wikipedia. *Proceedings of the 52nd Annual Meeting of the Association for Computational Linguistics*, pages 458–463.

Jauhar, S. and Specia, L. (2012). UOW-SHEF: SimpLex–lexical simplicity ranking based on contextual and psycholinguistic features. *First Joint Conference on Lexical and Computational Semantics*, pages 477–481.

Kauchak, D. (2013). Improving text simplification language modeling using unsimplified text data. In *Proceedings of the 51st Annual Meeting of the Association for Computational Linguistics*, pages 1537–1546, Sofia, Bulgaria. Association for Computational Linguistics.

Kauchak, D. and Barzilay, R. (2006). Paraphrasing for automatic evaluation. *Proceedings of the Main Conference on Human Language Technology Conference of the North American Chapter of the Association of Computational Linguistics.*

Keskisärkkä, R. (2012). Automatic text simplification via synonym replacement.

Leroy, G., Endicott, E. J., Kauchak, D., Mouradi, O., and Just, M. (2013). User evaluation of the effects of a text simplification algorithm using term familiarity on perception, understanding, learning, and information retention. *Journal of Medical Internet Research (JMIR).*

Nunes, B. P., Kawase, R., Siehndel, P., Casanova, M. a., and Dietze, S. (2013). As Simple as It Gets - A Sentence Simplifier for Different Learning Levels and Contexts. *2013 IEEE 13th International Conference on Advanced Learning Technologies.*

Paetzold, G. H. and Specia, L. (2013). Text simplification as tree transduction. In *Proceedings of the 9th Brazilian Symposium in Information and Human Language Technology.*

Rello, L., Baeza-Yates, R., Bott, S., and Saggion, H. (2013). Simplify or help?: text simplification strategies for people with dyslexia. *Proceedings of the 10th W4A*.

Rudell, A. P. (1993). Frequency of word usage and perceived word difficulty: Ratings of Kuera and Francis words. *Behavior Research Methods*.

Sedding, J. and Kazakov, D. (2004). Wordnet-based text document clustering. In *Proceedings of the 3rd Workshop on Robust Methods in Analysis of Natural Language Data*. Association for Computational Linguistics.

Shardlow, M. (2013a). A Comparison of Techniques to Automatically Identify Complex Words. *ACL (Student Research Workshop)*, pages 103–109.

Shardlow, M. (2013b). *Proceedings of the Second Workshop on Predicting and Improving Text Readability for Target Reader Populations*, chapter The CW Corpus: A New Resource for Evaluating the Identification of Complex Words, pages 69–77. Association for Computational Linguistics.

Shardlow, M. (2014). A Survey of Automated Text Simplification. *International Journal of Advanced Computer Science and Applications 2014*, pages 58–70.

Sinha, R. (2012). UNT-S IMPRANK : Systems for Lexical Simplification Ranking. pages 493–496.

Specia, L., Jauhar, S. K., and Mihalcea, R. (2012). Semeval-2012 task 1: English lexical simplification. In *Proceedings of the First Joint Conference on Lexical and Computational Semantics*. Association for Computational Linguistics.

Watanabe, W. and Junior, A. (2009). Facilita: reading assistance for low-literacy readers. *Proceedings of the 2010 international cross-disciplinary workshop on Web accessibility*.

Yamamoto, T. (2013). Selecting Proper Lexical Paraphrase for Children. *Proceedings of the Twenty-Fifth Conference on Computational Linguistics and Speech Processing (ROCLING 2013)*.

Analyzing Newspaper Crime Reports for Identification of Safe Transit Paths

Vasu Sharma[1] **Rajat Kulshreshtha**[2] **Puneet Singh**[1] **Nishant Agrawal**[3]
Akshay Kumar[4]

Indian Institute Of Technology,Kanpur[1] IIT,Guwahati[2] IIIT,Hyderabad[3]
VIT Chennai[4]

vasus@iitk.ac.in rk.kuls@gmail.com pun.singh92@gmail.com nash007@gmail.com
akshay.kumar2011@vit.ac.in

Abstract

In this paper, we propose a method to find the safest path between two locations, based on the geographical model of crime intensities. We consider the police records and news articles for finding crime density of different areas of the city. It is essential to consider news articles as there is a significant delay in updating police crime records. We address this problem by updating the crime intensities based on current news feeds. Based on the updated crime intensities, we identify the safest path. It is this real time updation of crime intensities which makes our model way better than the models that are presently in use. Our model would also inform the user of crime sprees in a particular area thereby ensuring that user avoids these crime hot spots.

Keywords: Crime detection, Hotspot identification, Safest Path, Topic Modeling, Latent Dirichlet Allocation, Latent Semantic Analysis, Natural Language Processing.

1 Introduction

In today's society, reports of criminal activity are on the rise. Newspapers each day are replete with news articles about incidents of crime from different parts of our cities. Crime is not spread evenly across a city, the level of criminal activity varies with region. In traveling from one spot to another within a city, people naturally desire not to be a victim to criminal activity. In general, the likelihood of falling victim to criminal activity is greater in areas with elevated crime levels, hence the path one travels must preferentially avoid areas with higher levels of crime.

Our objective in this paper, is to find the safest possible path between any two points on the street map, based on actual or inferred knowledge of prior criminal activity. The map may be viewed as a graph, where junctions are vertices in the graph, and streets are edges. The problem of finding a path from an origin to a destination is simply that of finding a path between the corresponding vertices in the graph. For the purpose of this paper we have focused on the city of New Delhi, India, a city which has recently gained notoriety as being particularly unsafe for commuters especially women.

We can now cast our "safest-path" problem as a graph search problem. Each vertex and edge in the graph can be assigned a risk. The safest path between junction A and junction B is the least risky path, or, assuming the risk to be a cost, the least-cost path between the graph vertices a and b. Thus now we can restate the problem as finding the least-cost path between vertices.

Given a graph, the algorithm for finding the least-cost path between vertices is well known. We use the well known Dijkstra's algorithm (Dijkstra, 1959). The greater challenge now is that of *specifying* the graph. The structure of the graph, as mentioned earlier, is simply the street map of the city. The real challenge becomes that of assigning costs to the vertices and edges, which reflect the risk of crime in the junctions and streets they represent. We will do so by assigning the cumulative count of the number of instances of crime that were reported at any street or junction as the cost of the corresponding edge.

We do not have a direct way of assigning these costs, since detailed, updated crime information is

Proceedings of NAACL-HLT 2015 Student Research Workshop (SRW), pages 17–24,
Denver, Colorado, June 1, 2015.

generally not available for the city. So we will try to infer this information using a variety of sources. We will use police records to assign costs based on historical data, and to compute *a priori* information for further inference. For more updated scores, we mine the newspaper reports. However mining newspaper articles is not easy, since the articles are in natural language. Moreover, they are often imprecise in locating the reported crimes and don't specify the roads or the junctions. So, we use a Bayesian formalism to determine the locations from the article.

Following the above mentioned steps, we can assign costs to our graph and thus find the safest path between any two locations. However, for simplicity we have not considered the actual road networks for finding the path, but do so based on neighborhoods, which we then map on to the road network. Our results show that we are able to infer location from newspapers reports with relatively high accuracy, and that moreover, the hypothesized paths are highly plausible.

The paper is organized as follows. Related literature is reviewed in Section 2. Section 3 presents our data collection strategy. Sections 4-7 present detailed methodology. Results and discussion are presented in Section 8. Our conclusions are presented in Section 9.

2 Literature Review

The majority of the literature on crime-data mining focuses on analyzing data and crime records to identify patterns and predict crime. (Chen et al. , 2004) propose a generic machine learning framework for various clustering and inference tasks that may be used to detect or predict crime based on observed activity. Other traditional approaches to crime data mining focus on finding relations between attributes of the crimes, or finding hot-spots from a set of crime incidents. Another approach to detect patterns within police records was presented in (Sukanya et al. , 2012), where an expert based semi-supervised learning method was used to cluster police crime records based on their attributes. Weights were introduced to the attributes, and various patterns were identified from subsets of attributes. A step further in this direction is crime forecasting, which was presented in (Yu et al. , 2011), which developed a model in collaboration with police, aiming at predicting the location, time and likelihood of future residential burglary based on temporal and spacial (over grids) information taken from police records. Various classification techniques are used to develop a model that best relates attributes to crimes. This is pertinent to our model, as the group has investigated data mining techniques to forecast crime.

For our purpose, it is sufficient to identify news articles that pertain to relevant criminal activity, and find the distribution of such crimes across the city. Our challenge, then, is to automatically identify news articles that relate to specific types of crime, and to automatically locate the crime that is reported with sufficient specificity that we can build a "path-safety map". As it turns out, little of the literature on crime-data mining actually directly relates to this task. The task of identifying news reports has its closest analog in the literature on document classification (Sebastiani , 2002), although we have not specifically encountered many that relate in particular to crime data.(Chau et al. , 2002) report on the use of machine learning algorithms to derive named entities from formal police reports, but do not specify the techniques used. As we see later from our work, we do not require sophisticated algorithms; simple classifiers can do this particular task quite effectively.

The current literature on crime mapping, e.g. (Maltz et al. , 2000) , (Leong et al. , 2000) does not significantly address the issue of generating maps from free-form text report. An interesting idea is division of the city into a grid, which is an intuitive method of quantizing the locations. In our model, we have assumed police stations to be a strong indicator of population (and consequently crime) density, and have mapped each locality to it's police station. Perhaps the most relevant work is done in (Mahendiran et al. , 2011), where the problem of identifying patterns in combined data sources is approached by inferring clusters from spatial and temporal distribution. Bayesian Belief Networks are used to find a probabilistic relation between crime, time and location. Creation of a "heat map" to represent unsafe areas was suggested but not part of this report. The group has collated crime reports from various websites. The distinguishing feature of our model is that we have combined crime reports and news feeds, and that we mapped our crime distribution into a graph with edges weighted according to crime intensities.

3 Data Collection

For the experiments reported in this paper we focus on Delhi, India, a city which has recently acquired some notoriety because of the spate of crimes reported from there, particularly against women. This recent notoriety particularly motivates people to try to find safe routes from origin to destination, making the solution reported in this paper especially relevant there.

In our proposed system, we gather data from disparate sources such as the reports from the Delhi Police Website [1]. Here we have ignored the gravity of crime and used only the number of crimes for allocating a cost to a location. We have used 42768 police crime records over a period of 3 years for the state of Delhi to form our historical prior. We parse the records and extract the location and type of crime from the records. We now tag the records to their nearest police station and maintain counts of the number of crimes committed in the jurisdiction area of every police station. This count is what we have considered as 'crime intensity' for that area. These are used to derive the *a priori* probability distribution of crime in the various precincts. A total of 162 locations were considered, one for each police station in Delhi.

We used a web crawler to obtain news articles from various news paper websites[2] to get crime related news articles. A total of 32000 news articles were obtained using the crawler out of which half were crime related and the other half were not crime related. These articles formed the prior for our k-nearest neighbor and LDA based approach used for classification as crime/non-crime and location identification described in the later sections.

[1]The police recoreds were obtained from : `http://delhipolice.serverpeople.com/firwebtemp/Index.aspx`

[2]The newspaper articles were obtained from:

- `http://timesofindia.indiatimes.com/` (Times of India online portal)
- `http://indiatoday.intoday.in/` (India Today news portal)
- `http://www.ndtv.com` (NDTV news portal)

4 Classification of Article as Crime or Non Crime

The news articles picked from news paper websites are not annotated. Besides, we are concerned only with crimes which affect safety of a person traveling through that region. For example cyber crimes, suicides , etc., do not affect the safety of a person traveling through a region and should not be classified as commuter affecting crimes by the model.

Therefore, in order to proceed with the "safety-map" generation, we must first classify the news articles as "crime" or "non-crime". We find that the language used to refer to such crime in the news articles is diverse, ranging from direct to oblique references. Even among the direct references, a variety of different vocabularies and constructs may be employed. Direct analysis of language and vocabulary may consequently require complicated classification schemes to account for all possible variations.

Instead, we work on a simpler hypothesis – we hypothesize that regardless of the manner in which the crimes are being referred to, there exist underlying *semantic* levels at which they are all similar, and that by expressing the documents in terms of their representation within these levels, we must be able to perform the requisite classification relatively simply.

Uncovering the underlying semantic structure must be performed in an unsupervised manner. A variety of statistical models such as latent semantic analysis, probabilistic latent semantic analysis (Hoffmann , 1999), latent Dirichlet allocation (Blei et al. , 2003) etc. have been proposed for this purpose. We employ a relatively lightweight, simple algorithm, latent semantic analysis (LSA)(Dumais , 2004). LSA is a singular-value decomposition (SVD) (Kumar , 2009) based statistical model of word usage that attempts to recover abstract equivalents of semantic structure from the co-occurrence statistics of words in documents. Given a collection of documents, it first composes a term-count matrix, where each column represents a document, and each row represents a particular word. The total number of columns represents the number of documents in the collection being analyzed, and the total number of rows represents the "vocabulary" of words being considered. The $(i, j)^{\text{th}}$ entry of the term-count matrix represents the number of times the ith word in the vocabulary occurs in the jth document. The term-count matrix is decomposed using SVD. The M most significant left singular vectors recovered, corresponding to the M highest singular values, are assumed to represent the M directions of the underlying latent semantic space. Any document can be represented in this space as the projection of the term-count vector of the document (comprising a vector of counts of the words from the vocabulary in the document) onto the set of M singular vectors. The projection is assumed to exist in the corresponding semantic space.

To compute our model, we first stem our corpus, and eliminate all stop word such as "a", "an', "the', etc. We compose a term-document matrix from the documents, and employ LSA to reduce the dimensionality of the data. All documents are represented in the lower dimensional semantic space.

We annotate our training data instances to identify if they belong to the "crime" category or not. Subsequently, given any test document, we use a k-nearest neighbor classifier to classify it: we identify the k closest training instances, where closeness is computed based on cosine distance. If the majority of the k instances are crime-related, we classify the article as a crime article, otherwise we classify it as non-crime.

5 Identification of Location of the Article

After identifying crime-related articles, we must next identify the location where the reported crime occurred. Again, we observe that newspaper articles often do not make explicit identification of the location of the crime, often not providing more than city-level information explicitly. The exact location must be inferred from the text used to describe the area, and sometimes from other incidental information that the articles may contain. Identification of the location thus becomes a challenging problem. Unlike the problem of identifying that the article refers to a crime, this is a closed-set problem in that the reported crime has indeed occurred, and hence *must* have occurred in one of the areas of the city. Thus, we only need to identify which of the various locations in the city was the spot of occurrence of the crime. We do so by a combination of methods. In the First, we employ a named-entity extractor to identify potential location-related words from the document, in case the location may be inferred from direct references. Then we use a Naive Bayes classifier based on a representation derived from latent Dirichlet allocation analysis (Blei et al. , 2003) of the articles to identify the location. We describe both below.

5.1 Named Entity Recognition

Named Entity Recognition (Klein et al. , 2003) is a Natural Language Processing technique which can identify named entities like names, locations, organizations etc. from text. Specifically, we use the technique described in the aforementioned work, to identify locations from articles. It uses decision trees and Conditional Random Fields(CRF's) (Wallach , 2004) to identify named entities. Conditional random fields (CRFs) are a class of statistical modeling method often applied in pattern recognition and machine learning, where they are used for structured prediction. Whereas an ordinary classifier predicts a label for a single sample without regard to "neighboring" samples, a CRF can take context into account; e.g., the linear chain CRF popular in natural language processing predicts sequences of labels for sequences of input samples. Given the nature of our problem we determined this technique to be most appropriate for our data.

5.2 LDA-based Naive Bayes for Location Determination

Named entity recognition cannot pull up location information when it is not actually specified in the article. Even when it is mentioned, the reference may not be unambiguous. In order to deal with such articles we use a simple Naive Bayes classifier based on features derived using Latent Dirichlet Allocation (LDA) (Blei et al. , 2003).

LDA is a well-known document-analysis technique which assumes a 'latent' or underlying pattern in the pattern of words in it. The model assumes that documents are composed of topics. Topics are distinguished by the probability distributions of words associated with the topic – different topics have different distributions over words. For instance, a sports-related topic may have a higher prevalence of sports-related words, while a politics-related topic will have a higher prevalence of politics-related words. The generative model for LDA assume that in order to compose a document, for each word in the document a topic is selected according to a document-specific probability distribution over topics, and subsequently a word is drawn from the topic. Mathematically, the collection of words $\{w \in D\}$ in any article A are assumed to have been drawn from a distribution $P(w|t;\theta)P(t|A)$, where $P(t|A)$ represents the probability distribution over topics t within article, and $P(w|t)$ is the probability distribution of words within topic t. The probability distributions $P(t|w)$ are learned from training data. The probability distribution $P(t|w)$ of topics within any document is also drawn from an *a priori* Dirichlet distribution, the parameters of which are also learned from training data.

We employ the distribution over topics as the fundamental characterization of documents. We derive a set of T topics from a training corpus comprising crime-related news reports. Every article A is now decomposed into these topics. The probability distribution $P(t|A)$ of topics t in the article, which is derived using LDA, is now used as a representation for the documents.

We view each document as bag of topics, and $P(t|A)$ as a normalized count of the number of times the topic appears in the document. Now we cast the location classification problem as follows.

We associate locations with police stations. The city is partitioned into regions, one corresponding to the jurisdiction of each station. We tag a number of training articles with the location of the crime they report. We ensure that every station is adequately represented in the training set. Each article is now decomposed into a topic histogram $P(t|A)$.

We now compute a probability distribution of topics with respect to each location to be identified using the following maximum likelihood estimator:

$$P(t|L) = \frac{1}{|\{A \in L\}|} \sum_{A \in L} P(t|A)$$

where $A \in L$ represents the set of all training articles that refer to crimes in location L.

In order to appropriately represent the natural bias of crime in the city, we derive *a priori* probability distribution of crime in the various precincts, $P(L)$ from historical police FIR records as

$$P(L) = \frac{|C \in L|}{\sum_L |C \in L|}$$

where $C \in L$ represents the set of all FIR records of crimes reported at location L.

We can now apply the following Bayesian classifier to identify the location $\hat{L}(A)$ of the crime reported in any article A:

$$\hat{L}(A) = \arg\max_A P(L|A) \qquad (1)$$

In other words, we are assigning the crime to the location that is most probable *a posteriori*, given the information in the article.

Using the usual modification of the above equation, the classification reduces to

$$\hat{L}(A) = \arg\max_A P(A|L)P(L) \qquad (2)$$

and working in the log domain, taking into account the monotonicity of the log function:

$$\hat{L}(A) = \arg\max_A \log P(A|L) + \log P(L) \qquad (3)$$

$\log p(L)$ in the above equation is directly obtained from the *a priori* probability distribution $P(L)$. We only need to compute $\log P(A|L)$ to perform the computation in Equation 3. To do so, we assume that the article being classified has been obtained by drawing topics from the location specific topic distribution $P(t|L)$ repeatedly. This leads us to the following equation for $P(A|L)$.

$$p(A|L) = \prod_t P(t|L)^{\lambda P(t|A)}$$

$$\log P(A|L) = \lambda \sum_t P(t|A) \log P(t|L)$$

where, as mentioned earlier, $P(t|A)$ is the normalized count of the times topic t in the article A, as computed using LDA. The term λ is required because we only know the *normalized* count of topic occurrence; this must be scaled to obtain the true counts. The overall classification rule thus becomes

$$\hat{L}(A) = \arg\max_A \lambda \sum_t P(t|A) \log P(t|L) + \log P(L) \qquad (4)$$

In principle λ is article specific. In practice, we derive a global value of λ by optimizing over a development training set.

6 Mapping Crime Intensities

We apply the combination of the document-identification and location-detection algorithms to news articles and use it to generate a "heat map" of crime for the city. Every new incoming article that has been classified as relating to crime, and assigned to any police station, is used to increment the crime count for that station. In our work we have worked with a fixed number of articles, resulting in a fixed heat map; in practice, to prevent the entire map from being saturated, a forgetting factor must be employed to assign greater weight to more recent crimes. We associate the total crime count for any station with every junction in its jurisdiction. Crime counts for junctions that span multiple jurisdictions accumulate the counts of all the stations that cover them. This results in a crime-weighted street map that we can now use to find the safest path between locations.

7 Identifying Safest Path

Once the safety map showing the crime intensities is known, we can convert the safest path problem to a shortest path problem by modeling the edge weights as the sum of crime frequencies of the two connecting nodes. Now that we have a graph with well defined positive edge weights, we can apply Dijkstra's algorithm(Dijkstra, 1959) to identify the shortest path which is the safest path here.

8 Results and Validation

The validation of the model is two-fold.In the first step we check the effectiveness of the classification of the article as crime or non crime. Then we check how well does the model identify the location of the article.

8.1 Result of Crime/Non Crime Classification

The test for crime/non-crime classification was done on 5000 articles (3000 crime and 2000 non-crime articles were taken) and various values of k were experimented with. The results of which are as follows:

Value of k	Accuracy	F-score
1	82.14%	0.78
3	84.86%	0.81
5	86.52%	0.82
7	87.94%	0.83
9	**89.36%**	**0.84**
11	87.60%	0.82

Table 1: Results of Classifying articles into Crime/Non-crime categories

As the experiments demonstrated the most suitable value for k was found to be 9.

8.2 Result of Identification of location

Method Used	Accuracy	F-score
NER	81.48%	0.78
LDA	79.38%	0.75
LDA+NER	**83.64%**	**0.81**

Table 2: Location Identification results

Clearly the combination of LDA and NER techniques yields the best results.

8.3 Result for Safest Path search

We did a survey for 1200 commuters to use our model for finding the safest transit path between two locations and rate the path suggested by our model on a scale of 1 to 10 based on their prior experience of commuting between these locations. We received an average rating of 8.75/10 from the 1200 users.

9 Conclusions

The model is able to predict the safest path between 2 locations to a very high degree of accuracy. The accuracy of the model depends on the correct classification of the article as crime/non crime and on the correct identification of crime's location from article. Clearly the model achieves both of these with very high degrees of accuracy as can be seen from Tables 1 and 2. The model also maps this safest path correctly on the map and informs the user of the route he should opt for to avoid crime prone regions.

10 Assumptions used and Future Work

Our model presently doesn't take into account the actual road networks and instead gives the path from one region(represented by that region's police station) to the other based on the assumption that a region is connected directly only to it's nearest neighbors.

In the near future we plan to do away with this assumption by incorporating the actual road network in our model.

Other future work includes identifying safest paths which also take into account the time of the day and the traffic density of various routes.We also plan to identify the exact type of crime and assign different weights to different kinds of crimes in the near future.

11 Acknowledgments

We would like to acknowledge the efforts of Dr. Bhiksha Raj and Dr. Rita Singh of Carnegie Mellon University without whose constant support and guidance this project would not have been possible.

References

[Klein et al. 2003] D. Klein and J. Smarr and H. Nguyen and C.D. Manning 2003. *Named Entity Recognition with Character-Level Model. Proceedings the Seventh Conference on Natural Language Learning.*

[Dumais 2004] Susan T. Dumais. 2004. *Latent Semantic Analysis. Annual Review of Information Science and Technology*

[Hoffmann 1999] Thomas Hoffmann. 1999. *Probabilistic Latent Semantic Analysis Uncertainty in Artificial Intelligence*

[Blei et al. 2003] David M. Blei and Andrew Y. Ng and Michael I. Jordan 2003. *Latent Dirichlet Allocation. The Journal of Machine Learning Research,*

[Maltz et al. 2000] Michael D. Maltz and Andrew C. Gordon and Warren Friedman 2000. *Mapping Crime in Its Community Setting: Event Geography Analysis.* Springer Verlag.

[Sebastiani 2002] Fabrizio Sebastian 2002. *Machine learning in automated text categorization.* ACM Computing Surveys.

[Leong et al. 2000] Kelvin Leong and Stephen Chan. 2000. *A content analysis of web-based crime mapping in the world's top 100 highest GDP cities. Mapping Crime in Its Community Setting: Event Geography Analysis. Springer Verlag*

[Ku et al. 2011] Chih-Hao Ku and Gondy Leroy. 2011. A crime reports analysis system to identify related crimes . *Journal of the American Society for Information Science and Technology.*

[Deerwester et al. 1990] S. Deerwester and S. T Dumais and G W Furnas and T K Landauer and R. Harshman. 1990. Indexing by Latent Semantic Analysis. *Journal of the American Society for Information Science.*

[Kumar 2009] Ch. Aswani Kumar. 2009. Analysis of Unsupervised Dimensionality Reduction Techniques . *COMSIS.*

[Wallach 2004] Hanna M. Wallach. 2004. Conditional Random Fields: An Introduction . *University of Pennsylvania CIS Technical Report MS-CIS-04-21.*

[BeyondNormality 2013] BeyondNormality. 2013. Wikipedia Entry .

[Dijkstra1959] Dijkstra's, E.W. 1959. A note on two problems in connexion with graphs . *Numerische Mathematik.*

[Chau et al. 2002] Michael Chau and Jennifer J. Zu and Hisnchun Chen. 2002. Extracting meaningful entities from police narrative reports . *Proceedings of the 2002 annual national conference on Digital government research.*

[Zhang et al. 2010] Yin Zhang,Rong Zim,Zhi Hua Zhou. 2010. Understanding Bag-of-Words Model: A Statistical Framework . *International Journal of Machine Learning and Computing.*

[Wang et al. 2004] Tong Wang and Cynthia Rudin and Daniel Wagner and Rich Sevieri. 2004. Learning to Detect Patterns of Crime . *Machine Learning and Knowledge Discovery in Databases. Springer Berlin Heidelberg*

[Hu 2013] Ruijuan Hu. 2013. Data Mining in the Application of Criminal Cases Based on Decision Tree . *International Journal of Engineering Sciences.*

[Yu et al. 2011] C.H. Yu and Max W. Ward and M. Morabito and W. Ding. 2011. Crime Forecasting Using Data Mining Techniques . *IEEE 11th International Conference on Data Mining Workshops.*

[Mahendiran et al. 2011] Aravindan Mahendiran and Michael Shuffett and Sathappan Muthiah and Rimy Malla and Gaoqiang Zhang. 2011. Forecasting Crime Incidents using Cluster Analysis and Bayesian Belief Networks .

[Nath 2006] Shyam Varan Nath. 2006. Crime Pattern Detection Using Data Mining . *Web Intelligence and Intelligent Agent Technology Workshops, 2006. WI-IAT 2006 Workshops. 2006 IEEE/WIC/ACM International Conference.*

[Bajpai 2012] Devesh Bajpai. 2012. Emerging Trends in Utilization of Data Mining in Criminal Investigation: An Overview . *Springer.*

[Sukanya et al. 2012] Sukanya, M. and Kalaikumaran, T.

and Karthik, S.. 2012. Criminals and crime hotspot detection using data mining algorithms: clustering and classification . *International Journal of Advanced Research in Computer Engineering and Technology (IJARCET).*

[Chen et al. 2004] Chen, H. and Chung, W. and Xu, J.J. and Wang, G. and Qin, Y. and Chau, M.. 2004. Crime data mining: A general framework and some examples . *IEEE Computer.*

Relation extraction pattern ranking using word similarity

Konstantinos Lambrou-Latreille
(1) École Polytechnique de Montréal
(2) Centre de Recherche Informatique de Montréal
Montréal, Québec, Canada
konstantinos.lambrou-latreille@polymtl.ca

Abstract

Our thesis proposal aims at integrating word similarity measures in pattern ranking for relation extraction bootstrapping algorithms. We note that although many contributions have been done on pattern ranking schemas, few explored the use of word-level semantic similarity. Our hypothesis is that word similarity would allow better pattern comparison and better pattern ranking, resulting in less semantic drift commonly problematic in bootstrapping algorithms. In this paper, as a first step into this research, we explore different pattern representations, various existing pattern ranking approaches and some word similarity measures. We also present a methodology and evaluation approach to test our hypothesis.

1 Introduction

In this thesis, we look at the problem of information extraction from the web; more precisely at the problem of extracting structured information, in the form of triples (predicate, subject, object), e.g. (ObjectMadeFromMaterial, table, wood) from unstructured text. This topic of Relation Extraction (RE), is a current and popular research topic within NLP, given the large amount of unstructured text on the WWW.

In the literature, machine learning algorithms have shown to be very useful for RE from textual resources. Although supervised (Culotta and Sorensen, 2004; Bunescu and Mooney, 2005) and unsupervised learning (Hasegawa et al., 2004; Zhang et al., 2005) have been used for RE, in this thesis, we will focus on semi-supervised bootstrapping algorithms.

In such algorithms (Brin, 1999; Agichtein and Gravano, 2000; Alfonseca et al., 2006a), the input is a set of related pairs called *seed instances* (e.g., (table,wood), (bottle, glass)) for a specific *relation* (e.g., ObjectMadeFromMaterial). These seed instances are used to collect a set of *candidate patterns* representing the relation in a corpus. A subset containing the best candidate patterns is added in the set of *promoted patterns*. The promoted patterns are used to collect *candidate instances*. A subset containing the best candidate instances is selected to form the set of *promoted instances*. The promoted instances are either added to the initial seed set or used to replace it. With the new seed set, the algorithm is repeated until a stopping criterion is met.

The advantage of bootstrapping algorithms is that they require little human annotation. Unfortunately, the system may introduce wrongly extracted instances. Due to its iterative approach, errors can quickly cumulate in the next few iterations; therefore, precision will suffer. This problem is called *semantic drift*. Different researchers have studied how to counter *semantic drift* by using better pattern representations, by filtering unreliable patterns, and filtering wrongly extracted instances (Brin, 1999; Agichtein and Gravano, 2000; Alfonseca et al., 2006a). Nevertheless, this challenge is far from being resolved, and we hope to make a contribution in that direction.

The semantic drift is directly related to which candidate patterns become promoted patterns. A crucial decision at that point is how to establish pattern confidence so as to rank the patterns. There are many ways to estimate the confidence of a pattern.

Proceedings of NAACL-HLT 2015 Student Research Workshop (SRW), pages 25–32,
Denver, Colorado, June 1, 2015.

Blohm et al. (2007) identified general types of pattern filtering functions for well-known systems. As we review pattern ranking approaches, we note that many include a notion of "resemblance", as either comparing patterns between successive iterations, or comparing instances generated at an iteration to instances in the seed set, etc. Although this notion of resemblance seems important to many ranking schemas, we do not find much research which combines word similarity approaches within pattern ranking. This is where we hope to make a research contribution and where our hypothesis lies, that using word similarity would allow for better pattern ranking.

In order to suggest better pattern ranking approaches incorporating word similarity, we need to look at the different pattern representations suggested in the literature and understand how they affect pattern similarity measures. This is introduced in Section 2. Then, section 3 provides a non-exhaustive survey of pattern ranking approaches with an analysis of commonality and differences; Section 4 presents a few word similarity approaches; Section 5 presents the challenges we face, as well as our methodology toward the validation of our hypothesis; Section 6 briefly explores other anticipated issues (e.g. seed selection) in relation to our main contribution and Section 7 presents the conclusion.

2 Pattern representation

In the literature, pattern representations are classified as lexical or syntactic.

Lexical patterns represent lexical terms around a relation instance as a pattern. For relation instance (*X,Y*) where *X* and *Y* are valid noun phrases, Brin (1999), Agichtein and Gravano (2000), Pasca et al. (2006), Alfonseca et al. (2006a) take *N* words before *X*, *N* words after *Y* and all intervening words between *X* and *Y* to form a pattern (e.g., *well-known author X worked on Y daily.*). Extremes for the choice of N exist, as in the CPL subsystem of NELL (Carlson et al., 2010) setting $N = 0$ and the opposite in Espresso (Pantel and Pennacchiotti, 2006) where the whole sentence is used.

Syntactic patterns convert a sentence containing a relation instance to a structured form such as a parse tree or a dependency tree. Yangarber (2003) and Stevenson and Greenwood (2005) use Subject-Verb-Object (SVO) dependency tree patterns such as [Company appoint Person] or [Person quit]. Culotta (2004) uses full dependency trees on which a tree kernel will be used to measure similarity. Bunescu and Mooney (2005) and Sun and Grishman (2010) use the shortest dependency path (SDP) between a relation instance in the dependency tree as a pattern (e.g., "nsubj ← met → prep_in"). Zhang et al. (2014) add a semantic constraint to the SDP; they define the semantic shortest dependency path (SSDP) as a SDP containing at least one *trigger word* representing the relation, if any. Trigger words are defined as words most representative of the target relation (e.g. *home*, *house*, *live*, for the relation *PersonResidesIn*).

We anticipate the use of word similarity to be possible when comparing either lexical or syntactic patterns, adapting to either words in sequence, or nodes within parse or dependency trees. In fact, as researchers have explored pattern generalization, some have already looked at ways of grouping similar words. For example, Alfonseca et al. (2006a) present a simple algorithm to generalize the set of lexical patterns using an edit-distance similarity. Also, Pasca et al. (2006) add term generalization to a pattern representation similar to Agichtein and Gravano (2000); terms are replaced with their corresponding classes of distributionally similar words, if any (e.g., let CL3 = {March, October, April,...} in the pattern *CL3 00th : X's Birthday (Y)*).

3 Pattern ranking approaches

We now survey pattern ranking algorithms to better understand in which ones similarity measures would be more likely to have an impact. We follow a categorization introduced in Blohm et al. (2007) as they quantified the impact of different relation pattern/instance filtering functions on their generic bootstrapping algorithm. The filtering functions proposed by Brin (1999), Agichtein and Gravano (2000), Pantel and Pennacchiotti (2006) and Etzioni et al. (2004) were described in their work.

Although non-exhaustive, our survey includes further pattern ranking approaches found in the literature, in order to best illustrate Blohm's different categories. A potential use of those categories would be to define a pattern ranking measure composed of voting experts representing each category. A combination of these votes might provide a better confidence measure for a pattern.

We define the following notation, as to allow the description of the different measures in a coherent way. Let p be a pattern and i be an instance; I is the set of promoted instances; P is the set of promoted patterns; $H(p)$ is the set of unique instances matched by p; $K(i)$ is the set of unique patterns matching i; $count(i, p)$ is the number of times p matches i; $count(p)$ is the number of p occurs in a corpus; S is the set of seed instances.

3.1 Syntactic assessment

This filtering assessment is purely based on the syntactic criteria (e.g., length, structure, etc.) of the pattern. Brin (1999) uses the length of the pattern to measure its specificity.

3.2 Pattern comparison

Blohm et al. (2007) named this category *inter-pattern comparison*. Their intuition was that candidate patterns could be rated based on how similar their generated instances are in comparison to the instances generated by the promoted patterns. We generalize this category to also include rating of candidate patterns based directly on their semantic similarity with promoted pattern.

Stevenson and Greenwood (2005) assign a score on a candidate pattern based on the similarity with promoted patterns. The pattern scoring function uses the Jiang and Conrath (1997) WordNet-based word similarity for pattern similarity. They represent the SVO pattern as a vector (e.g., [subject_COMPANY, verb_fired, object_ceo], or [subject_chairman, verb_resign]). The similarity between two pattern vectors is measured as :

$$sim(\vec{a}, \vec{b}) = \frac{\vec{a} \times W \times \vec{b^T}}{|\vec{a}| \times |\vec{b}|} \tag{1}$$

where W is a matrix that contains the word similarity between every possible element-filler pairs (e.g., subject_COMPANY, verb_fired, object_ceo) contained in every SVO pattern extracted from a corpus. The top-*N* (e.g., 4) patterns with a score larger than 95% are promoted.

Zhang et al. (2014) defines a bottom-up kernel (BUK) to filter undesired relation patterns. The BUK measures the similarity between two dependency tree patterns. The system accepts new patterns that are the most similar to seed patterns. The BUK defines a matching function t and a similarity function k on dependency trees. Let dep be the pair (rel, w) where rel is the dependency relation and w is the word of the relation (e.g., (nsubj, son)). The matching function is defined as:

$$t(dep_1, dep_2) = \begin{cases} 1 & if\ dep_1.w, dep_2.w \in W_{tr} \\ 0 & \text{otherwise} \end{cases} \tag{2}$$

where W_{tr} is the set of trigger words for the target relation. The similarity function is defined as:

$$k(dep_1, dep_2) = \begin{cases} \gamma_1 + \gamma_2 & if\ dep_1.rel = dep_2.rel\ \&\&\ dep_1.w = dep_2.w \\ \gamma_1 & if\ dep_1.w = dep_2.w \\ 0 & \text{otherwise} \end{cases} \tag{3}$$

where γ_1 and γ_2 are manually defined weights for attributes $dep.w$ and $dep.rel$ respectively. The word comparison is string-based.

3.3 Support-based assessment

This ranking assessment estimates the quality of a pattern based on the set of occurrences/patterns that generated this pattern. This assessment is usually used for patterns that were created by a generalization procedure. For example, if pattern *X BE mostly/usually made of/from Y* was generated by patterns *X is usually made of Y* and *X are mostly made from Y*, then the quality of the generalized pattern will be based on the last two patterns. Brin (1999) filters patterns if $(specificity(p) \times n) > t$, where n is the occurrence count of pattern p applied in a corpus and t is a manually set threshold.

3.4 Performance-based assessment

The quality of a candidate pattern can be estimated by the comparing its correctly produced instances with the set of promoted instances.

Blohm et al. (2007) defines a precision formula similar to Agichtein and Gravano (2000) to approximate a performance-based precision:

$$prec(p) = \frac{|H(p) \cap S|}{|H(p)|} \tag{4}$$

Alfonseca et al. (2006b) propose a procedure to measure the precision of candidate patterns in order to filter overly-general patterns. For every relation, and every hook *X* and target *Y* of the set of promoted instances (*X,Y*), a hook and target corpus is extracted from corpus *C*; *C* contains only sentences which contain *X* or *Y*. For every pattern p, instances of $H(p)$ are extracted. Then, a set of heuristics label every instance as correct/incorrect. The precision of p is number of correct extracted instances divided by the total number of extracted instances.

NELL (Carlson et al., 2010) ranks relation patterns by their precision:

$$prec(p) = \frac{\sum_{i \in I} count(i,p)}{count(p)} \quad (5)$$

Sijia et al. (2013) filters noisy candidate relation patterns that generate instances which appear in the seed set of relations other than the target relation.

3.5 Instance-Pattern correlation

Pattern quality can be assessed by measuring its correlation with the set of promoted instances. These measures estimate the correlation by counting pattern occurrences, promoted instance occurrences, and pattern occurrences with a specific promoted instance.

Blohm et al. (2007) classified Espresso (Pantel and Pennacchiotti, 2006) and KnowItAll (Etzioni et al., 2004) in this category.

Pantel et Pennacchiotti (2006) ranks candidate relation patterns by the following reliability score:

$$r_\pi(p) = \frac{\sum_{i \in I} \left(\frac{pmi(i,p)}{max_{pmi}} \times r_l(i) \right)}{|I|} \quad (6)$$

where max_{pmi} is the maximum PMI between all pattern and all instances, and $pmi(i,p)$ can be estimated using the following formula:

$$pmi(i,p) = \log \left(\frac{|x,p,y|}{|x,*,y| \times |*,p,*|} \right) \quad (7)$$

where i is an instance (*x,y*), $|x,p,y|$ is the occurrence of pattern *p* with terms *x* and *y* and (*) represents a wildcard. The reliability of an instance $r_l(i)$ is defined as:

$$r_l(i) = \frac{\sum_{p \in P} \left(\frac{pmi(i,p)}{max_{pmi}} \times r_\pi(p) \right)}{|P|} \quad (8)$$

Since $r_l(i)$ and $r_\pi(p)$ are defined recursively, $r_l(i) = 1$ for any seed instance. The top-*N* patterns are promoted where *N* is the number of patterns of the previous bootstrapping iteration plus one.

Sun and Grishman (2010) accept the top-*N* ranked candidate pattern by the following confidence formula:

$$Conf(p) = \frac{Sup(p)}{|H(p)|} \times \log Sup(p) \quad (9)$$

where $Sup(p) = \sum_{i \in H(p)} Conf(i)$ is the support candidate pattern *p* can get from the set of matched instances. Every relation instance in Sun and Grishman (2010) has a cluster membership, where a cluster contains similar patterns. The confidence of an newly extracted instance i is defined as:

$$Conf(i) = 2 \times \frac{Semi\_Conf(i) \times Cluster\_Conf(i)}{Semi\_Conf(i) + Cluster\_Conf(i)} \quad (10)$$

$$Semi\_Conf(i) = 1 - \prod_{p \in K(p)} (1 - Prec(p)) \quad (11)$$

$$Cluster\_Conf(i) = Prob(i \in C_t) = \frac{\sum_{p \in C_t} count(i,p)}{|K(i)|} \quad (12)$$

where C_t is the target cluster where the patterns of the target relation belong, $Semi\_Conf(i)$ is defined as the confidence given by the patterns matching the candidate relation instance and $Cluster\_Conf(i)$ is defined how strongly a candidate instance is associated with the target cluster.

4 Word similarity

Within the pattern ranking survey, we often saw the idea of comparing patterns and/or instances, but only once, was there a direct use of word similarity measures. Stevenson and Greenwood (2005) assign a score to a candidate pattern based on its similarity to promoted patterns using a WordNet-based word similarity measure (Jiang and Conrath, 1997). This measure is only one among many WordNet-based approaches, as can be found in (Lesk, 1986; Wu and Palmer, 1994; Resnik, 1995; Jiang and Conrath, 1997; Lin, 1998; Leacock and Chodorow, 1998; Banerjee and Pedersen, 2002).

There are limitations to these approaches, mainly that WordNet (Miller, 1995), although large, is still incomplete. Other similarity approaches are corpus-based (e.g. (Agirre et al., 2009)) where the distributional similarity between words is measured. Words are no longer primitives, but they are represented by a feature vector. The feature vector could contain the co-occurrences, the syntactic dependencies, etc. of the word with their corresponding frequencies from a corpus. The cosine similarity (among many possible measures) between the feature vector of two words indicates their semantic similarity.

Newer approaches to word similarity are based on neural network word embeddings. Mikolov et al. (2013) present algorithms to learn those distributed word representations which can then be compared to provide word similarity estimations.

Word similarity could be in itself the topic of a thesis. Therefore, we will not attempt at developing new word similarity measures, but rather we will search for measures which are intrinsically good and valuable for the pattern ranking task. The few mentioned above are a good start toward a more extensive survey. The methods found can be evaluated on existing datasets such as RG (Rubenstein and Goodenough, 1965), MC (Miller and Charles, 1991), WordSim353 (Finkelstein et al., 2001; Agirre et al., 2009), MTurk (Radinsky et al., 2011) and MEN (Bruni et al., 2013) datasets. However, these datasets are limited, since they contain only nouns (except MEN). When using word similarity in pattern ranking schemas, we will likely want to measure similarity between nouns, verbs, adjectives and adverbs. Still, these datasets provide a good starting point for evaluation of word similarity.

5 Word similarity in pattern ranking

The hypothesis of our research is that the use of word similarity will allow better pattern ranking to better prevent semantic drift. We face three main challenges in supporting this hypothesis. First, we need to understand the interdependence of the three elements presented in the three previous sections: pattern representation, pattern confidence estimation, and word similarity. Second, we need to devise an appropriate set-up to perform our bootstrapping approach. Third, we need to properly evaluate the role of the different variations in preventing semantic drift.

An important exploration will be to decide where the word similarity has the largest potential. For example, in the work of Stevenson and Greenwood (2005), similarity is directly applied on parts of the triples found (Subject, Verb predicate or Object), or in the work of Zhang et al. (2014), word similarity would be integrated in the matching and similarity functions over dependency trees, instead of using string equality.

As we see, the integration of word similarity measures would be different depending on the type of pattern representation used. Furthermore, in some representation, there is already a notion of pattern generalisation, such as in the work of Pasca et al. (2006), where words are replaced with more general classes, if any. In such case, word similarity measures are used at the core of the pattern representation, and will further impact pattern ranking.

As we will eventually be building a complex system, we intend to follow a standard methodology of starting with a baseline system for which we have an evaluation, and then further evaluate the different variations to measure their impact. As the number of combination of possible variations will be too large, time will be spent also on partial evaluation, to determine most promising candidates among word similarity measures, and/or pattern representation and/or pattern confidence estimation, to understand strength and weaknesses of each aspect independently of the others.

Our proposed methodology is to take promising ranking approaches among the one presented in Section 3, and promising pattern representations from what was presented in Section 2. We can evaluate their combined performance through N different iteration intervals and incorporate different similarity measures (some best measures chosen from the evaluation on known datasets) to measure the performance of the system.

As our baseline system, we are inspired by CPL subsystem of NELL (Carlson et al., 2010) since it is one of the largest, currently active, bootstrapping system in the literature. As in NELL, we will use ClueWeb[1] as our corpus, and for the set of relations, we will use the same seed instances and relations as in the evaluation of NELL (Carlson et al., 2010).

As for the bootstrapping RE system, to evaluate the precision, we will randomly sample knowledge from the knowledge base and evaluate them by sev-

[1] http://www.lemurproject.org/clueweb09/

eral human judges. The extracted knowledge could be validated using a crowdsourcing application such as MTurk. This method is based on NELL (Carlson et al., 2010). To evaluate its recall, we have to concentrate on already annotated relations. For example, Pasca et al. (2006) evaluates the relation *Person-BornIN-Year*. As a Gold Standard, 6617 instances were automatically extracted from Wikipedia. Instead of measuring recall for specific relation, we could use relative recall (Pantel et al., 2004; Pantel and Pennacchiotti, 2006). We can evaluate our contributions by the relative recall of system A (our system) given system B (baseline).

6 Related issues in pattern ranking

Our main contribution on the impact of word similarity on pattern ranking will necessarily bring forward other interesting questions that we will address within our thesis.

6.1 Choice of seed

As we saw, pattern ranking is often dependent on the comparison of instances found from one iteration to the next. At iteration 0, we start with a seed of instances. We can imagine that the manual selection of these seeds will have an impact on the following decisions. As our similarity measures are used to compare candidate instances to seed instances, and as we will start with NELL seed set, we will want to evaluate its impact on the bootstrapping process.

It was shown that the performance of bootstrapping algorithms highly depend on the seed instance selection (Kozareva and Hovy, 2010). Ehara et al. (2013) proposed an iterative approach where unlabelled instances are chosen to be labelled depending on their similarity with the seed instances and are added in the seed set.

6.2 Automatic selection of patterns

Something noticeable among our surveyed pattern ranking approaches is the inclusion of empirically set thresholds that will definitely have an impact on the semantic drift, but which impact is not discussed. Most authors (e.g (Carlson et al., 2010; Sun and Grishman, 2010; McIntosh and Yencken, 2011; Zhang et al., 2014) among recent ones) select the top-N best ranked patterns to be promoted to next iteration. Other authors (Pasca et al., 2006; Dang and Aizawa, 2008; Carlson et al., 2010) select the top-M ranked instances to add in the seed set for the next iteration. Other authors (Brin, 1999; Agichtein and Gravano, 2000; Sijia et al., 2013) only apply a filtering step without limiting pattern/instance selection.

In our work, including word similarity within pattern ranking will certainly impact the decision on the number of patterns to be promoted. We hope to contribute in developing a pattern selection mechanism that will be based on the pattern confidence themselves rather than on an empirically set N or M.

7 Conclusion

In this paper, we have presented our research proposal, aiming at determining the impact of employing word similarity measures within pattern ranking approaches in bootstrapping systems for relation extraction. We presented two aspects of pattern ranking on which the integration of word similarity will be dependent, that of pattern representation and pattern ranking schemas. We showed that there are minimally lexical and syntactic pattern representations on which different methods of generalizations can be applied. We performed a non-exhaustive survey of pattern ranking measures classified in five different categories. We also briefly looked into different word similarity approaches.

This sets the ground for the methodology that we will pursue, that of implementing a baseline bootstrapping system (inspired by NELL, and working with ClueWeb as a corpus), and then measuring the impact of modifying the pattern representation and the pattern ranking approaches, with and without the use of word similarity measures. There is certainly a complex intricate mutual influence of the preceding aspects which we need to look into. Lastly, we briefly discussed two related issues: the choice of seed set and better estimation of number of patterns to promote.

Acknowledgments

This work has seen the day with the help and advice of Caroline Barrière, my research supervisor at CRIM. This research project is partly funded by an NSERC grant RDCPJ417968-11, titled *Toward a second generation of an automatic product coding system*.

References

Eugene Agichtein and Luis Gravano. 2000. Snowball: Extracting Relations from Large Plain-Text Collections. In *Proceedings of the fifth ACM conference on Digital libraries - DL '00*, pages 85–94, New York, New York, USA. ACM Press.

Eneko Agirre, Enrique Alfonseca, Keith Hall, Jana Kravalova, Marius Paşca, and Aitor Soroa. 2009. A study on similarity and relatedness using distributional and WordNet-based approaches. In *Proceedings of Human Language Technologies: The 2009 Annual Conference of the North American Chapter of the Association for Computational Linguistics on - NAACL '09*, pages 19–27, Morristown, NJ, USA. Association for Computational Linguistics.

Enrique Alfonseca, Pablo Castells, Manabu Okumara, and Maria Ruiz-Casado. 2006a. A Rote Extractor with Edit Distance-based Generalisation and Multi-corpora Precision Calculation. In *COLING-ACL'06 Proceedings of the COLING/ACL Poster Session*, pages 9–16, Morristown, NJ, USA. Association for Computational Linguistics.

Enrique Alfonseca, Maria Ruiz-Casado, Manabu Okumura, and Pablo Castells. 2006b. Towards Large-scale Non-taxonomic Relation Extraction : Estimating the Precision of Rote Extractors. In *Proceedings of the second workshop on ontology learning and population, Coling-ACL'2006*, pages 49–56.

Satanjeev Banerjee and Ted Pedersen. 2002. An Adapted Lesk Algorithm for Word Sense Disambiguation Using WordNet. In Alexander Gelbukh, editor, *Computational linguistics and intelligent text processing*, volume 2276 of *Lecture Notes in Computer Science*, pages 136–145. Springer Berlin Heidelberg, Berlin, Heidelberg, February.

Sebastian Blohm, Philipp Cimiano, and E Stemle. 2007. Harvesting Relations from the Web - Quantifiying the Impact of Filtering Functions. In *Proceedings of the National Conference on Artificial Intelligence*, pages 1316–1321.

Sergey Brin. 1999. Extracting Patterns and Relations from the World Wide Web. In Paolo Atzeni, Alberto Mendelzon, and Giansalvatore Mecca, editors, *The World Wide Web and Databases*, Lecture Notes in Computer Science, chapter Extracting, pages 172–183. Springer Berlin Heidelberg, Berlin, Heidelberg, March.

Elia Bruni, Nam Khan Tran, and Marco Baroni. 2013. Multimodal distributional semantics. *Journal of Artificial Intelligence Research*, 48:1–47.

Razvan C Bunescu and Raymond J Mooney. 2005. A Shortest Path Dependency Kernel for Relation Extraction. In *Proceedings of Human Language Technology Conference and Conference on Empirical Methods in Naural Language Processing (HLT/EMNLP)*, pages 724–731, Vancouver, Canada.

Andrew Carlson, Justin Betteridge, and Bryan Kisiel. 2010. Toward an Architecture for Never-Ending Language Learning. In *Proceedings of the Conference on Artificial Intelligence (AAAI)*, pages 1306–1313.

Aron Culotta and Jeffrey Sorensen. 2004. Dependency tree kernels for relation extraction. In *Proceedings of the 42nd Annual Meeting on Association for Computational Linguistics - ACL '04*, pages 423–429, Morristown, NJ, USA. Association for Computational Linguistics.

VB Dang and Akiko Aizawa. 2008. Multi-class named entity recognition via bootstrapping with dependency tree-based patterns. In *Proceedings of the 12th Pacific-Asia conference on Advances in knowledge discovery and data mining*, pages 76–87.

Yo Ehara, Issei Sato, Hidekazu Oiwa, and Hiroshi Nakagawa. 2013. Understanding seed selection in bootstrapping. In *Proceedings of the TextGraphs-8 Workshop*, pages 44–52, Seattle, Washington, USA.

Oren Etzioni, Michael Cafarella, Doug Downey, Stanley Kok, Ana-maria Popescu, Tal Shaked, Stephen Soderland, Daniel S Weld, and Alexander Yates. 2004. Web-scale information extraction in knowitall: (preliminary results). In *Proceedings of the 13th conference on World Wide Web - WWW '04*, page 100, New York, New York, USA. ACM Press.

Lev Finkelstein, Evgeniy Gabrilovich, Yossi Matias, Ehud Rivlin, Zach Solan, Gadi Wolfman, and Eytan Ruppin. 2001. Placing search in context. In *Proceedings of the tenth international conference on World Wide Web - WWW '01*, pages 406–414, New York, New York, USA. ACM Press.

Takaaki Hasegawa, Satoshi Sekine, and Ralph Grishman. 2004. Discovering relations among named entities from large corpora. In *Proceedings of the 42nd Annual Meeting on Association for Computational Linguistics - ACL '04*, pages 415–422, Morristown, NJ, USA. Association for Computational Linguistics.

JJ Jiang and DW Conrath. 1997. Semantic similarity based on corpus statistics and lexical taxonomy. In *In the Proceedings of ROCLING X, Taiwan*, pages 19–33.

Zornitsa Kozareva and Eduard Hovy. 2010. Not All Seeds Are Equal : Measuring the Quality of Text Mining Seeds. In *Proceeding HLT '10 Human Language Technologies: The 2010 Annual Conference of the North American Chapter of the Association for Computational Linguistics*, pages 618–626.

Claudia Leacock and Martin Chodorow. 1998. Combining Local Context and WordNet Similarity for Word Sense Identification. In Christiane Fellbaum, editor,

WordNet: An electronic lexical database., pages 265–283. MIT Press.

Michael Lesk. 1986. Automatic sense disambiguation using machine readable dictionaries. In *Proceedings of the 5th annual international conference on Systems documentation - SIGDOC '86*, pages 24–26, New York, New York, USA. ACM Press.

Dekang Lin. 1998. An Information-Theoretic Definition of Similarity. In *ICML '98 Proceedings of the Fifteenth International Conference on Machine Learning*, pages 296–304.

T McIntosh and Lars Yencken. 2011. Relation guided bootstrapping of semantic lexicons. In *Proceeding HLT '11 Proceedings of the 49th Annual Meeting of the Association for Computational Linguistics: Human Language Technologies: short papers - Volume 2*, pages 266–270.

Tomas Mikolov, Greg Corrado, Kai Chen, and Jeffrey Dean. 2013. Efficient Estimation of Word Representations in Vector Space. In *Proceedings of the International Conference on Learning Representations (ICLR 2013)*, pages 1–12.

George A. Miller and Walter G. Charles. 1991. Contextual correlates of semantic similarity. *Language and Cognitive Processes*, 6(1):1–28.

George A. Miller. 1995. WordNet: A Lexical Database for English. *Communications of the ACM*, 38(11):39–41.

Patrick Pantel and Marco Pennacchiotti. 2006. Espresso: leveraging generic patterns for automatically harvesting semantic relations. In *Proceedings of the 21st International Conference on Computational Linguistics and the 44th annual meeting of the ACL - ACL '06*, pages 113–120, Morristown, NJ, USA. Association for Computational Linguistics.

Patrick Pantel, Deepak Ravichandran, and Eduard Hovy. 2004. Towards terascale knowledge acquisition. In *Proceedings of the 20th international conference on Computational Linguistics COLING 04*, pages 771–777.

M Pasca, Dekang Lin, Jeffrey Bigham, Andrei Lifchits, and A Jain. 2006. Organizing and searching the world wide web of facts-step one: the one-million fact extraction challenge. *AAAI*, 6:1400–1405.

Kira Radinsky, Eugene Agichtein, Evgeniy Gabrilovich, and Shaul Markovitch. 2011. A word at a time: computing word relatedness using temporal semantic analysis. In *Proceedings of the 20th international conference on World wide web - WWW '11*, page 337, New York, New York, USA. ACM Press.

Philip Resnik. 1995. Using IC to Evaluation the Semantic Similarity in a Taxonomy. In *Proceeding IJCAI'95 Proceedings of the 14th international joint conference on Artificial intelligence - Volume 1*, pages 448–453.

Herbert Rubenstein and John B. Goodenough. 1965. Contextual correlates of synonymy. *Communications of the ACM*, 8(10):627–633, October.

Chen Sijia, Li Yan, and Chen Guang. 2013. Reducing semantic drift in bootstrapping for entity relation extraction. In *Proceedings 2013 International Conference on Mechatronic Sciences, Electric Engineering and Computer (MEC)*, pages 1947–1950. Ieee, December.

Mark Stevenson and Mark A Greenwood. 2005. A semantic approach to IE pattern induction. In *Proceedings of the 43rd Annual Meeting on Association for Computational Linguistics - ACL '05*, pages 379–386, Morristown, NJ, USA. Association for Computational Linguistics.

Ang Sun and Ralph Grishman. 2010. Semi-supervised Semantic Pattern Discovery with Guidance from Unsupervised Pattern Clusters. In *Proceedings of the 23rd International Conference on Computational Linguistics: Posters*, pages 1194–1202, Beijing.

Zhibiao Wu and Martha Palmer. 1994. Verbs semantics and lexical selection. In *Proceedings of the 32nd annual meeting on Association for Computational Linguistics -*, pages 133–138, Morristown, NJ, USA. Association for Computational Linguistics.

Roman Yangarber. 2003. Counter-training in discovery of semantic patterns. In *Proceedings of the 41st Annual Meeting on Association for Computational Linguistics - ACL '03*, volume 1, pages 343–350, Morristown, NJ, USA. Association for Computational Linguistics.

Min Zhang, Jian Su, Danmei Wang, Guodong Zhou, and Chew Lim Tan. 2005. Discovering Relations Between Named Entities form a Large Raw Corpus Using Tree Similarity-based Clustering. In Robert Dale, Kam-Fai Wong, Jian Su, and Oi Yee Kwong, editors, *Natural Language Processing – IJCNLP 2005*, Lecture Notes in Computer Science, pages 378–389. Springer Berlin Heidelberg, Berlin, Heidelberg.

Chunyun Zhang, Weiran Xu, Sheng Gao, and Jun Guo. 2014. A bottom-up kernel of pattern learning for relation extraction. In *The 9th International Symposium on Chinese Spoken Language Processing*, pages 609–613. IEEE, September.

Towards a Better Semantic Role Labeling of Complex Predicates

Glorianna Jagfeld
Institute for Natural Language Processing
University of Stuttgart
Pfaffenwaldring 5b, 70569 Stuttgart, Germany
jagfelga@ims.uni-stuttgart.de

Lonneke van der Plas
Institute of Linguistics
University of Malta
Tal-Qroqq, Msida, Malta
lonneke.vanderplas@um.edu.mt

Abstract

We propose a way to automatically improve the annotation of verbal complex predicates in PropBank which until now has been treating language mostly in a compositional manner. In order to minimize the manual re-annotation effort, we build on the recently introduced concept of *aliasing* complex predicates to existing PropBank rolesets which encompass the same meaning and argument structure. We suggest to find aliases automatically by applying a multilingual distributional model that uses the translations of simple and complex predicates as features. Furthermore, we set up an annotation effort to obtain a frequency balanced, realistic test set for this task. Our method reaches an accuracy of 44% on this test set and 72% for the more frequent test items in a lenient evaluation, which is not far from the upper bounds from human annotation.

1 Introduction

Semantic Role Labeling (SRL) aims at determining 'who' did 'what' to 'whom' in sentences by identifying and associating predicates with their semantic arguments. This information is useful for many downstream applications, for example for question answering (Shen, 2007). The PropBank corpus (PB) (Palmer et al., 2005) is one of the most widely used resources for training SRL systems. It provides senses of (mostly verbal) predicates with their typical semantic arguments annotated in a corpus and accompanied by a lexical resource. The sense of a predicate is referred to as a 'roleset' because it lists all required and possible semantic roles for the predicate used in a specific sense.

The 12K rolesets in PB describe mostly single word predicates, to a great part leaving aside multiword expressions (MWEs). Complex predicates (CPs), 'predicates which are multi-headed: they are composed of more than one grammatical element' (Ramisch, 2012), are most relevant in the context of SRL. Light verb constructions (LVCs), e.g. *take care*, and verb particle constructions (VPCs), e.g. *watch out*, are the most frequently occurring types of CPs. As Bonial et al. (2014) stated 'PB has previously treated language as if it were purely compositional, and has therefore lumped the majority of MWEs in with lexical verb usages'. For example the predicates in the CPs *take a hard line, take time* and many others are all annotated with a sense of *take*, meaning *acquire, come to have, chose, bring with you from somewhere*. This results in a loss of semantic information in the PB annotations.

This is especially critical because CPs are a frequent phenomenon. The Wiki50 corpus (Vincze et al., 2011), which provides a full coverage MWE annotation, counts 814 occurrences of LVCs and VPCs in 4350 sentences. This makes for one CP in every fifth sentence.

Recently, Bonial et al. (2014) have introduced an approach to improve the handling of MWEs in PB while keeping annotation costs low. The process is called *aliasing*. Instead of creating new frames for CPs, human annotators map them to existing PB rolesets which encompass the same semantic and argument structure. For example, the CP *give (a) talk* could be mapped to the alias *lecture.01*. While this

Proceedings of NAACL-HLT 2015 Student Research Workshop (SRW), pages 33–39,
Denver, Colorado, June 1, 2015.

method significantly reduces the effort to create new rolesets, the time consuming manual mapping is still required. To address this problem, our work extends this approach by proposing a method to find the aliases automatically.

One way to find the most suitable alias roleset for a given CP is to group predicates by their rolesets assigned by an automatic SRL system and compute the most similar roleset group by searching for (near-) synonymous predicates of the CP. The roleset of the most similar roleset group is selected as alias for the CP.

Finding synonyms, both single-word and multi-word, from corpora has been done successfully with the multilingual variant of the distributional hypothesis (Van der Plas and Tiedemann, 2006; Van der Plas et al., 2011). The idea behind this approach is that words or MWEs that share many translations are probably synonymous. We use the word alignments in a parallel corpus to find the translations of CPs and single predicates. The predicates are automatically annotated with rolesets by an SRL system. This allows us to compute the most suitable roleset for a given CP fully automatically.

Our contributions are as follows: To the best of our knowledge, this work is the first to address the handling of CPs for SRL in an automatic way. We are thus able to scale up previous work that relies on manual intervention. In addition, we set up an annotation effort to gather a frequency-balanced, data-driven evaluation set that is larger and more diverse than the annotated set provided by Bonial et al. (2014).

2 Representing CPs for SRL

Previous work on representing CPs for SRL has mostly focused on PB. The currently available version of the PB corpus represents most CPs as if they were lexical usages of the verb involved in the predicate. Figure 1 shows an example for the annotation of the LVC *take care* in PB.[1] The CP is split up into its two components that are each assigned their own roleset. This annotation ignores the semantic unity of the CP and is unable to capture its single meaning of *being concerned with* or *caring for* something.

[1]We show an excerpt of the original sentence found in the currently available version of PB (Proposition Bank I).

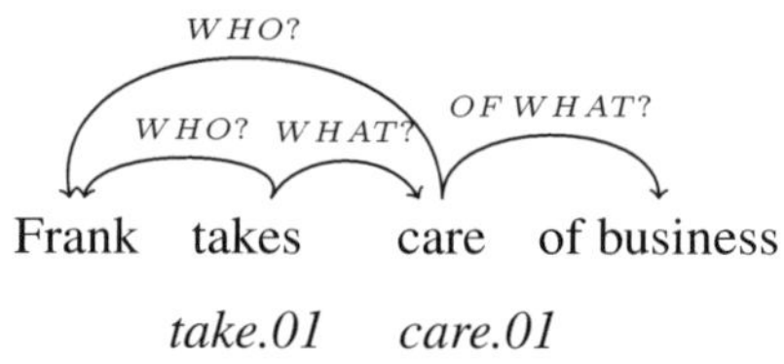

Figure 1: Current PB representation of the CP *take care*

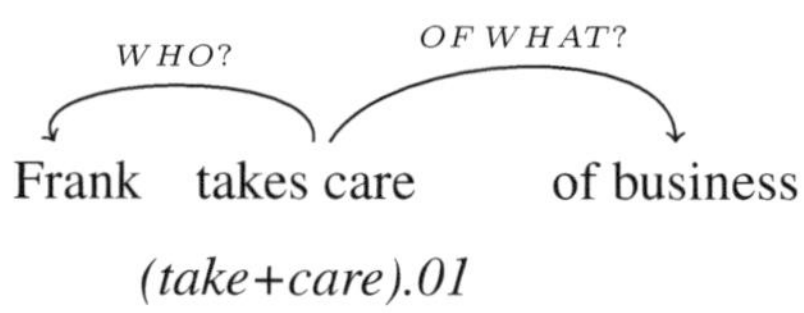

Figure 2: Improved representation of the CP *take care* adopted from (Hwang et al., 2010; Duran et al., 2011)

In contrast to this, Hwang et al. (2010) suggest a new annotation scheme for LVCs that assigns the argument structure of the LVC independently from the argument structure of its components. First, the arguments of the light verb and true predicate are annotated with roles regarding their relationship to the *combination* of the light verb and true predicate. Then, the light verb and predicate lemmas are joined into a single predicate. The result of this process is shown in Figure 2.

Duran et al. (2011) discuss the analysis of Brazilian Portuguese CPs. Similarly to Hwang et al. (2010) they argue that CPs should be treated as single predicates, not only for LVCs but for all CPs. They automatically extract CP candidates from a corpus and represent, if possible, the meaning of the CPs with one or more single-verb paraphrases.

Atkins et al. (2003) describe a way in which LVCs can be annotated in FrameNet (Baker et al., 1998), a framework that describes the semantic argument structure of predicates with semantic roles specific to the meaning of the predicate. In contrast to the proposals for PB by Hwang et al. (2010) and Duran et al. (2011), they suggest to annotate the light verb and its counterpart separately.

The *aliasing* process introduced by Bonial et al. (2014) tries to extend the coverage of PB for CPs while keeping the number of rolesets that should be newly created to a minimum. Bonial et al. (2014) conducted a pilot study re-annotating 138 CPs involving the verb *take*. As a first step, the annotators determined the meaning(s) of the CP by looking at their usage in corpora. If they found that the CP is already adequately represented by the existing rolesets for *take*, no further action was needed (18/138). Otherwise, they were instructed to propose as alias an existing PB entry that encompasses the same semantics and argument structure as the CP (100/138). If unable to find an alias, they could suggest to create a new roleset for this CP (20/138). Expressions for which the annotators were unable to determine the meaning were marked as idiomatic expressions that need further treatment (4/138).[2]

According to this process, *take care* could be aliased to the existing PB roleset *care.01* whose entry is shown in Figure 3. This alias replaces *(take+care).01* shown in Figure 2 and thus avoids the creation of a new roleset.

Roleset id: care.01, *to be concerned*
Arg0: carer, agent
Arg1: thing cared for/about

Figure 3: alias PB roleset for the predicate *take care*

Encouraged by the high proportion of CPs that could successfully be aliased in the pilot study by Bonial et al. (2014), we created a method to automatically find aliases for CPs in order to decrease the amount of human intervention, thereby scaling up the coverage of CPs in PB.

3 Method

The task of finding aliases for CPs automatically is related to finding (near-) synonymous predicates and their accompanying roleset for the CPs. To find the near-synonyms, we apply the distributional hypothesis which states that we can assess the similarity of expressions by looking at their contexts (Firth, 1957). As previous work (Van der Plas and Tiedemann, 2006) has shown that multilingual contexts work better for synonym acquisition than monolingual syntactic contexts, we use the translations of the CPs and other predicates to all 20 languages available via the word alignments in a multilingual parallel corpus as context.

Figure 4 shows an overview of the architecture of our system. First, we extract the CPs and all predicates that share a PB roleset (PB roleset groups) from the parallel corpus. For example, all verbs that were assigned to the roleset *care.01* by the SRL system belong to the PB roleset group of *care.01*. The CPs stem from the gold standard MWE annotation in the Wiki50 corpus (Vincze et al., 2011). We parsed this corpus to obtain lemmas, POS and syntactic dependencies and extracted this information for all VPCs and LVCs annotated in the corpus.[3] Figure 5 shows the two patterns we identified that the majority of the CPs followed.[4] We used these two patterns to search for occurrences of the CPs in Europarl.

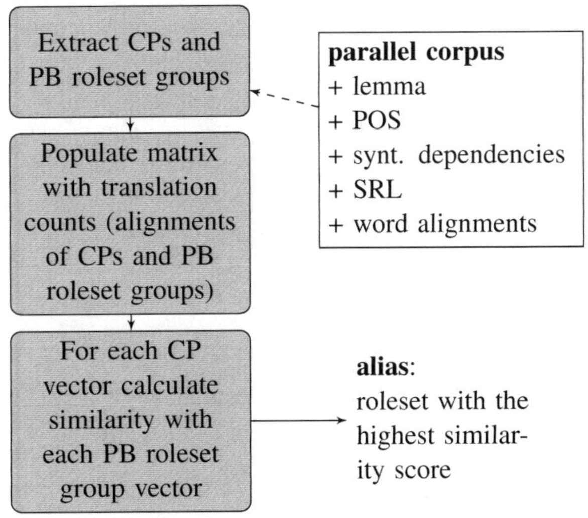

Figure 4: Overview of the alias finder

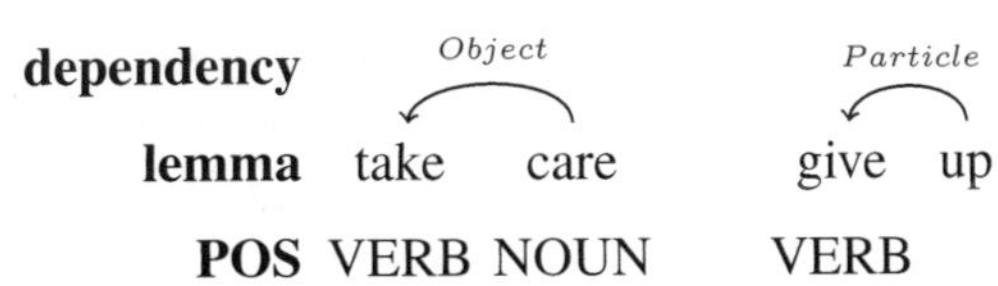

Figure 5: Patterns used for finding occurrences of CPs

Next, we build a co-occurrence matrix containing as head terms the CP and all PB roleset groups found in the parallel corpus. Figure 6 shows a toy example of such a matrix for the CP *take care*. The

[2]Note that the numbers do not add up to 138 because four MWEs obtained two different strategies.

[3]We concentrate on VPCs and LVCs because they are the most frequent types of CP in English.

[4]Here we use the example CPs *take care* and *give up*, but the lemmas were of course introduced as variables.

head words are listed in the rows, the translations (i.e. features) in the columns. Note that in contrast to previous work on distributional semantics we include PB roleset groups as head words. These contain several distinct verbal predicates but they share the same sense. Consequently, polysemous verbs are found in several distinct PB roleset groups.

	ter cuidado (es)	achten (de)	prendre soin (fr)	penser a (fr)
take care	3	3	5	0
care.01	4	3	7	1
think.01	0	2	1	6

Figure 6: Toy example co-occurrence matrix

Finally, we measure the similarity between CPs and roleset groups using the cosine similarity because it worked best in previous experiments for finding synonyms (Van der Plas, 2008). This results in a similarity ranking of PB roleset groups for each CP, from which we select the roleset with the highest cosine value as alias.

4 Experiments

4.1 Tools and Data

We processed the English section of the Europarl corpus (Koehn, 2005) (about 2 million sentences) with the MATE tools (Björkelund et al., 2010) to obtain lemmas, part-of-speech (POS) tags, dependency structures and semantic role labels. These annotations are used to find occurrences of the CPs and words assigned with PB rolesets in the English part. The word alignments produced with the grow-diag-final-and-heuristics (Koehn et al., 2003) provided by the OPUS project (Tiedemann, 2012) are then used to find their alignments to all other 20 languages in the corpus and exploited as features in the distributional model.

4.2 Evaluation Framework

Human Annotation. In order to evaluate our system, we set up an annotation effort loosely following the guidelines provided by Bonial et al. (2014). We selected 50 LVCs and 50 VPCs from the Wiki50 corpus (Vincze et al., 2011) divided equally over two frequency groups: Half of the expressions occur only once in the Wiki50 corpus (low-frequency subgroup) and the other half occur at least twice (high-frequency subgroup). All occurrences of these 100 CP types in the corpus were selected to account for the polysemy of CPs. Different instances of the same CP could get assigned to different aliases. This resulted in a total of 197 annotated instances.

Four annotators were presented with the CP in their original sentence context and were asked to propose one or several PB aliases which encompass the same meaning and argument structure. One annotator (A, one of the authors of this article) labeled the whole set of 100 expressions. The three other annotators (B,C,D) each labeled one third of the expressions assigned randomly, so that every expression was annotated by two annotators.

First, they were asked to decide if there is already an appropriate PB roleset for the CP and then provide it. The annotators were requested to divide these cases into semantically compositional CPs (e.g. obtain permission with the roleset *obtain.01*) and uncompositional CPs for which PB already provides a multi-word predicate (e.g. *open.03* for *open_up*). For the remaining CPs, they were asked to suggest PB rolesets (aliases) that share the same semantics and argument structure as the CP.

The simple inter-annotator agreement[5] was 67% for annotator A%B, 51% for A&C and 44% for A&D. These agreement figures are higher than the figures in Bonial et al. (2014), and actual agreement is probably even higher, because synonymous rolesets are regarded as disagreements. Annotator A discussed the annotations with the other annotators and they were able to reach a consensus that resulted in a final agreed-upon test set.

Table 1 shows the final decisions with respect to the complete set of 197 expressions. In line with the results from Bonial et al. (2014) who aliased 100 out of 138 uncompositional *take* MWEs, we were also able to alias most of the CPs in our annotation set.

The final Wiki50 set consists of 154[7] instances of

[5]Kappa scores (Cohen, 1960) are not suited to the present multi-label and multi-class setting: Annotators could choose from roughly 6K classes and were encouraged to provide multiple synonymous rolesets.

[6]Discarded CPs contained spelling or annotation errors in the Wiki50 corpus.

[7]We removed two CPs from the 'aliased' group because our extraction patterns do not cover LVCs formed with an adjective.

Decision	Count	MWE example
aliased	96	take part
multi-word PB pred.	60	open up
compositional	18	obtain permission
no alias found	16	go into politics
discarded[6]	7	take conrol

Table 1: Final decisions on the 197 annotated expressions

CPs from the categories 'aliased' and 'multi-word PB predicate' (low-frequency: 34, high-frequency: 120). The latter were included because the predicted roleset of the SRL only coincides with the gold standard for 23 out of 60 instances. This means that for the majority of the CPs, even if an adequate PB roleset exists, this roleset was not selected by the SRL system. We hope to also improve these cases with our method. All CPs were labeled with one to four appropriate PB alias rolesets.

In addition, we evaluated our system on the dataset from Bonial et al. (2014), restricted to the type of CP our system handles (LVCs and VPCs) and verb aliases (as opposed to aliases being a noun or adjective roleset). We used 70 of the 100 MWEs from their annotations.

Evaluation Measures and Baseline. We report the accuracy of our system's predictions as compared to the gold standard. For the STRICT ACCURACY, an alias is counted as correct if it corresponds exactly to one of the gold aliases. This evaluation is very rigid and regards synonymous rolesets as incorrect. Thus, we also compute a more LENIENT ACCURACY, which counts an alias as correct if it belongs to the same VerbNet (Kipper-Schuler, 2006) verb class as the gold alias. VerbNet (VN) is a hierarchically organized lexicon of English verbs. It consists of syntactically and semantically coherent verb classes, which are extensions of the classes proposed by Levin (1993). For the PB-VN mappings, we rely on the resource provided by the SemLink project[8] (Loper et al., 2007) and use the most-specific (deepest) layer of the verb classes. Since the mapping provided in SemLink is not complete (only 58% of the rolesets found in PB have a mapping to a corresponding VN class), we discard rolesets that are not found in SemLink, unless they are correct according to the gold standard in the first place.

We compared our system with a baseline system that distinguishes between VPCs and LVCs. For VPCs, it checks whether there exists a PB multi-word predicate for the expression and selects the first roleset of that predicate (e.g. there exists a predicate called *open_up (open.03)* for the VPC 'open up'). For LVCs, it checks whether the noun has a corresponding verb predicate in PB and selects the first roleset of this predicate (e.g. *walk.01* for *take a walk*). Note that this is an informed baseline that is very hard to beat and only fails in case of lack in coverage.

5 Results and Discussion

We evaluated our approach on the 160 CPs annotated in the course of this work (Wiki50 set), as well as on the 70 *take* CPs from Bonial et al. (2014) (*take* set) and compare our results to the baseline. Table 2 shows percentage coverage, accuracy and the harmonic mean of coverage and accuracy for our system and the baseline. We report results on the two evaluation sets in the strict and lenient evaluation.

The first five rows of Table 2 show the results for the Wiki50 set and its subsets. We see that our system scores 44.1 accuracy on the whole test set in the strict evaluation and 69.0 in the lenient evaluation. These numbers seem quite low, but they are not that far apart from the micro averaged IAA from our annotation effort (53%). Our system outperforms the baseline with very high coverage numbers. It beats the baseline in terms of the harmonic mean for all subsets except the multiword PB predicate subset. This is not surprising as the test items in this subset have a corresponding multiword PB predicate and all the baseline has to do is select the right sense. The high performance of the baseline on the multiword PB predicates leads to the high accuracy numbers for the baseline in all (sub-)sets except from the alias subset, which contains the expressions for which a true alias was provided. Our system beats the baseline in terms of strict accuracy for the alias subset. This is good news because the actual task is to find new aliases for CPs that are not covered in PB. The performance on the low-frequency subset is lower than on the high-frequency subset, as expected for a distributional method.

[8] http://verbs.colorado.edu/semlink/

Set	Strict Cov	Strict Acc	Strict Hm	Lenient Cov	Lenient Acc	Lenient Hm
Wiki50 all	**98.7** (65.6)	44.1 (**54.5**)	**60.9** (59.5)	**98.0** (59.5)	69.0 (**85.9**)	**81.0** (70.3)
alias	**98.9** (50.0)	**36.6** (34.0)	**53.4** (40.5)	**98.4** (40.5)	60.0 (**68.8**)	**74.5** (51.0)
mw. PB pred.	**98.3** (86.7)	55.9 (**71.2**)	71.3 (**78.1**)	**97.6** (84.6)	82.5 (**97.7**)	89.4 (**90.7**)
high-freq.	**100.0** (68.3)	45.0 (**52.4**)	**62.1** (59.3)	**100.0** (62.7)	72.0 (**84.4**)	**83.7** (72.0)
low-freq.	**94.1** (50.0)	40.6 (**58.5**)	**56.8** (54.1)	**92.6** (41.4)	60.0 (**91.7**)	**72.8** (57.0)
take	67.1 (**71.4**)	25.5 (**32.0**)	37.0 (**44.2**)	56.6 (**64.9**)	**60.0** (45.0)	**58.3** (53.8)

Table 2: Percentage coverage (Cov), accuracy (Acc) and the harmonic mean (Hm) of coverage and accuracy of the predicted aliases in the Wiki50 set (+ four of its subsets) and the *take* set; The results of the baseline are in brackets

The results on the *take* set are shown in the last row of Table 2. Compared to the Wiki50 set, they are substantially lower. We would like to stress that the *take* set is far from what we expect to find in an actual corpus. This set comprises only CPs that contain the word *take*. Many test items have been extracted from WordNet and possibly have a very low frequency in a general corpus. This is reflected in the coverage number, which shows the proportion of CPs for which our system was able to suggest at least one alias: It is above 94% for all Wiki50 (sub)sets, but only 67% for the take set. We constructed the Wiki50 set to allow us to get a better estimate of how our method would fare in a natural setting.

5.1 Error analysis

We examined all expressions from the full Wiki50 set for which the top ranked predicted alias was incorrect. Due to space limitations we only mention the main reasons for errors we identified. First of all, the limited language domain of the Europarl corpus caused a low frequency of some rolesets selected as gold alias, like *fuse.01* ('melt into lump') for the VPC *melt down*. This problem could be solved by adding more parallel data from different domains.

Another source of errors is the fact that our approach requires the output of an SRL system which, in turn, we want to improve. For 45 out of 160 CPs our system suggested the roleset as alias that was assigned to the verb by the SRL system, e.g. *leave.02* for *leave for*. But the automatically attributed roleset is only correct in 21 cases, which means that we reproduced the errors of the SRL in 24 cases.

Some LVCs keep their light verb structure in other languages, i.e. they receive multi-word translations. This diminishes the overlap of translations between the LVC and the PB roleset groups. PB rolesets are assigned to simplex verbs and therefore predominantly receive simplex translations. As more frequent rolesets have more diverse translations that contain more MWEs, these are promoted as aliases. Applying frequency weights to the roleset matrix could remedy this problem.

Lastly, our system adheres to the most frequent sense baseline due to lack of word sense disambiguation of the CPs and assigns the alias that fits the most dominant sense of the CP in the corpus.

6 Conclusions

We have presented an approach to handle CPs in SRL that extends on work from Bonial et al. (2014). We automatically link VPCs and LVCs to the PB roleset that best describes their meaning, by relying on word alignments in parallel corpora and distributional methods. We set up an annotation effort to gather a frequency-balanced, contextualized evaluation set that is more natural, varied and larger than the pilot annotations provided by Bonial et al. (2014). Our method can be used to alleviate the manual annotation effort by providing a correct alias in 44% of the cases (up to 72% for the more frequent test items when taking synonymous rolesets into account). These results are not too far from the upper bounds we calculate from human annotations.

In future work, we would like to improve our method by incorporating the methods discussed in the error analysis section. Additionally, we plan to evaluate the impact of the new CP representation on downstream applications by retraining an SRL system on the new annotations.

Acknowledgments

We thank Anna Konobelkina and two anonymous annotators for their efforts as well as the anonymous reviewers.

References

Sue Atkins, Charles J. Fillmore, and Christopher R. Johnson. 2003. Lexicographic relevance: selecting information from corpus evidence. *International Journal of Lexicography*, 16.3.

Collin F. Baker, Charles J. Fillmore, and John B. Lowe. 1998. The berkeley framenet project. In *Proceedings of the 36th Annual Meeting of the Association for Computational Linguistics and 17th International Conference on Computational Linguistics - Volume 1*, ACL '98, Stroudsburg, PA, USA.

Anders Björkelund, Bernd Bohnet, Love Hafdell, and Pierre Nugues. 2010. A high-performance syntactic and semantic dependency parser. In *Coling 2010: Demonstrations*, Beijing, China.

Claire Bonial, Meredith Green, Jenette Preciado, and Martha Palmer. 2014. An approach to take multi-word expressions. In *Proceedings of the 10th Workshop on Multiword Expressions (MWE)*, Gothenburg, Sweden.

Jacob Cohen. 1960. A Coefficient of Agreement for Nominal Scales. *Educational and Psychological Measurement*, 20(1).

Magali Sanches Duran, Carlos Ramisch, Sandra Maria Aluísio, and Aline Villavicencio. 2011. Identifying and analyzing brazilian portuguese complex predicates. In *Proceedings of the Workshop on Multiword Expressions: From Parsing and Generation to the Real World*, MWE '11, Stroudsburg, PA, USA.

John Rupert Firth. 1957. A synopsis of linguistic theory 1930-55. 1952-59.

Jena D. Hwang, Archna Bhatia, Clare Bonial, Aous Mansouri, Ashwini Vaidya, Nianwen Xue, and Martha Palmer. 2010. Propbank annotation of multilingual light verb constructions. In *Proceedings of the Fourth Linguistic Annotation Workshop*, LAW IV '10, Stroudsburg, PA, USA.

Karin Kipper-Schuler. 2006. *VerbNet: A Broad-Coverage, Comprehensive Verb Lexicon*. Ph.D. thesis, University of Pennsylvania.

Philipp Koehn, Franz Josef Och, and Daniel Marcu. 2003. Statistical phrase-based translation. In *Proceedings of the 2003 Conference of the North American Chapter of the Association for Computational Linguistics on Human Language Technology - Volume 1*, NAACL '03, Stroudsburg, PA, USA.

Philipp Koehn. 2005. Europarl: A Parallel Corpus for Statistical Machine Translation. In *Conference Proceedings: the Tenth Machine Translation Summit*, Phuket, Thailand.

Beth Levin. 1993. *English verb classes and alternations: a preliminary investigation*. University of Chicago Press, Chicago and London.

Edward Loper, Szu-Ting Yi, and Martha Palmer. 2007. Combining lexical resources: Mapping between propbank and verbnet. In *Proceedings of the 7th International Workshop on Computational Linguistics*, Tilburg, the Netherlands.

Martha Palmer, Daniel Gildea, and Paul Kingsbury. 2005. The proposition bank: An annotated corpus of semantic roles. *Computational Linguistics Journal*, 31(1).

Carlos Ramisch. 2012. *A generic and open framework for multiword expressions treatment: from acquisition to applications*. Ph.D. thesis, University of Grenoble (France) and Federal University of Rio Grande do Sul (Brazil).

Dan Shen. 2007. Using semantic role to improve question answering. In *Proceedings of EMNLP 2007*.

Jörg Tiedemann. 2012. Parallel data, tools and interfaces in opus. In *Proceedings of the Eight International Conference on Language Resources and Evaluation (LREC'12)*, Istanbul, Turkey.

Lonneke van der Plas and Jörg Tiedemann. 2006. Finding synonyms using automatic word alignment and measures of distributional similarity. In *Proceedings of ACL-COLING 2006*, Sydney, Australia.

Lonneke van der Plas, Jörg Tiedemann, and Ismail Fahmi. 2011. Automatic extraction of medical term variants from multilingual parallel translations. In *Interactive Multi-modal Question Answering*, Theory and Applications of Natural Language Processing. Springer-Verlag, Berlin.

Lonneke van der Plas. 2008. *Automatic lexico-semantic acquisition for question answering*. Ph.D. thesis, University of Groningen.

Veronika Vincze, István Nagy T., and Gábor Berend. 2011. Multiword expressions and named entities in the wiki50 corpus. In *Proceedings of the International Conference Recent Advances in Natural Language Processing 2011*, Hissar, Bulgaria.

Exploring Relational Features and Learning under Distant Supervision for Information Extraction Tasks

Ajay Nagesh
Dept. of Computer Science and Engineering, IIT Bombay.
Faculty of Information Technology, Monash University.
ajaynagesh@cse.iitb.ac.in

Abstract

Information Extraction (IE) has become an indispensable tool in our quest to handle the data deluge of the information age. IE can broadly be classified into Named-entity Recognition (NER) and Relation Extraction (RE). In this thesis, we view the task of IE as finding patterns in unstructured data, which can either take the form of features and/or be specified by constraints. In NER, we study the categorization of complex relational[1] features and outline methods to learn feature combinations through induction. We demonstrate the efficacy of induction techniques in learning : i) rules for the identification of named entities in text – the novelty is the application of induction techniques to learn in a very expressive declarative rule language ii) a richer sequence labeling model – enabling optimal learning of discriminative features. In RE, our investigations are in the paradigm of *distant supervision*, which facilitates the creation of large albeit noisy training data. We devise an inference framework in which constraints can be easily specified in learning relation extractors. In addition, we reformulate the learning objective in a max-margin framework. To the best of our knowledge, our formulation is the first to optimize multi-variate non-linear performance measures such as F_β for a latent variable structure prediction task.

1 Introduction

Most of the content that we come across in the digital media in the form of emails, blogs, webpages, enterprise data and so on are authored in natural language and have very little structure to them. With the dawn of the information age, we produce a colossal amount of unstructured data everyday. This presents an enormous challenge for machines to process, curate, search and reason in such data.

The process of automatically identifying and disambiguating entities, their attributes and relationships in unstructured data sources is termed as *Information Extraction (IE). IE* facilitates a rich and structured representation of data, enabling downstream applications to process unstructured documents like a standard database. The richness present in natural language text, presupposition of world knowledge and the rapid rate of content creation makes IE a highly challenging task. As a result, it has been a very active area of research in the computational linguistics community for over two decades (Sarawagi, 2008).

A few of the challenges faced when performing information extraction: (i) *Entity Disambiguation*: `Jeff Bezos` and `Bezos` refer to the same entity. `Washington` could be either a city, a state, or a person depending on the context. (ii) *Scope Resolution*: Certain Entities such as `Washington` in "`Washington Post`" should not be labeled as a location name because the entire textual span is an organization name (iii) *Type Disambiguation*: In the sentence, *" England beat Australia 2 - 0"*. `England` and `Australia` are sports organizations. (iv) *Relation mention detection*: The co-occurrence of `Obama` and `US` in a sentence is not a sure indication that the `President` relation (obtained from a database of facts) is expressed in it.

1.1 Contributions of the thesis

The problem of Information Extraction can be viewed as that of finding patterns in the data. These patterns can either take the form of features or can be specified as constraints on the search space.

Data-driven Patterns : Feature Combinations

Let us suppose that we are given a set of basic features (*e.g.* `Caps` - *a capitalized token*; `LastName` - *occurrence in a dictionary of last-names*). Named-

[1] Terminology is borrowed from *logic*, where relational logic is more powerful than propositional logic with the inclusion of quantifiers, but is a subset of first-order logic

Proceedings of NAACL-HLT 2015 Student Research Workshop (SRW), pages 40–47,
Denver, Colorado, June 1, 2015.

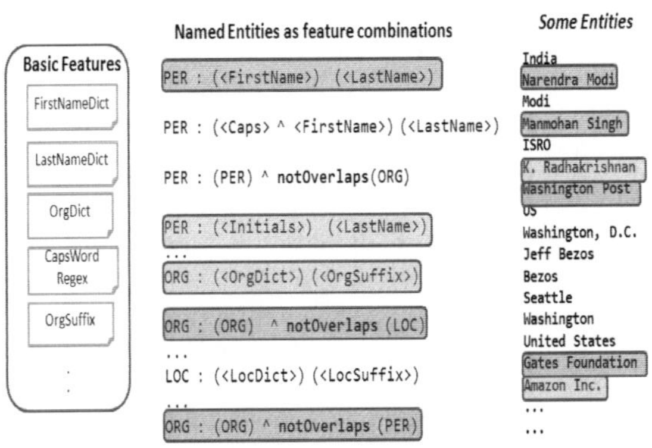

Figure 1: Patterns as Feature Combinations

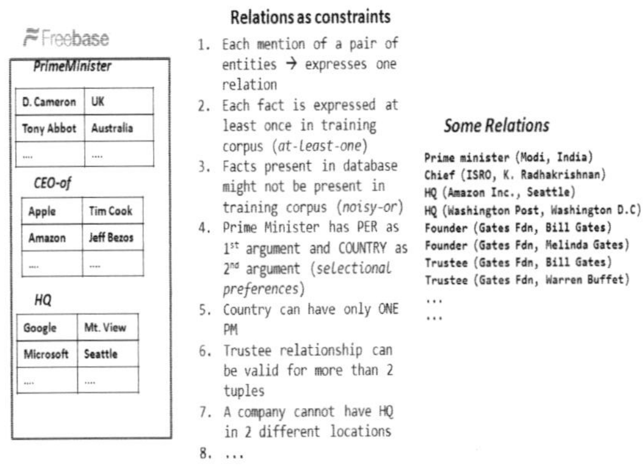

Figure 2: Patterns as Constraints

entities can be discovered by learning combinations of such features. For instance, *"if a span of text contains two tokens,* `Caps` *followed by* `LastName`*, then it is most probably a person named entity"*. We consider the previous statement as a pattern, leading to a named-entity.

Figure 1 depicts some of the basic features, a number of patterns (basic feature combinations) and the entities in text that can potentially match with these patterns. Named-entity recognition (NER) can immensely benefit from such patterns, some of which are domain-specific and others, domain-independent. Several patterns are non-trivial combinations of basic features. For instance, *"if a* `location` *name overlaps with an* `organization`*, then it is not a* `location` *named-entity"*. (*e.g.* `Washington` in `Washington Post`).

These patterns are very large in number and we could define them as feature classes. The set of features defined by them form a feature space. Since the number patterns are many and we are not sure which ones are triggered in a given piece of text, we would like to learn / induce such patterns.

In this thesis, we study the categorization of the feature classes. We also define various methods to learn feature combinations through induction. The features induced are consumed by a rule-based NER system to learn compact and "interpretable" rules that have a reasonable accuracy. We also demonstrate the use of these features in max-margin based sequence labeling models.

User-Specified Patterns : Constraints

Consider the problem of identifying relationships between entities in text. Here we can look at patterns as constraints that need to be enforced on relations extracted. Some of these are listed in Figure 2. They are few compared to the entity recognition case and can be specified by the user to restrict the search space.

For instance, we would like to enforce the following constraint: *For a* `Prime-minister` *relation, the first argument has to be a* `person` *and the second argument has to be a* `country`.

In this thesis, we look at a specific paradigm of relation extraction called *distant supervision* (Mintz et al., 2009). The goal is to learn relation extraction models by aligning facts in a database (Figure 2) to sentences in a large unlabeled corpus. Since the individual sentences are not hand labeled, the facts in the database act as "weak" or "distant" labels, and hence, the learning scenario is termed as distantly supervised. We look at ways in which constraints can be specified while learning relation extractors in this setting. We formulate an integer linear programming-based framework to facilitate the addition of constraints.

Existing distant supervision-based systems are often trained by optimizing performance measures (such as conditional log-likelihood or error rate) that are not directly related to the task-specific non-linear performance measure, *e.g.*, the F_1-score. We present a novel max-margin learning approach to optimize non-linear performance measures for distantly supervised relation extraction models.

2 Learning for Named-Entity Extraction

Several problems in Machine Learning are immensely benefited from a rich structural representation of the data (Flach and Lachiche, 1999; Roth and Yih, 2001). Specifically, the tasks in Information Extraction are relation-intensive and the usage of relational features has been shown to be quite effective in practice (Califf, 1998; Roth and Yih, 2001). In this section, we define categories of predicates and discuss the complexity-based classification of relational features followed by techniques to induce features in several of these categories.

Feature Space Categorization

The relational features are in a language that is similar in expressive power as *first order definite clauses* (Horn, 1951). Predicates are defined on textual spans. The head predicate is the class label of a textual span.

We define two types of body predicates, namely, *relation* and *basic feature* predicates. A *relation* predicate is a binary predicate that represents the relationship between two *spans* of text. *E.g.* `overlaps(X,Y)`. A *basic feature* predicate is an assertion of a situation or a property of a *span* or a *subspan*. For example, `FirstName(X)` states that the span of text X occurs in a dictionary of first names. We illustrate each of these feature classes with an example of a typical definite clause belonging to the feature class.

1. **Simple Conjuncts (SCs)**:
   `Org(X) :- OrgGazeteer(X),CapsWord(X).`
   e.g. Microsoft
2. **Candidate Definition Features (CDs)** : These consist of the two following feature classes.
   (a) **Absolute Features (AFs)**: non-overlapping evidence predicates chained by relation predicates.
   `person-AF(X) :- contains(X, X1), FirstNameDict(X1), CapsWord(X1), before(X1,X2), contains(X, X2), CapsWord(X2).` *e.g.:* Sachin Tendulkar
   (b) **Composite Features (CFs)**: Defined as a conjunction of two AFs that share the same head predicate.
   `person(X) :- person-AF (X), leftContext(X, 1, L2), Salutation(L2).` *e.g.:* Mr. Sachin Tendulkar (note the presence of contextual clues such as salutation)
3. **Candidate Refinement Features (CRs)**: The body of the clause is defined by head predicates that belong to different class labels, and can contain negations in the body (hence, not a definite clause)
   `Loc(X) :- Loc1(X),org1(Y),¬overlaps(X,Y).`
   A span of text is a location, *"if it matches a location feature and does not overlap with an organization feature"*. *e.g.:* Washington in "Washington Post" will not be marked as a location, due to this feature.

2.1 Feature Induction in a Rule-based Setting

Rule-based systems for NER achieve state-of-the-art accuracies (Chiticariu et al., 2010). However, manually building and customizing rules is a complex and labor-intensive process. In this work, we outline an approach that facilitates the process of building customizable rules for NER through rule induction. Given a set of basic feature predicates and an annotated document collection, our goal is to generate with reasonable accuracy an initial set of rules that are interpretable and thus can be easily refined by a human developer. Our contributions include (i) an efficient rule induction process in a declarative rule language, (ii) usage of induction biases to enhance rule interpretability, and (iii) definition of extractor complexity as a first step to quantify the interpretability of an extractor. We present initial promising results with our system and study the effect of induction bias and customization of basic features on the accuracy and complexity of induced rules. We demonstrate through experiments that the induced rules have good accuracy and low complexity, according to our complexity measure.

Our induction system is modeled on a four-stage manual rule development process since the overall structure of the induced rules must be similar in spirit to that which a developer who follows best practices would write. The stages of rule development and the corresponding phases of induction are summarized in Figure 3. In our system, we combine several induction techniques such as *least general generalization (LGG)*, iterative clustering, propositional rule learning in order to induce NER rules in a declarative rule language known as *Annotation Query Language (AQL)*. A brief overview of the salient aspects of our induction system is presented

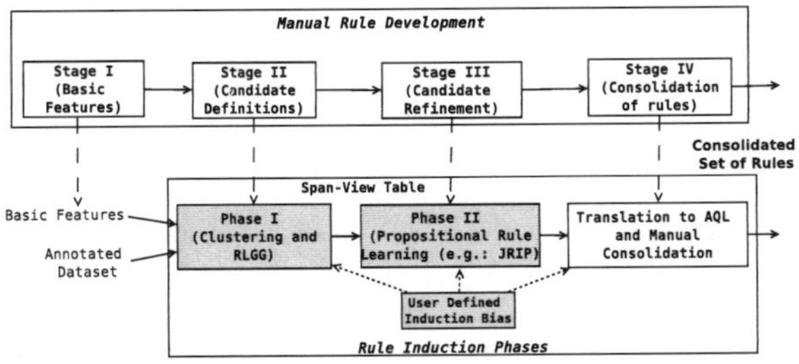

Figure 3: Correspondence between Manual Rule development and Rule Induction

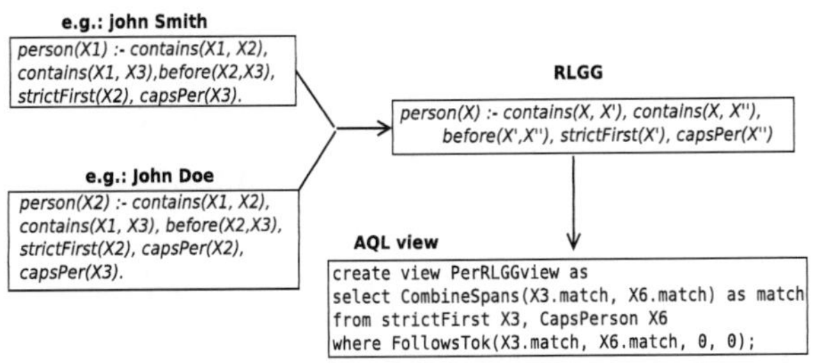

Figure 4: Relative Least General Generalization

in the following paragraphs.

Background Knowledge. We represent each example in the form of *first order definite clauses*, in conjunction with relevant background knowledge. This background knowledge will serve as input to our induction system.

Clustering and RLGG. The first phase of induction uses a combination of *clustering* and *relative least general generalization (RLGG)* techniques (Nienhuys-Cheng and Wolf, 1997; Muggleton and Feng, 1992). Using clustering, we group the examples based on the similarity of their background knowledge. This process is interleaved by RLGG where we take a set of examples and find their generalization that is analogous to the *least upper bound*. We recursively find pairwise-RLGGs of all examples in a cluster. At the end of this phase, we have a number of CD features.

The representation of an example and the RLGG procedure is shown in Figure 4.

Propositional Rule Learning. In the second phase, we begin by forming a structure known as the *span-view table*. Broadly speaking, this is an attribute-value table formed by all the features induced in the first phase along with the textual spans generated by them. The attribute-value table is used as input to a propositional rule learner such as *JRIP* to learn accurate compositions of a useful (as determined by the learning algorithm) subset of the CD features. This forms the second phase of our system. The rules learnt from this phase are in the space of CR features.

Induction Biases. At various phases, several induction biases are introduced to enhance the interpretability of rules. These biases capture the expertise gleaned from manual rule development and constrain the search space in our induction system.

Extractor Complexity. Since our goal is to generate extractors with manageable complexity, we must introduce a quantitative measure of extractor complexity, in order to (1) judge the complexity of the extractors generated by our system, and (2) reduce the search space considered by the induction system. To this end, we define a simple complexity score that is a function of the number of rules, and the number of predicates in the body of each rule of the extractor. Our simple notion of rule length is motivated by existing literature in the area of database systems.

AQL and SystemT : Advantages. The *hypothesis language* of our induction system is *AQL*, and we employ *SystemT* as the *theorem prover*. SystemT provides a very fast rule execution engine and is crucial to our induction system because we test multiple hypotheses in the search for the more promising ones. AQL provides a very expressive rule representation language that has proven to be capable of encoding all the paradigms that any rule-based representation can encode. The dual advantages of *rich rule-representation* and *execution efficiency* are the main motivations behind our choice.

We experimented with three different starting sets of basic feature predicates (with increasing accuracy and complexity) and observed that the complexity of the final set of induced rules is directly proportional to that of the initial set, both in terms of accuracy and complexity. We compared our induced set of rules with the manual rules. We achieve upto 75% accuracy of the state-of-the-art manual rules with a decrease in extractor complexity of upto 61%. For a more detailed exposition of the system and discussion of experiments, please refer to our work (Nagesh et al., 2012).

2.2 Feature Induction in a Max-margin Setting

In this piece of work, we view the problem of NER from the perspective of sequence labeling. The goal is to investigate the effectiveness of using relational features in the input space of a max-margin based sequence labeling model. Our work is based on StructHKL (Nair et al., 2012) and standard StructSVM formulations. We propose two techniques to learn a richer sequence labeling model by using relational features discussed above.

In one technique, we leverage an existing system that is known to learn optimal feature conjunctions (SCs) in order to learn relational features such as AFs and CFs. To achieve this, we propose a two-step process : (i) enumerate a good set of AFs using existing induction techniques (ii) use the StructHKL framework, which learns optimal conjunctions to learn CFs.

In the other technique, we leverage the StructSVM framework. We define a subsequence kernel to implicitly capture the relational features and reformulate the training objective.

Our experiments in sequence labeling tasks reinforce the importance of induction bias and the need for interpretability to achieve high-quality NER rules, as observed in the experiments of our previous work on rule induction.

3 Learning for Relation Extraction

In the second part of the thesis, we investigate another important problem in IE, namely, *relation extraction*. The task of extracting relational facts that pertains to a set of entities from natural language text is termed as *relation extraction*. For example, given a natural language sentence, *"On Friday, President Barack Obama defended his administration's mass collection of telephone and Internet records in the United States"*, we can infer the relation, `President(Barack Obama, United States)` between the entities `Barack Obama` and `United States`.

Our framework is motivated by distant supervision for learning relation extraction models (Mintz et al., 2009). Prior work casts this problem as a multi-instance multi-label learning problem (Hoffmann et al., 2011; Surdeanu et al., 2012). It is multi-instance because for a given entity-pair, only the label of the bag of sentences that contains both entities (aka mentions) is given. It is multi-label because a bag of mentions can have multiple labels. The interdependencies between relation labels and (hidden) mention labels are modeled by a Markov Random Field (Hoffmann et al., 2011).

3.1 Constrained Distant Supervision

Various models have been proposed in recent literature to align the facts in the database to their mentions in the corpus. In this work, we discuss and critically analyze a popular alignment strategy called the *"at least one"* heuristic. We provide a simple, yet effective relaxation to this strategy.

Our work extends the work by Hoffmann et al. (2011). We formulate the inference procedures in training as integer linear programming (*ILP*) problems and implement the relaxation to the *"at least one "* heuristic through a soft constraint in this formulation. This relaxation is termed as *"noisy-or"*. The idea is to model the situation where a fact is present in the database but it is not instantiated in the text.

Additionally, our inference formulation enables us to model additional type of constraints such as selectional preferences of arguments. Empirically, we demonstrate that this simple strategy leads to a better performance under certain settings when compared to the existing approaches. For additional details, please refer to our paper (Nagesh et al., 2014).

3.2 Distant Supervision in a Max-margin Setting

Rich models with latent variables are popular in many problems in natural language processing. For instance, in IE, one needs to predict the relation labels that an entity-pair can take based on the hidden relation mentions, *i.e.*, the relation labels for occurrences of the entity-pair in a given corpus. These models are often trained by optimizing performance measures (such as conditional log-likelihood or error rate) that are not directly related to the task-specific non-linear performance measure, *e.g.*, the F_1-score. However, better models may be trained by optimizing the task-specific performance measure while allowing latent variables to adapt their values accordingly.

Large-margin methods have been shown to be a

compelling approach to learn rich models detailing the inter-dependencies among the output variables. Some methods optimize loss functions decomposable over the *training instances* (Taskar et al., 2003; Tsochantaridis et al., 2004) compared to others that optimize non-decomposable loss functions (Ranjbar et al., 2013; Tarlow and Zemel, 2012; Rosenfeld et al., 2014; Keshet, 2014). They have also been shown to be powerful when applied to latent variable models when optimizing for decomposable loss functions (Wang and Mori, 2011; Felzenszwalb et al., 2010; Yu and Joachims, 2009).

In this work (Haffari et al., 2015), we describe a novel max-margin learning approach to optimize non-linear performance measures for distantly-supervised relation extraction models. Our approach can be generally used to learn latent variable models under multivariate non-linear performance measures, such as F_β-score.

Our approach involves solving the hard-optimization problem in learning by interleaving Concave-Convex Procedure with dual decomposition. Dual decomposition allowed us to solve the hard sub-problems independently. A key aspect of our approach involves a local-search algorithm that has led to a speed-up of 7,000 times in our experiments over an exhustive search baseline proposed in previous work (Ranjbar et al., 2012; Joachims, 2005).

Our work is the first to make use of max-margin training in distant supervision of relation extraction models. We demonstrate the effectiveness of our proposed method compared to two strong baseline systems which optimize for the error rate and conditional likelihood, including a state-of-the-art system by Hoffmann et al. (2011). On several data conditions, we show that our method outperforms the baseline and results in up to 8.5% improvement in the F_1-score.

4 Conclusion

Our thesis can be summarized as shown in Figure 5. The broad theme of each work along with its publication forum is indicated. In the entity extraction setting, we work in the paradigm of *relational feature space exploration*, and in the relation extraction setting, our research has been in the paradigm of *learning under distant supervision.*

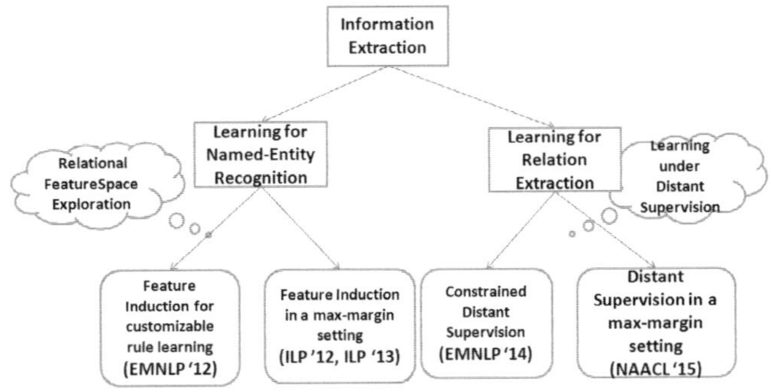

Figure 5: Thesis Summary

The design of our feature induction approach is aimed at producing accurate rules that can be understood and refined by humans, by placing special emphasis on low complexity and efficient computation of the induced rules. According to our complexity measure, the induced rules have good accuracy and low complexity. While our complexity measure informs the biases in our system and leads to simpler, smaller extractors, it captures extractor interpretability only to a certain extent. Therefore, we believe more work is required to devise a more comprehensive quantitative measure for interpretability. Another interesting direction of future work, is the designing of human-computer interaction experiments, to present the induced rules to a manual rule-developer and evaluating the quality of rules induced.

In the distantly supervised relation extraction, our ILP formulation provides a good framework to add new types of constraints to the problem. In the future, we would like to experiment with other constraints such as modeling the selectional preferences of entity types.

Our max-margin framework for distant supervision provided a way to optimize F_1 score while training the model. Although we solved the hard optimization problem with an efficient dual-decomposition formulation, our algorithms do not scale very well to large datasets. As part of future work, we would like to investigate distributed optimization algorithms as an extension to our solutions. In addition, we would like to maximize other performance measures, such as area under the curve, for information extraction models. We would also like to explore our approach for other latent variable models in NLP, such as those in machine translation.

References

Mary Elaine Califf. 1998. *Relational Learning Techniques for Natural Language Information Extraction*. Ph.D. thesis, Department of Computer Sciences, University of Texas, Austin, TX, August. Also appears as Artificial Intelligence Laboratory Technical Report AI 98-276.

Laura Chiticariu, Rajasekar Krishnamurthy, Yunyao Li, Frederick Reiss, and Shivakumar Vaithyanathan. 2010. Domain adaptation of rule-based annotators for named-entity recognition tasks. In *EMNLP*.

Pedro F. Felzenszwalb, Ross B. Girshick, David A. McAllester, and Deva Ramanan. 2010. Object detection with discriminatively trained part-based models. *IEEE Trans. Pattern Anal. Mach. Intell.*, 32(9):1627–1645.

Peter Flach and Nicolas Lachiche. 1999. 1bc: a first-order bayesian classifier. In *Proceedings Of the 9th International workshop on Inductive Logic Programming, Volume 1634 of Lecture Notes in Artificial Intelligence*, pages 92–103. Springer-Verlag.

Gholamreza Haffari, Ajay Nagesh, and Ganesh Ramakrishnan. 2015. Optimizing multivariate performance measures for learning relation extraction models. In *Human Language Technologies: Conference of the North American Chapter of the Association of Computational Linguistics, Proceedings, May 31 - Jun 5, 2015, Denver, Colorado, USA*. The Association for Computational Linguistics.

Raphael Hoffmann, Congle Zhang, Xiao Ling, Luke Zettlemoyer, and Daniel S. Weld. 2011. Knowledge-based weak supervision for information extraction of overlapping relations. In *Proceedings of the 49th Annual Meeting of the Association for Computational Linguistics: Human Language Technologies - Volume 1*, HLT '11, pages 541–550, Stroudsburg, PA, USA. Association for Computational Linguistics.

Alfred Horn. 1951. On sentences which are true of direct unions of algebras. *The Journal of Symbolic Logic*, 16(1):pp. 14–21.

T. Joachims. 2005. A support vector method for multivariate performance measures. In *International Conference on Machine Learning (ICML)*, pages 377–384.

Joseph Keshet. 2014. Optimizing the measure of performance in structured prediction. In Sebastian Nowozin, Peter V. Gehler, Jeremy Jancsary, and Christoph H. Lampert, editors, *Advanced Structured Prediction*. The MIT Press.

Mike Mintz, Steven Bills, Rion Snow, and Dan Jurafsky. 2009. Distant supervision for relation extraction without labeled data. In *Proceedings of the Joint Conference of the 47th Annual Meeting of the ACL*, ACL '09, pages 1003–1011, Stroudsburg, PA, USA. Association for Computational Linguistics.

Stephen Muggleton and C. Feng. 1992. Efficient induction in logic programs. In *ILP*.

Ajay Nagesh, Ganesh Ramakrishnan, Laura Chiticariu, Rajasekar Krishnamurthy, Ankush Dharkar, and Pushpak Bhattacharyya. 2012. Towards efficient named-entity rule induction for customizability. In *Proceedings of the 2012 Joint Conference on Empirical Methods in Natural Language Processing and Computational Natural Language Learning*, EMNLP-CoNLL '12, pages 128–138, Stroudsburg, PA, USA. Association for Computational Linguistics.

Ajay Nagesh, Gholamreza Haffari, and Ganesh Ramakrishnan. 2014. Noisy or-based model for relation extraction using distant supervision. In *Proceedings of the 2014 Conference on Empirical Methods in Natural Language Processing (EMNLP)*, Doha, Qatar, October. Association for Computational Linguistics.

Naveen Nair, Amrita Saha, Ganesh Ramakrishnan, and Shonali Krishnaswamy. 2012. Rule ensemble learning using hierarchical kernels in structured output spaces. In *AAAI*.

Shan-Hwei Nienhuys-Cheng and Ronald de Wolf. 1997. *Foundations of Inductive Logic Programming*.

Mani Ranjbar, Arash Vahdat, and Greg Mori. 2012. Complex loss optimization via dual decomposition. In *2012 IEEE Conference on Computer Vision and Pattern Recognition, Providence, RI, USA, June 16-21, 2012*, pages 2304–2311.

Mani Ranjbar, Tian Lan, Yang Wang, Stephen N. Robinovitch, Ze-Nian Li, and Greg Mori. 2013. Optimizing nondecomposable loss functions in structured prediction. *IEEE Trans. Pattern Anal. Mach. Intell.*, 35(4):911–924.

Nir Rosenfeld, Ofer Meshi, Amir Globerson, and Daniel Tarlow. 2014. Learning structured models with the auc loss and its generalizations. In *Proceedings of the 17th International Conference on Artificial Intelligence and Statistics (AISTATS)*.

D. Roth and W. Yih. 2001. Propositionalization of relational learning: An information extraction case study. Number UIUCDCS-R-2001-2206.

Sunita Sarawagi. 2008. Information extraction. *Found. Trends databases*, 1(3):261–377, March.

Mihai Surdeanu, Julie Tibshirani, Ramesh Nallapati, and Christopher D. Manning. 2012. Multi-instance multi-label learning for relation extraction. In *Proceedings of the 2012 Joint Conference on Empirical Meth-*

ods in Natural Language Processing and Computational Natural Language Learning, EMNLP-CoNLL '12, pages 455–465, Stroudsburg, PA, USA. Association for Computational Linguistics.

Daniel Tarlow and Richard S Zemel. 2012. Structured output learning with high order loss functions. In *Proceedings of the 15th Conference on Artificial Intelligence and Statistics*.

Benjamin Taskar, Carlos Guestrin, and Daphne Koller. 2003. Max-margin markov networks. In *NIPS*.

Ioannis Tsochantaridis, Thomas Hofmann, Thorsten Joachims, and Yasemin Altun. 2004. Support vector machine learning for interdependent and structured output spaces. In *Proceedings of the twenty-first international conference on Machine learning*, ICML '04, pages 104–, New York, NY, USA. ACM.

Yang Wang and Greg Mori. 2011. Hidden part models for human action recognition: Probabilistic versus max margin. *IEEE Trans. Pattern Anal. Mach. Intell.*, 33(7):1310–1323.

Chun-Nam John Yu and Thorsten Joachims. 2009. Learning structural svms with latent variables. In *Proceedings of the 26th Annual International Conference on Machine Learning, ICML 2009, Montreal, Quebec, Canada, June 14-18, 2009*, page 147.

Entity/Event-Level Sentiment Detection and Inference

Lingjia Deng
Intelligent Systems Program
University of Pittsburgh
lid29@pitt.edu

Abstract

Most of the work in sentiment analysis and opinion mining focuses on extracting explicit sentiments. Opinions may be expressed implicitly via inference rules over explicit sentiments. In this thesis, we incorporate the inference rules as constraints in joint prediction models, to develop an entity/event-level sentiment analysis system which aims at detecting both explicit and implicit sentiments expressed among entities and events in the text, especially focusing on but not limited to sentiments toward events that positively or negatively affect entities (*+/-effect events*).

1 Introduction

Nowadays there is an increasing number of opinions expressed online in various genres, including reviews, newswire, editorial, blogs, etc. To fully understand and utilize the opinions, much work in sentiment analysis and opinion mining focuses on more-fined grained levels rather than document-level (Pang et al., 2002; Turney, 2002), including sentence-level (Yu and Hatzivassiloglou, 2003; McDonald et al., 2007), phrase-level (Choi and Cardie, 2008), aspect-level (Hu and Liu, 2004; Titov and McDonald, 2008), etc. Different from them, this works contributes to the sentiment analysis at the **entity/event-level**. A system that could recognize sentiments toward entities and events would be valuable in an application such as Automatic Question Answering, to support answering questions such as "Who is negative/positive toward X?" (Stoyanov et al., 2005). It could also be used to facilitate the entity and event resolution (e.g. wikification system (Ratinov et al., 2011)). A recent NIST evaluation – The Knowledge Base Population (KBP) Sentiment track[1] — aims at using corpora to collect information regarding sentiments expressed toward or by named entities. We will compare the entity/event-level sentiment analysis task to other fine-grained level sentiment analysis tasks in Section 2, and propose to annotate a new entity/event-level sentiment corpus in Section 3.

The ultimate goal of this proposal is to develop an entity/event-level sentiment analysis system which aims at detecting both explicit and implicit sentiments expressed among entities and events in the text. Previous work in sentiment analysis mainly focuses on detecting explicit opinions (Wiebe et al., 2005; Johansson and Moschitti, 2013; Yang and Cardie, 2013). But not all the opinions are expressed in a straight forward way (i.e. explicitly). Consider the example below.

EX(1) It is great that the bill was defeated.

There is a positive sentiment, *great*, explicitly expressed. It is toward the clause *the bill was defeated*. In other words, the writer is explicitly positive toward the event *defeating bill*. Previous work may stop here. However, it is indicated in the sentence that the writer is negative toward *the bill* because (s)he is happy to see that the bill was defeated. The negative sentiment is implicit. Compared to detecting the explicit sentiment, it requires inference to recognize the implicit sentiment.

[1] http://www.nist.gov/tac/2014/KBP/Sentiment/index.html

Proceedings of NAACL-HLT 2015 Student Research Workshop (SRW), pages 48–56,
Denver, Colorado, June 1, 2015.

Now consider example Ex(2).

Ex(2) It is great that the bill was passed.

In Ex(2), the writer's sentiment toward *the bill* is positive, because (s)he is happy to see that the bill was passed. The writer is positive toward the events in both Ex(1) and Ex(2). But different events lead to different sentiments toward the bill. The *defeat* event is harmful to the bill, while the *pass* event is beneficial to the bill. We call such events are named ***+/-effect events*** (Deng et al., 2013) [2]. Many implicit sentiments are expressed via the +/-effect events, as we have seen in Ex(1) and Ex(2). Previously we have developed rules to infer the sentiments toward +/-effect events (Deng and Wiebe, 2014). An introduction of the rules will be given in Section 4.

This proposal aims at embedding the inference rules and incorporating +/-effect event information into a computational framework, in order to detect and infer both explicit and implicit entity/event-level sentiments. An overview of this proposed work will be presented in Section 5. Later, we will discuss the methods we propose to extract explicit entity/event-level sentiment in Section 6, and talk about how to incorporate the rules to jointly infer implicit sentiments and disambiguate the ambiguities in each step in Section 7. The contributions of this thesis proposal are summarized in Section 8.

2 Related Work

Sentiment Corpus. Annotated corpora of reviews (e.g., (Hu and Liu, 2004; Titov and McDonald, 2008)), widely used in NLP, often include target annotations. Such targets are often aspects or features of products or services, which can be seen as entities or events that are related to the product. However, the set of aspect terms is usually a pre-defined and closed set. (As stated in SemEval-2014: "we annotate only aspect terms naming particular aspects".) For an event in newsire (e.g. a terrorist attack), it is difficult to define a closed set of aspects. Recently, to create the Sentiment Treebank (Socher et al., 2013), researchers crowdsourced annotations of movie review data and then overlaid the annotations onto syntax trees. Thus, the targets are not limited to aspects of products/services. However, turkers were asked to annotate small and then increasingly larger segments of the sentence. Thus, all the information of the sentence is not shown to turkers when they annotate the span. Moreover, in both corpora of reviews and Sentiment Treebank, the sources are limited to the writer.

+/-Effect Event. Some work have mined various syntactic patterns (Choi and Cardie, 2008), proposed linguistic templates (Zhang and Liu, 2011; Anand and Reschke, 2010; Reschke and Anand, 2011) to find events similar to +/-effect events. There has been work generating a lexicon of patient polarity verbs (Goyal et al., 2012). We define that a *+effect* event has positive effect on the theme (e.g. pass, save, help), while a *-effect* event has negative effect on the theme (e.g. defeat, kill, prevent) (Deng et al., 2013). A +/-effect event has four components: the agent, the +/-effect event, the polarity, and the theme. Later, Choi and Wiebe (2014) have developed sense-level +/-effect event lexicons.

Sentiment Analysis. Most work in sentiment analysis focuses on classifying explicit sentiments and extracting explicit opinion expressions, sources and targets (Wiebe et al., 2005; Wiegand and Klakow, 2012; Johansson and Moschitti, 2013; Yang and Cardie, 2013). There is some work investigating features that directly indicate implicit sentiments (Zhang and Liu, 2011; Feng et al., 2013). In contrast, to bridge between explicit and implicit sentiments via inference, we have defined a generalized set of inference rules and proposed a graph-based model to achieve sentiment propagation between the sentiments toward the agents and themes of +/-effect events (Deng and Wiebe, 2014). But it requires each component of an +/-effect event from manual annotations as input. Later we use an Integer Linear Programming framework to reduce the need of manual annotations in the same task (Deng et al., 2014).

3 Corpus of Entity/Event-Level Sentiment: MPQA 3.0

The MPQA 2.0 (Wiebe et al., 2005; Wilson, 2007) is a widely-used, rich opinion resource. It includes editorials, reviews, news reports, and scripts of interviews from different news agencies, and covers

[2] It was initially named as **goodFor/badFor event** (Deng et al., 2013; Deng and Wiebe, 2014). Later we renamed it as +/-effect event (Deng et al., 2014; Choi and Wiebe, 2014).

a wide range of topics [3]. The MPQA annotations consist of *private states*, states of a *source* holding an *attitude*, optionally toward a *target*. Since we focus on sentiments, we only consider the attitudes which types are sentiments [4]. MPQA 2.0 also contains *expressive subjective element* (*ESE*) annotations, which pinpoint specific expressions used to express subjectivity (Wiebe et al., 2005). We only consider ESEs whose polarity is positive or negative (excluding those marked neutral).

To create MPQA 3.0, we propose to add entity-target and event-target (***eTarget***) annotations to the MPQA 2.0 annotations. An **eTarget** is an entity or event that is the target of an opinion (identified in MPQA 2.0 by a sentiment attitude or positive/negative ESE span). The eTarget annotation is anchored to the head word of the NP or VP that refers to the entity or event.

Let's consider some examples. The annotations in MPQA 2.0 are in the brackets, with the subscript indicating the annotation type. The eTargets we add in MPQA 3.0 are boldfaced.

> Ex(3) When the Imam [issued the fatwa against]$_{\text{sentiment}}$ [Salman **Rushdie** for **insulting** the Prophet]$_{\text{target}}$ ...

In Ex(3), *Imam* has a negative sentiment (*issued the fatwa against*) toward the target span, *Salman Rushdie for insulting the Prophet*, as annotated in MPQA 2.0. We find two eTargets in the target span: *Rushdie* himself and his act of *insulting*. Though *the Prophet* is another entity in the target span, we don't mark it because it is not negative. This shows that within a target span, the sentiments toward different entities may be different. Thus it is necessary to manually annotate the eTargets of a particular sentiment or ESE.

In the following example, the target span is short.

> Ex(4) [**He**]$_{\text{target}}$ is therefore [**planning** to **trigger wars**]$_{\text{sentiment}}$ ...

He is George W. Bush; this article appeared in the early 2000s. The writer is negative toward Bush because (the writer claims) he is planning to trigger wars. As shown in the example, the MPQA 2.0 target span is only *He*, for which we do create an eTarget. But there are three additional eTargets, which are not included in the target span. The writer is negative toward Bush planning to trigger wars; we infer that the writer is negative toward the idea of triggering wars and thus toward war itself.

We carried out an agreement study to show the feasibility of this annotation task (Deng and Wiebe, 2015). Two annotators together annotated four documents, including 292 eTargets in total. To evaluate the results, the same agreement measure is used for both attitude and ESE eTargets. Given an attitude or ESE, let set A be the set of eTargets annotated by annotator X, and set B be the set of eTargets annotated by annotator Y. Following (Wilson and Wiebe, 2003; Johansson and Moschitti, 2013), which treat each set A and B in turn as the gold-standard, we calculate the average F-measure $agr(A, B) = (|A \cap B|/|B| + |A \cap B|/|A|)/2$. The $agr(A, B)$ is 0.82 on average over the four documents, showing that this annotation task is feasible. In the future we will continue annotating the MPQA corpus.

We believe that the corpus will be a valuable new resource for developing entity/event-level sentiment analysis systems and facilitating other NLP applications in the future.

4 Inference Rules

Previously we have proposed rules to infer sentiments toward +/-effect events and the components (Deng and Wiebe, 2014). The rule used to infer sentiments in Ex(1) in Section 1 is listed below.

> *writer* positive (E_2 -effect E_3) $\Rightarrow$
> *writer* positive E_2 & *writer* negative E_3

The rule above can be explained as: the writer is positive toward the defeating event (-effect) with the agent (E_2) being implicit and the bill (E_3) being the theme, so that the writer is negative toward the bill. However, these rules are limited to sentiments toward the particular type of event, +/-effect events. Later we develop more rules to infer sentiments toward all types of entities and events (Wiebe and Deng, 2014). One of the rules and an example sentence is:

[3] Available at http://mpqa.cs.pitt.edu

[4] The other types of attitudes include belief, arguing, etc.

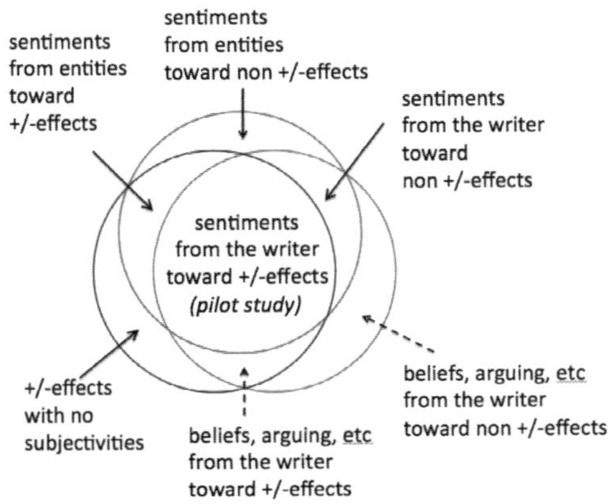

Figure 1: Overview of Subtasks.

E_1 positive (E_2 positive E_3) $\Rightarrow$
E_1 positive E_2 & E_1 positive E_3

Ex(5) Great! Mike praised my project!

The rule above can be explained as: if *Mike* (E_2) is positive toward *project* (E_3), and the speaker (E_1) is positive about that positive sentiment, then we could infer: (1) the speaker is positive toward Mike, because the speaker is glad that Mike holds the sentiment, implying that the two entities agree with each other. (2) Because the speaker agrees with Mike, the speaker is positive toward project.

5 Overview

The ultimate goal of this proposed work is to utilize the +/-effect events information and inference rules to improve detecting entity/event-level sentiments in the documents. There are ambiguities in each step of the whole task. We decompose this task into several subtasks, as shown in Figure 1. In this section, we illustrate what are the ambiguities in each subtask.

(1) The region in the blue circle in Figure 1 represents the +/-effect events and the components to be identified. The ambiguities come from: (1.1) Which spans are +/-effect events? (1.2) Which NPs are the agents, which are the themes? (1.3) What is the polarity of the +/-effect event? (1.4) Is the polarity reversed (e.g. negated)?

(2) The region in the red circle represents sentiments we need to extract from the document. The ambiguities are: (2.1) Is there any explicit sentiment? (2.2) What are the sources, targets and polarities of the explicit sentiments? (2.3) Is there any implicit sentiment inferred? (2.4) What are the sources, targets and polarities of the implicit sentiments?

(3) The region in the green circle represents all types of subjectivities of the *writer*, including sentiments, beliefs and arguing . The ambiguities are similar to those in the red circle: (3.1) Is there any subjectivity of the *writer*? (3.2) What are the targets and polarities of the subjectivity?

Though there are many ambiguities, they are interdependent. Inference rules in Section 4 define dependencies among these ambiguities. Our pilot study identifies and infers the writer's sentiments toward +/-effect events and the components (Deng et al., 2014). We first develop local classifiers using traditional methods to generate the candidates of each ambiguity. Each candidate is defined as a variable in an Integer Linear Programming (ILP) framework and four inference rules are incorporated as constraints in the framework. The pilot study corresponds to the intersection of the three regions in Figure 1. The success of it encourages us to extend from the intersection to all the regions with *solid lines* pointed to: the sources of sentiments are not limited to only the writer but all entities , and the targets of sentiments are not only the +/-effect events and the components, but all the entities and events. The pilot study used a simplified version of the set of rules in (Wiebe and Deng, 2014). In this proposal, we will use the full set.

In summary, this proposal focuses on (a) extracting +/-effect events and the components, and (b) extracting explicit and implicit sentiments. For subtask (a), we propose to utilize the +/-effect event lexicon (Choi and Wiebe, 2014) and semantic role labeling tools to generate candidates of each ambiguity. For subtask (b), we will discuss how to extract explicit sentiments in the next section. Finally, we will discuss how to simultaneously infer implicit sentiments and disambiguate the ambiguities listed above in a joint model in Section 7.

Gold Standard. The MPQA 3.0 proposed in Section 3 and the KBP sentiment dataset will be used as gold standard in this thesis.

Note that, although the two regions with *dashed lines* pointed to are out of scope in this proposal, we can adopt the framework in this proposal to jointly analyze sentiments and beliefs in the future.

6 Explicit Entity/Event-Level Sentiment

To fully utilize the off-the-shelf resources and tools in the span-level and phrase-level sentiment analysis (Wiegand and Klakow, 2012; Johansson and Moschitti, 2013; Yang and Cardie, 2013; Socher et al., 2013; Yang and Cardie, 2014), we will use the opinion spans and source spans extracted by previous work. To extract **eTarget**s, which are newly annotated in the MPQA 3.0 corpus, we propose to model this subtask as a classification problem: Given an extracted opinion span returned by the resources, a discriminative classifier judges whether a head of NP/VP in the same sentence is the correct eTarget of the extracted opinion. Two sets of features will be considered.

Opinion Span Features. Several common features used to extract targets will be used, including Part-Of-Speech, path in the dependency parse graph, distance of the constituents on the parse tree, etc (Yang and Cardie, 2013; Yang and Cardie, 2014).

Target Span Features. Among the off-the-shelf systems and resources, some work extracts the target spans in addition to the opinions. We will investigate features depicting the relations between a NP/VP head and the extracted target spans, such as whether the head overlaps with the target span. However, some off-the-shelf systems only extract the opinion spans, but do not extract any target span. For a NP/VP head, if the target span feature is false, there may be two reasons: (1) There is a target span extracted, but the target span feature is false (e.g. the head doesn't overlap with the target span). (2) There is no target span extracted by any tool at all.

Due to this fact, we propose three ways to define target span features. The simplest method (M1) is to assign zero to a false target span feature, regardless of the reason. A similar method (M2) is to assign different values (e.g. 0 or -1) to a false target span feature, according to the reason that causes the feature being false. For the third method (M3), we propose the Max-margin SVM (Chechik et al., 2008). Unlike the case where a feature exists but its value is not observed or false, here this model focus on the case where a feature may not even exist (structurally absent) for some of the samples (Chechik et al., 2008). In other words, the Max-margin SVM deals with features that are known to be non-existing, rather than have an unknown value. This allows us to fully utilize the different structures of outputs from different state-of-the-art resources.

7 Implicit Entity/Event-Level Sentiment

The explicit sentiments extracted from Section 6 above are treated as input for inferring the implicit sentiment. We are pursing such **a joint prediction model** that combines the probabilistic calculation of many ambiguities under the constraints of the dependencies of the data, defined by inference rules in the first order logic. Every candidate of every ambiguity is represented as a variable in the joint model. The goal is to find an optimal configuration of all the variables, thus the ambiguities are solved. Models differ in the way constraints are expressed. We plan to mainly investigate undirected lifted graphical models, including Markov Logic Network, and Probabilistic Soft Logics.

Though our pilot study (Deng et al., 2014) and many previous work in various applications of NLP (Roth and Yih, 2004; Punyakanok et al., 2008; Choi et al., 2006; Martins and Smith, 2009; Somasundaran and Wiebe, 2009) have used Integer Linear Programming (ILP) as a joint model, by setting the dependencies as constraints in the ILP framework, there is one limitation of ILP: we have to manually translate the first order logic rules into the linear equations and inequations as constraints. Now we have more complicated rules. In order to choose a framework that computes the first order logic directly, we propose the Markov Logic Network (MLN) (Richardson and Domingos, 2006).

The MLN is a framework for probabilistic logic that employ weighted formulas in first order logic to compactly encode complex undirected probabilistic graphical models (i.e., Markov networks) (Beltagy et al., 2014). It has been applied to various NLP tasks to achieves good results (Poon and Domingos, 2008; Fahrni and Strube, 2012; Dai et al., 2011; Kennington and Schlangen, 2012; Yoshikawa et al., 2009; Song et al., 2012; Meza-Ruiz and Riedel, 2009). It consists of a set of first order logic formula, each associated with a weight. The goal of the MLN is to find an optimal grounding which maximizes the values of all the satisfied first order logic formula in the knowledge base (Richardson and Domingos,

2006). We use the inference rules in Section 4 as the set of first order logic formula in MLN, and define atoms in the logic corresponding to our various kinds of ambiguities. Thus, solving the MLN is to assign true or false value to each atom, that is solving the ambiguities at the same time. For example, THEME(x,y) represents that the +/-effect event x has a theme y, TARGET(x,y) represents that the sentiment x has a target y, POS(s,x) represents that s is positive toward x. The inferences used in Ex(1) and Ex(5) are shown in Table 1.

It is great that the bill was defeated.
(THEME(x, y) $\wedge$ POLARITY(x, *-effect*)) $\Rightarrow$ (POS(s, x) $\Leftrightarrow$ NEG(s, y))
(THEME(defeat, bill) $\wedge$ POLARITY(defeat, *-effect*)) $\Rightarrow$ (POS(writer, defeat) $\Leftrightarrow$ NEG(writer, bill))
Great! Mike praised my project!
(TARGET(x, y) $\wedge$ POLARITY(x, *positive*)) $\Rightarrow$ (POS(s, x) $\Leftrightarrow$ POS(s, y))
(TARGET(praised, project) $\wedge$ POLARITY(praised, *positive*)) $\Rightarrow$ (POS(speaker, praised) $\Leftrightarrow$ POS(speaker, project))

Table 1: Examples and Inference Rules. In each box, line 1: sentence. Line 2: inference rule. Line 3: presenting the sentence in the rule.

Though MLN is a good choice of our task, it has a limitation. Each atom in the first order formula in MLN is boolean value. However, as we stated above, each atom represents an candidate of ambiguity returned by local classifiers, which may be numerical value. We can manually set thresholds for the numerical values to be boolean values, or train a regression over different atoms to select thresholds, but both methods need more parameters and may lead to over-fitting. Therefore, we propose another method, Probabilistic Soft Logic (PSL) (Broecheler et al., 2010). PSL is a new model of statistical relation learning and has been quickly applied to solve many NLP and other machine learning tasks in recent years (Beltagy et al., 2014; London et al., 2013; Pujara et al., 2013; Bach et al., 2013; Huang et al., 2013; Memory et al., 2012; Beltagy et al., 2013). Instead of only being boolean value, the atom in PSL could have numerical values. Given the atoms being numerical, PSL uses the *Lukasiewicz t-norm* and its corresponding co-norm to quantify the degree to which a grounding of the logic formula is satisfied (Kimmig et al., 2014).

Not limited to the lifted graphical models proposed above, other graphical models are attractive to explore. The Latent Dirichelet Allocation (LDA) (Blei et al., 2003), is widely used in sentiment analysis (Titov and McDonald, 2008; Si et al., 2013; Lin and He, 2009; Li et al., 2010). Li et al. (2010) proposed a LDA model assuming that sentiments depend on each other, which is similar to our assumption that the implicit sentiments depend on explicit sentiment by the inference rules. There is work combining LDA and PSL together (Ramesh et al., 2014), which may be another exploration for us.

8 Contributions

The proposed thesis mainly contributes to sentiment analysis and opinion mining in various genres such as newswire, blogs, editorials, etc.

- Develop MPQA 3.0, an entity/event-level sentiment corpus. It will be a valuable new resource for developing entity/event-level sentiment analysis systems, which are useful for various NLP applications including opinion-oriented Question Answering systems, wikification systems, etc.
- Propose a classification model to extract explicit entity/event-level sentiments. Different from previous classifications in sentiment analysis, we propose to distinguish opinion span features, which are applicable to all the data samples, and target span features, which may be structure absent for some samples (i.e. features do not exist at all).
- Propose a joint prediction framework aims at utilizing the +/-effect events information and inference rules to improve detecting entity/event-level sentiments in the documents and disambiguate the followed ambiguities in each step simultaneously.

Acknowledgement. Thank my advisor Dr. Janyce Wiebe for her very helpful suggestions in this thesis proposal. Thank the anonymous reviewers for their useful comments.

References

Pranav Anand and Kevin Reschke. 2010. Verb classes as evaluativity functor classes. In *Interdisciplinary Workshop on Verbs. The Identification and Representation of Verb Features*.

Stephen H Bach, Bert Huang, and Lise Getoor. 2013. Learning latent groups with hinge-loss markov random fields. In *Inferning: ICML Workshop on Interactions between Inference and Learning*.

Islam Beltagy, Cuong Chau, Gemma Boleda, Dan Garrette, Katrin Erk, and Raymond Mooney. 2013. Montague meets markov: Deep semantics with probabilistic logical form. In *2nd Joint Conference on Lexical and Computational Semantics: Proceeding of the Main Conference and the Shared Task, Atlanta*, pages 11–21. Citeseer.

Islam Beltagy, Katrin Erk, and Raymond Mooney. 2014. Probabilistic soft logic for semantic textual similarity. In *Proceedings of the 52nd Annual Meeting of the Association for Computational Linguistics (Volume 1: Long Papers)*, pages 1210–1219, Baltimore, Maryland, June. Association for Computational Linguistics.

David M Blei, Andrew Y Ng, and Michael I Jordan. 2003. Latent dirichlet allocation. *the Journal of machine Learning research*, 3:993–1022.

Matthias Broecheler, Lilyana Mihalkova, and Lise Getoor. 2010. Probabilistic similarity logic. In *Uncertainty in Artificial Intelligence (UAI)*.

Gal Chechik, Geremy Heitz, Gal Elidan, Pieter Abbeel, and Daphne Koller. 2008. Max-margin classification of data with absent features. *The Journal of Machine Learning Research*, 9:1–21.

Yejin Choi and Claire Cardie. 2008. Learning with compositional semantics as structural inference for subsentential sentiment analysis. In *Proceedings of the Conference on Empirical Methods in Natural Language Processing*, pages 793–801. Association for Computational Linguistics.

Yoonjung Choi and Janyce Wiebe. 2014. +/-effectwordnet: Sense-level lexicon acquisition for opinion inference. In *Proceedings of the 2014 Conference on Empirical Methods in Natural Language Processing (EMNLP)*, pages 1181–1191, Doha, Qatar, October. Association for Computational Linguistics.

Yejin Choi, Eric Breck, and Claire Cardie. 2006. Joint extraction of entities and relations for opinion recognition. In *Proceedings of the 2006 Conference on Empirical Methods in Natural Language Processing*, EMNLP '06, pages 431–439, Stroudsburg, PA, USA. Association for Computational Linguistics.

Hong-Jie Dai, Richard Tzong-Han Tsai, Wen-Lian Hsu, et al. 2011. Entity disambiguation using a markov-logic network. In *IJCNLP*, pages 846–855. Citeseer.

Lingjia Deng and Janyce Wiebe. 2014. Sentiment propagation via implicature constraints. In *Proceedings of the 14th Conference of the European Chapter of the Association for Computational Linguistics*, pages 377–385, Gothenburg, Sweden, April. Association for Computational Linguistics.

Lingjia Deng and Janyce Wiebe. 2015. Mpqa 3.0: An entity/event-level sentiment corpus. In *Conference of the North American Chapter of the Association of Computational Linguistics: Human Language Technologies*.

Lingjia Deng, Yoonjung Choi, and Janyce Wiebe. 2013. Benefactive/malefactive event and writer attitude annotation. In *ACL 2013 (short paper)*. Association for Computational Linguistics.

Lingjia Deng, Janyce Wiebe, and Yoonjung Choi. 2014. Joint inference and disambiguation of implicit sentiments via implicature constraints. In *Proceedings of COLING 2014, the 25th International Conference on Computational Linguistics: Technical Papers*, pages 79–88, Dublin, Ireland, August. Dublin City University and Association for Computational Linguistics.

Angela Fahrni and Michael Strube. 2012. Jointly disambiguating and clustering concepts and entities with Markov logic. In *Proceedings of COLING 2012*, pages 815–832, Mumbai, India, December. The COLING 2012 Organizing Committee.

Song Feng, Jun Sak Kang, Polina Kuznetsova, and Yejin Choi. 2013. Connotation lexicon: A dash of sentiment beneath the surface meaning. In *Proceedings of the 51th Annual Meeting of the Association for Computational Linguistics (Volume 2: Short Papers)*, Sofia, Bulgaria, Angust. Association for Computational Linguistics.

Amit Goyal, Ellen Riloff, and Hal Daum III. 2012. A computational model for plot units. *Computational Intelligence*, pages 466–488.

Minqing Hu and Bing Liu. 2004. Mining and summarizing customer reviews. In *Proceedings of the tenth ACM SIGKDD international conference on Knowledge discovery and data mining*, pages 168–177. ACM.

Bert Huang, Angelika Kimmig, Lise Getoor, and Jennifer Golbeck. 2013. A flexible framework for probabilistic models of social trust. In *Social Computing, Behavioral-Cultural Modeling and Prediction*, pages 265–273. Springer.

Richard Johansson and Alessandro Moschitti. 2013. Relational features in fine-grained opinion analysis. *Computational Linguistics*, 39(3):473–509.

Casey Kennington and David Schlangen. 2012. Markov logic networks for situated incremental natural language understanding. In *Proceedings of the 13th An-*

nual Meeting of the Special Interest Group on Discourse and Dialogue, pages 314–323. Association for Computational Linguistics.

Angelika Kimmig, Lilyana Mihalkova, and Lise Getoor. 2014. Lifted graphical models: a survey. *Machine Learning*, pages 1–45.

Fangtao Li, Minlie Huang, and Xiaoyan Zhu. 2010. Sentiment analysis with global topics and local dependency. In *AAAI*.

Chenghua Lin and Yulan He. 2009. Joint sentiment/topic model for sentiment analysis. In *Proceedings of the 18th ACM conference on Information and knowledge management*, pages 375–384. ACM.

Ben London, Sameh Khamis, Stephen H. Bach, Bert Huang, Lise Getoor, and Larry Davis. 2013. Collective activity detection using hinge-loss Markov random fields. In *CVPR Workshop on Structured Prediction: Tractability, Learning and Inference*.

André F. T. Martins and Noah a. Smith. 2009. Summarization with a joint model for sentence extraction and compression. In *Proceedings of the Workshop on Integer Linear Programming for Natural Langauge Processing - ILP '09*, pages 1–9, Morristown, NJ, USA. Association for Computational Linguistics.

Ryan McDonald, Kerry Hannan, Tyler Neylon, Mike Wells, and Jeff Reynar. 2007. Structured models for fine-to-coarse sentiment analysis. In *Annual Meeting-Association For Computational Linguistics*, volume 45, page 432. Citeseer.

Alex Memory, Angelika Kimmig, Stephen Bach, Louiqa Raschid, and Lise Getoor. 2012. Graph summarization in annotated data using probabilistic soft logic. In *Proceedings of the 8th International Workshop on Uncertainty Reasoning for the Semantic Web (URSW 2012)*, volume 900, pages 75–86.

Ivan Meza-Ruiz and Sebastian Riedel. 2009. Multilingual semantic role labelling with markov logic. In *Proceedings of the Thirteenth Conference on Computational Natural Language Learning: Shared Task*, pages 85–90. Association for Computational Linguistics.

Bo Pang, Lillian Lee, and Shivakumar Vaithyanathan. 2002. Thumbs up?: sentiment classification using machine learning techniques. In *Proceedings of the ACL-02 conference on Empirical methods in natural language processing-Volume 10*, pages 79–86. Association for Computational Linguistics.

Hoifung Poon and Pedro Domingos. 2008. Joint unsupervised coreference resolution with Markov Logic. In *Proceedings of the 2008 Conference on Empirical Methods in Natural Language Processing*, pages 650–659, Honolulu, Hawaii, October. Association for Computational Linguistics.

Jay Pujara, Hui Miao, Lise Getoor, and William Cohen. 2013. Knowledge graph identification. In *The Semantic Web–ISWC 2013*, pages 542–557. Springer.

Vasin Punyakanok, Dan Roth, and Wen-tau Yih. 2008. The importance of syntactic parsing and inference in semantic role labeling. *Computational Linguistics*, 34(2):257–287.

Arti Ramesh, Dan Goldwasser, Bert Huang, Hal Daume III, and Lise Getoor. 2014. Understanding mooc discussion forums using seeded lda. In *9th ACL Workshop on Innovative Use of NLP for Building Educational Applications*. ACL.

Lev Ratinov, Dan Roth, Doug Downey, and Mike Anderson. 2011. Local and global algorithms for disambiguation to wikipedia. In *Proceedings of the 49th Annual Meeting of the Association for Computational Linguistics: Human Language Technologies-Volume 1*, pages 1375–1384. Association for Computational Linguistics.

Kevin Reschke and Pranav Anand. 2011. Extracting contextual evaluativity. In *Proceedings of the Ninth International Conference on Computational Semantics*, IWCS '11, pages 370–374, Stroudsburg, PA, USA. Association for Computational Linguistics.

Matthew Richardson and Pedro Domingos. 2006. Markov logic networks. *Machine learning*, 62(1-2):107–136.

Dan Roth and Wen-tau Yih. 2004. A linear programming formulation for global inference in natural language tasks. In *CONLL*.

Jianfeng Si, Arjun Mukherjee, Bing Liu, Qing Li, Huayi Li, and Xiaotie Deng. 2013. Exploiting topic based twitter sentiment for stock prediction. In *ACL (2)*, pages 24–29.

Richard Socher, Alex Perelygin, Jean Y Wu, Jason Chuang, Christopher D Manning, Andrew Y Ng, and Christopher Potts. 2013. Recursive deep models for semantic compositionality over a sentiment treebank. In *Proceedings of the Conference on Empirical Methods in Natural Language Processing (EMNLP)*, pages 1631–1642. Citeseer.

Swapna Somasundaran and Janyce Wiebe. 2009. Recognizing stances in online debates. In *Proceedings of the Joint Conference of the 47th Annual Meeting of the ACL and the 4th International Joint Conference on Natural Language Processing of the AFNLP*, pages 226–234, Suntec, Singapore, August. Association for Computational Linguistics.

Yang Song, Jing Jiang, Wayne Xin Zhao, Sujian Li, and Houfeng Wang. 2012. Joint learning for coreference resolution with markov logic. In *Proceedings of the 2012 Joint Conference on Empirical Methods in Natural Language Processing and Computational Natu-*

ral Language Learning, pages 1245–1254. Association for Computational Linguistics.

Veselin Stoyanov, Claire Cardie, and Janyce Wiebe. 2005. Multi-Perspective Question Answering using the OpQA corpus. In *Proceedings of the Human Language Technologies Conference/Conference on Empirical Methods in Natural Language Processing (HLT/EMNLP-2005)*, pages 923–930, Vancouver, Canada.

Ivan Titov and Ryan T McDonald. 2008. A joint model of text and aspect ratings for sentiment summarization. In *ACL*, volume 8, pages 308–316. Citeseer.

Peter D Turney. 2002. Thumbs up or thumbs down?: semantic orientation applied to unsupervised classification of reviews. In *Proceedings of the 40th annual meeting on association for computational linguistics*, pages 417–424. Association for Computational Linguistics.

Janyce Wiebe and Lingjia Deng. 2014. An account of opinion implicatures. *arXiv*, 1404.6491[cs.CL].

Janyce Wiebe, Theresa Wilson, and Claire Cardie. 2005. Annotating expressions of opinions and emotions in language ann. *Language Resources and Evaluation*, 39(2/3):164–210.

Michael Wiegand and Dietrich Klakow. 2012. Generalization methods for in-domain and cross-domain opinion holder extraction. In *Proceedings of the 13th Conference of the European Chapter of the Association for Computational Linguistics*, pages 325–335. Association for Computational Linguistics.

Theresa Wilson and Janyce Wiebe. 2003. Annotating opinions in the world press. In *Proceedings of the 4th ACL SIGdial Workshop on Discourse and Dialogue (SIGdial-03)*, pages 13–22.

Theresa Wilson. 2007. *Fine-grained Subjectivity and Sentiment Analysis: Recognizing the Intensity, Polarity, and Attitudes of private states*. Ph.D. thesis, Intelligent Systems Program, University of Pittsburgh.

Bishan Yang and Claire Cardie. 2013. Joint inference for fine-grained opinion extraction. In *ACL (1)*, pages 1640–1649.

Bishan Yang and Claire Cardie. 2014. Context-aware learning for sentence-level sentiment analysis with posterior regularization. In *Proceedings of ACL*.

Katsumasa Yoshikawa, Sebastian Riedel, Masayuki Asahara, and Yuji Matsumoto. 2009. Jointly identifying temporal relations with markov logic. In *Proceedings of the Joint Conference of the 47th Annual Meeting of the ACL and the 4th International Joint Conference on Natural Language Processing of the AFNLP: Volume 1-Volume 1*, pages 405–413. Association for Computational Linguistics.

Hong Yu and Vasileios Hatzivassiloglou. 2003. Towards answering opinion questions: Separating facts from opinions and identifying the polarity of opinion sentences. In *Proceedings of the 2003 conference on Empirical methods in natural language processing*, pages 129–136. Association for Computational Linguistics.

Lei Zhang and Bing Liu. 2011. Identifying noun product features that imply opinions. In *Proceedings of the 49th Annual Meeting of the Association for Computational Linguistics: Human Language Technologies*, pages 575–580, Portland, Oregon, USA, June. Association for Computational Linguistics.

Initial Steps for Building a Lexicon of Adjectives with Scalemates

Bryan Wilkinson
Dept. of Computer Science and Electrical Engineering
University of Maryland, Baltimore County
1000 Hilltop Circle
Baltimore, MD 21250
bryan.wilkinson@umbc.edu

Abstract

This paper describes work in progress to use clustering to create a lexicon of words that engage in the lexico-semantic relationship known as grading. While other resources like thesauri and taxonomies exist detailing relationships such as synonymy, antonymy, and hyponymy, we do not know of any thorough resource for grading. This work focuses on identifying the words that may participate in this relationship, paving the way for the creation of a true grading lexicon later.

1 Introduction

Many common adjectives, like *small* and *tiny*, can be defined in terms of intensities of other adjectives. These relations, known as grading, intensification, magnification and others, are hypothesized to be one of the more important types in a lexicon (Evens, 1980). This type of relationship has applications in question answering and ontological representations (de Marneffe et al., 2010; Raskin and Nirenburg, 1996).

While the existence of this relationship is widely agreed upon, the study of it has fallen far behind that of synonymy, antonymy, and hyponymy, especially in the computational linguistics community. Recent work has brought renewed attention to this area of research, but there is still no large resource of words that participate in this relationship (van Miltenburg, 2015; Ruppenhofer et al., 2014).

The phenomenon of grading is not the same as gradability, although there is significant overlap among the adjectives that have it. Gradability refers to an adjective's ability to be combined with adverbs like *very* or be used in comparative expressions. It is possible that words like *lukewarm*, which are not considered gradable by most linguists, still have the lexico-semantic relation of grading. Similarly, a word like *spotted*, which is gradable, and in fact can be viewed on its own scale, does not express the relationship of grading with any other words in English.

There is no agreement on what types of adjectives express this relationship. Paradis and Kennedy & McNally propose two similar views that were influential to this work. Kennedy and McNally (2005) focus on the structure of scales, whether they are open at both ends (*tall, short*), closed at both ends (*visible, invisible*), or a combination of the two (*bent, straight* and *safe, dangerous*). Paradis (1997) on the other hand, defines three classes of gradable adjectives, limit adjectives, extreme adjectives, and scalar adjectives. For her, *dead* and *alive* are gradable adjectives but of the limit variety, meaning there is a definite boundary between the two. Extreme and scalar adjectives, such as *terrible* and *good* respectively, are both conceptualized as being on a scale, although extreme adjectives share some properties with limit adjectives as well. Paradis also points out that many adjectives can easily have a scalar interpretation, such as someone being *very Swedish.*

The study of grading has focused on a small number of adjectives (van Tiel et al., 2014). Many previous approaches of automatically learning the relation have relied on existing ontologies such as WordNet and FrameNet to choose which words occur on scales (Sheinman et al., 2013; Ruppenhofer et al.,

Proceedings of NAACL-HLT 2015 Student Research Workshop (SRW), pages 57–63,
Denver, Colorado, June 1, 2015.

2014). The issues with using ontologies like these as starting points are pointed out by Van Miltenburg (2015). He notes that words like *difficult* and *impossible* are not grouped together and that limiting scales to WordNet networks prevents ad-hoc scales as introduced by Hirschenberg (1985) from being studied. To this we can add our own observation that many times an ontology can be too broad, including *puffy*, *rangy*, and *large-mouthed* under *size* alongside expected senses of *big*, *small*, and others. Westney investigated what might be necessary for a word to be on a scale while recent work in cognitive science has focused on the acquisition of scalar implicatures in children (Westney, 1986; Verbuk, 2007).

We demonstrate work in progress to cluster adjectives into those that participate in grading and those that do not. While our metrics do not currently match the supervised solution of (Hatzivassiloglou and Wiebe, 2000), the lack of large amounts of training data encourages us to continue to pursue the unsupervised approach. Clustering the adjectives is a critical first step to support further research into semantic intensities of adjectives, which is outlined in section 2.

1.1 Adverb Types

As shown above, adverbs can play a large role in the study of adjectives. Many types of adverbs have been recognized in the literature, with many studies being derived from the classification of Quirk (1985). Many of these studies have been done with an emphasis on adverbs' interactions with verbs. Moryzcki (2008) has noted that at least the subject oriented class (*deliberately, purposely, willfully, etc.*) and what he terms "remarkably adverbs" (*astoundingly, disappointingly, remarkably, etc.*) occur with adjectives as well.

The group of adverbs that have received the most attention in regards to their combinations with adjectives has been degree adverbs. In addition to Kennedy and McNally's use of co-occurrence with degree adverbs to arrive at the scale structures mentioned earlier, Paradis (1997) performed detailed research on this class of adverbs. She found that certain adverbs combine only with certain types of gradable adjectives. Adverbs she terms scalar modifiers (*fairly, slightly, very, etc.*) combine only with scalar adjectives while maximizer adverbs like *absolutely* combine with extreme adjectives.

	rather	pretty
high	175929.0	42533.0
long	141152.0	31229.0
low	161944.0	22953.0
odd	55147.0	3424.0
short	119977.0	8251.0
bad	30308.0	127592.0
funny	13350.0	19563.0
good	79737.0	817421.0
hard	87502.0	110704.0
tough	9620.0	37633.0

Table 1: Co-occurrence matrix from Google syntactic ngrams corpus

This type of pattern of co-occurrence has not only been observed between the classes of adjectives and adverbs but also within them. Desaguilier (2014) showed that *rather* combined more often with words like *long* and *high* while *pretty* combined more often with words like *good* and *stupid*, yet both are considered not only scalar modifiers, but a subtype known as moderators according to (Paradis, 1997). This effect can be seen in the co-occurrence matrix shown in Table 1.

2 Related Work

While this is the first attempt we know of to create a general lexicon of adjectives that participate in grading, several related studies have occurred. We first discuss work on defining gradable and non-gradable adjectives and then discuss several recent works on automatically ordering adjectives.

Using the intuition that gradability is a good indicator of subjectivity Hatzivassiloglou and Wiebe (2000) use the co-occurrence of adjectives with adverbs as well as a word's ability to be inflected for gradability in a classification task. They classified all adjectives that occurred more than 300 times in the 1987 WSJ corpus as gradable or non-gradable, for a total of 496 adjectives. When counting the co-occurrence with adverbs, they used only two features, the number of times an adjective occurred with any of the degree modifiers from a manually created list of 73, and the number of times it occurred with any other type of adverb. The classifier was trained on 100 randomly selected subsets of 300 adjectives and tested on randomly selected subsets of 100 adjectives.

Since Hatzivassiloglou and Wiebe was published, a great number of corpora have been produced. One issue we now face is that the class of degree adverbs is generally agreed to be a closed class in English, while other adverbs are not. This means we can reasonably expect the number of non-modifier adverbs would dominate the other features in an unsupervised situation. Additionally, while the degree adverb class is considered closed, we have not found a comprehensive list of all of them, leading to further reservations about simply counting adverbs as degree modifying and non degree modifying based on a list.

Several works have looked at automatically ordering a group of adjectives by intensity given that they occur on the same scale. Van Miltenburg (van Miltenburg, 2015) uses patterns to find scalemates from a large corpus. He is particularly interested in pairs of words for use in reasoning about scalar implicatures. The candidate pairs generated by the patterns are then validated by using various similarity measures, such as LSA or being under the same attribute in WordNet. This pattern based approach has also been taken by Sheinman (Sheinman et al., 2013), although she starts out with the words on a scale from WordNet and uses the patterns to order the words. As pointed out by (Ruppenhofer et al., 2014), pattern based approaches do not have wide applicability, a fact backed up by the results of van Miltenburg. Out of 32470 pairs identified, only 121 occur in 4 or more of the 6 patterns used.

Ruppenhoffer (2014) has also investigated the automatic ordering of adjectives on a scale. Using adjectives taken from FrameNet, they compare the occurrence of adjectives with 3 "end-of-scale" modifiers and 3 "normal" modifiers, using (Kennedy and McNally, 2005) as a guide. They achieve good correlations to human standards on the 4 scales they chose to investigate using this method, though it should be noted that once these co-occurrence metrics were computed, the scale was constructed manually.

Shivade, et al. (2015) use a combination of clustering and patterns in their approach to ordering not only adjectives, but adverbs as well. To determine scale membership, they cluster 256 adjectives known to occur on scales by their co-occurrence with nouns. They then match patterns of parse trees rather than at string level to derive features for ordering. The order is computed using Mixed Linear Integer Programming as done in (de Melo and Bansal, 2013). Our contribution can be seen as a precursor to their pipeline, providing a list of adjectives that are known to participate in grading to the clustering algorithm.

3 Methodology

While the group of gradable adjectives and those that participate in grading do not entirely overlap, it is a good starting point to build a lexicon of graded adjectives. There are rare cases, like *lukewarm*, but it is not believed there are many other words that would be missed by this assumption.

For a given set of adjectives that we wish to derive a lexicon from, we first build a co-occurrence matrix using the Google syntactic ngrams to select adverbs that are dependent on adjectives (Goldberg and Orwant, 2013). We used the arc relations in this dataset that represent a direct dependency between two words. The adverbs were required to participate in the advmod dependency with the adjective. To ensure a wide representation of adverbs, we use the degree modifiers discussed by Paradis (1997), the remarkably adverbs discussed by Moryzcki (2008), the subject oriented adverbs discussed by Moryzcki and enumerated by Quirk (1985), and the viewpoint and time adverbs from Quirk as our features. This gives us a total of 84 features, which we call the Manual feature set in Table 2. We also produce a variation of the feature set with only five features, where the adjectives are grouped together by type as defined above, denoted by Manual Collapsed in Table 2. A third feature set we investigated was the 1000 most frequent adverbs in the corpus, regardless of their occurrence with adjectives, denoted by Top 1000 Advs.

The matrix is weighted with PPMI as implemented in DISSECT (Dinu et al., 2013). We then run k-means(k=2) clustering to split the adjectives into a group of gradable adjectives and a group of non-gradable adjectives.

As previously discussed, being gradable does not

guarantee an adjective participates in the grading lexico-semantic relation. As an approximation of finding only adjectives that occur on the same scale as others, we run anomaly detection on the adjectives which were clustered into the gradable group. We used local outlier factor (LOF) due to its ability to find anomalies locally, rather than on a global scale, better approximating adjectives without scalemates (Breunig et al., 2000).

4 Evaluation

As Hatzivassiloglou and Wiebe did, we use the Collins COBUILD Dictionary for our evaluation (Sinclair et al., 1987). The dictionary classifies adjectives as either classifying or qualitative which correspond approximately to non-gradable and gradable. The distinction here is the narrow sense of gradable, meaning the adjectives can be modified by only scalar modifiers, not maximizers or approximators. This is the best resource we know of at this time however, and it allows comparisons to earlier work. We follow Hatzivassiloglou and Wiebe in removing adjectives from the dataset that we could not reliably label as classifying or qualitative when different senses had conflicting labels.

We ran the clustering and anomaly detection on the 500 and 1000 most common adjectives in the Google syntactic ngrams corpus, removing any that were not labeled as an adjective by COBUILD. This gives of datasets of length 427 (237 gradable and 190 non-gradable) and 838 (461 gradable and 377 non-gradable) respectively. Due to many of the words having conflicting senses, we ran another dataset consisting of only the words for which all senses unanimously chose the same classification.

The results of evaluating the clustering can be seen in Table 2. The data set that should be compared to (Hatzivassiloglou and Wiebe, 2000) who report a precision of .9355, recall of .8224, and accuracy of .8797, is the 500 most frequent adjectives. While we don't achieve as high a precision, our recall is much higher. Partial reasons for this could be that using COBUILD is a flawed choice, as it assigns words like *far* to the classifying class of adjectives in all senses, even though it can be inflected as *farther* and *farthest*. The words that were labeled by COBUILD as non-gradable but clustered as gradable by our method from the 500 words dataset using the 1000 most frequent adverbs are shown in figure 1. While some of the words are true errors, words like *dead* and *alive* are commonly discussed in linguistic literature, with many considering them gradable (Kennedy and McNally, 2005). Other words that were misclustered can easily be placed on a scale, such as *silent* or *everyday*. Ultimately we are using a broader definition of gradable than COBUILD. Additionally it is more likely for a word not traditionally viewed as gradable to appear in gradable context rather than vice-versa. This leads to a high recall due to the fact that the gradable adjectives rarely appear in non-gradable contexts.

able above absolute actual additional alive available average based central chief chronic comprehensive constant contemporary continuous corresponding criminal current dead dear double east entire equivalent eternal everyday extreme facial far fatal fellow few fewer free front fundamental future gay giant global horizontal identical illegal induced inevitable intermediate known lateral left like logical natural neutral objective occasional ongoing operational overall parallel particular past positive possible potential present previous principal proper pure ready real related responsible right same separate silent single solid special specific subject subsequent sufficient temporary top total traditional ultimate unable unique universal unknown up usual various vertical very whole

Figure 1: Words labeled by COBUILD as non-gradable, but clustered with gradable words in our data

The most interesting outcome is that the use of manual features does not provide an advantage. This is promising for future work, especially for applications in other languages. Constructing manual features requires the existence of detailed descriptive grammars for the language in question.

Testing against only the words that were assigned one label in the dictionary performed the worst under all conditions. This may be because the distribution of these terms is heavily skewed towards the

Data Set	Feature Set	Precision	Recall	F_1	Accuracy
1000	Manual	.7061	.9696	.8171	.7613
	Manual Collapsed	.7154	.9652	**.8217**	.7697
	Top 1000 Advs	.6931	.9848	.8136	.7517
500	Manual	.7030	.9789	.8183	7587
	Manual Collapsed	.7285	.8945	.8030	.7564
	Top 1000 Advs	.7005	.9873	**.8196**	.7587
Unanimous	Manual	.6493	.9765	.78	.7417
	Manual Collapsed	.6445	.9843	.7789	.7380
	Top 1000 Advs	.6791	.9921	**.8063**	.7765
(Hatzivassiloglou and Wiebe, 2000)	Custom Features	.9355	.8224	**.8753**	.8797

Table 2: Evaluation against COBUILD classifications

less frequent words of the top 1000, rather than any effect from the classification itself.

One group of words that is reliably identified as not having any scalemates are demonyms like *American* and *Swedish*. As another heuristic on our algorithm, we use the list of denonymic names from Wikipedia [1]. We found that 100% of these were correctly excluded from the final list for all feature sets.

While we have no evaluation for the effectiveness of the anomaly detection, the words with the 10 highest LOF are shown in Table 3. Of these, *able* and *logical* are identified by COBUILD as classifying adjectives. If we assume that the synonyms and antonyms given by COBOUILD could be scalemates for these words, we find that only *consistent* and *historic* do not have scalemates in the dataset. This suggests that at least LOF is not a good estimate of words sharing a scale, and possibly anomaly detection in general.

word	LOF
able	34.78
consistent	4.98
realistic	3.42
loyal	2.92
better	2.57
historic	2.56
hungry	2.50
logical	2.46
attractive	2.43
extensive	2.41

Table 3: Top 10 Highest LOF

5 Future Work

There are many areas for improvement. In the methodology, we feel that there is currently too much manual selection of the features. This includes both the selection of adverbs that apply to a wider range of adjectives as well as the ability to automatically group the adverbs into classes similar to those defined in section 2.1.

While using more semantically related feature sets revealed no large improvement, we still believe this could be a productive avenue of further work. One possible source of inspiration for this would be biclustering often used in biology. This works on the assumption that the underlying data has a checkerboard pattern. The problem with this assumption is that this may actually separate the related adjectives and adverbs more. The idea of of grouping the adverbs and adjectives simultaneously is an attractive one however.

Once the adjectives have been placed into preliminary groupings, we need to determine which of the words to not have any scalemates. It was shown above that LOF does not appear to be a viable solution. Several promising solutions to this are still available for exploration. Hypernym identification as performed in (Lenci and Benotto, 2012) has traditionally been used on nouns to build taxonomies, but may have some applications to adjective taxonomies

[1] http://en.wikipedia.org/wiki/List_of_adjectival_and_demonymic_forms_for_countries_and_nations

as well. Additionally, (Kanzaki et al., 2004) have exploited the relationship between abstract nouns and adjectives to build a hierarchy of adjectives in Japanese.

Another area of improvement is the need for a better evaluation. In addition to the issue of COBUILD using a narrower version of gradability than us, there is no resource to reliably check if the words produced do in fact have scalemates. Work by (van Miltenburg, 2015) on finding pairs of scalemates used in scalar implicature is a possible solution but notes that their techniques also face evaluation issues.

The relationship between gradability, subjectivity and the lexical relationship we investigate in this paper needs to be further explored. While we do not believe they are the same, they may serve as resources for both the creation of our lexicon as well as evaluation.

Beyond the creation of the lexicon, it will have many potential uses once created. For linguists, it will provide new data on which to test theoretical models of scales, scale structures, and gradability. For the NLP community, it will serve as a resource in investigations into scalar implicature as well as the automatic ordering of adjectives.

6 Conclusion

In this paper we discuss a method to automatically build a lexicon of words that appear on a scale. Our clustering step achieved F_1 scores between .78 and .82. While these are not as high as the those achieved by (Hatzivassiloglou and Wiebe, 2000), we have demonstrated that using an unsupervised method comes close to a supervised one. In addition, we have pointed out many potential flaws with the current evaluation, and provided several future directions on which to further improve the lexicon.

References

Markus Breunig, Hans-Peter Kriegel, Raymond Ng, and Jörg Sander. 2000. LOF: Identifying density-based local outliers. *SIGMOD Rec.*, 29(2):93–104, May.

Marie-Catherine de Marneffe, Christopher D Manning, and Christopher Potts. 2010. Was it good? it was provocative. learning the meaning of scalar adjectives. In *Proceedings of the 48th Annual Meeting of the Association for Computational Linguistics*, pages 167–176. Association for Computational Linguistics.

Gerard de Melo and Mohit Bansal. 2013. Good, great, excellent: Global inference of semantic intensities. *Transactions of the Association for Computational Linguistics*, 1:279–290.

Guillaume Desagulier. 2014. Visualizing distances in a set of near-synonyms. *Corpus Methods for Semantics: Quantitative studies in polysemy and synonymy*, 43:145.

Georgiana Dinu, Nghia The Pham, and Marco Baroni. 2013. Dissect: Distributional semantics composition toolkit. In *Proceedings of the System Demonstrations of ACL 2013 (51st Annual Meeting of the Association for Computational Linguistics)*, East Stroudsburg PA. Association for Computational Linguistics.

Martha W Evens. 1980. *Lexical-semantic relations : a comparative survey*. Linguistic Research, Carbondale [Ill.].

Yoav Goldberg and Jon Orwant. 2013. A dataset of syntactic-ngrams over time from a very large corpus of english books. In *Second Joint Conference on Lexical and Computational Semantics (* SEM)*, volume 1, pages 241–247.

Vasileios Hatzivassiloglou and Janyce Wiebe. 2000. Effects of adjective orientation and gradability on sentence subjectivity. In *Proceedings of the 18th Conference on Computational Linguistics*, volume 1 of *COLING '00*, pages 299–305, Stroudsburg, PA, USA. Association for Computational Linguistics.

Julia Hirschberg. 1985. *A theory of scalar implicature*. Ph.D. thesis, University of Pennsylvania.

Kyoko Kanzaki, Eiko Yamamoto, Hitoshi Isahara, and Qing Ma. 2004. Construction of an objective hierarchy of abstract concepts via directional similarity. In *Proceedings of the 20th international conference on Computational Linguistics*, page 1147. Association for Computational Linguistics.

Chris Kennedy and Louise McNally. 2005. Scale structure, degree modification, and the semantics of gradable predicates. *Language*, 81(2):345–381.

Alessandro Lenci and Giulia Benotto. 2012. Identifying hypernyms in distributional semantic spaces. In *Proceedings of First Joint Conference on Lexical and Computational Semantics (*SEM)*, pages 75–79, Stroudsburg, PA, USA. Association for Computational Linguistics.

Marcin Morzycki. 2008. Adverbial modification in AP: Evaluatives and a little beyond. In Johannes Dölling and Tatjana Heyde-Zybatow, editors, *Event Structures in Linguistic Form and Interpretation*, pages 103–126. Walter de Gruyter, Berlin.

Carita Paradis. 1997. *Degree modifiers of adjectives in spoken British English*, volume 92 of *Lund studies in English*. Lund University Press.

Randolph Quirk, Sidney Greenbaum, Geoffrey Leech, and Jan Svartvik. 1985. *A Comprehensive Grammar of the English Language (General Grammar)*. Longman, 2nd revised edition edition.

Victor Raskin and Sergei Nirenburg. 1996. Adjectival modification in text meaning representation. In *Proceedings of the 16th conference on Computational Linguistics*, volume 2, pages 842–847. Association for Computational Linguistics.

Josef Ruppenhofer, Michael Wiegand, and Jasper Brandes. 2014. Comparing methods for deriving intensity scores for adjectives. In *Proceedings of the 14th Conference of the European Chapter of the Association for Computational Linguistics*, pages 117–122. Association for Computational Linguistics.

Vera Sheinman, Christiane Fellbaum, Isaac Julien, Peter Schulam, and Takenobu Tokunaga. 2013. Large, huge or gigantic? identifying and encoding intensity relations among adjectives in WordNet. *Language Resources and Evaluation*, 47(3):797–816, 1 September.

Chaitanya Shivade, Marie-Catherine de Marneffe, Eric Folser-Lussier, and Albert Lai. 2015. Corpus-based discovery of semantic intensity scales. In *In Proceedings of NAACL-HTL 2015*, Denver, CO. Association for Computational Linguistics.

John Sinclair, Patrick Hanks, Gwyneth Fox, Rosamund Moon, Penny Stock, et al. 1987. *Collins COBUILD English language dictionary*. Collins London.

Emiel van Miltenburg. 2015. Detecting and ordering adjectival scalemates. In *MAPLEX*, Yamagata, Japan.

Bob van Tiel, Emiel van Miltenburg, Natalia Zevakhina, and Bart Geurts. 2014. Scalar diversity. *Journal of Semantics*, 23 December.

Anna Verbuk. 2007. *Acquisition of scalar implicatures*. Ph.D. thesis, University of Massachusetts Amherst.

Paul Westney. 1986. Notes on scales. *Lingua*, 69(4):333–354, August.

A Preliminary Evaluation of the Impact of Syntactic Structure in Semantic Textual Similarity and Semantic Relatedness Tasks

Ngoc Phuoc An Vo
Fondazione Bruno Kessler,
University of Trento
Trento, Italy
ngoc@fbk.eu

Octavian Popescu
IBM Research, T.J. Watson
Yorktown, US
o.popescu@us.ibm.com

Abstract

The well related tasks of evaluating the Semantic Textual Similarity and Semantic Relatedness have been under a special attention in NLP community. Many different approaches have been proposed, implemented and evaluated at different levels, such as lexical similarity, word/string/POS tags overlapping, semantic modeling (LSA, LDA), etc. However, at the level of syntactic structure, it is not clear how significant it contributes to the overall accuracy. In this paper, we make a preliminary evaluation of the impact of the syntactic structure in the tasks by running and analyzing the results from several experiments regarding to how syntactic structure contributes to solving these tasks.

1 Introduction

Since the introduction of Semantic Textual Similarity (STS) task at SemEval 2012 and the Semantic Relatedness (SR) task at SemEval 2014, a large number of participating systems have been developed to resolve the tasks.[1,2] The systems must quantifiably identify the degree of similarity, relatedness, respectively, for pair of short pieces of text, like sentences, where the similarity or relatedness is a broad concept and its value is normally obtained by averaging the opinion of several annotators. A semantic similarity/relatedness score is usually a real number in a semantic scale, [0-5] in STS, or [1-5] in SR, in the direction from *no relevance* to *semantic equivalence*. Some examples from the dataset *MSRpar* of STS 2012 with associated similarity scores (by human judgment) are as below:

- *The bird is bathing in the sink.* vs. *Birdie is washing itself in the water basin.* (score = 5.0)
- *Shares in EDS closed on Thursday at $18.51, a gain of 6 cents.* vs. *Shares of EDS closed Thursday at $18.51, up 6 cents on the New York Stock Exchange.* (score = 3.667)
- *Vivendi shares closed 3.8 percent up in Paris at 15.78 euros.* vs. *Vivendi shares were 0.3 percent up at 15.62 euros in Paris at 0841 GMT.* (score = 2.6)
- *John went horse back riding at dawn with a whole group of friends.* vs. *Sunrise at dawn is a magnificent view to take in if you wake up early enough for it.* (score = 0)

From our reading of the literature (Marelli et al., 2014b; Agirre et al., 2012; Agirre et al., 2013; Agirrea et al., 2014), most of STS/SR systems rely on pairwise similarity, such as lexical similarity using taxonomies (WordNet (Fellbaum, 1998)) or distributional semantic models (LDA (Blei et al., 2003), LSA (Landauer et al., 1998), ESA (Gabrilovich and Markovitch, 2007), etc), and word/n-grams overlap as main features to train a support vector machines (Joachims, 1998) regression model (supervised), or use a word-alignment metric (unsupervised) aligning the two given texts to compute their semantic similarity.

Intuitively, the syntactic structure plays an important role for human being to understand the mean-

[1] http://www.cs.york.ac.uk/semeval-2012/task6
[2] http://alt.qcri.org/semeval2014/task1

Proceedings of NAACL-HLT 2015 Student Research Workshop (SRW), pages 64–70,
Denver, Colorado, June 1, 2015.

ing of a given text. Thus, it also may help to identify the semantic equivalence/relatedness between two given texts. However, in the STS/SR tasks, very few systems provide evidence of the contribution of syntactic structure in its overall performance. Some systems report partially on this issue, for example, iKernels (Severyn et al., 2013) carried out an analysis on the STS 2012, but not on STS 2013 datasets. They found that syntactic structure contributes 0.0271 and 0.0281 points more to the overall performance, from 0.8187 to 0.8458 and 0.8468, for adopting constituency and dependency trees, respectively.

In this paper, we analyze the impact of syntactic structure on the STS 2014 and SICK datasets of STS/SR tasks. We consider three systems which are reported to perform efficiently and effectively on processing syntactic trees using three proposed approaches Syntactic Tree Kernel (Moschitti, 2006), Syntactic Generalization (Galitsky, 2013) and Distributed Tree Kernel (Zanzotto and Dell'Arciprete, 2012).

The remainder of the paper is as follows: Section 2 introduces three approaches to exploit the syntactic structure in STS/SR tasks, Section 3 describes Experimental Settings, Section 4 discusses about the Evaluations and Section 5 is the Conclusions and Future Work.

2 Three Approaches for Exploiting the Syntactic Structure

In this section, we describe three different approaches exploiting the syntactic structure to be used in the STS/SR tasks, which are **Syntactic Tree Kernel** (Moschitti, 2006), **Syntactic Generalization** (Galitsky, 2013), and **Distributed Tree Kernel** (Zanzotto and Dell'Arciprete, 2012). All these three approaches learn the syntactic information either from the dependency parse trees produced by the Stanford Parser (standard PCFG Parser) (Klein and Manning, 2003) or constituency parse trees obtained by OpenNLP.[3] The output of each approach is normalized to the standard semantic scale of STS [0-5] or SR [1-5] tasks to evaluate its standalone performance, or combined with other features in our baseline system for assessing its contribution to the overall accuracy by using the same WEKA machine learning tool (Hall et al., 2009) with as same configurations and parameters as our baseline systems.

2.1 Syntactic Tree Kernel (STK)

Given two trees T1 and T2, the functionality of tree kernels is to compare two tree structures by computing the number of common substructures between T1 and T2 without explicitly considering the whole fragment space. According to the literature (Moschitti, 2006), there are three types of fragments described as the subtrees (STs), the subset trees (SSTs) and the partial trees (PTs). A subtree (ST) is a node and all its children, but terminals are not STs. A subset tree (SST) is a more general structure since its leaves need not be terminals. The SSTs satisfy the constraint that grammatical rules cannot be broken. When this constraint is relaxed, a more general form of substructures is obtained and defined as partial trees (PTs).

Syntactic Tree Kernel (STK) (Moschitti, 2006) is a tree kernels approach to learn the syntactic structure from syntactic parsing information, particularly, the Partial Tree (PT) kernel is proposed as a new convolution kernel to fully exploit dependency trees. The evaluation of the common PTs rooted in nodes n1 and n2 requires the selection of the shared child subsets of the two nodes, e.g. [S [DT JJ N]] and [S [DT N N]] have [S [N]] (2 times) and [S [DT N]] in common.

In order to learn the similarity of syntactic structure, we seek for a corpus which should fulfill the two requirements, (1) sentence-pairs contain similar syntactic structure, and with (2) a variety of their syntactic structure representations (in their parsing trees). However, neither SICK nor STS corpus seems to be suitable. As the SICK corpus is designed for evaluating compositional distributional semantic models through semantic relatedness and textual entailment, the syntactic structure of sentence pairs are quite simple and straightforward. In contrast, the STS corpus contains several different datasets derived from different sources (see Table 1) which carry a large variety of syntactic structure representations, but lack of learning examples due to no human annotation given for syntactic structure similarity (only annotation for semantic similarity exists); and it is difficult to infer the syntactic structure

[3] https://opennlp.apache.org

similarity from general semantic similarity scores in STS datasets. Hence, having assumed that paraphrased pairs would share the same content and similar syntactic structures, we decide to choose the Microsoft Research Paraphrasing Corpus (Dolan et al., 2005) which contains 5,800 sentence pairs extracted from news sources on the web, along with human annotations indicating whether each pair captures a paraphrase/semantic equivalence relationship.[4] This corpus is split into Training set (4,076 pairs) and Testing set (1,725 pairs).

We use Stanford Parser (PCFG Parser) trained on Penn TreeBank (Klein and Manning, 2003) to obtain the dependency parsing from sentence pairs. Then we use the machine learning tool svm-light-tk 1.2 which uses Tree Kernel approach to learn the similarity of syntactic structure to build a binary classifying model on the Train dataset.[5] According to the assumption above, we label paraphrased pairs as 1, -1 otherwise. We test this model on the Test dataset and obtain the Accuracy of 69.16%, with Precision/Recall is: 69.04%/97.21%.

We apply this model on the STS and SICK data to predict the similarity between sentence pairs. The output predictions are probability confidence scores in [-1,1], corresponds to the probability of the label to be positive. Thus, we convert the prediction value into the semantic scale of STS and SR tasks to compare to the human annotation. The example data (including train, test, and predictions) of this tool is available here.[6]

2.2 Syntactic Generalization (SG)

Given a pair of parse trees, the Syntactic Generalization (SG) (Galitsky, 2013) finds a set of maximal common subtrees. Though generalization operation is a formal operation on abstract trees, it yields semantics information from commonalities between sentences. Instead of only extracting common keywords from two sentences, the generalization operation produces a syntactic expression. This expression maybe semantically interpreted as a common meaning held by both sentences. This syntactic parse tree generalization learns the semantic information differently from the kernel methods which compute a kernel function between data instances, whereas a kernel function is considered as a similarity measure. Other than the kernel methods, SG is considered as structure-based and deterministic, in which linguistic features remain their structure, not as value presentations.

The toolkit "relevance-based-on-parse-trees" is an open-source project which evaluates text relevance by using syntactic parse tree-based similarity measure.[7] Given a pair of parse trees, it measures the similarity between two sentences by finding a set of maximal common subtrees, using representation of constituency parse trees via chunking. Each type of phrases (NP, VP, PRP etc.) will be aligned and subject to generalization. It uses the OpenNLP system to derive dependency trees for generalization (chunker and parser).[8] This tool is made to give as a tool for text relevance which can be used as a black box, no understanding of computational linguistics or machine learning is required. We apply the tool on the SICK and STS datasets to compute the similarity of syntactic structure of sentence pairs. The similarity score from this tool is converted into the semantic scale of STS and SR tasks for comparison against the human annotation.

2.3 Distributed Tree Kernel (DTK)

Distributed Tree Kernel (DTK) (Zanzotto and Dell'Arciprete, 2012) is a tree kernels method using a linear complexity algorithm to compute vectors for trees by embedding feature spaces of tree fragments in low-dimensional spaces. Then a recursive algorithm is proposed with linear complexity to compute reduced vectors for trees. The dot product among reduced vectors is used to approximate the original tree kernel when a vector composition function with specific ideal properties is used.

Firstly, we use Stanford Parser (PCFG Parser) trained on Penn TreeBank (Klein and Manning, 2003) to obtain the dependency parsing of sentences, and feed them to the software "distributed-tree-kernels" to produce the distributed trees.[9] Then, we compute the Cosine similarity between the vectors of distributed trees of each sentence pair. This

[4] http://research.microsoft.com/en-us/downloads/607d14d9-20cd-47e3-85bc-a2f65cd28042

[5] http://disi.unitn.it/moschitti/SIGIR-tutorial.htm

[6] http://disi.unitn.it/moschitti/Tree-Kernel.htm

[7] https://code.google.com/p/relevance-based-on-parse-trees

[8] https://opennlp.apache.org

[9] https://code.google.com/p/distributed-tree-kernels

cosine similarity score is converted to the scale of STS and SR for evaluation.

3 Experiments

In this section, we describe the two corpora we use for experiments with several different settings to evaluate the contribution of each syntactic structure approach and in combination with other features in our baseline systems.

3.1 Datasets

We run our experiments on two datasets from two different tasks at SemEval 2014 as follows:

- The SICK dataset (Marelli et al., 2014a) is used in Task# 1 "Evaluation of compositional distributional semantic models on full sentences through semantic relatedness and textual entailment".[10] It consists of 10,000 English sentence pairs, built from two paraphrase sets: the 8K ImageFlickr dataset and the STS 2012 Video Descriptions dataset.[11,12] Each sentence pair was annotated for relatedness score in scale [1-5] and entailment relation. It is split into three parts: Trial (500 pairs), Training (4,500 pairs) and Testing (4,927 pairs).

- The STS dataset is used in Task #10 "Multilingual Semantic Textual Similarity" (STS English subtask) which consists of several datasets in STS 2012 (Agirre et al., 2012), 2013 (Agirre et al., 2013) and 2014 (Agirrea et al., 2014). Each sentence pair is annotated the semantic similarity score in the scale [0-5]. Table 1 shows the summary of STS datasets and sources over the years. For training, we use all data in STS 2012 and 2013; and for evaluation, we use STS 2014 datasets.

year	dataset	pairs	source
2012	MSRpar	1500	newswire
2012	MSRvid	1500	video descriptions
2012	OnWN	750	OntoNotes, WordNet glosses
2012	SMTnews	750	Machine Translation evaluation
2012	SMTeuroparl	750	Machine Translation evaluation
2013	headlines	750	newswire headlines
2013	FNWN	189	FrameNet, WordNet glosses
2013	OnWN	561	OntoNotes, WordNet glosses
2013	SMT	750	Machine Translation evaluation
2014	headlines	750	newswire headlines
2014	OnWN	750	OntoNotes, WordNet glosses
2014	Deft-forum	450	forum posts
2014	Deft-news	300	news summary
2014	Images	750	image descriptions
2014	Tweet-news	750	tweet-news pairs

Table 1: Summary of STS datasets in 2012, 2013, 2014.

3.2 Baselines

In order to evaluate the significance of syntactic structure in the STS/SR tasks, we not only examine the syntactic structure alone, but also combine it with some features learned from common approaches, such as bag-of-words, pairwise similarity, n-grams overlap, etc. Therefore, we use two baseline systems for evaluations, the weak and the strong ones. The weak baseline is the basic one used for evaluation in all the STS tasks, namely **tokencos**. It uses the bag-of-words approach which represents each sentence as a vector in the multidimensional token space (each dimension has 1 if the token is present in the sentence, 0 otherwise) and computes the cosine similarity between vectors.

Besides the weak baseline, we use **DKPro Similarity** (Bär et al., 2012) as a strong baseline which is an open source software and intended to use as a baseline-system in the share task STS at *SEM 2013.[13] It uses a simple log-linear regression model (about 18 features), to combine multiple text similarity measures of varying complexity ranging from simple character/word n-grams and common subsequences to complex features such as Explicit Semantic Analysis vector comparisons and aggregation of word similarity based on lexical-semantic resources (WordNet and Wiktionary).[14,15]

4 Evaluations and Discussions

In this section, we present twelve different settings for experimenting the contribution of syntactic structure individually and in combination with typi-

[10] http://alt.qcri.org/semeval2014/task1

[11] http://nlp.cs.illinois.edu/HockenmaierGroup/data.html

[12] http://www.cs.york.ac.uk/semeval-2012/task6/index.php?id=data

[13] https://code.google.com/p/dkpro-similarity-asl/wiki/SemEval2013

[14] http://wordnet.princeton.edu

[15] http://en.wiktionary.org/wiki/Wiktionary:Main_Page

Settings	deft-forum	deft-news	headlines	images	OnWN	tweet-news	STS2014 Mean	SICK-test
Tokencos (0)	0.353	0.596	0.510	0.513	0.406	0.654	0.5054	0.501
DKPro (1)	0.4314	0.7089	0.6887	0.7671	0.8125	0.6932	0.6836	0.6931
STK (2)	0.1163	0.2369	0.0374	*-0.1125*	0.0865	*-0.0296*	0.0558	0.0757
SG (3)	0.2816	0.3808	0.4078	0.4449	0.4934	0.5487	0.4262	0.4498
DTK (4)	0.0171	0.1	*-0.0336*	*-0.109*	0.0359	*-0.0986*	*-0.0147*	0.2657
STK & SG & DTK	0.2402	0.3886	0.3233	0.2419	0.4066	0.4489	0.3416	0.4822
(0) & (2)	0.3408	0.5738	0.4817	0.4184	0.4029	0.6016	0.4699	**0.5074**
(0) & (3)	**0.3735**	0.5608	**0.5367**	**0.5432**	**0.4813**	**0.6736**	**0.5282**	**0.522**
(0) & (4)	**0.3795**	**0.6343**	**0.5399**	0.5096	**0.4504**	0.6539	**0.5279**	**0.5018**
(0), (2), (3) & (4)	**0.3662**	0.5867	**0.5265**	0.464	**0.4758**	0.6407	**0.51**	**0.5252**
(1) & (2)	**0.4423**	0.7019	**0.6919**	0.7653	0.8122	**0.7105**	**0.6874**	**0.7239**
(1) & (3)	**0.4417**	0.7067	0.6844	0.7636	0.812	0.6777	0.6810	**0.6948**
(1) & (4)	0.4314	0.7089	0.6887	0.7671	0.8125	0.6932	0.6836	**0.6953**
(1), (2), (3) & (4)	**0.4495**	0.7032	**0.6902**	0.7627	0.8115	**0.6974**	**0.6857**	**0.7015**

Table 2: Experiment Results on STS 2014 and SICK datasets.

cal similarity features to the overall performance of computing similarity/relatedness score on SICK and STS datasets. The results reported here are obtained with Pearson correlation, which is the official measure used in both tasks.[16] We have some discussions from the results in Table 2 as below:

Baseline comparison. The strong baseline DKPro is superior than the bag-of-word baseline on most of datasets (both STS and SICK), except the *tweet-news* where their performances are close as the *tweet-news* dataset contains little or no syntactic information compared to others.

Individual approach evaluation. Each syntactic approach is weaker than both baselines. Though the STK and DTK both use the tree kernel approach, just different representations, the performance is similar only on the dataset *images*. The STK still performs better than DTK on most of STS datasets, but much lower on SICK dataset. This is reasonable as the SICK dataset is created for evaluating distributional semantics which suits the DTK approach. Both approaches have some negative results on STS datasets; especially, both methods obtain negative correlation on two datasets *"images"* and *"tweet-news"*. It seems that both methods struggle to learn the semantic information (in parsing) extracted from these two datasets. Moreover, due to the fact that Twitter data is informal text which carries lot of noise created by users, and very different from formal text from other STS datasets, the syntactic approach does not seem to capture correct meaning, thus, the result confirms that syntactic approach is not suitable and beneficial for social media text.

In contrast, the SG performs better than other two approaches to obtain better correlation with human judgment; yet it is still below the bag-of-word baseline (only better on *OnWN* dataset). Hence, using any of these syntactic approaches is not sufficient to solve the STS/SR task as its performance is still lower than the weak baseline. Some examples with gold-standard and system scores as below:

- *Blue and red plane in mid-air flight.* vs. *A blue and red airplane while in flight.* (gold=4.8; STK=3.418; DTK=3.177; SG=3.587)
- *Global online #education is a key to democratizing access to learning and overcoming societal ills such as poverty* vs. *Op-Ed Columnist: Revolution Hits the Universities* (gold=0.6; STK=3.054; DTK=3.431; SG=2.074)
- *you are an #inspiration! #Keepfighting* vs. *The front lines in fight for women* (gold=0.4; STK=3.372; DTK=3.479; SG=2.072)
- *CGG - 30 die when bus plunges off cliff in Nepal* vs. *30 killed as bus plunges off cliff*

[16]http://en.wikipedia.org/wiki/Pearson_product-moment_correlation_coefficient

in Nepal (gold=5; STK=3.155; DTK=3.431; SG=3.402)

The combination of three approaches. These three methods do not collaborate well on STS datasets, it even decreases the overall performance of the best method SG by a large margin of 8%. However, it improves the result on SICK dataset by a medium margin around 4%. Finally, the combination of three methods still returns a lower result than the weak baseline. Thus, this combination of syntactic approaches alone cannot solve the STS/SR tasks.

Combination with bag-of-word approach. The combination of syntactic information and bag-of-word approach more or less improves the performance over the weak baseline.

- The STK does not improve but has negative impact to the overall performance on STS with a decrease of 4%. However, it gains a small improvement on SICK of 1%.
- Though the DTK returns 3.5% better result than STK on STS and slightly improves the performance on SICK for less than 1%, it is 0.5% lower than the weak baseline.
- The SG improves the performance 2-12% on most of STS and SICK datasets. It performs 4-8% better than the weak baseline, but still dramatically 11-14% lower than the DKPro baseline.
- The combination of three methods with the bag-of-word results 3-8% better performance than the weak baseline on STS/SICK datasets. However, this combination brings negative effect of 0.5% to the overall result on STS in comparison to the performance of SG.

Combination with DKPro. Perhaps DKPro baseline consists of several strong features which make syntactic features insignificant in the combination. Hence, using a strong baseline like DKPro is not a good way to evaluate the significance of syntactic information.

- The STK gains small improvement on SICK (3%) and some STS datasets (1%), whereas other datasets remain unchanged.
- The DTK does not have any effect to the result of DKPro standalone. This shows that DTK has no integration with DKPro features.
- The SG only makes slight improvement on SICK (0.2%) and *deft-forum* (1%), whereas little decrease on other datasets. This shows that SG does not collaborate well with DKPro either.
- On STS, this total combination returns few small improvements around 1% on some datasets *deft-forum, headlines, tweet-news* and mean value, whereas 1-3% better on SICK dataset.

In conclusion, despite the fact that we experiment different methods to exploit syntactic information on different datasets derived from various data sources, the results in Table 2 confirms the positive impact of syntactic structure in the overall performance on STS/SR tasks. However, syntactic structure does not always work well and effectively on any dataset, it requires a certain level of syntactic presentation in the corpus to exploit. In some cases, applying syntactic structure on poor-structured data may cause negative effect to the overall performance.

5 Conclusions and Future Work

In this paper, we deploy three different approaches to exploit and evaluate the impact of syntactic structure in the STS/SR tasks. We use a freely available STS system, DKPro, which is using similarity features for computing the semantic similarity/relatedness scores as a strong baseline. We also evaluate the contribution of each syntactic structure approach and different combinations between them and the typical similarity approach in the baseline. From our observation, in the mean time with recent proposed approaches, the results in Table 2 shows that the syntactic structure does contribute individually and together with typical similarity approaches for computing the semantic similarity/relatedness scores between given sentence pairs. However, compared to the baselines, the contribution of syntactic structure is not significant to the overall performance. For future work, we may expect to see more effective ways for exploiting and learning syntactic structure to have better contribution into the overall performance in the STS/SR tasks.

References

Eneko Agirre, Mona Diab, Daniel Cer, and Aitor Gonzalez-Agirre. 2012. Semeval-2012 task 6: A pilot on semantic textual similarity. In *Proceedings of the First Joint Conference on Lexical and Computational Semantics-Volume 1: Proceedings of the main conference and the shared task, and Volume 2: Proceedings of the Sixth International Workshop on Semantic Evaluation*, pages 385–393. Association for Computational Linguistics.

Eneko Agirre, Daniel Cer, Mona Diab, Aitor Gonzalez-Agirre, and Weiwei Guo. 2013. sem 2013 shared task: Semantic textual similarity, including a pilot on typed-similarity. In *In* SEM 2013: The Second Joint Conference on Lexical and Computational Semantics. Association for Computational Linguistics*. Citeseer.

Eneko Agirrea, Carmen Baneab, Claire Cardiec, Daniel Cerd, Mona Diabe, Aitor Gonzalez-Agirrea, Weiwei Guof, Rada Mihalceab, German Rigaua, and Janyce Wiebeg. 2014. Semeval-2014 task 10: Multilingual semantic textual similarity. *SemEval 2014*, page 81.

Daniel Bär, Chris Biemann, Iryna Gurevych, and Torsten Zesch. 2012. Ukp: Computing semantic textual similarity by combining multiple content similarity measures. In *Proceedings of the First Joint Conference on Lexical and Computational Semantics-Volume 1: Proceedings of the main conference and the shared task, and Volume 2: Proceedings of the Sixth International Workshop on Semantic Evaluation*, pages 435–440. Association for Computational Linguistics.

David M Blei, Andrew Y Ng, and Michael I Jordan. 2003. Latent dirichlet allocation. *the Journal of machine Learning research*, 3:993–1022.

Bill Dolan, Chris Brockett, and Chris Quirk. 2005. Microsoft research paraphrase corpus. *Retrieved March*, 29:2008.

Christiane Fellbaum. 1998. *WordNet*. Wiley Online Library.

Evgeniy Gabrilovich and Shaul Markovitch. 2007. Computing semantic relatedness using wikipedia-based explicit semantic analysis. In *IJCAI*, volume 7, pages 1606–1611.

Boris Galitsky. 2013. Machine learning of syntactic parse trees for search and classification of text. *Engineering Applications of Artificial Intelligence*, 26(3):1072–1091.

Mark Hall, Eibe Frank, Geoffrey Holmes, Bernhard Pfahringer, Peter Reutemann, and Ian H Witten. 2009. The weka data mining software: an update. *ACM SIGKDD explorations newsletter*, 11(1):10–18.

Thorsten Joachims. 1998. *Text categorization with support vector machines: Learning with many relevant features*. Springer.

Dan Klein and Christopher D Manning. 2003. Accurate unlexicalized parsing. In *Proceedings of the 41st Annual Meeting on Association for Computational Linguistics-Volume 1*, pages 423–430. Association for Computational Linguistics.

Thomas K Landauer, Peter W Foltz, and Darrell Laham. 1998. An introduction to latent semantic analysis. *Discourse processes*, 25(2-3):259–284.

M Marelli, S Menini, M Baroni, L Bentivogli, R Bernardi, and R Zamparelli. 2014a. A SICK cure for the evaluation of compositional distributional semantic models. In *Proceedings of LREC 2014, Reykjavik (Iceland): ELRA*.

Marco Marelli, Luisa Bentivogli, Marco Baroni, Raffaella Bernardi, Stefano Menini, and Roberto Zamparelli. 2014b. Semeval-2014 task 1: Evaluation of compositional distributional semantic models on full sentences through semantic relatedness and textual entailment. *SemEval-2014*.

Alessandro Moschitti. 2006. Efficient convolution kernels for dependency and constituent syntactic trees. In *Machine Learning: ECML 2006*, pages 318–329. Springer.

Aliaksei Severyn, Massimo Nicosia, and Alessandro Moschitti. 2013. ikernels-core: Tree kernel learning for textual similarity. *Atlanta, Georgia, USA*, page 53.

Fabio Massimo Zanzotto and Lorenzo Dell'Arciprete. 2012. Distributed tree kernels. *arXiv preprint arXiv:1206.4607*.

Benchmarking Machine Translated Sentiment Analysis for Arabic Tweets

Eshrag Refaee
Interaction Lab, Heriot-Watt University
EH144AS Edinburgh, UK
eaar1@hw.ac.uk

Verena Rieser
Interaction Lab, Heriot-Watt University
EH144AS Edinburgh, UK
v.t.rieser@hw.ac.uk

Abstract

Traditional approaches to Sentiment Analysis (SA) rely on large annotated data sets or wide-coverage sentiment lexica, and as such often perform poorly on under-resourced languages. This paper presents empirical evidence of an efficient SA approach using freely available machine translation (MT) systems to translate Arabic tweets to English, which we then label for sentiment using a state-of-the-art English SA system. We show that this approach significantly outperforms a number of standard approaches on a gold-standard held-out data set, and performs equally well compared to more cost-intense methods with 76% accuracy. This confirms MT-based SA as a cheap and effective alternative to building a fully fledged SA system when dealing with under-resourced languages.

Keywords: Sentiment Analysis, Arabic, Twitter, Machine Translation

1 Introduction

Over the past decade, there has been a growing interest in collecting, processing and analysing user-generated text from social media using Sentiment Analysis (SA). SA determines the *polarity* of a given text, i.e. whether its overall sentiment is *negative* or *positive*. While previous work on SA for English tweets reports an overall accuracy of 65-71% on average (Abbasi et al., 2014), recent studies investigating Arabic tweets only report accuracy scores ranging between 49-65% (Mourad and Darwish, 2013; Abdul-Mageed et al., 2012; Refaee and Rieser, 2014b). Arabic SA faces a number of challenges: first, Arabic used in social media is usually a mixture of Modern Standard Arabic (MSA) and one or more of its dialects (DAs). Standard toolkits for Natural Language Processing (NLP) mainly cover the former and perform poorly on the latter [1]. These tools are vital for the performance of machine learning (ML) approaches to Arabic SA: traditionally, ML approaches use a "bag of words" (BOW) model (e.g. Wilson et al. (2009)). However, for morphologically rich languages, such as Arabic, a mixture of stemmed tokens and morphological features have shown to outperform BOW approaches (Abdul-Mageed et al., 2011; Mourad and Darwish, 2013), accounting for the fact that Arabic contains a very large number of inflected words. In addition (or maybe as a result), there is much less interest from the research community in tackling the challenge of Arabic SA for social media. As such, there are much fewer open resources available, such as annotated data sets or sentiment lexica. We therefore explore an alternative approach to Arabic SA on social media, using off-the-shelf Machine Translation systems to translate Arabic tweets into English and then use a state-of-the-art sentiment classifier (Socher et al., 2013) to assign sentiment labels. To the best of our knowledge, this is the first study to measure the impact of automatically translated data on the accuracy of sentiment analysis of Arabic tweets. In particular, we address the following research questions:

1. How does off-the-shelf MT on Arabic social data influence SA performance?

[1] Please note the ongoing efforts on extending NLP tools to DAs (e.g. (Pasha et al., 2014; Salloum and Habash, 2012)).

Proceedings of NAACL-HLT 2015 Student Research Workshop (SRW), pages 71–78,
Denver, Colorado, June 1, 2015.

2. Can MT-based approaches be a viable alternative to improve sentiment classification performance on Arabic tweets?
3. Given the linguistic resources currently available for Arabic and its dialects, is it more effective to adapt an MT-based approach instead of building a new system from scratch?

2 Related Work

There are currently two main approaches to automatic sentiment analysis: using a sentiment lexicon or building a classifier using machine learning. Lexicon-based approaches, on the one hand, utilise sentiment lexica to retrieve and annotate sentiment bearing word tokens for their sentiment orientation and then utilise a set of rules to assign the overall sentiment label (Taboada et al., 2011). Machine Learning (ML) approaches, on the other hand, frequently make use of annotated data sets, to learn a statistical classifier (Mourad and Darwish, 2013; Abdul-Mageed et al., 2011; Wilson et al., 2009). These approaches gain high performance for English tweets: a benchmark test on commercial and freely-available SA tools report accuracy levels between 65% - 71% on English tweets (Abbasi et al., 2014).

For Arabic tweets, one of the best results for SA to date is reported in Mourad and Darwish (2013) with 72.5% accuracy using 10-fold-cross validation and SVM on a manually annotated data set (2300 tweets). However, this performance drops dramatically to 49.65% - 65.32% accuracy when testing an independent held-out set (Abdul-Mageed et al., 2012; Refaee and Rieser, 2014c). One possible explanation is the time-changing nature of twitter (Eisenstein, 2013): models trained on data collected at one point in time will not generalise to tweets collected at a later stage, due to changing topics and vocabulary. As such, current work investigates Distant Supervision (DS) to collect and annotate large data sets in order to train generalisable models (e.g. Go et al. (2009)). Recent work by Refaee and Rieser (2014b) has evaluated DS approaches on Arabic Tweets. They report accuracy scores of around 57% which significantly outperforms a majority baseline and a fully supervised ML approach, but it is still considerably lower than scores achieved on English tweets.

In the following, we compare these previous approaches to an approach using automatic Machine Translation (MT). So far, there is only limited evidence that this approach works for languages lack large SA training data-set, such as Arabic. Bautin et al. (2008) investigate MT to aggregate sentiment from multiple news documents written in a number of different languages. The authors argue that despite the difficulties associated with MT, e.g. information loss, the translated text still maintains a sufficient level of captured sentiments for their purposes. This work differs from our work in terms of domain and in measuring summary consistency rather than SA accuracy. Balahur and Turchi (2013) investigate the use of an MT system (Google) to translate an annotated corpus of English tweets into four European languages in order to obtain an annotated training set for learning a classifier. The authors report an accuracy score of 64.75% on the English held-out test set. For the other languages, reported accuracy scores ranged between 60 - 62%. Hence, they conclude that it is possible to obtain high quality training data using MT, which is an encouraging result to motivate our approach.

Wan (2009) proposes a co-training approach to tackle the lack of Chinese sentiment corpora by employing Google Translate as publicly available machine translation (MT) service to translate a set of annotated English reviews into Chinese. Using a held-out test set, the best reported accuracy score was at 81.3% with SVM on binary classification task: positive vs negative.

Our approach differs from the ones described, in that we use automatic MT to translate Arabic tweets into English and then perform SA using a state-of-the-art SA classifier for English (Socher et al., 2013). Most importantly, we empirically benchmark its performance towards previous SA approaches, including lexicon-based, fully supervised and distant supervision SA.

3 Experimental Setup

3.1 Data-set

We follow a similar approach to Refaee and Rieser (2014a) for collecting the held-out data set we use for benchmarking. First, we randomly retrieve tweets from the Twitter public stream. We restrict the language of all retrieved tweets to Arabic by setting the language parameter to *ar*. The data-set was manually labeled with gold-standard sentiment orientation by two native speakers of Arabic, obtaining a Kappa score of 0.81, which indicates highly reliable annotations. Table 1 summarises the data set and its distribution of labels. For SA, we perform binary classification using *positive* and *negative* tweets. We apply a number of common pre-processing steps following Go et al. (2009) and Pak and Paroubek (2010) to account for noise introduced by Twitter. The data set will be released as part of this submission.

Sentiment	Pos.	Neg.	Total
no. of tweets	470	467	937
no. of tokens	4,516	5,794	10,310
no. of tok. types	2,664	3,200	5,864

Table 1: Evaluation data-set.

3.2 MT-based approach

In order to obtain the English translation of our Twitter data-set, we employ two common and freely-available MT systems: Google Translate and Microsoft Translator Service. We then use the Stanford Sentiment Classifier (SSC) developed by Socher et al. (2013) to automatically assign sentiment labels (positive, negative) to translated tweets. The classifier is based on a deep learning (DL) approach, using recursive neural models to capture syntactic dependencies and compositionality of sentiments. Socher et al. (2013) show that this model significantly outperforms previous standard models, such as Naïve Bayes (NB) and Support Vector Machines (SVM) with an accuracy score of 85.4% for binary classification (positive vs. negative) at sentence level [2]. The authors observe that the recursive models work well on shorter text while BOW features with NB and SVM perform well only on longer sentences. Using Socher et al. (2013)'s approach for directly training a sentiment classifier will require a larger training data-set, which is not available yet for Arabic [3].

3.3 Baseline Systems

We benchmark the MT-approach against three baseline systems representing current standard approaches to SA: a lexicon-based approach, a fully supervised machine learning approach and a distant supervision approach (also see Section 2). The **lexicon-based baseline** combines three sentiment lexica. We exploit two existing subjectivity lexica: a manually annotated Arabic subjectivity lexicon (Abdul-Mageed and Diab, 2012) and a publicly available English subjectivity lexicon, called MPQA (Wilson et al., 2009), which we automatically translate using Google Translate, following a similar technique to Mourad and Darwish (2013). The translated lexicon is manually corrected by removing translations with a no clear sentiment indicator [4]. This results in 2,627 translated instances after correction. We then construct a third dialectal lexicon of 484 words that we extract from an independent Twitter development set and manually annotate for sentiment. All lexica are merged into a combined lexicon of 4,422 annotated sentiment words (duplicates removed). In order to obtain automatic labels for positive and negative instances, we follow a simplified version of the rule-based aggregation approach of Taboada et al. (2011). First, all lexicons and tweets are lemmatised using MADAMIRA (Pasha et al., 2014). For each tweet, matched sentiment words are marked with either (+1) or (-1) to incorporate the semantic orientation of individual constituents. This achieves a coverage level of 76.62% (which is computed as a percentage of tweets with at least one lexicon word) using the combined lexicon. To account for negation, we reverse the polarity (switch negation) following Taboada et al. (2011). The sentiment orientation of the entire tweet is then computed by summing up the sentiment scores of all sentiment words in a given tweet into a single score that automatically determines the label as being: positive or negative. Instances where the score equals zero are excluded from the training set as they

[2] SSC distinguishes between 5 sentiments, including very-positive, positive, neutral, negative, and very-negative. For our purposes, all very-positive and very-negative were mapped to the standard positive and negative classes.

[3] SSC was trained using a set of 215,154 unique and manually labeled phrases.

[4] For instance, *the day of judgement* is assigned with a negative label while its Arabic translation is neutral considering the context-independent polarity.

Metrics	Google-Trans.+DL		Microsoft-Trans.+DL		Lexicon-based		Distant Superv.		Fully-supervised	
	Pos.	Neg.	Pos.	Neg.	Pos.	Neg.	Pos.	Neg.	Pos.	Neg.
precision	44.64	92.52	56.60	91.60	75.87	77.72	52.1	73.3	48.2	59.7
avg. precision	68.58		74.10		**76.79**		63.5		54.3	
recall	21.27	55.67	25.53	53.74	36.81	32.12	86.6	31.7	89.4	14.1
avg. recall	38.47		39.63		34.46		**57.1**		49.7	
F-score	28.81	69.52	35.19	67.74	49.57	45.45	65.1	44.2	0.627	22.8
avg. F-score	49.16		51.46		47.51		**53.9**		41.6	
accuracy	71.28		76.34		**76.72**		57.06		49.65	

Table 2: Benchmarking Arabic sentiment classification: results for positive vs. negative

represent mixed-sentiment instances with an even number of sentiment words.

The **fully-supervised ML baseline** uses a freely available corpus of gold-standard annotated Arabic tweets (Refaee and Rieser, 2014c) to train a classifier using word n-grams and SVMs (which we found to achieve the best performance amongst a number of other machine learning schemes we explored).

The **Distant Supervision (DS) baseline** uses lexicon-based annotation to create a training set of 134,069 automatically labeled tweets (using the approach we described for the lexicon-based baseline), where the identified sentiment-bearing words are replaced by place-holders to avoid bias. We then use these noisy sentiment labels to train a classifier using SVMs. Note that previous work has also experimented with emoticon-based DS, but has found that a lexicon-based DS approach leads to superior results (Refaee and Rieser, 2014b).

4 Experiment Results

Table 2 summarises the results for comparing the above baselines to our MT-based approaches (using Google and Microsoft MT), reporting on per-class and average recall, precision and F-measure. We also measure statistical significance by performing a planned comparison between the top-performing approaches (namely, the lexicon-based baseline and the two MT systems) using χ^2 with Bonferroni correction on binary accuracy values (see Table 3). We observe the following:

- In general, MT-based approaches reach a similar performance to the more resource-intense baseline systems. There is no significant distance in accuracy between the MT-based approaches and the overall best performing lexicon-based approach.
- Microsoft MT significantly outperforms Google MT for this task.
- Overall, the fully supervised baseline performs worst. A possible explanation for that is the time-changing nature of Twitter resulting in issues like topic-shift resulting in word token-based features being less effective in such a medium (Refaee and Rieser, 2014c).
- MT-based SA approaches in general have a problem of identifying positive tweets (low recall and precision), often misclassifying them as negative. The reverse it true for the DS and fully supervised baselines, which find it hard to identify negative tweets. This is in line with results reported by Refaee and Rieser (2014b) which evaluate DS approaches to Arabic SA. Only the lexicon-approach is balanced between the positive and negative class. Note that our ML baseline systems as well as the English SA classifier by Socher et al. (2013) are trained on balanced data sets, i.e. we can assume no prior bias towards one class.

Planned Contrasts	χ^2 (p)	Effect Size (p)
Google MT vs. Microsoft MT	273.67 (p=0.000)*	0.540 (p=0.000)*
Microsoft MT vs. lexicon-based	1.64 (p=0.206)	0.042 (p=0.200)
lexicon-based vs. Google MT	3.32 (p=0.077)	0.060 (p=0.068)

Table 3: Comparison between top approaches with respect to accuracy; * indicates a sig. difference at p<0.001

4.1 Error Analysis

The above results highlight the potential of an MT-based approach to SA for languages that lack a large

	Example Tweet	Human Translation	Auto Translation	Manual	Auto Label
1	ولي عهد بريطَانيَا طَالع كشخه في الزي السعودي	Crown Prince of Britain looks very elegant in the Saudi attire	Crown Prince of Britain climber Kchkh in Saudi outfit	positive	negative
2	هذَا الشبل من ذَاك الَاسد، الّله يعَافيك و يطول بعمرك	That cub is from that lion, God bless you with a healthy and long life	That drops of Assad God heal and go on your age	positive	negative
3	فرّحه محمد بَالهدف	Muhammad's happiness with scoring a goal	Farahhh Muhammad goal	positive	negative
4	يَا الّله امطر اِهل سوريَا بَالَامن وَالرزق	Oh God, shower people of Syria with safety and livelihood	Oh God rained folks Syria security and livelihood	positive	negative
5	وعشَان انكم معَايَا انَا امتليت حيَاه، امتليت حب	Because you are with me, I'm full of life and love	And Ashan you having I Amtlat Amtlat love life	positive	negative
6	القمه الحكوميه في دبي بصرَاحه عمل يستحق التقدير، روعه	Frankly, the Government Summit in Dubai is a splended work that deserves recognition	Government summit in Dubai Frankly work deserves recognition, splendor	positive	negative

Table 4: Examples of misclassified tweets

training data-set annotated for sentiment analysis, such as Arabic. In the following, we conduct a detailed error analysis to fully understand the strength and weaknesses of this approach. First, we investigate the superior performance of Microsoft over Google MT by manually examining examples where Microsoft translated data is assigned the correct SA label, but the reverse is true for Google translated data, which is the case for 108 instances of our test set (11.5%). This analysis reveals that the main difference is the ability of Microsoft MT to maintain a better sentence structure (see Table 5).

For the following example-based error analysis of the MT approach, we therefore only consider examples where both MT systems lead to the same SA label, taking a random sample of 100 misclassified tweets. We observe the following cases of incorrectly classified tweets (see examples in Table 4):

1. Example 1 fails to translate the sentiment-bearing dialectical word, 'elegant', transcribing it as Kchkh but not translating it.
2. Incorrectly translated sentiment-bearing phrases/idioms, see e.g. *that cub is from that lion* in example 2.
3. Misspelled and hence incorrectly translated sentiment-bearing words in the original text, see example 3 'Farahhh' ('happpiness') with repeated letters. This problem is also highlighted by Abbasi et al. (2014) as one of challenges facing sentiment analysis for social networks.
4. Example 4 shows a correctly translated tweet, but with an incorrect sentiment label. We assume that this is a case of cultural differences: the phrase "oh God" can have a negative connotation in English (Strapparava et al., 2012). Note that the Stanford Sentiment classifier makes use of a manually labeled English sentiment phrase-based lexicon, which may introduce a cultural bias.
5. Example 5 represents a case of correctly translated sentiment-bearing words (love, life), but failed to translate surrounding text ('Ashan' and 'Amtlat'). Bautin et al. (2008) point out that this type of contextual information loss is one of the main challenges of MT-based SA.
6. Example 6 represents a case of a correctly translated tweet, but with an incorrectly assigned sentiment label. We assume that this is due to changes in sentence structure introduced by the MT system. Balahur and Turchi (2013) state that word ordering is one of the most prominent causes of SA misclassification. In order to confirm this hypothesis, we manually

corrected sentence structure before feeding it into the SA classifier. This approach led to the correct SA label, and thus, confirmed that the cause of the problem is word-ordering. Note that the Stanford SA system pays particular attention to sentence structure due to its "deep" architecture that adds to the model the feature of being sensitive to word ordering (Socher et al., 2013). In future work, we will verify this by comparing these results to other high performing English SA tools (see for example Abbasi et al. (2014)).

Example Tweet	تويتر مَاَاقدر اوصف شنَاعته
Google Trans.	I really appreciate what Twitter Describe the Hnaath
Microsoft Trans.	Twitter what I describe his ugliness
Human Trans.	I cannot describe how ugly is Twitter

Table 5: Example tweet along with its Google, Microsoft and human translations

In sum, one of the major challenges of this approach seems to be the use of Arabic dialects in social media, such as Twitter. In order to confirm this hypothesis, we automatically label Dialectal Arabic (DA) vs. Modern Standard Arabic (MSA) using AIDA (Elfardy et al., 2014) and analyse the performance of MT-based SA. The results in Fig. 1 show a significant correlation (Pearson, $p<0.05$) between language class and SA accuracy, with MSA outperforming DA. This confirms DA as a major source of error in the MT-based approach. Issues like dialectal variation and the vowel-free writing system still present a challenge to machine-translation (Zbib et al., 2012). This is especially true for tweets as they tend to be less formal resulting in issues like misspelling and individual spelling variations. However, with more resources being released for informal Arabic and Arabic dialects, e.g. (Cotterell and Callison-Burch, 2014; Refaee and Rieser, 2014a), we assume that off-the-shelf MT systems will improve their performance in the near future.

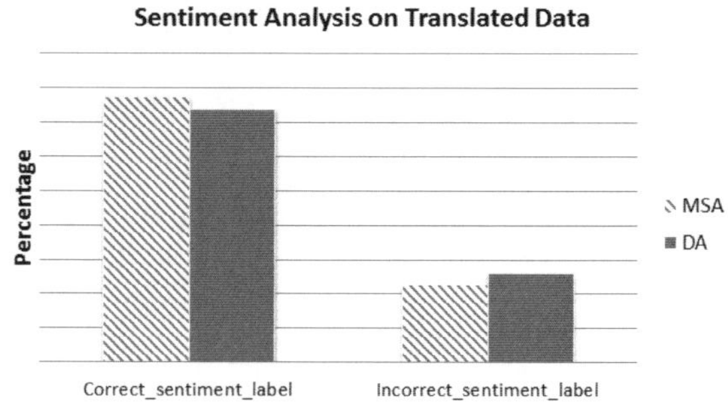

Figure 1: Performance of the sentiment classifier with respect to language class (MSA or DA)

5 Conclusion

This paper is the first to investigate and empirically evaluate the performance of Machine Translation (MT)-based Sentiment Analysis (SA) for Arabic Tweets. In particular, we make use of off-the-shelf MT tools, such as Google and Microsoft MT, to translate Arabic Tweets into English. We then use the Stanford Sentiment Classifier (Socher et al., 2013) to automatically assign sentiment labels (positive, negative) to translated tweets. In contrast to previous work, we benchmark this approach on a gold-standard test set of 937 manually annotated tweets and compare its performance to standard SA approaches, including lexicon-based, supervised and distant supervision approaches. We find that MT approaches reach a comparable performance or significantly outperform more resource-intense standard approaches. As such, we conclude that using off-the-shelf tools to perform SA for under-resourced languages, such as Arabic, is an effective and efficient alternative to building SA classifiers from scratch.

Future directions of this work include quantifying the impact of the used off-the-shelf tools, e.g. by using alternative high performing English SA tools. In addition, we plan to investigate multi-classifier systems, given the strength and weaknesses identified for each of the approaches.

References

Ahmed Abbasi, Ammar Hassan, and Milan Dhar. 2014. Benchmarking twitter sentiment analysis tools. In *Proceedings of the Ninth International Conference on Language Resources and Evaluation (LREC'14)*, Reykjavik, Iceland, may. European Language Resources Association (ELRA).

Muhammad Abdul-Mageed and Mona Diab. 2012. AWATIF: A multi-genre corpus for modern standard Arabic subjectivity and sentiment analysis. In *Proceedings of the Eight International Conference on Language Resources and Evaluation (LREC'12)*, Istanbul, Turkey. European Language Resources Association (ELRA).

Muhammad Abdul-Mageed, Mona T. Diab, and Mohammed Korayem. 2011. Subjectivity and sentiment analysis of modern standard Arabic. In *Proceedings of the 49th Annual Meeting of the Association for Computational Linguistics: Human Language Technologies: short papers - Volume 2*, HLT '11, pages 587–591, Stroudsburg, PA, USA. Association for Computational Linguistics.

Muhammad Abdul-Mageed, Sandra Kuebler, and Mona Diab. 2012. SAMAR: A system for subjectivity and sentiment analysis of Arabic social media. In *Proceedings of the 3rd Workshop in Computational Approaches to Subjectivity and Sentiment Analysis*, pages 19–28. Association for Computational Linguistics.

Alexandra Balahur and Marco Turchi. 2013. Improving sentiment analysis in twitter using multilingual machine translated data. In *Proceedings of the International Conference Recent Advances in Natural Language Processing RANLP 2013*, pages 49–55, Hissar, Bulgaria, September. INCOMA Ltd. Shoumen, BULGARIA.

Mikhail Bautin, Lohit Vijayarenu, and Steven Skiena. 2008. International sentiment analysis for news and blogs. In *ICWSM*.

Ryan Cotterell and Chris Callison-Burch. 2014. A multi-dialect, multi-genre corpus of informal written Arabic. In *The 9th edition of the Language Resources and Evaluation Conference*, Reykjavik, Iceland, May. European Language Resources Association.

Jacob Eisenstein. 2013. What to do about bad language on the internet. In *Proceedings of NAACL-HLT*, pages 359–369.

Heba Elfardy, Mohamed Al-Badrashiny, and Mona Diab. 2014. AIDA: Identifying code switching in informal Arabic text. *EMNLP 2014*, page 94.

Alec Go, Richa Bhayani, and Lei Huang. 2009. Twitter sentiment classification using distant supervision. *CS224N Project Report, Stanford*, pages 1–12.

Ahmed Mourad and Kareem Darwish. 2013. Subjectivity and sentiment analysis of modern standard Arabic and Arabic microblogs. *WASSA 2013*, page 55.

A. Pak and P. Paroubek. 2010. Twitter as a corpus for sentiment analysis and opinion mining. In *Proceedings of LREC*.

Arfath Pasha, Mohamed Al-Badrashiny, Mona Diab, Ahmed El Kholy, Ramy Eskander, Nizar Habash, Manoj Pooleery, Owen Rambow, and Ryan Roth. 2014. MADAMIRA: A fast, comprehensive tool for morphological analysis and disambiguation of Arabic. In *Proceedings of the Ninth International Conference on Language Resources and Evaluation (LREC'14)*, Reykjavik, Iceland, may. European Language Resources Association (ELRA).

Eshrag Refaee and Verena Rieser. 2014a. An Arabic twitter corpus for subjectivity and sentiment analysis. In *9th International Conference on Language Resources and Evaluation (LREC'14)*.

Eshrag Refaee and Verena Rieser. 2014b. Evaluating distant supervision for subjectivity and sentiment analysis on Arabic twitter feeds. In *Proceedings of the EMNLP 2014 Workshop on Arabic Natural Language Processing (ANLP)*.

Eshrag Refaee and Verena Rieser. 2014c. Subjectivity and sentiment analysis of Arabic twitter feeds with limited resources. In *Workshop on Free/Open-Source Arabic Corpora and Corpora Processing Tools (OSACT)*.

Wael Salloum and Nizar Habash. 2012. Elissa: A dialectal to standard Arabic machine translation system. In *COLING (Demos)*, pages 385–392.

Richard Socher, Alex Perelygin, Jean Y Wu, Jason Chuang, Christopher D Manning, Andrew Y Ng, and Christopher Potts. 2013. Recursive deep models for semantic compositionality over a sentiment treebank. In *Proceedings of the conference on empirical methods in natural language processing (EMNLP)*, volume 1631, page 1642. Citeseer.

Carlo Strapparava, Oliviero Stock, and Ilai Alon. 2012. Corpus-based explorations of affective load differences in arabic-hebrew-english. In *COLING (Posters)*, pages 1201–1208.

Maite Taboada, Julian Brooke, Milan Tofiloski, Kimberly Voll, and Manfred Stede. 2011. Lexicon-based methods for sentiment analysis. *Computational linguistics*, 37(2):267–307.

Xiaojun Wan. 2009. Co-training for cross-lingual sentiment classification. In *Proceedings of the Joint Conference of the 47th Annual Meeting of the ACL and the 4th International Joint Conference on Natural Language Processing of the AFNLP: Volume 1-Volume 1*, pages 235–243. Association for Computational Linguistics.

Theresa Wilson, Janyce Wiebe, and Paul Hoffmann. 2009. Recognizing contextual polarity: An exploration of features for phrase-level sentiment analysis. *Computational Linguistics*, 35(3):399–433.

Rabih Zbib, Erika Malchiodi, Jacob Devlin, David Stallard, Spyros Matsoukas, Richard Schwartz, John

Makhoul, Omar F Zaidan, and Chris Callison-Burch. 2012. Machine translation of Arabic dialects. In *Proceedings of the 2012 Conference of the North American Chapter of the Association for Computational Linguistics: Human Language Technologies*, pages 49–59. Association for Computational Linguistics.

Learning Kernels for Semantic Clustering: A Deep Approach

Ignacio Arroyo-Fernández
Universidad Nacional Autónoma de México (UNAM)
iarroyof@iingen.unam.mx

Abstract

In this thesis proposal we present a novel semantic embedding method, which aims at consistently performing semantic clustering at sentence level. Taking into account special aspects of *Vector Space Models (VSMs)*, we propose to learn *reproducing kernels* in classification tasks. By this way, capturing spectral features from data is possible. These features make it theoretically plausible to model *semantic similarity criteria* in Hilbert spaces, i.e. the embedding spaces. We could improve the semantic assessment over embeddings, which are criterion-derived representations from traditional semantic vectors. The learned kernel could be easily *transferred* to clustering methods, where the Multi-Class Imbalance Problem is considered (e.g. semantic clustering of definitions of terms).

1 Introduction

Overall in Machine Learning algorithms (Duda et al., 2012), knowledge is statistically embedded via the Vector Space Model (VSM), which is also named *the semantic space* (Landauer et al., 1998; Padó and Lapata, 2007; Baroni and Lenci, 2010). Contrarily to it is usually conceived in text data analysis (Manning et al., 2009; Aggarwal and Zhai, 2012), not any data set is suitable to embed into ℓ_p metric spaces, including euclidean spaces ($p = 2$) (Riesz and Nagy, 1955). This implies that, in particular, clustering algorithms are being adapted to some ℓ_p-derived metric, but not to semantic vector sets (clusters) (Qin et al., 2014).

The above implication also means that semantic similarity measures are commonly not consistent, e.g. the cosine similarity or transformation-based distances (Sidorov et al., 2014). These are mainly based on the concept of triangle. Thus if the triangle inequality does not hold (which induces norms for *Hilbert spaces* exclusively), then the case of the cosine similarity becomes mathematically inconsistent[1]. Despite VSMs are sometimes not mathematically analyzed, traditional algorithms work well enough for global semantic analysis (hereinafter *global analysis*, i.e. at document level where Zipf's law holds). Nevertheless, for local analysis (hereinafter *local analysis*, i.e., at sentence, phrase or word level) the issue remains still open (Mikolov et al., 2013).

In this thesis proposal, we will address the main difficulties raised from traditional VSMs for local analysis of text data. We consider the latter as an ill-posed problem (which implies unstable algorithms) in the sense of some explicit *semantic similarity criterion* (hereinafter *criterion*), e.g. topic, concept, etc. (Vapnik, 1998; Fernandez et al., 2007). The following feasible reformulation is proposed. By learning a kernel in classification tasks, we want to induce an embedding space (Lanckriet et al., 2004; Cortes et al., 2009). In this space, we will consider relevance (weighting) of spectral features of data, which are in turn related to the shape of semantic vector sets (Xiong et al., 2014). These vectors would be derived from different *Statistical Language Models (SLMs)*; i.e. countable things, e.g. *n*-grams, bag-of-words (BoW), etc.; which in turn encode *language*

[1] Riesz (1955) gives details about Hilbert spaces.

Proceedings of NAACL-HLT 2015 Student Research Workshop (SRW), pages 79–87,
Denver, Colorado, June 1, 2015.

aspects (e.g. semantics, syntax, morphology, etc.). Learned kernels are susceptible to be transferred to clustering methods (Yosinski et al., 2014; Bengio et al., 2014), where spectral features would be properly *filtered* from text (Gu et al., 2011).

When both learning and clustering processes are performed, the kernel approach is tolerant enough for data scarcity. Thus, eventually, we could have any criterion-derived amount of semantic clusters regardless of the Multi-Class Imbalance Problem (MCIP) (Sugiyama and Kawanabe, 2012). It is a rarely studied problem in Natural Language Processing (NLP), however, contributions can be helpful in a number of tasks such as IE, topic modeling, QA systems, opinion mining, Natural Language Understanding, etc.

This paper is organized as follows: In Section 2 we show our case study. In Section 3 we show the embedding framework. In Section 4 we present our learning problem. Sections 5 and 6 respectively show research directions and related work. In Section 7, conclusions and future work are presented.

2 A case study and background

A case study. Semantic clustering of definitions of terms is our case study. See the next extracted[2] examples for the terms *window* and *mouse*. For each of them, the main acception is showed first, and afterwards three secondary acceptions:

1. *A* ***window*** *is a* ***frame*** *including a* ***sheet of glass*** *or other material capable of admitting light...*
   (a) *The window is the* ***time*** *elapsed since a* ***passenger*** *calls to* ***schedule****...*
   (b) *A window is a* ***sequence*** *region of 20-codon length on an alignment of* ***homologous genes****...*
   (c) *A window is any* ***GUI element*** *and is usually identified by a Windows handle...*
2. *A* ***mouse*** *is a* ***mammal*** *classified in the order* ***Rodentia****, suborder* ***Sciurognathi****....*
   (a) *A mouse* ***is a small object*** *you can roll along a hard, flat surface...*
   (b) *A mouse is a* ***handheld pointing device*** *used to position a cursor on a* ***computer****...*
   (c) *The Mouse is a* ***fictional character*** *in* ***Alice's Adventures*** *in Wonderland by* ***Lewis Carroll****...*

In the example 1, it is possible to assign the four acceptions to four different semantic groups (the window (1), transport services (1a), genetics (1b) and computing (1c)) by using lexical features (bold terms). This example also indicates how abstract concepts are always latent in the definitions. The example 2 is a bit more complex. Unlike to example 1, there would be three clusters because there are two semantically similar acceptions (2a and 2b are related to computing). However, they are lexically very distant. See that in both examples the amount of semantic clusters can't be defined a priory (unlike to Wikipedia). Additionally, it is impossible to know what topic the users of an IE system could be interested in. These issues, point out the need for analyzing the way we are currently treating semantic spaces in the sense of stability of algorithms (Vapnik, 1998), i.e. the existence of semantic similarity consistence, although Zipf's law scarcely holds (e.g. in local analysis).

Semantic spaces and embeddings. Erk (2012) and Brychcín (2014) showed insightful empiricism about well known semantic spaces for different cases in global analysis. In this work we have special interest in local analysis, where semantic vectors are representations (*embeddings*) derived from learned feature maps for specific semantic assessments (Mitchell and Lapata, 2010). These feature maps are commonly encoded in Artificial Neural Networks (ANNs) (Kalchbrenner et al., 2014).

ANNs have recently attracted worldwide attention. Given their surprising adaptability to unknown distributions, they are used in NLP for embedding and feature learning in local analysis, i.e. *Deep Learning* (DL) (Socher et al., 2011; Socher et al., 2013). However, we require knowledge transfer towards clustering tasks. It is still not feasible by using ANNs (Yosinski et al., 2014). Thus, theoretical access becomes ever more necessary, so it is worth extending *Kernel Learning* (KL) studies as alternative feature learning method in NLP (Lanckriet et al., 2004). Measuring subtle semantic displacements, according to a criterion, is theoretically attainable in a well defined (learned) *reproducing kernel Hilbert space* (RKHS), e.g. some subset of L_2 (Aronszajn, 1950). In these spaces, features are latent *abstraction levels*[3] of data spectrum, which improves kernel scaling (Dai et al., 2014; Anandkumar et al., 2014).

[2] www.describe.com.mx

[3] Mainly in *DL*, it is known there are different hierarchies of generality of features learned by a learning machine.

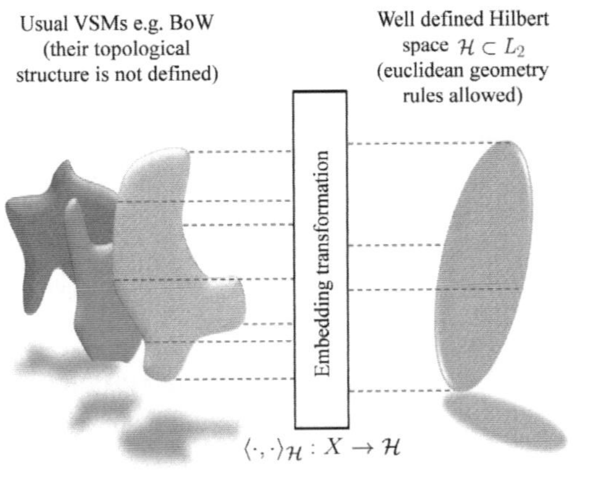

Figure 1: General schema of the transformation framework from some traditional VSM (left) to a well defined embedding space (right).

3 RKHS and semantic embeddings

We propose mapping sets of semantic vectors (e.g. BoW) into well defined function spaces (RKHSs), prior to directly endowing such sets (not elliptical or at least convex (Qin et al., 2014)) with the euclidean norm, $\|.\|_2$ (see Figure 1). For the aforesaid purpose, we want to take advantage of the RKHSs.

Any semantic vector $x_o \in X$ could be consistently embedded (*transformed*) into a well defined Hilbert space by using the *reproducing property* of a kernel $k(\cdot,\cdot)$ (Shawe-Taylor and Cristianini, 2004):

$$f_{x_o}(x) = \langle f(\cdot), k(\cdot, x) \rangle_{\mathcal{H}}; \ \forall x \in X \quad (1)$$

where: $\mathcal{H} \subset L_2$ is a RKHS, $f_{x_o}(\cdot) \in \mathcal{H}$ is the embedding derived from x_o, which can be seen as fixed parameter of $k(\cdot, x_o) = f(\cdot) \in \mathcal{H}$. This embedding function is defined over the vector domain $\{x\} \subset X$ and $\langle \cdot,\cdot \rangle_{\mathcal{H}} : X \to \mathcal{H}$ is the inner product in $\mathcal{H}$.

Always that (1) holds, $k(\cdot,\cdot)$ is a positive definite (PD) kernel function, so X does not need even to be a vector space and even then, convergence of any sequence $\{f_n(x) : f_n \in \mathcal{H}; n \in \mathbb{N}\}$ can be ensured. The above is a highly valuable characteristic of the resulting function space (Smola et al., 2007):

$$\lim_{n\to\infty} f_n = f \iff \lim_{n\to\infty} k_n(\cdot, x) = k(\cdot, x). \quad (2)$$

The result (2) implies that convergence of summation of initial guessing kernel functions $k_n(\cdot,\cdot) \in \mathcal{H}$ always occurs, hence talking about the existence of a suitable kernel function $k(\cdot,\cdot) \in \mathcal{H}$ in (1) is absolutely possible. It means that L_2 operations can be consistently applied, e.g. the usual norm $\|\cdot\|_2$, trigonometric functions (e.g. $\cos\theta$) and distance $d_2 = \|f_n - f_m\|_2 : m \neq n$. Thus, from right side of (2), in order that (1) holds convergence of the Fourier series decomposition of $k(\cdot,\cdot)$ towards the spectrum of desired features from data is necessary; i.e., by learning parameters and hyperparameters[4] of the series (Ong et al., 2005; Băzăvan et al., 2012).

3.1 Learnable kernels for language features

Assume (1) and (2) hold. For some SLM a encoded in a traditional semantic space, it is possible to define a learnable kernel matrix K_a as follows (Lanckriet et al., 2004; Cortes et al., 2009):

$$K_a := \sum_{i=1}^{p} \beta_i K_i, \quad (3)$$

where $\{K_i\}_{i=1}^{p} \subset \mathcal{K}$ is the set of p initial guessing kernel matrices (belonging to the family $\mathcal{K}$, e.g. Gaussian) with fixed hyperparameters and β_i's are parameters weighting K_i's. Please note that, for simplicity, we are using matrices associated to kernel functions $k_i(\cdot,\cdot), k_a(\cdot,\cdot) \in \mathcal{H}$, respectively.

In the Fourier domain and bandwidth. In fact (3) is a Fourier series, where β_i's are decomposition coefficients of K_a (Băzăvan et al., 2012). This kernel would be fitting the spectrum of some SLM that encodes some latent language aspect from text (Landauer et al., 1998). On one hand, in Fourier domain operations (e.g. the error vector norm) are closed in L_2, i.e., according to (2) convergence is ensured as a Hilbert space is well defined. Moreover, the L_2-regularizer is convex in terms of the Fourier series coefficients (Cortes et al., 2009). The aforementioned facts imply benefits in terms of computational complexity (scaling) and precision (Dai et al., 2014). On the other hand, hyperparameters of initial guessing kernels are learnable for detecting the bandwitdh of data (Ong et al., 2005; Băzăvan et al., 2012; Xiong et al., 2014). Eventually, the latter fact would lead us to know (learning) bounds for

[4] So called in order to make distinction between weights (kernel parameters or coefficients) and the basis function parameters (hyperparameters), e.g. mean and variance.

the necessary amount of data to properly train our model (*the Nyquist theorem*).

Cluster shape. A common shape among clusters is considered even for unseen clusters with different, independent and imbalanced prior probability densities (Vapnik, 1998; Sugiyama and Kawanabe, 2012). For example, if data is Guassian-distributed in the input space, then shape of different clusters tend to be elliptical (the utopian ℓ_2 case), although their densities are not regular or even very imbalanced. Higher abstraction levels of the data spectrum possess mentioned traits (Ranzato et al., 2007; Baktashmotlagh et al., 2013). We will suggest below a more general version of (3), thereby considering higher abstraction levels of text data.

4 Learning our kernel in a RKHS

A transducer is a setting for learning parameters and hyperparameters of a multikernel linear combination like the Fourier series (3) (Băzăvan et al., 2012).

Overall, the above setting consists on defining a multi-class learning problem over a RKHS: let $\mathcal{Y}_\theta = \{y_\ell\}_{y_\ell \in \mathbb{N}}$ be a sequence of targets inducing a semantic criterion θ, likewise a training set $\mathcal{X} = \{x_\ell\}_{x_\ell \in \mathbb{R}^n}$ and a set of initial guessing kernels $\{K_{\sigma_i}\}_{i=1}^p \subset \mathcal{K}$ with the associated hyperparameter vector $\sigma_a = \{\sigma_i\}_{i=1}^p$. Then for some SLM $a \in \mathcal{A}$, we would learn the associated kernel matrix K_a by optimizing the SLM empirical risk functional:

$$\mathcal{J}_\mathcal{A}(\sigma_a, \beta_a) = L_\mathcal{A}(K_a, \mathcal{X}, \mathcal{Y}_\theta) + \psi(\sigma_a) + \xi(\beta_a), \tag{4}$$

where in $\mathcal{J}_\mathcal{A}(\cdot,\cdot)$ we have:

$$K_a = \sum_{1 \leq i \leq p} \beta_i K_{\sigma_i}. \tag{5}$$

The learning is divided in two interrelated stages: at the first stage, the free parameter vector $\beta_a = \{\beta_i\}_{i=1}^p$ in (5) (a particular version of (3)), is optimized for learning a partial kernel $\widehat{K}_a$, given a fixed (sufficiently small) σ_a and by using the regularizer $\xi(\beta_a)$ over the SLM prediction loss $L_\mathcal{A}(\cdot,\cdot)$ in (4). Conversely at the second stage σ_a is free, thus by using the regularizer $\psi(\sigma_a)$ over the prediction loss $L_\mathcal{A}(\cdot,\cdot)$, given that the optimal β_a^* was found at the first stage, we could have the optimal σ_a^* and therefore K_a^* is selected.

At higher abstraction levels, given the association $\{\mathcal{X}, \mathcal{Y}_\theta\}$, the transducer setting would learn a kernel function that fits a multi-class partition of X via summation of K_a's. Thus, we can use learned kernels K_a^* as new initial guesses in order to learn a compound kernel matrix K_θ for a higher abstraction level:

$$\mathcal{J}(\gamma_\theta) = L(K_\theta, \mathcal{X}, \mathcal{Y}_\theta) + \zeta(\gamma_\theta), \tag{6}$$

where in the general risk functional $\mathcal{J}(\cdot)$ we have:

$$K_\theta = \sum_{a \in \mathcal{A}} \gamma_a K_a^*. \tag{7}$$

In (6) the vector $\gamma_\theta = \{\gamma_a\}_{a \in \mathcal{A}}$ weights semantic representations K_a^* associated to each SLM and $\zeta(\gamma_\theta)$ is a proper regularizer over the general loss $L(\cdot,\cdot)$. The described learning processes can even be jointly performed (Băzăvan et al., 2012). The aforementioned losses and regularizers can be conveniently defined (Cortes et al., 2009).

4.1 The learned kernel function

In order to make relevant features to emerge from text, we would use our learned kernel K_θ^*. Thus if $\{\gamma_\theta^*, \{\beta_a^*, \sigma_a^*\}_{a \in \mathcal{A}}\}$ is the solution set of the learning problems (4) and (6), then combining (5) and (7) gives the embedding kernel function, for $|\mathcal{A}|$ different SLMs as required (see Figure 2):

Definition 1. *Given a semantic criterion θ, then the learned parameters $\{\gamma_\theta^*, \{\beta_a^*, \sigma_a^*\}_{a \in \mathcal{A}}\}$ are eigenvalues of kernels $\{K_a^*\}_{a \in \mathcal{A}} \prec K_\theta^*$, respectively*[5]*. Thus according to (1), we have for any semantic vector $x_o \in X$ its representation $f_{x_o}(x) \in \mathcal{H}$:*

$$\begin{aligned} f_{x_o}(x) &:= \sum_{a \in \mathcal{A}} \sum_{i=1}^{p} \gamma_a^* \beta_i^* k_i(x, x_o) \\ &= k_\theta(x, x_o) \approx K_\theta^* x_o. \end{aligned} \tag{8}$$

In (8), $k_i(\cdot,\cdot), k_\theta(\cdot,\cdot) \in \mathcal{H} \subset L_2$ are reproducing kernel functions associated to matrices K_{σ_i} and K_θ, respectively. The associated $\{\sigma_a^*\}_{a \in \mathcal{A}}$ would be optimally fitting the bandwidth of data. $X \supset \mathcal{X}$ is a compounding semantic space from different SLMs

[5] *(i)* The symbol '$\prec$' denotes subordination (from right to left) between operators, i.e. hierarchy of abstraction levels. *(ii)* See (Shawe-Taylor and Cristianini, 2004; Anandkumar et al., 2014) for details about eigendecompositions.

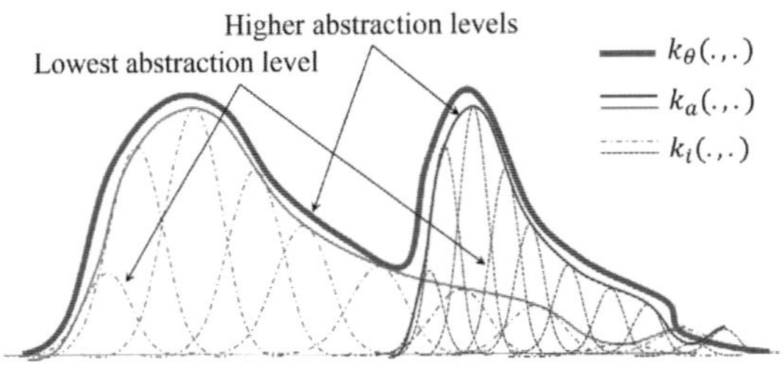

Figure 2: Sketch (bold plot) of the abstraction levels of some learned kernel function $k_\theta(\cdot,\cdot) \in \mathcal{H} \subset L_2$.

$a \in \mathcal{A}$ (Băzăvan et al., 2012). According to θ, semantic clustering could be consistently performed in $\mathcal{H}$ by computing any L_2 similarity measure between embeddings $\{f_{x_n}, f_{x_m}\}$, which are derived from any semantic vectors $x_n, x_m \in X$, e.g. *(i)* the kernel correlation coefficient $\rho_\theta = \mu k_\theta(x_n, x_m) \in [0, 1]$; with $\mu = \frac{1}{\|f_{x_n}\|\|f_{x_m}\|}$, and *(ii)* the distance by simply computing $d_2 = \|f_{x_n} - f_{x_m}\|_2$.

Please note that we could extend Definition 1 to deeper levels (layers) associated to abstraction levels of SLMs. These levels could explicitly encode morphology, syntax, semantics or compositional semantics, i.e. $\{K_a\}_{a \in \mathcal{A}} = K_{SLMs} \prec K_{aspects}$.

5 Research directions

Our main research direction is to address in detail linguistic interpretations associated to second member of (8), which is still not clear. There are potential ways of interpreting *pooling operations* over the expansion of either eigenvalues or eigenfunctions of $f_{x_o}(\cdot)$. This fact could lead us to an alternative way of analyzing written language, i.e. in terms of the spectral decomposition of $\mathcal{X}$ given θ.

As another direction we consider data scarcity (low annotated resources). It is a well handled issue by spectral approaches like the proposed one, so it is worth investigating hyperparameter learning techniques. We consider hyperparameters as the lowest abstraction level of the learned kernel and they are aimed at data bandwidth estimation (i.e. by tuning the σ_i associated to each $k_i(\cdot, \cdot)$ in (8)). This estimation could help us to try to answer the question of how much training data is enough. This question is also related to the quality bounds of a learned kernel. These bounds could be used to investigate the possible relation among the number of annotated clusters, the training set size and the generalization ability. The latter would be provided (transferred) by the learned kernel to a common clustering algorithm for discovering imbalanced unseen semantic clusters. We are planning to perform the above portrayed experiments at least for a couple of semantic criteria[6], including term acception discovering (Section 2). Nevertheless, much remains to be done.

6 Related work

Clustering of definitional contexts. Molina (2009) processed snippets containing definitions of terms (Sierra, 2009). The obtained PD matrix is not more than a homogeneous quadratic kernel that induces a Hilbert space: The *Textual Energy* of data (Fernandez et al., 2007; Torres-Moreno et al., 2010). Hierarchical clustering is performed over the resulting space, but some semantic criterion was not considered. Thus, such as Cigarran (2008), they ranked retrieved documents by simply relying on lexical features (global analysis). ML analysis was not performed, so their approach suffers from high sensibility to lexical changes (instability) in local analysis.

Paraphrase extraction from definitional sentences. Hashimoto, et.al. (2011) and Yan, et.al. (2013) engineered vectors from contextual, syntactical and lexical features of definitional sentence paraphrases (similarly to Lapata (2007) and Ferrone (2014)). As training data they used a POS annotated corpus of sentences that contain noun phrases. It was trained a binary SVM aimed at both paraphrase detection and multi-word term equivalence assertion (Choi and Myaeng, 2012; Abend et al., 2014). More complex constructions were not considered, but their feature mixure performs very well.

Socher et al., (2011) used ANNs for paraphrase detection. According to labeling, the network unsupervisedly capture as many language features as latent in data (Kalchbrenner et al., 2014). The network supervisedly learns to represent desired contents inside phrases (Mikolov et al., 2013); thus paraphrase detection is highly generalized. Nevertheless, it is notable the necessity of a tree parser. Unlike to (Socher et al., 2013), the network must to learn syntactic features separately.

[6]For example: SemEval-2014; Semantic Evaluation Exercises.

Definitional answer ranking. Fegueroa (2012) and (2014) proposed to represent definitional answers by a Context Language Model (CLM), i.e. a Markovian process as probabilistic language model. A knowledge base (WordNET) is used as an annotated corpus of specific domains (limited to Wikipedia). Unlike to our approach, queries must be previously disambiguated; for instance: *"what is a computer virus?"*, where "computer virus" disambiguates "virus". Answers are classified according to relevant terms (Mikolov et al., 2013), similarly to the way topic modeling approaches work (Fernandez et al., 2007; Lau et al., 2014).

Learning kernels for clustering. Overall for knowledge transfer from classification (source) tasks to clustering (target) tasks, the state of the art is not bast. This setting is generally explored by using toy Gaussian-distributed data and predefined kernels (Jenssen et al., 2006; Jain et al., 2010). Particularly for text data, Gu et.al. (2011) addressed the setting by using multi-task kernels for global analysis. In their work, it was not necessary neither to discover clusters nor to model some semantic criterion. Both them are assumed as a presetting of their analysis, which differs from our proposal.

Feasibility of KL over DL. We want to perform clustering over an embedding space. At the best of our knowledge there exist two dominant approaches for feature learning: KL and DL. However, knowledge transfer is equally important for us, so both procedures should be more intuitive by adopting the KL approach instead of DL. We show the main reasons: *(i) Interpretability.* The form (8) has been deducted from punctual items (e.g. SLMs encoding language aspects), which leads us to think that a latent statistical interpretation of language is worthy of further investigation. *(ii) Modularity.* Any kernel can be transparently transferred into kernelized and non-kernelized clustering methods (Schölkopf et al., 1997; Aguilar-Martin and De Mántaras, 1982; Ben-Hur et al., 2002). *(iii) Mathematical support.* Theoretical access provided by kernel methods would allow for future work on semantic assessments via increasingly abstract representations. *(iv) Data scarcity.* It is one of our principal challenges, so kernel methods are feasible because of their generalization predictability (Cortes and Vapnik, 1995).

Regardless of its advantages, our theoretical framework exhibit latent drawbacks. The main of them is that feature learning is not fully unsupervised, which suggests the underlying possibility of preventing learning from some decisive knowledge related to, mainly, the tractability of the MCIP. Thus, many empirical studies are pending.

7 Conclusions and future work

At the moment, our theoretical framework analyzes semantic embedding in the sense of a criterion for semantic clustering. However, correspondences between linguistic intuitions and the showed theoretical framework (interpretability) are actually incipient, although we consider these challenging correspondences are described in a generalized way in the seminal work of Harris (1968). It is encouraging (not determinant) that our approach can be associated to his operator hypothesis on composition and separability of both linguistic entities and language aspects. That is why we consider it is worth investigating spectral decomposition methods for NLP as possible rapprochement to elucidate improvements in semantic assessments (e.g. semantic clustering). Thus, by performing this research we also expect to advance the state of the art in statistical features of written language.

As immediate future work we are planning to learn compositional distributional *operators* (kernels), which can be seen as stable solutions of operator equations (Harris, 1968; Vapnik, 1998). We would like to investigate this approach for morphology, syntax and semantics (Mitchell and Lapata, 2010; Lazaridou et al., 2013). Another future proposal could be derived from the abovementioned approach (operator learning), i.e. multi-sentence compression for automatic sumarization.

A further extension could be ontology learning. It would be proposed as a multi-structure KL framework (Ferrone and Zanzotto, 2014). In this case, IE and knowledge organization would be our main aims (Anandkumar et al., 2014).

Aknowledgements. This work is funded by CONACyT Mexico (grant: 350326/178248). Thanks to the UNAM graduate program in CS. Thanks to Carlos Méndez-Cruz, to Yang Liu and to anonymous reviewers for their valuable comments.

References

Omri Abend, B. Shay Cohen, and Mark Steedman. 2014. Lexical inference over multi-word predicates: A distributional approach. In *Proceedings of the 52nd Annual Meeting of the Association for Computational Linguistics (Volume 1: Long Papers)*, pages 644–654. ACL.

Charu C. Aggarwal and Cheng Xiang Zhai. 2012. An introduction to text mining. In Charu C Aggarwal and ChengXiang Zhai, editors, *Mining Text Data*, pages 1–10. Springer US.

J Aguilar-Martin and R De Mántaras. 1982. The process of classification and learning the meaning of linguistic descriptors of concepts. *Approximate Reasoning in Decision Analysis*, 1982:165–175.

Animashree Anandkumar, Rong Ge, Daniel Hsu, Sham M Kakade, and Matus Telgarsky. 2014. Tensor decompositions for learning latent variable models. *The Journal of Machine Learning Research*, 15(1):2773–2832.

Nachman Aronszajn. 1950. Theory of reproducing kernels. *Transactions of the American mathematical society*, pages 337–404.

Mahsa Baktashmotlagh, Mehrtash T Harandi, Brian C Lovell, and Mathieu Salzmann. 2013. Unsupervised domain adaptation by domain invariant projection. In *Computer Vision (ICCV), 2013 IEEE International Conference on*, pages 769–776. IEEE.

Marco Baroni and Alessandro Lenci. 2010. Distributional memory: A general framework for corpus-based semantics. *Computational Linguistics*, 36(4):673–721.

Eduard Gabriel Băzăvan, Fuxin Li, and Cristian Sminchisescu. 2012. Fourier kernel learning. In *Computer Vision–ECCV 2012*, pages 459–473. Springer.

Asa Ben-Hur, David Horn, Hava T Siegelmann, and Vladimir Vapnik. 2002. Support vector clustering. *The Journal of Machine Learning Research*, 2:125–137.

Yoshua Bengio, Ian J. Goodfellow, and Aaron Courville. 2014. Deep learning. Book in preparation for MIT Press.

Tomáš Brychcín and Miroslav Konopík. 2014. Semantic spaces for improving language modelling. *Computer Speech and Language*, 28:192–209.

Sung-Pil Choi and Sung-Hyon Myaeng. 2012. Terminological paraphrase extraction from scientific literature based on predicate argument tuples. *Journal of Information Science*, pages 1–19.

Juan Manuel Cigarrán Recuero. 2008. *Organización de resultados de búsqueda mediante análisis formal de conceptos*. Ph.D. thesis, Universidad Nacional de Educación a Distancia; Escuela Técnica Superior de Ingeniería Informática.

Corinna Cortes and Vladimir Vapnik. 1995. Support-vector networks. *Machine learning*, 20(3):273–297.

Corinna Cortes, Mehryar Mohri, and Afshin Rostamizadeh. 2009. L 2 regularization for learning kernels. In *Proceedings of the Twenty-Fifth Conference on Uncertainty in Artificial Intelligence*, pages 109–116. AUAI Press.

Bo Dai, Bo Xie, Niao He, Yingyu Liang, Anant Raj, Maria-Florina F Balcan, and Le Song. 2014. Scalable kernel methods via doubly stochastic gradients. In *Advances in Neural Information Processing Systems*, pages 3041–3049.

Richard O Duda, Peter E Hart, and David G Stork. 2012. *Pattern classification*. John Wiley & Sons.

Katrin Erk. 2012. Vector space models of word meaning and phrase meaning: A survey. *Language and Linguistics Compass*, 6(10):635–653.

Silvia Fernandez, Eric San Juan, and Juan-Manuel Torres-Moreno. 2007. Textual energy of associative memories: Performant applications of enertex algorithm in text summarization and topic segmentation. *MICAI 2007: Advances in Artificial Intelligence*, pages 861–871.

Lorenzo Ferrone and Fabio Massimo Zanzotto. 2014. Towards syntax-aware compositional distributional semantic models. In *Proceedings of COLING 2014: Technical Papers*, pages 721–730. Dublin City University and Association for Computational Linguistics (ACL).

Alejandro Figueroa and John Atkinson. 2012. Contextual language models for ranking answers to natural language definition questions. *Computational Intelligence*, pages 528–548.

Alejandro Figueroa and Günter Neumann. 2014. Category-specific models for ranking effective paraphrases in community question answering. *Expert Systems with Applications*, 41(10):4730–4742.

Quanquan Gu, Zhenhui Li, and Jiawei Han. 2011. Learning a kernel for multi-task clustering. In *Proceedings of the 25th AAAI conference on artificial intelligence*. Association for the Advancement of Artificial Intelligence (AAAI).

Zellig S. Harris. 1968. *Mathematical Structures of Language*. Wiley, New York, NY, USA.

Chikara Hashimoto, Kentaro Torisawa, Stijn De Saeger, Jun'ichi Kazama, and Sadao Kurohashi. 2011. Extracting paraphrases from definition sentences on the web. In *Proceedings of the 49th Annual Meeting of the Association for Computational Linguistics: Human Language Technologies-Volume 1*, pages 1087–1097.

Prateek Jain, Brian Kulis, and Inderjit S Dhillon. 2010. Inductive regularized learning of kernel functions. In

Advances in Neural Information Processing Systems, pages 946–954.

Robert Jenssen, Torbjørn Eltoft, Mark Girolami, and Deniz Erdogmus. 2006. Kernel maximum entropy data transformation and an enhanced spectral clustering algorithm. In *Advances in Neural Information Processing Systems*, pages 633–640.

Nal Kalchbrenner, Edward Grefenstette, and Phil Blunsom. 2014. A convolutional neural network for modelling sentences. *arXiv preprint arXiv:1404.2188*.

Gert R. G. Lanckriet, Nello Cristianini, Peter Bartlett, Laurent El Ghaoui, and Michael I. Jordan. 2004. Learning the kernel matrix with semidefinite programming. *J. Mach. Learn. Res.*, 5:27–72, December.

Thomas K Landauer, Peter W. Foltz, and Darrell Laham. 1998. An introduction to latent semantic analysis. *Discourse Processes*, 25(2-3):259–284.

Jey Han Lau, Paul Cook, Diana McCarthy, Spandana Gella, and Timothy Baldwin. 2014. Learning word sense distributions, detecting unattested senses and identifying novel senses using topic models. In *Proceedings of the 52nd Annual Meeting of the Association for Computational Linguistics, ACL 2014*, volume 1, pages 259–270.

Angeliki Lazaridou, Marco Marelli, Roberto Zamparelli, and Marco Baroni. 2013. Compositional-ly derived representations of morphologically complex words in distributional semantics. In *Proceedings of the 51st Annual Meeting of the Association for Computational Linguistics (Volume 1: Long Papers)*, pages 1517–1526.

Christopher D. Manning, Prabhakar Raghavan, and Hinrich Schütze. 2009. *An Introduction to Information Retrieval.* Cambridge UP.

Tomas Mikolov, Ilya Sutskever, Kai Chen, Greg S Corrado, and Jeff Dean. 2013. Distributed representations of words and phrases and their compositionality. In *Advances in Neural Information Processing Systems*, pages 3111–3119.

Jeff Mitchell and Mirella Lapata. 2010. Composition in distributional models of semantics. *Cognitive Science*, 34(34):1388–1429. Cognitive Science Society, ISSN: 1551-6709.

A Molina. 2009. Agrupamiento semántico de contextos definitorios. *Mémoire de Master, Universidad Nacional Autónoma de México–Posgrado en Ciencia e Ingeniería de la Computación, México*, 108.

Cheng S Ong, Robert C Williamson, and Alex J Smola. 2005. Learning the kernel with hyperkernels. In *Journal of Machine Learning Research*, pages 1043–1071.

Sebastian Padó and Mirella Lapata. 2007. Dependency-based construction of semantic space models. *Computational Linguistics*, 33(2):161–199.

Danfeng Qin, Xuanli Chen, Matthieu Guillaumin, and Luc V Gool. 2014. Quantized kernel learning for feature matching. In *Advances in Neural Information Processing Systems*, pages 172–180.

M Ranzato, Fu Jie Huang, Y-L Boureau, and Yann LeCun. 2007. Unsupervised learning of invariant feature hierarchies with applications to object recognition. In *Computer Vision and Pattern Recognition, 2007. CVPR'07. IEEE Conference on*, pages 1–8. IEEE.

F. Riesz and Sz Nagy. 1955. Functional analysis. *Dover Publications, Inc., New York. First published in*, 3(6):35.

Bernhard Schölkopf, Alexander Smola, and Klaus-Robert Müller. 1997. Kernel principal component analysis. In *Artificial Neural Networks–ICANN'97*, pages 583–588. Springer.

Jhon Shawe-Taylor and Nello Cristianini. 2004. *Kernel Methods for Pattern Analysis.* Cambridge UP. ISBN: 978-0-521-81397-6.

Grigori Sidorov, Alexander Gelbukh, Helena Gómez-Adorno, and David Pinto. 2014. Soft similarity and soft cosine measure: Similarity of features in vector space model. *Computación y Sistemas*, 18(3).

Gerardo Sierra. 2009. Extracción de contextos definitorios en textos de especialidad a partir del reconocimiento de patrones lingüísticos. *LinguaMÁTICA*, 2:13–38, Dezembro.

Alex Smola, Arthur Gretton, Le Song, and Bernhard Schölkopf. 2007. A hilbert space embedding for distributions. In *Algorithmic Learning Theory: 18th International Conference*, pages 13–31. Springer-Verlag.

Richard Socher, Eric H Huang, Jeffrey Pennin, Christopher D Manning, and Andrew Y Ng. 2011. Dynamic pooling and unfolding recursive autoencoders for paraphrase detection. In *Advances in Neural Information Processing Systems*, pages 801–809.

Richard Socher, Alex Perelygin, Jean Y Wu, Jason Chuang, Christopher D Manning, Andrew Y Ng, and Christopher Potts. 2013. Recursive deep models for semantic compositionality over a sentiment treebank. In *Proceedings of the Conference on Empirical Methods in Natural Language Processing (EMNLP)*, pages 1631–1642. Citeseer.

M. Sugiyama and M. Kawanabe. 2012. *Machine Learning in Non-stationary Environments: Introduction to Covariate Shift Adaptation.* Adaptive computation and machine learning. MIT Press.

Juan-Manuel Torres-Moreno, Alejandro Molina, and Gerardo Sierra. 2010. La energía textual como medida de distancia en agrupamiento de definiciones. In *Statistical Analysis of Textual Data*, pages 215–226.

Vladimir Naumovich Vapnik. 1998. *Statistical learning theory.* Wiley New York.

Yuanjun Xiong, Wei Liu, Deli Zhao, and Xiaoou Tang. 2014. Zeta hull pursuits: Learning nonconvex data hulls. In *Advances in Neural Information Processing Systems*, pages 46–54.

Yulan Yan, Chikara Hashimoto, Kentaro Torisawa, Takao Kawai, Jun'ichi Kazama, and Stijn De Saeger. 2013. Minimally supervised method for multilingual paraphrase extraction from definition sentences on the web. In *HLT-NAACL*, pages 63–73.

Jason Yosinski, Jeff Clune, Yoshua Bengio, and Hod Lipson. 2014. How transferable are features in deep neural networks? In *Advances in Neural Information Processing Systems*, pages 3320–3328.

Narrowing the Loop: Integration of Resources and Linguistic Dataset Development with Interactive Machine Learning

Seid Muhie Yimam
FG Language Technology
Department of Computer Science
Technische Universität Darmstadt
http://www.lt.tu-darmstadt.de
yimam@lt.informatik.tu-darmstadt.de

Abstract

This thesis proposal sheds light on the role of interactive machine learning and implicit user feedback for manual annotation tasks and semantic writing aid applications. First we focus on the cost-effective annotation of training data using an interactive machine learning approach by conducting an experiment for sequence tagging of German named entity recognition. To show the effectiveness of the approach, we further carry out a sequence tagging task on Amharic part-of-speech and are able to significantly reduce time used for annotation. The second research direction is to systematically integrate different NLP resources for our new semantic writing aid tool using again an interactive machine learning approach to provide contextual paraphrase suggestions. We develop a baseline system where three lexical resources are combined to provide paraphrasing in context and show that combining resources is a promising direction.

1 Introduction

Machine learning applications require considerable amounts of annotated data in order to achieve a good prediction performance (Pustejovsky and Stubbs, 2012). Nevertheless, the development of such annotated data is labor-intensive and requires a certain degree of human expertise. Also, such annotated data produced by expert annotators has limitations, such as 1) it usually does not scale very well since annotation of a very large data set is prohibitively expensive, and 2) for applications which should reflect dynamic changes of data over time, static training data will not serve its purpose. This issue is commonly known as *concept drift* (Kulesza et al., 2014).

There has been a lot of effort in automatically expanding training data and lexical resources using different techniques. One approach is the use of active learning (Settles et al., 2008) which aims at reducing the amount of labeled training data required by selecting most informative data to be annotated. For example it selects the instances from the training dataset about which the machine learning model is least certain how to label (Krithara et al., 2006; Settles, 2010; Raghavan et al., 2006; Mozafariy et al., 2012). Another recent approach to alleviate bottleneck in collecting training data is the usage of crowdsourcing services (Snow et al., 2008; Costa et al., 2011) to collect large amount of annotations from non-expert crowds at comparably low cost.

In an interactive machine learning approach, the application might start with minimal or no training data. During runtime, the user provides simple feedback to the machine learning process interactively by correcting suggestions or adding new annotations and integrating background knowledge into the modeling stage (Ware et al., 2002).

Similarly, natural language processing (NLP) tasks, such as information retrieval, word sense disambiguation, sentiment analysis and question answering require comprehensive external knowledge sources (electronic dictionaries, ontologies, or thesauri) in order to attain a satisfactory performance (Navigli, 2009). Lexical resources such as WordNet, Wordnik, and SUMO (Niles and Pease, 2001) also suffer from the same limitations that the machine learning training data faces.

Proceedings of NAACL-HLT 2015 Student Research Workshop (SRW), pages 88–95,
Denver, Colorado, June 1, 2015. ©2015 Association for Computational Linguistics

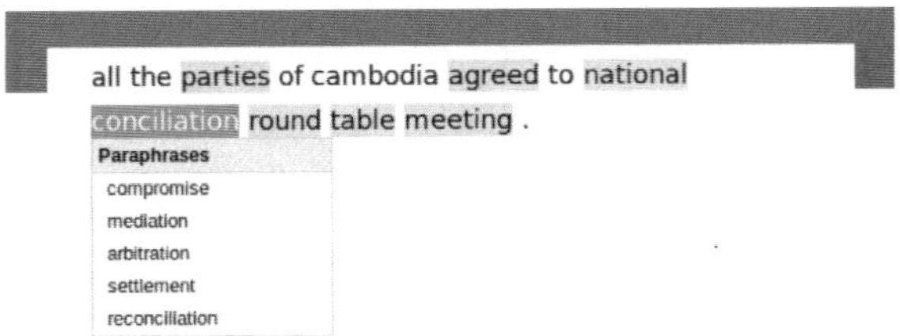

Figure 1: An online interface for the semantic writing aid application. Paraphrase suggestions are presented from a systematic combination of different NLP resources.

This proposal focuses on the development and enhancement of training data as well as on systematic combinations of different NLP resources for a semantic writing aid application. More specifically we address the following issues: 1) How can we produce annotated data of high quality using an interactive machine learning approach? 2) How can we systematically integrate different NLP resources? 3) How can we integrate user interaction and feedback into the interactive machine learning system? Moreover, we will explore the different paradigms of interactions (when should the machine learning produce a new model, how to provide useful suggestions to users, and how to control annotators behavior in the automation process). To tackle these problems, we will look at two applications, 1) an annotation task using a web-based annotation tool and 2) a semantic writing aid application, a tool with an online interface that provides users with paraphrase detection and prediction capability for a varying writing style. In principle, the two applications have similar nature except that the ultimate goal of the annotation task is to produce a fully annotated data whereas the semantic writing aid will use the improved classifier model instantly. We have identified a sequence tagging and a paraphrasing setup to explore the aforementioned applications.

Sequence tagging setup: We will employ an annotation tool similar to WebAnno (Yimam et al., 2014) in order to facilitate the automatic acquisition of training data for machine learning applications. Our goal is to fully annotate documents sequentially but interactively using the machine learning support in contrast to an active learning setup where the system presents portions of the document at a time.

Paraphrasing setup: The semantic writing aid tool is envisioned to improve readability of documents and provide varied writing styles by suggesting semantically equivalent paraphrases and remove redundant or overused words or phrases. Using several lexical resources, the system will detect and provide alternative contextual paraphrases as shown in Figure 1. Such paraphrasing will substitute words or phrases in context with appropriate synonyms when they form valid collocations with the surrounding words (Bolshakov and Gelbukh, 2004) based on the lexical resource suggestion or using statistics gathered from large corpora. While the work of Bhagat and Hovy (2013) shows that there are different approaches of paraphrasing or quasi-paraphrasing based on syntactical analysis, we will also further explore context-aware paraphrasing using distributional semantics (Biemann and Riedl, 2013) and machine learning classifiers for contextual similarity.

2 Related Work

There have been many efforts in the development of systems using an adaptive machine learning process. Judah et al. (2009) developed a system where the machine learning and prediction process incorporates user interaction. For example, for sensitive email detection system, the user is given the opportunity to indicate which features, such as body or title of the message, or list of participants, are important for prediction so that the system will accordingly learn the classification model based on the user preference. Similarly, recommender systems usually provide personalized suggestions of products to consumers (Desrosiers and Karypis, 2011). The recommendation problem is similar to an annotation task as both of them try to predict the correct suggestions based on the existing user preference.

CueFlik, a system developed to support Web image search (Amershi et al., 2011), demonstrates that active user interactions can significantly impact the effectiveness of the interactive machine learning process. In this system, users interactively define visual concepts of pictures such as product photos or pictures with quiet scenery, and they train the system so as to learn and re-rank web image search results.

JAAB (Kabra et al., 2013) is an interactive machine learning system that allows biologists to use machine learning in closed loop without assistance from machine learning experts to quickly train classifiers for animal behavior. The system allows users to start the annotation process with trustworthy examples and train an initial classifier model. Furthermore, the system enables users to correct suggestions and annotate unlabeled data that is leveraged in subsequent iteration.

Stumpf et al. (2007) investigate the impact of user feedback on a machine learning system. In addition to simple user feedback such as accepting and rejecting predictions, complex feedback like selecting the best features, suggestions for the reweighting of features, proposing new features and combining features significantly improve the system.

2.1 Combination and Generation of Resources

There are different approaches of using existing NLP resources for an application. Our approach mainly focuses on a systematic combination of NLP resources for a specific application with the help of interactive machine learning. As a side product, we plan to generate an application-specific NLP resource that can be iteratively enhanced.

The work by Lavelli et al. (2002) explores how thematic lexical resources can be built using an iterative process of learning previously unknown associations between terms and themes. The research is inspired by text categorization. The process starts with minimal manually developed lexicons and learns new thematic lexicons from the user interaction.

Jonnalagadda et al. (2012) demonstrate the use of semi-supervised machine learning to build medical semantic lexicons. They demonstrated that a distributional semantic method can be used to increase the lexicon size using a large set of unannotated texts.

The research conducted by Sinha and Mihalcea (2009) concludes that a combination of several lexical resources generates better sets of candidate synonyms where results significantly exceed the performance obtained with one lexical resource.

While most of the existing approaches such as UBY (Gurevych et al., 2012) strive at the construction of a unified resource from several lexical resources, our approach focuses on a dynamic and interactive approach of resource integration. Our approach is adaptive in such a way that the resource integration depends on the nature of the application.

3 Overview of the Problem

3.1 Interactive Machine Learning Approach

The generation of large amounts of high quality training data to train or validate a machine learning system at one pass is very difficult and even undesirable (Vidulin et al., 2014). Instead, an interactive machine learning approach is more appropriate in order to adapt the machine learning model iteratively using the train, learn, and evaluate technique.

Acquiring new knowledge from newly added training data on top of an existing trained machine learning model is important for incremental learning (Wen and Lu, 2007). An important aspect of such incremental and interactive machine learning approach is, that the system can start with minimal or no annotated training data and continuously presents documents to a user for annotation. On the way, the system can learn important features from the annotated instances and improve the machine learning model continuously. When a project requires to annotate the whole dataset, an interactive machine learning approach can be employed to incrementally improve the machine learning model.

3.2 Paraphrasing and Semantic Writing Aid

Acquisition and utilization of contextual paraphrases in a semantic writing aid ranges from integration of structured data sources such as ontologies, thesauri, dictionaries, and wordnets over semi-structured data sources such as Wikipedia and encyclopedia entries to resources based on unstructured data such as distributional thesauri. Paraphrases using ontologies such as YAGO (Suchanek et al., 2007) and SUMO provide particular semantic relations between lexical units. This approach is domain specific and limited to some predefined form of semantic relations. Structured data sources such as WordNet support paraphrase suggestions in the form of synonyms. Structured data sources have limited coverage and they usually do not capture contextual paraphrases. Paraphrases from unstructured sources can be collected using distributional similarity techniques from large corpora. We can also obtain paraphrase suggestions from monolingual comparable corpora, for example, using multiple translations of foreign novels (Ibrahim et al., 2003) or different news articles about the same topics (Wang and Callison-Burch, 2011). Moreover, paraphrases can also be extracted from bilingual parallel corpora by "pivoting" a shared translation and ranking paraphrases using the translation probabilities from the parallel text (Ganitkevitch and Callison-Burch, 2014).

The research problem on the one hand is the adaptation of such diverse resources on the target semantic writing aid application and on the other hand the combination of several such resources using interactive machine learning to suit the application.

4 Methodology: Paraphrasing Component

The combinations of lexical resources will be based on the approach of Sinha and Mihalcea (2009), where candidate synonymous from different resources are systematically combined in a machine learning framework. Furthermore, lexical resources induced in a data driven way such as distributional thesauri (DT) (Weeds and Weir, 2005), will be combined with the structured lexical resources in an interactive machine learning approach, which incrementally learns weights through a classifier. We will train a classifier model using features from resources, such as n-gram frequencies, co-occurrence statistics, number of senses from WordNet, different feature values from the paraphrase database (PPDB)[1] (Ganitkevitch and Callison-Burch, 2014), and syntactic features such as part of speech and dependency patterns. Training data will be acquired with crowdsourcing by 1) using existing crowdsourcing frameworks and 2) using an online interface specifically developed as a semantic writing aid tool (ref Figure 1).

While the way the system provides suggestions might be based on many possible conditions, we will particularly address at least the following ones: 1) non-fitting word detection, 2) detection of too many repetitions, and 3) detection of stylistic deviations.

Once we have the resource combining component in place, we employ an interactive machine learning to train a classifier based on implicit user feedback obtained as 1) users intentionally request paraphrasing and observe their actions (such as which of the suggestion they accept, if they ignore all suggestions, if the users provide new paraphrase by themselves, and so on), and 2) the system automatically suggests candidate paraphrases (as shown in Figure 1) and observe how the user interacts.

[1] http://paraphrase.org

5 Experiments and Evaluation

We now describe several experimental setups that evaluate the effectiveness of our current system, the quality of training data obtained, and user satisfaction in using the system. We have already conducted some preliminary experiments and simulated evaluations towards some of the tasks.

5.1 Annotation Task

As a preliminary experiment, we have conducted an interactive machine learning simulation to investigate the effectiveness of this approach for named entity annotation and POS tagging tasks. For the named entity annotation task, we have used the training and development dataset from the GermEval 2014 Named Entity Recognition Shared Task (Benikova et al., 2014) and the online machine learning tool MIRA[2] (Crammer and Singer, 2003). The training dataset is divided by an increasing size, as shown in Table 1 to train the system where every larger partition contains sentences from earlier parts. From Figure 2 it is evident that the interactive machine learning approach improves the performance of the system (increase in recall) as users continue correcting the suggestions provided.

Sentences	precision	recall	F-score
24	80.65	1.12	2.21
60	62.08	6.68	12.07
425	71.57	35.13	47.13
696	70.36	43.02	53.40
1264	71.35	47.15	56.78
5685	77.22	56.57	65.30
8770	77.83	60.16	67.86
10 812	78.06	62.72	69.55
15 460	78.14	64.96	70.95
24 000	80.15	68.82	74.05

Table 1: Evaluation result for the German named entity recognition task using an interactive online learning approach with different sizes of training dataset tested on the fixed development dataset.

[2] https://code.google.com/p/miralium/

Furthermore, an automation experiment is carried out for Amharic POS tagging to explore if interactive machine learning reduces annotation time. In this experiment, a total of 34 sentences are manually annotated, simulating different levels of precision and recall (ref Table 2) for automatic suggestions as shown in Figure 3. We have conducted this annotation task several times to measure the savings in time when using automatic annotation. When no suggestion is provided, it took about 67 minutes for an expert annotator to completely annotate the document. In contrast to this, the same annotation task with suggestions (e.g with recall of 70% and precision of 60%) took only 21 minutes, demonstrating a significant reduction in annotation cost.

		recall (%)			
		no Auto.	30	50	70
prec (%)	no Auto.	67	-	-	-
	60	-	53	33	21
	70	-	45	29	20
	80	-	42	28	18

Table 2: Experimentation of interactive machine learning for different precision and recall levels for Amharic POS tagging task. The cell with the precision/recall intersection records the total time (in minutes) required to fully annotate the dataset with the help of interactive automation. Without automation (no Auto.), annotation of all sentences took 67 minutes.

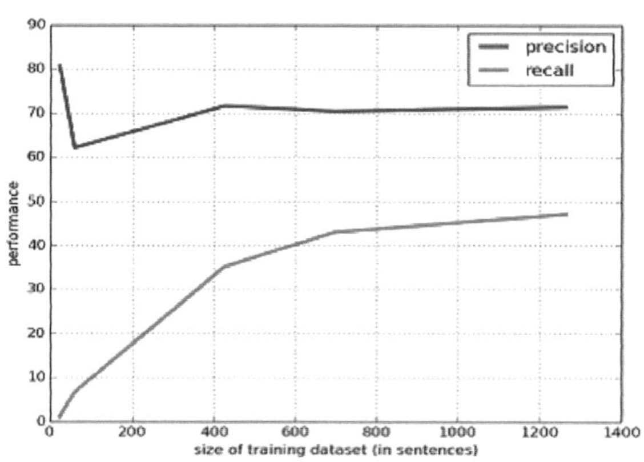

Figure 2: Learning curve showing the performance of interactive automation using different sizes of training data

5.2 Evaluation of Paraphrasing

For the semantic writing aid tool, we need to create a paraphrasing component (see Sec. 3.2). We conduct an evaluation by comparing automatic paraphrases against existing paraphrase corpora (Callison-Burch et al., 2008). The Microsoft Research Paraphrase Corpus (MSRPC) (Dolan et al., 2004) dataset, PPDB, and the DIRT paraphrase collections (Lin and Pantel, 2001) will be used for phrase-level evaluations. The TWSI dataset (Biemann, 2012) will be used for the word level paraphrase evaluation. We will use precision, recall, and machine translation metrics BLEU for evaluation.

Once the basic paraphrasing system is in place and evaluated, the next step will be the improvement of the paraphrasing system using syntagmatic and paradigmatic structures of language as features. The process will incorporate the implementation of distributional similarity based on syntactic structures such as POS tagging, dependency parsing, token n-grams, and patterns, resulting in a context-aware paraphrasing system, which offers paraphrases in context. Furthermore, interactive machine learning can be employed to train a model that can be used to provide context-dependent paraphrasing.

5.2.1 Preliminary Experiments

We have conducted preliminary experiments for a semantic writing aid system, employing the LanguageTools (Naber, 2004) user interface to display paraphrase suggestions. We have used WordNet, PPDB, and JobimText DT[3] to provide paraphrase

[3]http://goo.gl/0Z2Rcs

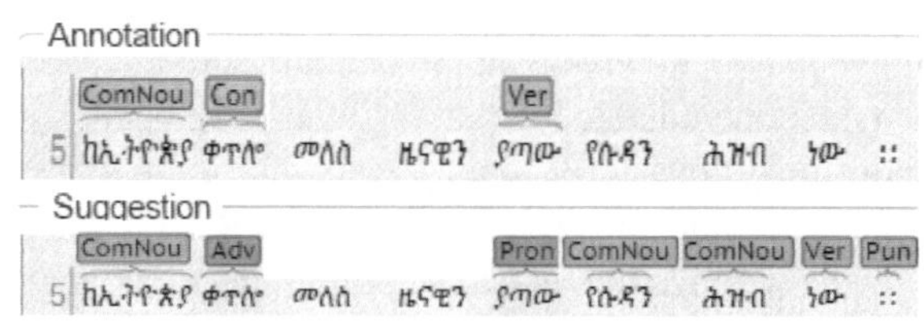

Figure 3: Amharic POS tagging. lower pane: suggestion provided to the user by the interactive classifier, upper pane: annotations by the user. When (grey) the suggestion in the lower pane is correct, the user will click the annotation and copy it to the upper pane. Otherwise (shown in red or no suggestion), the user should provide a new annotation in the upper pane.

suggestions. Paraphrases are first obtained from each individual resources and irrelevant or out-of-context paraphrases are discarded by ranking alternatives using an n-gram language model. Paraphrases suggested by most of the underlining resources (at least 2 out of 3) are provided as suggestions. Figure 1 shows an online interface displaying paraphrase suggestions based on our approach[4].

We have conducted experimental evaluation to assess the performance of the system using recall as a metric ($recall = \frac{s}{r}$ where s is the number of tokens in the source (paraphrased) sentence and r is the number of tokens in the reference sentence). We have used 100 sentences of paraphrase pairs (source and reference sentences) from the MSRPC dataset. The baseline result is computed using the original paraphrase pairs of sentences which gives us a recall of 59%. We took the source sentence and applied our paraphrasing technique for words that are not in the reference sentence and computed recall. Table 3 shows results for different settings, such as taking the first, top 5, and top 10 suggestions from the candidate paraphrases which outperforms the baseline result. The combination of different resources improves the performance of the paraphrasing system.

setups	Baseline	top 1	top 5	top 10
WordNet	59.0	60.3	61.4	61.9
ppdb	59.0	60.2	62.2	64.6
JoBimText	59.0	59.9	60.3	60.4
2in3	59.0	**60.7**	**65.3**	**66.2**

Table 3: Recall values for paraphrasing using different NLP resources and techniques. Top 1 is where we consider only the best suggestion and compute the score. top 5 and 10 considers the Top 5 and 10 suggestions provided by the system respectively. The row 2in3 shows the result where we consider a paraphrase suggestion to be a candidate when it appears at least in two of the three resources.

6 Conclusion and Future Work

We propose to integrate interactive machine learning for an annotation task and semantic writing aid application to incrementally train a classifier based on user feedback and interactions. While the goal of the annotation task is to produce a quality annotated data, the classifier is built into the semantic writing aid application to continuously improve the system. The proposal addresses the following main points: 1) How to develop a quality linguistic dataset using interactive machine learning approach for a given annotation task. 2) How to systematically combine different NLP resources to generate paraphrase suggestions for a semantic writing aid application. Moreover, how to produce an application specific NLP resource iteratively using an interactive machine learning approach. 3) How to integrate user interaction and feedback to improve the effectiveness and quality of the system.

We have carried out preliminary experiments for creating sequence tagging data for German NER and Amharic POS. Results indicate that integrating interactive machine learning into the annotation tool can substantially reduce the annotation time required for creating a high-quality dataset.

Experiments have been conducted for the systematic integrations of different NLP resources (WordNet, PPDB, and JoBimText DT) as a paraphrasing component into a semantic writing aid application. Evaluation with the recall metric shows that the combination of resources yields better performance than any of the single resources.

For further work within the scope of this thesis, we plan the following:

- Integrate an active learning approach for the linguistic dataset development
- Investigate crowdsourcing techniques for interactive machine learning applications.
- Integrate more NLP resources for the semantic writing aid application.
- Investigate different paradigms of interactions, such as when and how the interactive classifier should produces new model and study how suggestions are better provided to annotators.
- Investigate how user interaction and feedback can improve the linguistic dataset development and the semantic writing aid applications.
- Investigate how to improve the paraphrasing performance by exploring machine learning for learning resource combinations, as well as by leveraging user interaction and feedback.

[4] http://goo.gl/C0YkiA

References

Saleema Amershi, James Fogarty, Ashish Kapoor, and Desney Tan. Effective end-user interaction with machine learning. In *Proceedings of the 25th AAAI Conference on Artificial Intelligence*, San Francisco, CA, USA, 2011.

Darina Benikova, Chris Biemann, and Marc Reznicek. NoSta-D Named Entity Annotation for German: Guidelines and Dataset. In *Proceedings of the Ninth International Conference on Language Resources and Evaluation (LREC-2014)*, 2014.

Rahul Bhagat and Eduard Hovy. What is a paraphrase? In *Association for Computational Linguistics*. MIT Press, 2013.

Chris Biemann. *Structure Discovery in Natural Language*. Springer Berlin Heidelberg, 2012. ISBN 978-3-642-25922-7.

Chris Biemann and Martin Riedl. Text: now in 2D! A framework for lexical expansion with contextual similarity. *J. Language Modelling*, pages 55–95, 2013.

Igor A. Bolshakov and Alexander Gelbukh. Synonymous paraphrasing using wordnet and internet. In Farid Meziane and Elisabeth Métais, editors, *Natural Language Processing and Information Systems*, volume 3136 of *Lecture Notes in Computer Science*, pages 312–323. Springer Berlin Heidelberg, 2004.

Chris Callison-Burch, Trevor Cohn, and Mirella Lapata. Parametric: An automatic evaluation metric for paraphrasing. In *Proceedings of the 22nd International Conference on Computational Linguistics (Coling 2008)*, pages 97–104, Manchester, UK, 2008. Coling 2008 Organizing Committee.

Joana Costa, Catarina Silva, Mário Antunes, and Bernardete Ribeiro. On using crowdsourcing and active learning to improve classification performance. In *Intelligent Systems Design and Applications (ISDA)*, pages 469–474, San Diego, USA, 2011.

Koby Crammer and Yoram Singer. Ultraconservative online algorithms for multiclass problems. *J. Mach. Learn. Res.*, pages 951–991, 2003.

Christian Desrosiers and George Karypis. A comprehensive survey of neighborhood-based recommendation methods. *Recommender Systems Handbook*, 2011.

William Dolan, Chris Quirk, and Chris Brockett. Unsupervised construction of large paraphrase corpora: Exploiting massively parallel news sources. International Conference on Computational Linguistics, 2004.

Juri Ganitkevitch and Chris Callison-Burch. The multilingual paraphrase database. In *Proceedings of the Ninth International Conference on Language Resources and Evaluation (LREC-2014), Reykjavik, Iceland, May 26-31, 2014.*, pages 4276–4283, 2014.

Iryna Gurevych, Judith Eckle-Kohler, Silvana Hartmann, Michael Matuschek, Christian M. Meyer, and Christian Wirth. Uby - a large-scale unified lexical-semantic resource based on lmf. In *Proceedings of the 13th Conference of the European Chapter of the Association for Computational Linguistics (EACL 2012)*, pages 580–590, 2012.

Ali Ibrahim, Boris Katz, and Jimmy Lin. Extracting structural paraphrases from aligned monolingual corpora. In *Proceedings of the Second International Workshop on Paraphrasing - Volume 16*, PARAPHRASE '03, pages 57–64, 2003.

Siddhartha Jonnalagadda, Trevor Cohen, Stephen Wu, and Graciela Gonzalez. Enhancing clinical concept extraction with distributional semantics. In *Journal of Biomedical Informatics*, pages 129–140, San Diego, USA, 2012.

Kshitij Judah, Thomas Dietterich, Alan Fern, Jed Irvine, Michael Slater, Prasad Tadepalli, Melinda Gervasio, Christopher Ellwood, William Jarrold, Oliver Brdiczka, and Jim Blythe. User initiated learning for adaptive interfaces. In *IJCAI Workshop on Intelligence and Interaction*, Pasadena, CA, USA, 2009.

Mayank Kabra, Alice A Robie, Marta Rivera-Alba, Steven Branson, and Kristin Branson. Jaaba: interactive machine learning for automatic annotation of animal behavior. In *Nature Methods*, pages 64–67, 2013.

Anastasia Krithara, Cyril Goutte, MR Amini, and Jean-Michel Renders. Reducing the annotation burden in text classification. In *Proceedings of the 1st International Conference on Multidisciplinary Information Sciences and Technologies (InSciT 2006)*, Merida, Spain, 2006.

Todd Kulesza, Saleema Amershi, Rich Caruana, Danyel Fisher, and Denis Charles. Structured labeling to facilitate concept evolution in machine learning. In *Proceedings of CHI 2014*, Toronto, ON, Canada, 2014. ACM Press.

Alberto Lavelli, Bernardo Magnini, and Fabrizio Sebastiani. Building thematic lexical resources by bootstrapping and machine learning. In *Proc. of the workshop "Linguistic Knowledge Acquisition and Representation: Bootstrapping Annotated Language Data", wokshop at LREC-2002*, 2002.

Dekang Lin and Patrick Pantel. Dirt - discovery of inference rules from text. In *Proceedings of ACM Conference on Knowledge Discovery and Data Mining (KDD-01)*, pages 323–328, San Francisco, CA, USA, 2001.

Barzan Mozafariy, Purnamrita Sarkarz, Michael Franklinz, Michael Jordanz, and Samuel Madden. Active learning for crowdsourced databases. In *arXiv:1209.3686*. arXiv.org preprint, 2012.

Daniel Naber. A rule-based style and grammar checker. diploma thesis, Computer Science - Applied, University of Bielefeld, 2004.

Roberto Navigli. Word sense disambiguation: A survey. *ACM Comput. Surv.*, pages 10:1–10:69, 2009. ISSN 0360-0300.

Ian Niles and Adam Pease. Toward a Standard Upper Ontology. In *Proceedings of the 2nd International Conference on Formal Ontology in Information Systems (FOIS-2001)*, pages 2–9, 2001.

James Pustejovsky and Amber Stubbs. *Natural Language Annotation for Machine Learning*. O'Reilly Media, 2012. ISBN 978-1-4493-0666-3.

Hema Raghavan, Omid Madani, Rosie Jones, and Pack Kaelbling. Active learning with feedback on both features and instances. *Journal of Machine Learning Research*, 7, 2006.

Burr Settles. Active learning literature survey. Technical report, University of Wisconsin–Madison, 2010.

Burr Settles, Mark Craven, and Lewis Friedland. Active learning with real annotation costs. In *Proceedings of the NIPS Workshop on Cost-Sensitive Learning*, 2008.

Ravi Sinha and Rada Mihalcea. Combining lexical resources for contextual synonym expansion. In *Proceedings of the International Conference RANLP-2009*, pages 404–410, Borovets, Bulgaria, 2009. Association for Computational Linguistics.

Rion Snow, Brendan O'Connor, Daniel Jurafsky, and Andrew Ng. Cheap and fast – but is it good? evaluating non-expert annotations for natural language tasks. In *Proceedings of the 2008 Conference on Empirical Methods in Natural Language Processing*, pages 254–263, Honolulu, Hawaii, 2008.

Simone Stumpf, Vidya Rajaram, Lida Li, Margaret Burnett, Thomas Dietterich, Erin Sullivan, Russell Drummond, and Jonathan Herlocker. Toward harnessing user feedback for machine learning. In *Proceedings of the 12th International Conference on Intelligent User Interfaces*, pages 82–91, 2007.

Fabian M. Suchanek, Gjergji Kasneci, and Gerhard Weikum. Yago: A core of semantic knowledge. In *Proceedings of the 16th International Conference on World Wide Web*, WWW '07, pages 697–706, 2007. ISBN 978-1-59593-654-7.

Vedrana Vidulin, Marko Bohanec, and Matjaž Gams. Combining human analysis and machine data mining to obtain credible data relations. *Information Sciences*, 288:254–278, 2014.

Rui Wang and Chris Callison-Burch. Paraphrase fragment extraction from monolingual comparable corpora. In *Proceedings of the 4th Workshop on Building and Using Comparable Corpora: Comparable Corpora and the Web*, BUCC '11, pages 52–60, 2011.

Malcolm Ware, Eibe Frank, Geoffrey Holmes, Mark Hall, and Ian H Witten. Interactive machine learning: letting users build classifiers. In *International Journal of Human-Computer Studies*, pages 281–292, 2002.

Julie Weeds and David Weir. Co-occurrence retrieval: A flexible framework for lexical distributional similarity. In *Association for Computational Linguistics*, volume 31, pages 439–475, 2005.

Yi-Min Wen and Bao-Liang Lu. Incremental learning of support vector machines by classifier combining. In *Advances in Knowledge Discovery and Data Mining*, pages 904–911, Heidelberg, Germany, 2007.

Seid Muhie Yimam, Richard Eckart de Castilho, Iryna Gurevych, and Chris Biemann. Automatic annotation suggestions and custom annotation layers in WebAnno. In *Proceedings of the 52nd Annual Meeting of the Association for Computational Linguistics. System Demonstrations*, pages 91–96, Stroudsburg, PA 18360, USA, 2014. Association for Computational Linguistics.

Relation Extraction from Community Generated Question-Answer Pairs

Denis Savenkov
Emory University
dsavenk@emory.edu

Wei-Lwun Lu
Google
weilwunlu@google.com

Jeff Dalton
Google
jeffdalton@google.com

Eugene Agichtein
Emory University
eugene@mathcs.emory.edu

Abstract

Community question answering (CQA) websites contain millions of question and answer (QnA) pairs that represent real users' interests. Traditional methods for relation extraction from natural language text operate over individual sentences. However answer text is sometimes hard to understand without knowing the question, *e.g.*, it may not name the subject or relation of the question. This work presents a novel model for relation extraction from CQA data, which uses discourse of QnA pairs to predict relations between entities mentioned in question and answer sentences. Experiments on 2 publicly available datasets demonstrate that the model can extract from $\sim$20% to $\sim$40% additional relation triples, not extracted by existing sentence-based models.

1 Introduction

Recently all major search companies have adopted knowledge bases (KB), and as a result users now can get rich structured data as answers to some of their questions. However, even the largest existing knowledge bases, such as Freebase (Bollacker et al., 2008), DPpedia (Auer et al., 2007), NELL (Carlson et al., 2010), Google Knowledge Graph *etc.*, which store billions of facts about millions of entities, are far from being complete (Dong et al., 2014). A lot of information is hidden in unstructured data, such as natural language text, and extracting this information for knowledge base population (KBP) is an active area of research (Surdeanu and Ji, 2014).

One particularly interesting source of unstructured text data is CQA websites (*e.g.* Yahoo! Answers,[1] Answers.com,[2] *etc.*), which became very popular resources for question answering. The information expressed there can be very useful, for example, to answer future questions (Shtok et al., 2012), which makes it attractive for knowledge base population. Although some of the facts mentioned in QnA pairs can also be found in some other text documents, another part might be unique (*e.g.* in Clueweb[3] about 10% of entity pairs with existing Freebase relations mentioned in Yahoo!Answers documents cannot be found in other documents). There are certain limitations in applying existing relation extraction algorithms to CQA data, *i.e.*, they typically consider sentences independently and ignore the discourse of QnA pair text. However, often it is impossible to understand the answer without knowing the question. For example, in many cases users simply give the answer to the question without stating it in a narrative sentence (*e.g.* "*What does "xoxo" stand for? Hugs and kisses.*"), in some other cases the answer contains a statement, but some important information is omitted (*e.g.* "*What's the capital city of Bolivia? Sucre is the legal capital, though the government sits in La Paz*").

In this work we propose a novel model for relation extraction from CQA data, that uses discourse of a QnA pair to extract facts between entities mentioned in question and entities mentioned in answer sentences. The conducted experiments confirm that many of such facts cannot be extracted by existing sentence-based techniques and thus it is beneficial to combine their outputs with the output of our model.

2 Problem

This work targets the problem of relation extraction from QnA data, which is a collection of (q, a) pairs,

[1]http://answers.yahoo.com/

[2]http://www.answers.com

[3]http://www.lemurproject.org/clueweb12/

Proceedings of NAACL-HLT 2015 Student Research Workshop (SRW), pages 96–102,
Denver, Colorado, June 1, 2015.

where q is a question text (can contain multiple sentences) and a is the corresponding answer text (can also contain multiple sentences). By relation instance r we mean an ordered binary relation between $subject$ and $object$ entities, which is commonly represented as $[subject, predicate, object]$ triple. For example, the fact that Brad Pitt married Angelina Jolie can be represented as [Brad Pitt, married_to, Angelina Jolie]. In this work we use Freebase, an open schema-based KB, where all entities and predicates come from the fixed alphabets E and P correspondingly. Let e_1 and e_2 be entities that are mentioned together in a text (*e.g.* in a sentence, or e_1 in a question and e_2 in the corresponding answer), we will call such an entity pair with the corresponding context a mention. The same pair of entities can be mentioned multiple times within the corpus, and for all mentions $i = 1, ..., n$ the goal is to predict the expressed predicate ($z_i \in P$) or to say that none applies ($z_i = \emptyset$). Individual mention predictions $z_1, ..., z_n$ are combined to infer a set of relations $\mathbf{y} = \{y_i \in P\}$ between the entities e_1 and e_2.

3 Models

Our models for relation extraction from QnA data incorporates the topic of the question and can be represented as a graphical model (Figure 1). Each mention of a pair of entities is represented with a set of mention-based features x and question-based features x_t. A multinomial latent variable z represents a relation (or none) expressed in the mention and depends on the features and a set of weights w_x for mention-based and w_t for question-based features: $\hat{z} = \underset{z \in P \cup \emptyset}{arg\,max}\; p(z|x, x_t, w_x, w_t)$. To estimate this variable we use L2-regularized multinomial logistic regression model, trained using the distant supervision approach for relation extraction (Mintz et al., 2009), in which mentions of entity pairs related in Freebase are treated as positive instances for the corresponding predicates, and negative examples are sampled from mentions of entity pairs which are not related by any of the predicates of interest. Finally, to predict a set of possible relations $\mathbf{y}$ between the pair of entities we take logical OR of individual mention variables $\mathbf{z}$, *i.e.* $y_p = \vee_{i=1}^{M}[z_i = p, p \in P]$, where M is the number of mentions of this pair of entities.

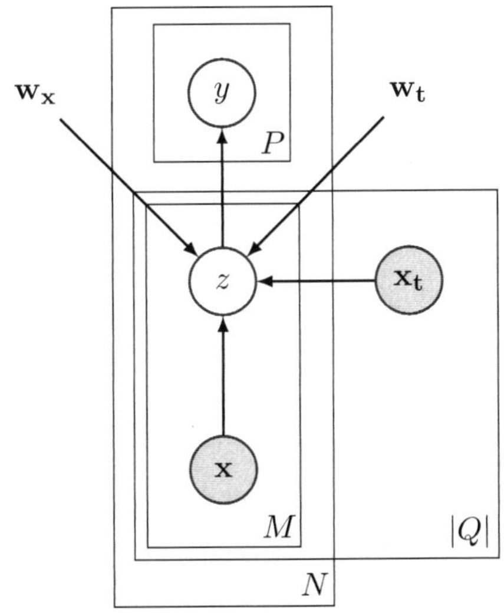

Figure 1: QnA-based relation extraction model plate diagram. N - number of different entity pairs, M - number of mentions of an entity pair, $|Q|$ - number of questions where an entity pair is mentioned, $\mathbf{x}$ and $\mathbf{x_t}$ - mention-based and question-based features, $\mathbf{w}$ and $\mathbf{w_t}$ - corresponding feature weights, latent variables z - relation expressed in an entity pair mention, latent variables y - relations between entity pair

3.1 Sentence-based baseline model

Existing sentence-based relation extraction models can be applied to individual sentences of a QnA pair and will work well for complete statements, *e.g.* “Who did Brad Pitt marry? Brad Pitt and Angelina Jolie married at secret ceremony”. In sentence-based scenario, when the set of question-based features is empty, the above model corresponds to the Mintz++ baseline described in Surdeanu et al. (2012), which was shown to be superior to the original model of Mintz et al. (2009), is easier to train than some other state of the art distant supervision models and produces comparable results.

3.2 Sentence-based model with question features

In many cases an answer statement is hard to interpret correctly without knowing the corresponding question. To give the baseline model some knowledge about the question, we include question features (Table 1), which are based on dependency tree and surface patterns of a question sentence. This

Table 1: Examples of features used for relation extraction for "*When was Mariah Carey born? Mariah Carey was born 27 March 1970*"

Sentence-based model	
Dependency path between entities	[PERSON]→nsubjpass(born)tmod←[DATE]
Surface pattern	[PERSON] be/VBD born/VBN [DATE]
Question features for sentence-based model	
Question template	when [PERSON] born
Dependecy path from a verb to the question word	(when)→advmod(born)
Question word + dependency tree root	when+born
QnA-based model	
Question template + answer entity type	Q: when [PERSON] born A:[DATE]
Dependency path from question word to entity	Q:(when)→advmod(born)nsubj←[PERSON]
and answer entity to the answer tree root	A: (born)tmod←[DATE]
Question word, dependency root and answer pattern	Q: when+born A:born [DATE]

information can help the model to account for the question topic and improve predictions in some ambiguous situations.

3.3 QnA-based model

The QnA model for relation extraction is inspired by the observation, that often an answer sentence do not mention one of the entities at all, *e.g.*, "*When was Isaac Newton born? December 25, 1642 Woolsthorpe, England*". To tackle this situation we make the following assumption about the discourse of a QnA pair: an entity mentioned in a question is related to entities in the corresponding answer and the context of both mentions can be used to infer the relation predicate. Our QnA-based relation extraction model takes an entity from a question sentence and entity from the answer as a candidate relation mention, represents it with a set features (Table 1) and predicts a possible relation between them similar to sentence-based models. The features are conjunctions of various dependency tree and surface patterns of question and answer sentences, designed to capture their topics and relation.

4 Experiments

4.1 Datasets

For experiments we used 2 publicly available CQA datasets: Yahoo! Answers Comprehensive Questions and Answers[4] and a crawl of WikiAnswers[5] (Fader et al., 2014). The Yahoo! Answers dataset contains 4,483,032 questions (3,894,644 in English) with the corresponding answers collected on 10/25/2007. The crawl of WikiAnswers has 30,370,994 question clusters, tagged by WikiAnswers users as paraphrases, and only 3,386,256 them have answers. From these clusters we used all possible pairs of questions and answers (19,629,443 pairs in total).

For each QnA pair we applied tokenization, sentence detection, named entity tagger, parsing and coreference resolution from Stanford CoreNLP (Manning et al., 2014). Our cascade entity linking approach is similar to Chang et al. (2011) and considered all noun phrase and named entity mentions as candidates. First all named entity mentions are looked up in Freebase names and aliases dictionary. The next two stages attempt to match mention text with dictionary of English Wikipedia concepts (Spitkovsky and Chang, 2012) and its normalized version. Finally for named entity mentions we try spelling correction using Freebase entity names dictionary. We didn't disambiguate entities and instead took top-5 ids for each coreference cluster (using the $p(entity|phrase)$ score from the dictionary or number of existing Freebase triples). All pairs of entities (or entity and date) in a QnA pair that are directly related[6] in Freebase were annotated with the corresponding relations.

[4] http://webscope.sandbox.yahoo.com/catalog.php?datatype=l
[5] http://wiki.answers.com

[6] We also consider some paths that come through a mediator node, *e.g.*/people/person/spouse_s./people/marriage/spouse

Table 2: Yahoo! Answers and WikiAnswers datasets statistics

	Y!A	WA
Number of QnA pairs	3.8M	19.6M
Average question length (in chars)	56.67	47.03
Average answer length (in chars)	335.82	24.24
Percent of QnA pairs with answers that do not have any verbs	8.8%	18.9%
Percent of QnA pairs with at least one pair of entities related in Freebase	11.7%	27.5%
Percent of relations between entity pairs in question sentences only	1.6 %	3.1%
Percent of relations between entity pairs in question and answer sentences only	28.1%	46.4%
Percent of relations between entity pairs in answer sentences only	38.6%	12.0%

Table 2 gives some statistics on the datasets used in this work. The analysis of answers that do not have any verbs show that ∼8.8% of all QnA pairs do not state the predicate in the answer text. The percentage is higher for WikiAnswers, which has shorter answers on average. Unfortunately, for many QnA pairs we were unable to find relations between the mentioned entities (for many of them no or few entities were resolved to Freebase). Among those QnA pairs, where some relation was annotated, we looked at the location of related entities. In Yahoo! Answers dataset 38.6% (12.0% for WikiAnswers) of related entities are mentioned in answer sentences and can potentially be extracted by sentence-based model, and 28.1% (46.4% for WikiAnswers) between entities mentioned in question and answer sentences, which are not available to the baseline model and our goal is to extract some of them.

4.2 Experimental setup

For our experiments we use a subset of 29 Freebase predicates that have enough unique instances annotated in our corpus, *e.g.* date of birth, profession, nationality, education institution, date of death, disease symptoms and treatments, book author, artist album, *etc.* We train and test the models on each dataset separately. Each corpus is randomly split for training (75%) and testing (25%). Knowledge base facts are also split into training and testing sets (50% each). QnA and sentence-based models predict labels for each entity pair mention, and we aggregate mention predictions by taking the maximum score for each predicate. We do the same aggregation to produce a combination of QnA- and sentence-based models, *i.e.*, all extractions produced by the models are combined and if there are multiple extractions of the same fact we take the maximum score as the final confidence. The precision and recall of extractions are evaluated on a test set of Freebase triples, *i.e.* an extracted triple is considered correct if it belongs to the test set of Freebase triples, which are not used for training (triples used for training are simply ignored). Note, that this only provides a lower bound on the model performance as some of the predicted facts can be correct and simply missing in Freebase.

4.3 Results

Figure 2 shows Precision-Recall curves for QnA-based and sentence-based baseline models and some numeric results are given in Table 3. As 100% recall we took all pairs of entities that can be extracted by either model. It is important to note, that since some entity pairs occur exclusively inside the answer sentences and some in pairs of question and answer sentences, none of the individual models is capable of achieving 100% recall, and maximum possible recalls for QnA- and sentence-based models are different.

Results demonstrate that from 20.5% to 39.4% of correct triples extracted by the QnA-based model are not extracted by the baseline model, and the combination of both models is able to achieve higher precision and recall. Unfortunately, comparison of sentence-based model with and without question-based features (Figure 2) didn't show a significant difference.

5 Error analysis and future work

To get an idea of typical problems of QnA-based model we sampled and manually judged extracted high confidence examples that are not present in

Table 3: Extraction results for QnA- and sentence-based models on both datasets

	Yahoo! Answers			WikiAnswers		
	QnA	Sentence	Combined	QnA	Sentence	Combined
F-1 score	0.219	0.276	0.310	0.277	0.297	0.332
Number of correct extractions	3229	5900	7428	2804	2288	3779
Correct triples not extracted by other model	20.5%	56.5%	-	39.4%	25.8%	-

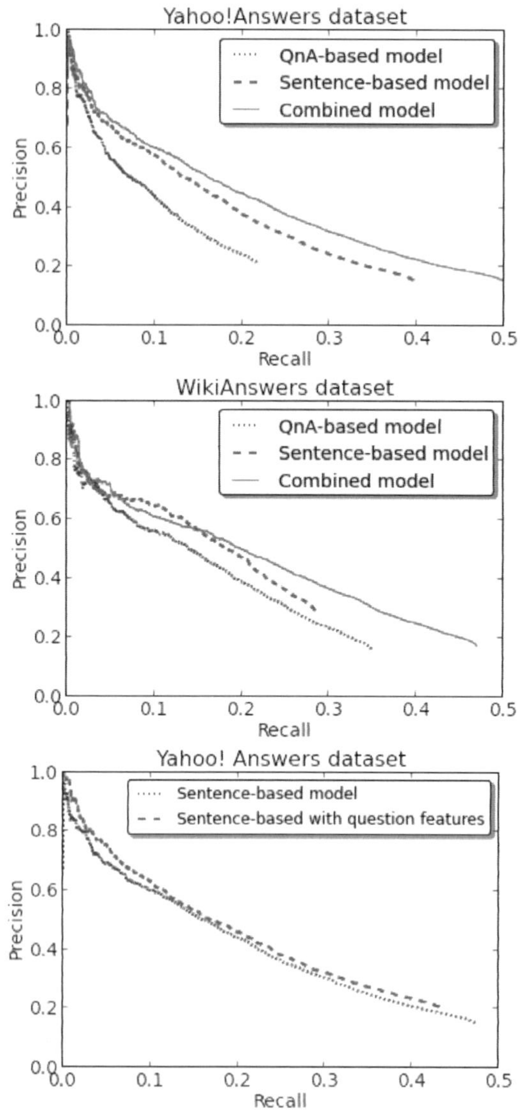

Figure 2: Precision-Recall curves for QnA-based vs sentence-based models and sentence-based model with and without question features

Freebase (and thus are considered incorrect for precision-recall analysis).

The major reason (40%) of false positive extractions is errors in entity linking. For example: "*Who is Tim O'Brien? He was born in Austin on October 1, 1946*". The model was able to correctly extract [Tim O'Brien, date_of_birth, October 1, 1946], however Tim O'Brien was linked to a wrong person. In a number of cases (16%) our discourse model turns out to be too simple and fails for answers, that mention numerous additional information, *e.g.* "*How old is Madonna really? ...Cher was born on 20 May 1946 which makes her older that Madonna...*". A possible solution would be to either restrict QnA-based model to cases when no additional information is present or design a better discourse model with deeper analysis of the answer sentence and its predicates and arguments. Some mistakes are due to distant supervision errors, for example for the music.composition.composer predicate our model extracts singers as well as composers (which are in many cases the same).

Of course, there are a number of cases, when our extractions are indeed correct, but are either missing (33%) or contradicting with Freebase (8%). An example of an extracted fact, that is missing in Freebase is "*Who is Wole Soyinka? He studied at the University College, Ibadan(1952-1954) and the University of Leeds (1954-1957)*", and [Wole Soyinka, institution, University of Leeds] is currently not present in Freebase. Contradictions with Freebase occur because of different precision levels ("pianist" vs "jazz pianist", city vs county, *etc.*), different calendars used for dates or "incorrect" information provided by the user. An example, when existing and extracted relation instance are different in precision is:"*Who is Edward Van Vleck? Edward Van Vleck was a mathematician born in Middletown, Connecticut*" we extract [Edward Van Vleck, place_of_birth, Middletown], however the Freebase currently has USA as his place of birth.

The problem of "incorrect" information provided in the answer is very interesting and worth special attention. It has been studied in CQA research, *e.g.* (Shah and Pomerantz, 2010), and an example of such QnA pair is: "*Who is Chandrababu Naidu? Nara Chandra Babu Naidu (born April 20, 1951)*". Other authoritative resources on the Web give April 20, 1950 as Chandrababu Naidu's date of birth. This raises a question of trust to the provided answer and expertise of the answerer. Many questions on CQA websites belong to the medical domain, *e.g.* people asking advices on different health related topics. How much we can trust the answers provided to extract them into the knowledge base? We leave this question to the future work.

Finally, we have seen that only a small fraction of available QnA pairs were annotated with existing Freebase relations, which shows a possible limitation of Freebase schema. A promising direction for future work is automatic extraction of new predicates, which users are interested in and which can be useful to answer more future questions.

6 Related work

Relation extraction from natural language text has been an active area of research for many years, and a number of supervised (Snow et al., 2004), semi-supervised (Agichtein and Gravano, 2000) and unsupervised (Fader et al., 2011) methods have been proposed. These techniques analyze individual sentences and can extract facts stated in them using syntactic patterns, sentence similarity, *etc.* This work focus on one particular type of text data, *i.e.* QnA pairs, and the proposed algorithm is designed to extract relations between entities mentioned in question and answer sentences.

Community question-answering data has been a subject of active research during the last decade. Bian et al. (2008) and Shtok et al. (2012) show how such data can be used for question answering, an area with a long history of research, and numerous different approaches proposed over the decades (Kolomiyets and Moens, 2011). One particular way to answer questions is to utilize structured KBs and perform semantic parsing of questions to transform natural language questions into KB queries. Berant et al. (2013) proposed a semantic parsing model that can be trained from QnA pairs, which are much easier to obtain than correct KB queries used previously. However, unlike our approach, which takes noisy answer text provided by a CQA website user, the work of Berant et al. (2013) uses manually created answers in a form of single or lists of KB entities. Later Yao and Van Durme (2014) presented an information extraction inspired approach, that predicts which of the entities related to an entity in the question could be the answer to the question. The key difference of this work from question answering is that our relation extraction model doesn't target question understanding problem and doesn't necessarily extract the answer to the question, but rather some knowledge it can infer from a QnA pair. Many questions on CQA websites are not factoid, and there are many advice and opinion questions, which simply cannot be answered with a KB entity or a list of entities. However, it is still possible to learn some information from them (*e.g.* from "*What's your favorite Stephen King book? The Dark Half is a pretty incredible book*" we can learn that the Dark Half is a book by Stephen King). In addition, answers provided by CQA users often contain extra information, which can also be useful (*e.g.* from "*Where was Babe Ruth born? He was born in Baltimore, Maryland on February 6th, 1895*" we can learn not only place of birth, but also date of birth of Babe Ruth).

7 Conclusion

In this paper we proposed a model for relation extraction from QnA data, which is capable of predicting relations between entities mentioned in question and answer sentences. We conducted experiments on 2 publicly available CQA datasets and showed that our model can extract triples not available to existing sentence-based techniques and can be effectively combined with them for better coverage of a knowledge base population system.

Acknowledgments

This work was funded by the Google Faculty Research Award. We gratefully thank Evgeniy Gabrilovich and Amar Subramanya for numerous valuable and insightful discussions, and anonymous reviewers for useful comments on the work.

References

Eugene Agichtein and Luis Gravano. 2000. Snowball: Extracting relations from large plain-text collections. In *Proceedings of the Fifth ACM Conference on Digital Libraries*, DL '00, pages 85–94, New York, NY, USA. ACM.

Sören Auer, Christian Bizer, Georgi Kobilarov, Jens Lehmann, Richard Cyganiak, and Zachary Ives. 2007. *Dbpedia: A nucleus for a web of open data*. Springer.

Jonathan Berant, Andrew Chou, Roy Frostig, and Percy Liang. 2013. Semantic parsing on freebase from question-answer pairs. In *Proceedings of the 2013 Conference on Empirical Methods in Natural Language Processing*, EMNLP'13, pages 1533–1544.

Jiang Bian, Yandong Liu, Eugene Agichtein, and Hongyuan Zha. 2008. Finding the right facts in the crowd: Factoid question answering over social media. In *Proceedings of the 17th International Conference on World Wide Web*, WWW '08, pages 467–476, New York, NY, USA. ACM.

Kurt Bollacker, Colin Evans, Praveen Paritosh, Tim Sturge, and Jamie Taylor. 2008. Freebase: A Collaboratively Created Graph Database for Structuring Human Knowledge. In *Proceedings of the 2008 ACM SIGMOD International Conference on Management of Data*, SIGMOD '08.

A. Carlson, J. Betteridge, B. Kisiel, B. Settles, E.R. Hruschka Jr., and T.M. Mitchell. 2010. Toward an Architecture for Never-Ending Language Learning. In *Proceedings of the Conference on Artificial Intelligence (AAAI)*, AAAI'10, pages 1306–1313. AAAI Press.

Angel X Chang, Valentin I Spitkovsky, Eneko Agirre, and Christopher D Manning. 2011. Stanford-ubc entity linking at tac-kbp, again. In *Proceedings of Text Analysis Conference*, TAC'11.

Xin Dong, Evgeniy Gabrilovich, Geremy Heitz, Wilko Horn, Ni Lao, Kevin Murphy, Thomas Strohmann, Shaohua Sun, and Wei Zhang. 2014. Knowledge vault: A web-scale approach to probabilistic knowledge fusion. In *Proceedings of the 20th ACM SIGKDD International Conference on Knowledge Discovery and Data Mining*, KDD '14, pages 601–610, New York, NY, USA. ACM.

Anthony Fader, Stephen Soderland, and Oren Etzioni. 2011. Identifying relations for open information extraction. In *Proceedings of the Conference on Empirical Methods in Natural Language Processing*, EMNLP '11, pages 1535–1545, Stroudsburg, PA, USA. Association for Computational Linguistics.

Anthony Fader, Luke Zettlemoyer, and Oren Etzioni. 2014. Open question answering over curated and extracted knowledge bases. In *Proceedings of the 20th ACM SIGKDD International Conference on Knowledge Discovery and Data Mining*, KDD '14, pages 1156–1165, New York, NY, USA. ACM.

Oleksandr Kolomiyets and Marie-Francine Moens. 2011. A survey on question answering technology from an information retrieval perspective. *Inf. Sci.*, 181(24):5412–5434, December.

Christopher D. Manning, Mihai Surdeanu, John Bauer, Jenny Finkel, Steven J. Bethard, and David McClosky. 2014. The Stanford CoreNLP natural language processing toolkit. In *Proceedings of 52nd Annual Meeting of the Association for Computational Linguistics: System Demonstrations*, pages 55–60.

Mike Mintz, Steven Bills, Rion Snow, and Dan Jurafsky. 2009. Distant supervision for relation extraction without labeled data. In *Proceedings of the Joint Conference of the 47th Annual Meeting of the Association for Computational Linguistics and the 4th International Joint Conference on Natural Language Processing of the AFNLP*, ACL '09.

Chirag Shah and Jefferey Pomerantz. 2010. Evaluating and predicting answer quality in community qa. In *Proceedings of the 33rd international ACM SIGIR conference on Research and development in information retrieval*, pages 411–418. ACM.

Anna Shtok, Gideon Dror, Yoelle Maarek, and Idan Szpektor. 2012. Learning from the past: Answering new questions with past answers. In *Proceedings of the 21st International Conference on World Wide Web*, WWW '12, pages 759–768, New York, NY, USA. ACM.

Rion Snow, Daniel Jurafsky, and Andrew Y Ng. 2004. Learning syntactic patterns for automatic hypernym discovery. *Advances in Neural Information Processing Systems 17*.

Valentin I Spitkovsky and Angel X Chang. 2012. A cross-lingual dictionary for english wikipedia concepts. In *LREC*, pages 3168–3175.

Mihai Surdeanu and Heng Ji. 2014. Overview of the english slot filling track at the tac2014 knowledge base population evaluation. In *Proc. Text Analysis Conference (TAC2014)*.

Mihai Surdeanu, Julie Tibshirani, Ramesh Nallapati, and Christopher D. Manning. 2012. Multi-instance multi-label learning for relation extraction. In *Proceedings of the 2012 Joint Conference on Empirical Methods in Natural Language Processing and Computational Natural Language Learning*, EMNLP-CoNLL '12, pages 455–465, Stroudsburg, PA, USA. Association for Computational Linguistics.

Xuchen Yao and Benjamin Van Durme. 2014. Information extraction over structured data: Question answering with freebase. In *Proceedings of ACL*, ACL'14.

Detecting Translation Direction: A Cross-Domain Study

Sauleh Eetemadi
Michigan State University, East Lansing, MI
Microsoft Research, Redmond, WA
saulehe@microsoft.com

Kristina Toutanova
Microsoft Research
Redmond, WA
kristout@microsoft.com

Abstract

Parallel corpora are constructed by taking a document authored in one language and translating it into another language. However, the information about the authored and translated sides of the corpus is usually not preserved. When available, this information can be used to improve statistical machine translation. Existing statistical methods for translation direction detection have low accuracy when applied to the realistic out-of-domain setting, especially when the input texts are short. Our contributions in this work are threefold: 1) We develop a multi-corpus parallel dataset with translation direction labels at the sentence level, 2) we perform a comparative evaluation of previously introduced features for translation direction detection in a cross-domain setting and 3) we generalize a previously introduced type of features to outperform the best previously proposed features in detecting translation direction and achieve 0.80 precision with 0.85 recall.

1 Introduction

Translated text differs from authored text (Baker, 1993). The main differences are simplification, explicitation, normalization and interference (Volansky et al., 2013). Statistical classifiers have been trained to detect Translationese[1]. Volansky et al. (2013) state two motivations for automatic detection of Translationese: empirical validation of Translationese linguistic theories and improving statistical machine translation (Kurokawa et al., 2009). Most of the prior work focus on in-domain Translationese detection (Baroni and Bernardini, 2006; Kurokawa et al., 2009). That is, the training and test set come from the same, usually narrow, domain. Cross-domain Translationese detection serves the two stated motivations better than in-domain detection. First, automatic classification validates linguistic theories only if it works independent of the domain. Otherwise, the classifier could perform well by memorizing lexical terms unique to a specific domain without using any linguistically meaningful generalizations. Second, a Translationese classifier can improve statistical machine translation in two ways: 1) By labeling the parallel training data with translation direction[2]; 2) By labeling input sentences to a decoder at translation time and use matching models. The accuracy of the classifier is the main factor determining its impact on statistical machine translation. Most parallel or monolingual training data sources do not contain translation direction meta-data. Also, the input sentences at translation time can be from any domain. Therefore, a cross-domain setting for translation direction detection is more appropriate for improving statistical machine translation as well. We develop a cross-domain training and test data set and compare some of the linguistically motivated features from prior work (Kurokawa et al., 2009; Volansky et al., 2013) in this setting. In addition, we introduce a new bilingual feature that outperforms all prior work in both

[1]Translated text is often referred to as "Translationese" (Volansky et al., 2013).

[2]Detection of *translation direction* refers to classifying a text block pair (A and B) as A was translated to B or vice versa. In contrast, *Translationese* detection usually refers to classifying a single block of text as "Translationese" versus "Original".

Proceedings of NAACL-HLT 2015 Student Research Workshop (SRW), pages 103–109,
Denver, Colorado, June 1, 2015.

in-domain and cross-domain settings.

Our work also differs from many prior works by focusing on sentence level, rather than block level classification. Although Kurokawa et al. (2009) compare sentence level versus block level detection accuracy, most other research focuses on block level detection (Baroni and Bernardini, 2006; Volansky et al., 2013). Sentence level classification serves the stated motivations above better than block level classification. For empirical validation of linguistic theories, features that are detectable at the sentence level are more linguistically meaningful than block level statistics. Sentence level detection is also more appropriate for labeling decoder input as well as some statistical machine translation training data.

In the rest of the paper, we first review prior work on sentence level and cross-domain translation direction detection. In Section 3 we motivate the selection of features used in this study. Next, we describe our cross-domain data set and the classification algorithm we use to build and evaluate models given a set of features. Experimental results are presented in Section 5.2.

2 Related Work

Volansky et al. (2013) provide a comprehensive list of monolingual features used for Translationese detection. These features include POS n-grams, character n-grams, function word frequency, punctuation frequency, mean word length, mean sentence length, word n-grams and type/token ratio. We are aware of only one prior work that presented a cross-domain evaluation. Koppel and Ordan (2011) use a logistic regression classifier with function word unigram frequencies to achieve 92.7% accuracy with ten fold cross validation on the EuroParl (Koehn, 2005) corpus and 86.3% on the IHT corpus. However testing the EuroParl trained classifier on the IHT corpus yields an accuracy of 64.8% (and the accuracy is 58.8% when the classifier is trained on IHT and tested on EuroParl). The classifiers in this study are trained and tested on text blocks of approximately 1500 tokens, and there is no comparative evaluation of models using different feature sets.

We are also aware of two prior works that investigate Translationese detection accuracy at the sentence level. First Kurokawa et al (2009) use the Hansard English-French corpus for their experiments. For sentence level translation direction detection they reach F-score of 77% using word n-grams and stay slightly below 70% F-score with POS n-grams using an SVM classifier. Second, Eetemadi and Toutanova (2014) leverage word alignment information by extracting POS tag minimal translation units (MTUs) (Quirk and Menezes, 2006) along with an online linear classifier trained on the Hansard English-French corpus to achieve 70.95% detection accuracy at the sentence level.

Label	Description
ENG.LEX	English word n-grams
FRA.LEX	French word n-grams
ENG.POS	English POS Tag n-grams
FRA.POS	French POS Tag n-grmas
ENG.BC	English Brown Cluster n-grams
FRA.BC	French Brown Cluster n-grams
POS.MTU	POS MTU n-grams
BC.MTU	Brown Cluster MTU n-grams

Table 1: Classification features and their labels.

3 Feature Sets

The goal of our study is to compare novel and previously introduced features in a cross-domain setting. Due to the volume of experiments required for comparison, for an initial study, we select a limited number of feature sets for comparison. Prior works claim POS n-gram features capture linguistic phenomena of translation and should generalize across domains (Kurokawa et al., 2009; Eetemadi and Toutanova, 2014). We chose source and target POS n-gram features for $n = 1 \ldots 5$ to test this claim. Another feature we have chosen is from the work of Eetemadi and Toutanova (2014) where they achieve higher accuracy by introducing POS MTU[3] n-gram features.

POS MTUs incorporate source and target side information in addition to word alignment. Prior work has also claimed lexical features such as word n-grams do not generalize across domains due to corpus specific vocabulary (Volansky et al., 2013). We test this hypothesis using source and target word n-gram features. Using n-grams of length 1 through 5 we run 45 (nine data matrix entries times n-gram lengths of five) experiments for each feature set mentioned above.

In addition to the features mentioned above, we

[3] Minimal Translation Units (Quirk and Menezes, 2006)

Corpus	Authored Language	Translation Language	Training Sentences	Test Sentences
EuroParl	English	French	62k	6k
EuroParl	French	English	43k	4k
Hansard	English	French	1,697k	169k
Hansard	French	English	567k	56k
Hansard-Committees	English	French	2,930k	292k
Hansard-Committees	French	English	636k	63k

Table 2: Cross-Domain Data Sets

make a small modification to the feature used to obtain the best previously reported sentence level performance (Eetemadi and Toutanova, 2014) to derive a new type of features. POS MTU n-gram features are the most linguistically informed features amongst prior work. We introduce Brown cluster (Brown et al., 1992) MTUs instead. Our use of Brown clusters is inspired by recent success on their use in statistical machine translation systems (Bhatia et al., 2014; Durrani et al., 2014). Finally, we also include source and target Brown cluster n-grams as a comparison point to better understand their effectiveness compared to POS n-grams and their contribution to the effectiveness of Brown cluster MTUs.

Given these 8 feature types summarized in Table 1, n-gram lengths of up to 5 and the 3×3 data matrix explained in the next section, we run 360 experiments for this cross-domain study.

4 Data, Preprocessing and Feature Extraction

We chose the English-French language pair for our cross-domain experiments based on prior work and availability of labeled data. Existing sentence-parallel datasets used for training machine translation systems, do not normally contain gold-standard translation direction information, and additional processing is necessary to compile a dataset with such information (labels). Kurokawa et al (2009) extract translation direction information from the English-French Hansard parallel dataset using speaker language tags. We use this dataset, and treat the two sections "main parliamentary proceedings" and "committee hearings" as two different corpora. These two corpora have slightly different domains, although they share many common topics as well. We additionally choose a third corpus, whose domain is more distinct from these two, from the EuroParl English-French corpus. Islam and Mehler (2012) provided a customized version of Europarl with translation direction labels, but this dataset only contains sentences that were authored in English and translated to French, and does not contain examples for which the original language of authoring was French. We thus prepare a new dataset from EuroParl and will make it publicly available for use. The original unprocessed version of EuroParl (Koehn, 2005) contains speaker language tags (original language of authoring) for the French and English sides of the parallel corpus. We filter out inconsistencies in the corpus. First, we filter out sections where the language tag is missing from one or both sides. We also filter out sections with conflicting language tags. Parallel sections with different number of sentences are also discarded to maintain sentence alignment. This leaves us with three data sets (two Hansard and one EuroParl) with translation direction information available, and which contain sentences authored in both languages. We hold out 10% of each data set for testing and use the rest for training. Our 3×3 corpus data matrix consists of all nine combinations of training on one corpus and testing on another (Table 2).

4.1 Preprocessing

First, we clean all data sets using the following simple techniques.

- Sentences with low alphanumeric density are discarded.
- A character n-gram based language detection tool is used to identify the language of each sentence. We discard sentences with a detected language other than their label.
- We discard sentences with invalid unicode characters or control characters.
- Sentences longer than 2000 characters are excluded.

Next, an HMM word alignment model (Vogel et al., 1996) trained on the WMT English-French corpus (Bojar et al., 2013) word-aligns sentence pairs.

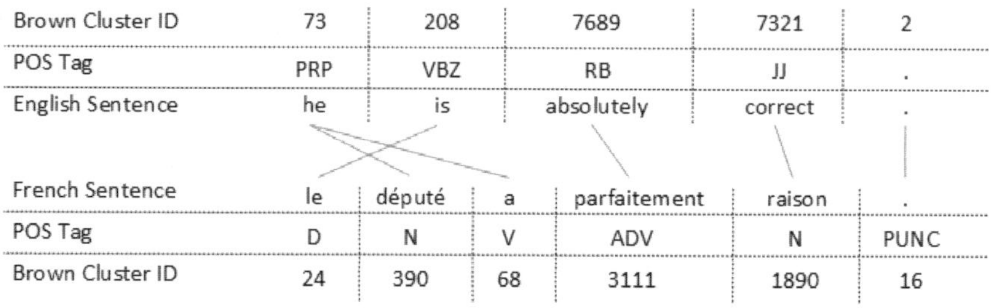

Figure 1: POS Tagged and Brown Cluster Aligned Sentence Pairs

We discard sentence pairs where the word alignment fails. We use the Stanford POS tagger (Toutanova and Manning, 2000) for English and French to tag all sentence pairs. A copy of the alignment file with words replaced with their POS tags is also generated. French and English Brown clusters are trained separately on the French and English sides of the WMT English-French corpus (Bojar et al., 2013). The produced models assign cluster IDs to words in each sentence pair. We create a copy of the alignment file with cluster IDs instead of words as well.

4.2 Feature Extraction

The classifier of our choice (Section 5) extracts n-gram features with n specified as an option. In preparation for classifier training and testing, feature extraction only needs to produce the unigram features while preserving the order (n-grams of higher length are automatically extracted by the classifier). POS, word, and Brown cluster n-gram features are generated by using the respective representation for sequences of tokens in the sentences. For POS and Brown cluster MTU features, the sequence of MTUs is defined as the left-to-right in source order sequence (due to reordering, the exact enumeration order of MTUs matters). For example, for the sentence pair in Figure 1, the sequence of Brown cluster MTUs is: 73⇒(390,68), 208⇒24, 7689⇒3111, 7321⇒1890, 2⇒16.

5 Experiments

We chose the Vowpal Wabbit (Langford et al., 2007) (VW) online linear classifier since it is fast, scalable and it has special (bag of words and n-gram generation) options for text classification. We found that VW was comparable in accuracy to a batch logistic regression classifier. For training and testing the classifier, we created balanced datasets with the same number of training examples in both directions. This was achieved by randomly removing sentence pairs from the English to French direction until it matches the French to English direction. For example, 636k sentence pairs are randomly chosen from the 2,930k sentence pairs in English to French Hansard-Committees corpus to match the number of examples in the French to English direction.

5.1 Evaluation Method

We are interested in comparing the performance of various feature sets in translation direction detection. Performance evaluation of different classification features objectively is challenging in the absence of a downstream task. Specifically, depending on the preferred balance between precision and recall, different features can be superior. Ideally an ROC graph (Fawcett, 2006) visualizes the tradeoff between precision and recall and can serve as an objective comparison between different classification feature sets. However, it is not practical to present ROC graphs for 360 experiments. Hence, we resort to the Area Under the ROC graph (AUC) measure as a good measure to provide an objective comparison. Theoretically, the area under the curve can be interpreted as the probability that the classifier scores a random negative example higher than a random positive example (Fawcett, 2006). As a point of reference, we also provide F-scores for experimental settings that are comparable to the prior work reviewed in Section 2.

5.2 Results

Figure 2 presents AUC points for all experiments. Rows and columns are labeled with corpus names for training and test data sets respectively. For example, the graph on the third row and first column corresponds to training on the Hansard-Committees corpus and testing on EuroParl. Within each graph we compare the AUC performance of different fea-

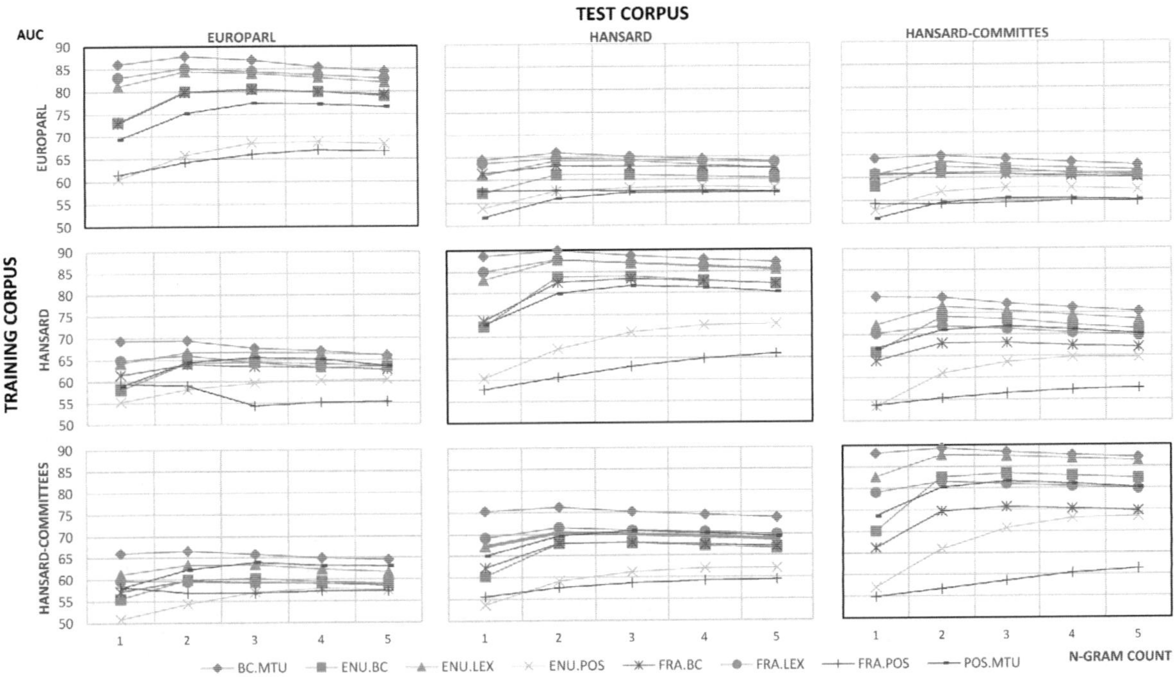

Figure 2: Comparing area under the ROC curve for the translation direction detection task when training and testing on different corpora using each of the eight feature sets. See Table 1 for experiment label description.

tures with n-gram lengths of 1 through 5.

Graphs on the diagonal correspond to in-domain detection and demonstrate higher performance compared to off diagonal graphs. This confirms the basic assumption that cross-domain translation direction detection is a more difficult task. The overall performance is also higher when trained on the Hansard corpus and tested on Hansard-Commitee and vice versa. This is because the Hansard corpus is more similar to the Hansard-Committees corpus compared to the EuroParl corpus. It is also observable that the variation in performance of different features diminishes as the training and test corpora become more dissimilar. For instance, this phenomenon can be observed on the second row of graphs where the features are most spread out when tested on the Hansard corpus. They are less spread out when tested on the Hansard-Committees corpus, and compressed together when tested on the EuroParl corpus. The same phenomenon can be observed for classifiers trained on other corpora.

For different feature types, different n-gram order of the features is best, depending on the feature granularity. To make it easier to observe patterns in the performance of different feature types, Figure 3 shows the performance for each feature type and each train-test corpus combination as a single point, by using the best n-gram order for that feature/data combination. Each of the 9 train/test data combinations is shown as a curve over feature types.

We can see that MTU features (which look at both languages at the same time) outperform individual source or target features (POS or Brown cluster) for all datasets. Brown clusters are unsupervised and can provide different levels of granularity. On the other hand, POS tags usually provide a fixed granularity and require lexicons or labeled data to train. We see that Brown clusters outperform corresponding POS tags across data settings. As an example, when training and testing on the Hansard corpus FRA.BC outperforms FRA.POS by close to 20 AUC points.

Lexical features outperform monolingual POS and Brown cluster features in most settings although their advantages diminish as the training and test corpus become more dissimilar. This is somewhat contrary to prior claims that lexical features will not generalize well across domains – we see that lexical features do capture important generalizations across domains and models that use only POS tag features have lower performance, both in and out-of-domain.

Figure 4 shows the rank of each feature amongst

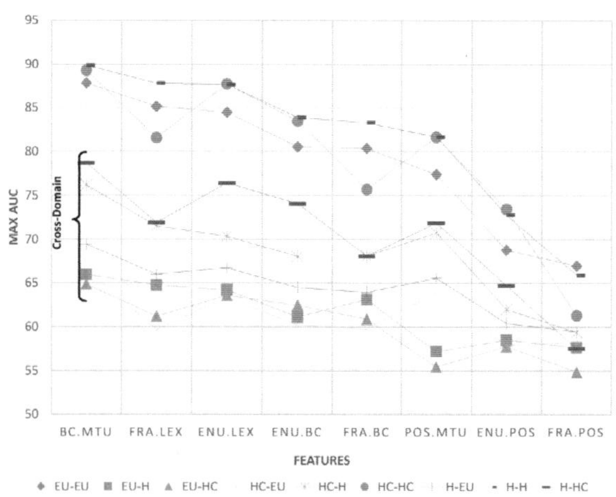

Figure 3: Translation detection performance matrix for training and testing on three different corpora - We ran experiments for n-grams of up to length five for each feature (See Table 1 for feature label descriptions). Unlike Figure 2 where we report AUC values for all n-gram lengths, in this graph we only present the highest AUC number for each feature. Each marker type indicates a training and test set combination. The format of experiment labels in the legend is [TrainingSet]-[TestSet] and **EU**: EuroParl, **H**: Hansard, **HC**: Hansard Committees. For example, EU-HC means training on EuroParl corpus and testing on Hansard Committees corpus.

all 8 different features for each entry in the cross-corpus data matrix (Similar to Figure 3 the highest performing n-gram length has been chosen for each feature). Brown cluster MTUs outperform all other features with rank one in all dataset combinations. Source and target POS tag features are the lowest performing features in 8 out of 9 data set combinations. The POS.MTU has its lowest ranks (7 and 8) when it is trained on the EuroParl corpus and its highest ranks (2 and 3) when trained on the Hansard-Committees corpus. High number of features in POS.MTU requires a large data set for training. The variation in performance for POS.MTU can be explained by the significant difference in training data size between EuroParl and Hansard-Committees. Finally, while FRA.LEX and ENG.LEX are mostly in rank 2 and 3 (after BC.MTU) they have their lowest ranks (6 and 4) in cross-corpus settings (HC-EU and HC-H).

Finally, we report precision and recall numbers to enable comparison between our experiments and previous work reported in Section 2. When training and testing on the Hansard corpus, BC.MTU achieves 0.80 precision with 0.85 recall. In comparison, ENG.POS achieves 0.65 precision with 0.64 recall and POS.MTU achieves 0.73 precision and 0.74 recall. These are the highest performance of each feature with n-grams of up to length 5.

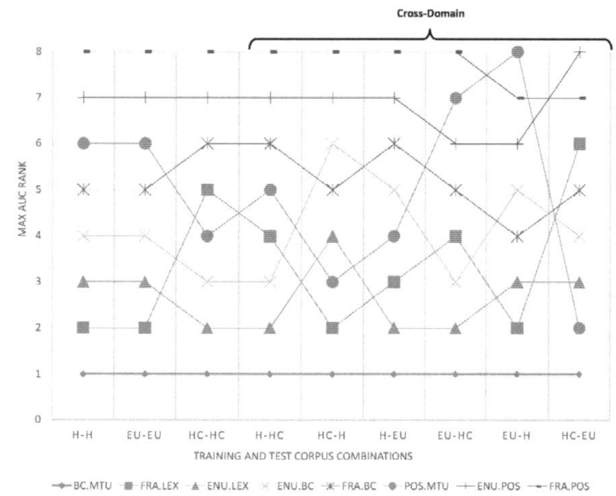

Figure 4: Translation direction detection AUC performance rank for each training and test set combination. For corpus combination abbreviations see description of Figure 3. For feature label descriptions see Table 1.

6 Conclusion and Future Work

From among eight studied sets of features, Brown cluster MTUs were the most effective at identifying translation direction at the sentence level. They were superior in both in-domain and cross-domain settings. Although English-Lexical features did not perform as well as Brown cluster MTUs, they performed better than most other methods. In future work, we plan to investigate lexical MTUs and to consider feature sets containing any subset of the eight or more basic feature types we have considered here. With these experiments we hope to gain further insight into the performance of feature sets in in out out-of-domain settings and to improve the state-of-the-art in realistic translation direction detection tasks. Additionally, we plan to use this classifier to extend the work of Twitto-Shmuel (2013) by building a more accurate and larger parallel corpus labeled for translation direction to further improve SMT quality.

References

Mona Baker. 1993. Corpus linguistics and translation studies: Implications and applications. *Text and technology: in honour of John Sinclair*, 233:250.

Marco Baroni and Silvia Bernardini. 2006. A new approach to the study of translationese: Machine-learning the difference between original and translated text. *Literary and Linguistic Computing*, 21(3):259–274.

Austin Matthews Waleed Ammar Archna Bhatia, Weston Feely, Greg Hanneman Eva Schlinger Swabha Swayamdipta, Yulia Tsvetkov, and Alon Lavie Chris Dyer. 2014. The cmu machine translation systems at wmt 2014. *ACL 2014*, page 142.

Ondrej Bojar, Christian Buck, Chris Callison-Burch, Christian Federmann, Barry Haddow, Philipp Koehn, Christof Monz, Matt Post, Radu Soricut, and Lucia Specia. 2013. Findings of the 2013 workshop on statistical machine translation. In *Proceedings of the Eighth Workshop on Statistical Machine Translation*, pages 1–44.

Peter F Brown, Peter V Desouza, Robert L Mercer, Vincent J Della Pietra, and Jenifer C Lai. 1992. Class-based n-gram models of natural language. *Computational linguistics*, 18(4):467–479.

Nadir Durrani, Philipp Koehn, Helmut Schmid, and Alexander Fraser. 2014. Investigating the usefulness of generalized word representations in smt. In *Proceedings of the 25th Annual Conference on Computational Linguistics (COLING), Dublin, Ireland*, pages 421–432.

Sauleh Eetemadi and Kristina Toutanova. 2014. Asymmetric features of human generated translation. In *Proceedings of the 2014 Conference on Empirical Methods in Natural Language Processing (EMNLP)*, pages 159–164. Association for Computational Linguistics.

Tom Fawcett. 2006. An introduction to roc analysis. *Pattern recognition letters*, 27(8):861–874.

Zahurul Islam and Alexander Mehler. 2012. Customization of the europarl corpus for translation studies. In *LREC*, page 2505–2510.

Philipp Koehn. 2005. Europarl: A Parallel Corpus for Statistical Machine Translation. In *Conference Proceedings: the tenth Machine Translation Summit*, pages 79–86, Phuket, Thailand. AAMT, AAMT.

Moshe Koppel and Noam Ordan. 2011. Translationese and its dialects. In *Proceedings of the 49th Annual Meeting of the Association for Computational Linguistics: Human Language Technologies-Volume 1*, page 1318–1326. Association for Computational Linguistics.

David Kurokawa, Cyril Goutte, and Pierre Isabelle. 2009. Automatic detection of translated text and its impact on machine translation. *Proceedings. MT Summit XII, The twelfth Machine Translation Summit International Association for Machine Translation hosted by the Association for Machine Translation in the Americas*.

J Langford, L Li, and A Strehl, 2007. *Vowpal wabbit online learning project*.

Chris Quirk and Arul Menezes. 2006. Do we need phrases?: Challenging the conventional wisdom in statistical machine translation. In *Proceedings of the Main Conference on Human Language Technology Conference of the North American Chapter of the Association of Computational Linguistics*, HLT-NAACL '06, pages 9–16, Stroudsburg, PA, USA. Association for Computational Linguistics.

Kristina Toutanova and Christopher D. Manning. 2000. Enriching the knowledge sources used in a maximum entropy part-of-speech tagger. In *Proceedings of the 2000 Joint SIGDAT Conference on Empirical Methods in Natural Language Processing and Very Large Corpora: Held in Conjunction with the 38th Annual Meeting of the Association for Computational Linguistics - Volume 13*, EMNLP '00, pages 63–70, Stroudsburg, PA, USA. Association for Computational Linguistics.

Naama Twitto-Shmuel. 2013. *Improving Statistical Machine Translation by Automatic Identification of Translationese*. Ph.D. thesis, University of Haifa.

Stephan Vogel, Hermann Ney, and Christoph Tillmann. 1996. Hmm-based word alignment in statistical translation. In *Proceedings of the 16th conference on Computational linguistics-Volume 2*, pages 836–841. Association for Computational Linguistics.

Vered Volansky, Noam Ordan, and Shuly Wintner. 2013. On the features of translationese. *Literary and Linguistic Computing*, page 31.

Improving the Translation of Discourse Markers for Chinese into English

David Steele
Department Of Computer Science
The University of Sheffield
Sheffield, UK
dbsteele1@sheffield.ac.uk

Abstract

Discourse markers (DMs) are ubiquitous cohesive devices used to connect what is said or written. However, across languages there is divergence in their usage, placement, and frequency, which is considered to be a major problem for machine translation (MT). This paper presents an overview of a proposed thesis, exploring the difficulties around DMs in MT, with a focus on Chinese and English. The thesis will examine two main areas: modelling cohesive devices within sentences and modelling discourse relations (DRs) across sentences. Initial experiments have shown promising results for building a prediction model that uses linguistically inspired features to help improve word alignments with respect to the implicit use of cohesive devices, which in turn leads to improved hierarchical phrase-based MT.

1 Introduction

Statistical Machine Translation (SMT) has, in recent years, seen substantial improvements, yet approaches are not able to achieve high quality translations in many cases. The problem is especially prominent with complex composite sentences and distant language pairs, largely due to computational complexity. Rather than considering larger discourse segments as a whole, current SMT approaches focus on the translation of single sentences independently, with clauses and short phrases being treated in isolation. DMs are seen as a vital contextual link between discourse segments and could be used to guide translations in order to improve accuracy. However, they are often translated into the target language in ways that differ from how they are used in the source language (Hardmeier, 2012a; Meyer and Popescu-Belis, 2012). DMs can also signal numerous DRs and current SMT approaches do not adequately recognise or distinguish between them during the translation process (Hajlaoni and Popescu-Belis, 2013). Recent developments in SMT potentially allow the modelling of wider discourse information, even across sentences (Hardmeier, 2012b), but currently most existing models appear to focus on producing well translated localised sentence fragments, largely ignoring the wider global cohesion.

Five distinct cohesive devices have been identified (Halliday and Hasan, 1976), but for this thesis the pertinent devices that will be examined are conjunction (DMs) and (endophoric) reference. Conjunction is pertinent as it encompasses DMs, whilst reference includes pronouns (amongst other elements), which are often connected with the use of DMs (e.g. 'Because John ..., therefore he ...').

The initial focus is on the importance of DMs within sentences, with special attention given to implicit markers (common in Chinese) and a number of related word alignment issues. However, the final thesis will cover two main areas:

- Modelling cohesive devices within sentences
- Modelling discourse relations across sentences and wider discourse segments.

This paper is organized as follows. In Section 2 a survey of related work is conducted. Section 3

Proceedings of NAACL-HLT 2015 Student Research Workshop (SRW), pages 110–117,
Denver, Colorado, June 1, 2015.

outlines the initial motivation and research including a preliminary corpus analysis. It covers examples that highlight various problems with the translation of (implicit) DMs, leading to an initial intuition. Section 4 looks at experiments and word alignment issues following a deeper corpus analysis and discusses how the intuition led towards developing the methodology used to study and improve word alignments. It also includes the results of the experiments that show positive gains in BLEU. Section 5 provides an outline of the future work that needs to be carried out. Finally, Section 6 is the conclusion.

2 Literature Review

This section is a brief overview of some of the pertinent important work that has gone into improving SMT with respect to cohesion. Specifically the focus is on the areas of: identifying and annotating DMs, working with lexical and grammatical cohesion, and translating implicit DRs.

2.1 Identifying and Annotating Chinese DMs

A study on translating English discourse connectives (DCs) (Hajlaoni and Popescu-Belis, 2013) showed that some of them in English can be ambiguous, signalling a variety of discourse relations. However, other studies have shown that sense labels can be included in corpora and that MT systems can take advantage of such labels to learn better translations (Pitler and Nenkova, 2009; Meyer and Popescu-Belis, 2012). For example, The Penn Discourse Treebank project (PDTB) adds annotation related to structure and discourse semantics with a focus on DRs and can be used to guide the extraction of DR inferences. The Chinese Discourse Treebank (CDTB) adds an extra layer to the annotation in the PDTB (Xue, 2005) focussing on DCs as well as structural and anaphoric relations and follows the lexically grounded approach of the PDTB.

The studies also highlight how anaphoric relations can be difficult to capture as they often have one discourse adverbial linked with a local argument, leaving the other argument to be established from elsewhere in the discourse. Pronouns, for example, are often used to link back to some discourse entity that has already been introduced. This essentially suggests that arguments identified in anaphoric relations can cover a long distance and Xue (2005) argues that one of the biggest challenges for discourse annotation is establishing the distance of the text span and how to decide on what discourse unit should be included or excluded from the argument.

English	Chinese DC
although(1)/but(2)	(1) 虽然，虽说，虽 (2)但，可是，却
because(1)/therefore(2)	(1) 因为，因，由于 (2)所以
if(1)/then(2)	(1) 如果，假如，若 (2)就

Table 1: Examples of Interchangeable DMs.

There are also some additional challenges such as variants or substitutions of DCs. Table 1 (Xue, 2005) shows a range of DCs that can be used interchangeably. The numbers indicate that any marker from (1) can be paired with any marker from (2) to form a compound sentence with the same meaning.

2.2 Lexical and Grammatical Cohesion

Previous work has attempted to address lexical and grammatical cohesion in SMT (Gong et al., 2011; Xiao et al., 2011; Wong and Kit, 2012; Xiong et al., 2013b) although their results are still relatively limited (Xiong et al., 2013a). Lexical cohesion is determined by identifying lexical items forming links between sentences in text (also lexical chains). A number of models have been proposed in order to try and capture document-wide lexical cohesion and when implemented they showed significant improvements over the baseline (Xiong et al., 2013a).

Lexical chain information (Morris and Hirst, 1991) can be used to capture lexical cohesion in text and it is already successfully used in a range of fields such as information retrieval and the summarisation of documents (Xiong et al., 2013b). The work of Xiong et al. (2013b) introduces two lexical chain models to incorporate lexical cohesion into document wide SMT and experiments show that, compared to the baseline, implementing these models substantially improves translation quality. Unfortunately with limited grammatical cohesion, propagated by DMs, translations can be difficult to understand, especially if there is no context provided by local discourse segments.

To achieve improved grammatical cohesion Tu et al. (2014) propose creating a model that generates transitional expressions through using complex sentence structure based translation rules alongside a generative transfer model, which is then incorporated into a hierarchical phrase-based system. The test results show significant improvements leading to smoother and more cohesive translations. One of the key reasons for this is through reserving cohesive information during the training process by converting source sentences into "tagged flattened complex sentence structures"(Tu et al., 2014) and then performing word alignments using the translation rules. It is argued that connecting complex sentence structures with transitional expressions is similar to the human translation process (Tu et al., 2014) and therefore improvements have been made showing the effectiveness of preserving cohesion information.

2.3 Translation of Implicit Discourse Relations

It is often assumed that the discourse information captured by the lexical chains is mainly explicit. However, these relations can also be implicitly signalled in text, especially for languages such as Chinese where implicitation is used in abundance (Yung, 2014). Yung (2014) explores DM annotation schemes such as the CDTB (2.1) and observes that explicit relations are identified with an accuracy of up to 94%, whereas with implicit relations this can drop as low as 20% (Yung, 2014). To overcome this, Yung proposes implementing a discourse-relation aware SMT system, that can serve as a basis for producing a discourse-structure-aware, document-level MT system. The proposed system will use DC annotated parallel corpora, that enables the integration of discourse knowledge. Yung argues that in Chinese a segment separated by punctuation is considered to be an elementary discourse unit (EDU) and that a running Chinese sentence can contain many such segments. However, the sentence would still be translated into one single English sentence, separated by ungrammatical commas and with a distinct lack of connectives. The connectives are usually explicitly required for the English to make sense, but can remain implicit in the Chinese (Yung, 2014). However, this work is still in the early stages.

3 Motivation

This section outlines the initial research, including a preliminary corpus analysis, examining difficulties with automatically translating DMs across distant languages such as Chinese and English. It draws attention to deficiencies caused from under-utilising discourse information and examines divergences in the usage of DMs. The final part of this section outlines the intuition garnered from the given examples and highlights the approach to be undertaken.

For the corpus analysis, research, and experiments three main parallel corpora are used:

- Basic Travel Expression Corpus (BTEC): Primarily made up of short simple phrases that occur in travel conversations. It contains 44,016 sentences in each language with over 250,000 Chinese characters and over 300,000 English words (Takezawa et al., 2012).

- Foreign Broadcast Information Service (FBIS) corpus: This uses a variety of news stories and radio podcasts in Chinese. It contains 302,996 parallel sentences with 215 million Chinese characters and over 237 million English words.

- Ted Talks corpus (TED): Made up of approved translations of the live Ted Talks presentations[1]. It contains over 300,000 Chinese characters and over 2 million English words from 156,805 sentences (Cettolo et al., 2012) .

Chinese uses a rich array of DMs including: simple conjunctions, composite conjunctions, and zero connectives where the meaning or context is strongly inferred across clauses with sentences having natural, allowable omissions, which can cause problems for current SMT approaches. Here a few examples[2] are outlined:

Ex (1) 他因为病了，没来上课。
he because ill, not come class.
Because he was sick, he didn't come to class[3].
He is ill, absent. (Bing)

[1] http://www.ted.com

[2] These examples (Steele and Specia, 2014) are presented as: Chinese sentence / literal translation / reference translation / automated translation - using either Google or Bing.

[3] (Ross and Sheng, 2006)

Ex (2) 你因为这个在吃什么药吗?
you because this (be) eat what medicine?
Have you been taking anything for this? (BTEC)
What are you eating because of this medicine? (Google)

Both examples show 'because' (因为) being used in different ways and in each case the automated translations fall short. In Ex1 the dropped (implied) pronoun in the second clause could be the problem, whilst in Ex2 significant reordering is needed as 'because' should be linked to 'this' (这个) - the topic - rather than 'medicine' (药). The 'this' (这个) refers to an 'ailment', which is hard to capture from a single sentence. Information preserved from a larger discourse segment may have provided more clues, but as is, the sentence appears somewhat exophoric and the meaning cannot necessarily be gleaned from the text alone.

Ex (3) 一有空位我们就给你打电话。
as soon as have space we then give you make phone.
We'll call you as soon as there is an opening. (BTEC)
A space that we have to give you a call. (Google)

In Ex3 the characters '一' and '就' are working together as coordinating markers in the form: ...一VP^a 就 VP^b. However, individually these characters have significantly different meanings, with '一' meaning 'a' or 'one' amongst many things. Yet, in the given sentence using the '一' and '就' constuct '一' has a meaning akin to 'as soon as' or 'once', while '就' implies a 'then' relation, both of which can be difficult to capture. Figure 1[4] shows an example where word alignment failed to map the 'as soon as ... then' structure to ...一...就... . That is, columns 7, 8, 9, which represent 'as soon as' in the English have no alignment points whatsoever. Yet, in this case, all three items should be aligned to the single element '一' which is on row 1 on the Chinese side. Additionally, the word 'returns' (column 11), which is currently aligned to '一' (row 1) should in fact be aligned to '回来' (return/come back) in row 2. This misalignment

[4]The boxes with a '#' inside are the alignment points and each coloured block (large or small) is a minimal-biphrase.

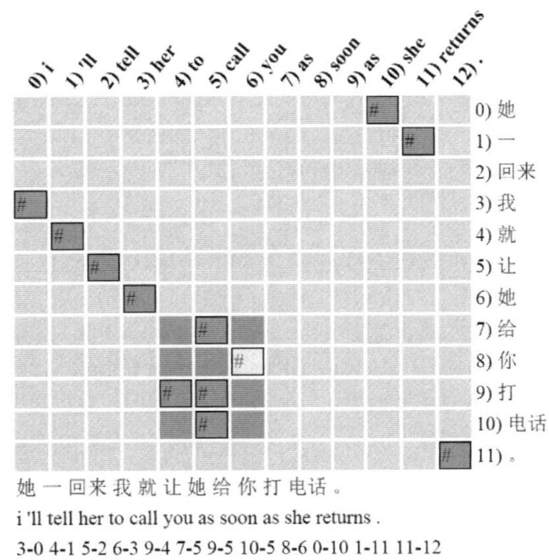

Figure 1: A visualisation of word alignments for the given parallel sentence, showing a non-alignment of 'as soon as'.

could be a direct side-effect of having no alignment for 'as soon as' in the first place. Consequently, the knock-on effect of poor word alignment, especially around markers - as in this case, will lead to the overall generation of poorer translation rules.

Ex (4) 他因为病了, 所以他没来上课。
he because ill, **so he** not come class.
Because he was sick, he didn't come to class.
He is ill, so he did not come to class. (Bing)

Ex4 is a modified version of Ex2, with an extra 'so'(所以) and 'he' (他) manually inserted in the second clause of the Chinese sentence. Grammatically these extra characters are not required for the Chinese to make sense, but are still correct. However, the interesting point is that the extra information (namely 'so' and 'he') has enabled the system to produce a much better final translation.

From the given examples it appears that both implicitation and the use of specific DM structures can cause problems when generating automated translations. The highlighted issues suggest that making markers (and possibly, by extension, pronouns) explicit, due to linguistic clues, more information becomes available, which can support the extraction of word alignments. Although making implicit markers explicit can seem unnatural and even unnecessary for human readers, it does follow that if the word alignment process is made easier by this explicitation it will lead to better translation rules and ultimately better translation quality.

4 Experiments and Word Alignments

This section examines the current ongoing research and experiments that aim to measure the extent of the difficulties caused by DMs. In particular the focus is on automated word alignments and problems around implicit and misaligned DMs. The work discussed in Section 3 highlighted the importance of improving word alignments, and especially how missing alignments around markers can lead to the generation of poorer rules.

Before progressing onto the experiments an initial baseline system was produced according to detailed criteria (Chiang, 2007; Saluja et al., 2014). The initial system was created using the ZH-EN data from the BTE parallel corpus (Paul, 2009) (Section 3). Fast-Align is used to generate the word alignments and the CDEC decoder (Dyer et al., 2010) is used for rule extraction and decoding. The baseline and subsequent systems discussed here are hierarchical phrase-based systems for Chinese to English translation.

Once the alignments were obtained the next step in the methodology was to examine the misalignment information to determine the occurrence of implicit markers. A variance list was created[5] that could be used to cross-reference discourse markers with appropriate substitutable words (as per Table 1). Each DM was then examined in turn (automatically) to look at what it had been aligned to. When the explicit English marker was aligned correctly, according to the variance list, then no change was made. If the marker was aligned to an unsuitable word, then an artificial marker was placed into the Chinese in the nearest free space to that word. Finally if the marker was not aligned at all then an artificial marker was inserted into the nearest free space by number[6]. A percentage of misalignments[7] across all occurrences of individual markers was also calculated.

DM	BTEC	FBIS	TED
if	25.70%	40.75%	23.35%
then	21.00%	50.85 %	40.47%
because	23.95%	32.80%	16.48%
but	29.40%	39.90%	27.08%

Table 2: Misalignment information for the 3 corpora.

System	DEV	TST
BTEC-Dawn (baseline)	34.39	35.02
BTEC-Dawn (if)	34.60	35.03
BTEC-Dawn (then)	34.69	35.04
BTEC-Dawn (but)	34.51	35.21
BTEC-Dawn (because)	34.41	35.02
BTEC-Dawn (all)	34.53	35.46

Table 3: BLEU Scores for the Experimental Systems

Table 2 shows the misalignment percentages for the four given DMs across the three corpora. The average sentence length in the BTE Corpus is eight units, in the FBIS corpus it is 30 units, and in the TED corpus it is 29 units. The scores show that there is a wide variance in the misalignments across the corpora, with FBIS consistently having the highest error rate, but in all cases the percentage is fairly significant.

Initially tokens were inserted for single markers at a time, but then finally with tokens for all markers inserted simultaneously. Table 3 shows the BLEU scores for all the experiments. The first few experiments showed improvements over the baseline of up to +0.30, whereas the final one showed improvements of up to +0.44, which is significant.

After running the experiments the visualisation of a number of word alignments (as per Figures 1,2,3) were examined and a single example of a 'then' sentence was chosen at random. Figure 2 shows the word alignments for a sentence from the baseline system, and Figure 3 shows the word alignments for

[5]The variance list is initially created by filtering good alignments and bad alignments by hand and using both on-line and off-line (bi-lingual) dictionaries/resources.

[6]The inserts are made according to a simple algorithm, and inspired by the examples in Section 3.

[7]A non-alignment is not necessarily a bad alignment. For example: '正反' = 'positive and negative', with no 'and' in the Chinese. In this case a non-alignment for 'and' is acceptable.

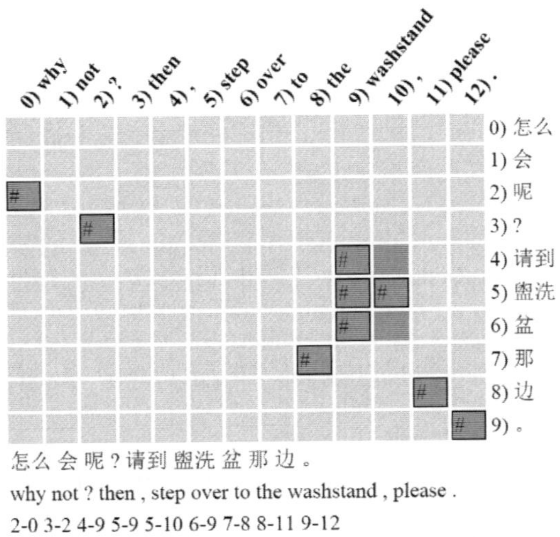

Figure 2: Visualisation of word alignments showing no alignment for 'then' in column 3.

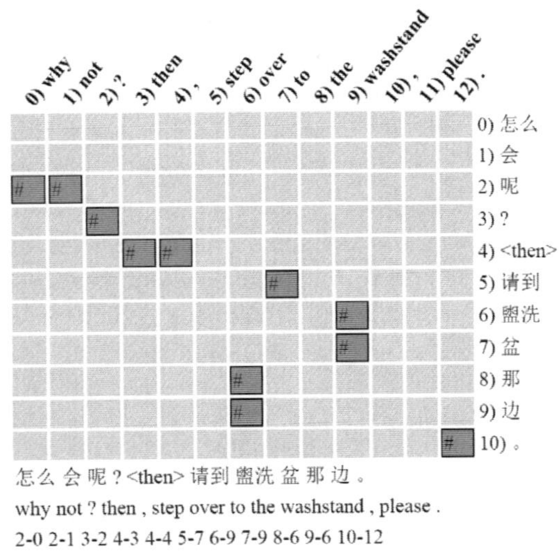

Figure 3: Visualisation of word alignments showing the artificial marker '<then>' and a smoother overall alignment.

the same sentence, but with an artificial marker automatically inserted for the unaligned 'then'.

The differences between the word alignments in the figures are subtle, but positive. For example, in Figure 3 more of the question to the left of 'then' is captured correctly. Moreover, to the right of 'then', 'over' has now been aligned quite well to '那边' (over there) and 'to' has been aligned to '请到' (please - go to). Perhaps most significantly though is the mish-mash of alignments to 'washstand' in Figure 2 has now been replaced by a very good alignment to '盥洗盆' (washbasin/washstand) showing an overall smoother alignment. These preliminary findings indicate that there is plenty of scope for further positive investigation and experimentation.

5 Ongoing Work

This section outlines the two main research areas (Section 1) that will be tackled in order to feed into the final thesis. Having addressed the limitations of current SMT approaches, the focus has moved on to looking at cohesive devices at the sentential level, but ultimately the overall aim is to better model DRs across wider discourse segments.

5.1 Modelling Cohesive Devices Within Sentences

Even at the sentence level there exists a local context, which produces dependencies between certain words. The cohesion information within the sentence can hold vital clues for tasks such as pronoun resolution, and so it is important to try to capture it.

Simply looking at the analysis in Section 4 provides insight into which other avenues should be explored for this part, including:

- Expanding the number of DMs being explored, including complex markers (e.g. as soon as).
- Improving the variance list to capture more variant translations of marker words. It is also important here to include automated filtering for difficult DMs (e.g. cases where 'and' or 'so' are not being used as specific markers can perhaps make them more difficult to align). Making significant use of parts of speech tagging and annotated texts could be useful.
- Develop better insertion algorithms to produce an improved range of insertion options, and reduce damage to existing word alignments.
- Looking at using alternative/additional evaluation metrics and tools to either replace or complement BLEU. This could produce more targeted evaluation that is better at picking up on individual linguistic components such as DMs and pronouns.

However, the final aim is to work towards a true prediction model using parallel data as a source of annotation. Creating such a model can be hard monolingually, whereas a bilingual corpus can be used as a source of additional implicit annotation or indeed a source of additional signals for discourse relations. The prediction model should make the word alignment task easier (through either guiding the process or adding constraints), which in turn will generate better translation rules and ultimately should improve MT.

5.2 Modelling Discourse Relations Across Sentences

This part will be an extension of the tasks in Section 5.1. The premise is that if the discourse information or local context within a sentence can be captured then it could be applied to wider discourse segments and possibly the whole document. Some inroads into this task have been trialled through using lexical chaining (Xiong et al., 2013b). However, more recently tools are being developed enabling document wide access to the text, which should provide scope for examining the links between larger discourse units - especially sentences and paragraphs.

6 Conclusions

The findings in Section 3 highlighted that implicit cohesive information can cause significant problems for MT and that by adding extra information translations can be made smoother. Section 4 extended this idea and outlined the experiments and methodology used to capture some effects of automatically inserting artificial tokens for implicit or misaligned DMs. It showed largely positive results, with some good improvements to the word alignments, indicating that there is scope for further investigation and experimentation. Finally, section 5 highlighted the two main research areas that will guide the thesis, outlining a number of ways in which the current methodology and approach could be developed.

The ultimate aim is to use bilingual data as a source of additional clues for a prediction model of Chinese implicit markers, which can, for instance, guide and improve the word alignment process leading to the generation of better rules and smoother translations.

References

Mauro Cettolo, Christian Girardi, and Marcello Federico. 2012 *Web Inventory of Transcribed and Translated Talks.* In: EAMT, pages 261-268. Trento, Italy.

David Chiang. 2007. *Hierarchical phrase-based translation.* Computational Linguistics, 33(2):201–228.

Chris Dyer, Adam Lopez, Juri Ganitkevitch, Johnathan Weese, Ferhan Ture, Phil Blunsom, Hendra Setiawan, Vladimir Eidelman, and Philip Resnik. 2010. *CDEC: A decoder, Alignment, and Learning Framework for Finite-state and Context-free Translation Models.* In Proceedings of ACL.

Zhengxian Gong, Min Zhang, and Guodong Zhou. 2011. *Cache-based Document-level Statistical Machine Translation.* In 2011 Conference on Empirical Methods in Natural Language Processing, pages 909-919. Edinburgh, Scotland, UK

Najeh Hajlaoui and Andre Popescu-Belis. 2013 *Translating English Discourse Connectives into Arabic: a Corpus-based analysis and an Evaluation Metric.* In: CAASL4 Workshop at AMTA (Fourth Workshop on Computational Approaches to Arabic Script-based Languages), San Diego, CA, pages 1-8.

M.A.K Halliday and Ruqaiya Hasan. 1976. *Cohesion in English (English Language Series* Longmen, London

Christian Hardmeier. 2012. *Discourse in Statistical Machine Translation: A Survey and a Case Study* Elanders Sverige, Sweden.

Christian Hardmeier, Sara Stymne, Jorg Tiedemann, and Joakim Nivre. 2012 *Docent: A Document-Level Decoder for Phrase-Based Statistical Machine Translation.* In: 51st Annual Meeting of the ACL. Sofia, Bulgaria, pages 193-198.

Christian Hardmeier. 2014 *Discourse in Statistical Machine Translation.* Elanders Sverige, Sweden.

Thomas Meyer and Andrei Popescu-Belis. 2012. *Using sense-labelled discourse connectives for statistical machine translation.* In: EACL Joint Workshop on Exploiting Synergies between IR and MT, and Hybrid Approaches to MT (ESIRMTHyTra), pages 129-138. Avignon, France.

Jane Morris and Graeme Hirst. March 1991 *Lexical Cohesion Computed by Thesaural Relations as an Indicator of the Structure of Text.* Computational Linguistics, 17(1):Pages 21-48.

Joseph Olive, Caitlin Christianson, and John McCary (editors). 2011, *Handbook of Natural Language Processing and Machine Translation: DARPA Global Autonomous Language Exploitation.* Springer Science and Business Media, New York.

Michael Paul. 2009. *Overview of the IWSLT 2009 evaluation campaign.* In Proceedings of IWSLT.

Emily Pitler and Ani Nenkova. 2009. *Using Syntax to Disambiguate Explicit Discourse Connectives in Text.* In: ACL-IJCNLP 2009 (47th Annual Meeting of the ACL and 4th International Joint Conference on NLP of the AFNLP), Short Papers, pages 13-16, Singapore.

Claudia Ross and Jing-heng Sheng Ma. 2006. *Modern Mandarin Chinese Grammar: A Practical Guide.* Routledge, London.

Avneesh Saluja, Chris Dyer, and Shay B. Cohen. 2014 *Latent-Variable Synchronous CFGs for Hierarchical Translation.* In: Empirical methods in Natural language processing (EMNLP), pages 1953-1964 Doha, Qatar.

David Steele and Lucia Specia. 2014. *Divergences in the Usage of Discourse Markers in English and Mandarin Chinese.* In: Text, Speech and Dialogue (17th International Conference TSD), pages 189-200, Brno, Czech Republic.

Toshiyuki Takezawa, Eiichiro Sumita, Fumiaki Sugaya, Hirofumi Yamamoto, and Seiichi Yamamoto. 2002 *Toward a Broad-coverage Bilingual Corpus for Speech Translation of Travel Conversations in the Real World.* In: LREC , pages 147-152. Las Palmas, Spain.

Mei Tu, Yu Zhou and Chengqing Zong. 2014. *Enhancing Grammatical Cohesion: Generating Transitional Expressions for SMT.* In: 52nd annual meeting of the ACL, June 23-25, Baltimore, USA.

Billy T.M. Wong and Chunyu Kit. 2012. *Extending Machine Translation Evaluation Metrics with Lexical Cohesion to Document Level.* In: 2012 Joint Conference on Empirical Methods in Natural Language Processing and Computational Natural Language Learning, pages 1060-1068. Jeju Island, Korea.

Tong Xiao, Jingbo Zhu, Shujie Yao, and Hao Zhang. September 2011. *Document-level Consistency Verification in Machine Translation.* In 2011 MT summit XIII, pages 131-138. Xiamen, China:

Deyi Xiong., Guosheng Ben, Min Zhang, Yajuan Lu, and Qun Liu. August 2013. *Modelling Lexical Cohesion for Document-level Machine Translation.* In: Twenty-Third International Joint Conference on Artificial Intelligence (IJCAI-13) Beijing, China.

Deyi Xiong, Yang Ding, Min Zhang, and Chew Lim Tan. 2013 *Lexical Chain Based Cohesion Models for Document-Level Statistical Machine Translation.* In: 2013 Conference on Empirical Methods in Natural Language Processing, pages: 1563-1573.

Jinxi Xu and Roger Bock. 2011. *Combination of Alternative Word Segmentations for Chinese Machine Translation.* DARPA Global Autonomous Language Exploitation. Springer Science and Business Media, New York.

Nianwen Xue. 2005. *Annotating Discourse Connectives in the Chinese Treebank.* In: ACL Workshop on Frontiers in Corpus Annotation 2: Pie in the Sky.

Frances Yung. 2014. *Towards a Discourse Relation-aware Approach for Chinese-English Machine Translation.* In: ACL Student Research Workshop, pages 18-25. Baltimore, Maryland USA.

Discourse and Document-level Information for Evaluating Language Output Tasks

Carolina Scarton
Department of Computer Science, University of Sheffield
Regent Court, 211 Portobello, Sheffield, S1 4DP, UK
c.scarton@sheffield.ac.uk

Abstract

Evaluating the quality of language output tasks such as Machine Translation (MT) and Automatic Summarisation (AS) is a challenging topic in Natural Language Processing (NLP). Recently, techniques focusing only on the use of outputs of the systems and source information have been investigated. In MT, this is referred to as Quality Estimation (QE), an approach that uses machine learning techniques to predict the quality of unseen data, generalising from a few labelled data points. Traditional QE research addresses sentence-level QE evaluation and prediction, disregarding document-level information. Document-level QE requires a different set up from sentence-level, which makes the study of appropriate quality scores, features and models necessary. Our aim is to explore document-level QE of MT, focusing on discourse information. However, the findings of this research can improve other NLP tasks, such as AS.

1 Introduction

Evaluation metrics for Machine Translation (MT) and Automatic Summarisation (AS) tasks should be able to measure quality with respect to different aspects (e.g. fluency and adequacy) and they should be fast and scalable. Human evaluation seems to be the most reliable (although it might introduce biases of reviewers). However, it is expensive and cumbersome for large datasets; it is also not practical for certain scenarios, such as *gisting* in MT and summarisation of webpages.

Automatic evaluation metrics (such as BLEU (Papineni et al., 2002) and ROUGE (Lin and Och, 2004)), based on human references, are widely used to evaluate MT and AS outputs. One limitation of these metrics is that if the MT or AS system outputs a translation or summary considerably different from the references, it does not really mean that it is a bad output. Another problem is that these metrics cannot be used in scenarios where the output of the system is to be used directly by end-users, for example a user reading the output of Google Translate[1] for a given news text cannot count on a reference for that translated text.

Quality Estimation (QE) approaches aim to predict the quality of MT systems without using references. Instead, features (that may be or may not be related to the MT system that produced this translations) are applied to source and target documents (Blatz et al., 2004; Bojar et al., 2013). The only requirement is data points with scores (e.g.: Human-targeted Translation Error Rate (HTER) (Snover et al., 2006) or even BLEU-style metrics). These data points can be used to train supervised machine learning models (regressors or classifiers) to predict the scores of unseen data. The advantage of these approaches is that we do not need to have all the words, sentences or documents of a task evaluated manually, we just need enough data points to train the machine learning model.

QE systems predict scores that reflect how good a translation is for a given scenario. For example, a widely predicted score in QE is HTER, which measures the effort needed to post-edit a sentence. A

[1] https://translate.google.com/

Proceedings of NAACL-HLT 2015 Student Research Workshop (SRW), pages 118–125,
Denver, Colorado, June 1, 2015.

user of a QE system predicting HTER could decide whether to post-edit or translate sentences from scratch based on the score predicted for each sentence.

The vast majority of work done on QE is at sentence level. Document-level predictions, on the other hand, are interesting in scenarios where one wants to evaluate the overall score of an MT system or where the end-user is interested in the quality of the document as whole. In addition, document-level features can also correlate well with quality scores, mainly because state-of-the-art MT systems translate documents at sentence level, disregarding discourse information. Therefore, it is expected that the outputs of these systems may contain discourse problems.

In this work we focus on document-level QE. Regarding features, discourse phenomena are being considered since they are linguistic phenomena that often manifest document-wide. These phenomena are related to how sentences are connected, how genre and domain of a document are identified, anaphoric pronouns, etc.

Regarding document-level prediction, we focus on finding the ideal quality label for the task. Traditional evaluation metrics tend to yield similar scores for different documents. This leads to low variation between the document quality scores with all these scores being close to the mean score. Therefore, a quality label that captures document quality in a more sensitive way is needed.

Research on the use of linguistic features for QE and the use of discourse for improving MT and MT evaluation are presented in Section 2. Section 3 presents the work done so far and the directions that we intend to follow. Conclusions and future work are presented in Section 4

2 Document-level information for QE and MT

Traditional systems translate documents at sentence level, disregarding document-wide information. This means that sentences are translated without considering the relations in the whole document. Therefore, information such as discourse structures can be lost in this process.

QE is also traditionally done at sentence level mainly because the majority of MT systems translate texts at this level. Another reason is that sentence-level approaches have more applications than other granularity levels, because they can explore the peculiarities of each sentence, being very useful for the post-edition task. On the other hand, sentence-level approaches do not consider the document as a whole and information regarding discourse is disregarded. Moreover, for scenarios in which post-edition is not possible, for example, *gisting*, quality predictions for the entire documents are more useful.

In this section we present related work on QE and the first research towards document-level QE. Research on the use of discourse phenomena for MT improvement and MT evaluation are also presented.

2.1 Quality Estimation of Machine Translation

Previous work on QE has used supervised machine learning (ML) approaches (mainly regression algorithms). Besides the specific ML method adopted, the choice of features is also a design decision that plays a crucial role.

Sentences (or documents) from source and target and also information from the MT system are used for designing features. The features extracted are used as input to train a QE model. In this training phase supervised ML techniques, such as regression, can be applied. A training set with quality labels is provided for an ML model. These quality labels are the scores that the QE model will learn to predict. Therefore, the QE model will be able to predict a quality score for a new, unseen data points. The quality labels can be *likert* scores, HTER, BLEU, just to cite some widely used examples. Also the ML algorithm can vary (SVM and Gaussian Process are the state-of-the-art algorithms for QE).

Some work in the area include linguistic information as features for QE (Avramidis et al., 2011; Pighin and Màrquez, 2011; Hardmeier, 2011; Felice and Specia, 2012; Almaghout and Specia, 2013) at sentence level. Only Scarton and Specia (2014) (predicting quality at document level) and Rubino et al. (2013) (sentence level) focus on the use of discourse information for QE.

It is important to notice that frameworks like QuEst[2] (Specia et al., 2013) are available for QE at

[2]http://www.quest.dcs.shef.ac.uk

sentence level. QuEst has modules to extract several features for QE from source and target documents and to experiment with ML techniques for predicting QE. Features are divided in two types: glass-box (dependent on the MT system) and black-box (independent on the MT system).

At document level, Soricut and Echihabi (2010) explore document-level QE prediction to rank documents translated by a given MT system, predicting BLEU scores. Features include text-based, language model-based, pseudo-reference-based, example-based and training-data-based. Pseudo-reference features are BLEU scores based on pseudo-references from an off-the-shelf MT system, for both the target and the source languages.

Scarton and Specia (2014) explore lexical cohesion and LSA (Latent Semantic Analysis) (Landauer et al., 1998) cohesion for document-level QE. The lexical cohesion features are repetitions (Wong and Kit, 2012) and the LSA cohesion is achieved following the work of Graesser et al. (2004). Pseudo-reference features are also applied in this work, according to the work of Soricut and Echihabi (2010). BLEU and TER (Snover et al., 2006) are used as quality labels. The best results were achieved with pseudo-reference features. However, LSA cohesion features alone also showed improvements over the baseline.

2.2 Discourse phenomena in MT

In the MT area, there have been attempts to use discourse information that can be used as inspiration source for QE features. The need of document-level information for improving MT is a widely accepted fact. However, it is hard to integrate discourse information into traditional state-of-the-art sentence-level MT systems. It is also challenging to build a document-level or discourse-based MT system from scratch. Therefore, the initiatives focus on the integration of discourse as features into the decoding phase or previously annotate discourse phenomena in the parallel corpora.

Lexical Cohesion is related to word usage: word repetitions, synonyms repetitions and collocations. Besides initiatives to improve MT system and outputs with lexical cohesion (Ture et al., 2012; Xiao et al., 2011; Ben et al., 2013), Wong and Kit (2012) apply lexical cohesion metrics for evaluation of MT systems at document level.

Coreference is related to coherence clues, such as pronominal anaphora and connectives. Machine translation can break coreference chains since it is done at sentence level. Initiatives for improvement of coreference in MT include anaphora resolution (Giménez et al., 2010; LeNagard and Kohen, 2010; Hardmeier and Federico, 2010; Hardmeier, 2014) and connectives (Popescu-Belis et al., 2012; Meyer and Popescu-Belis, 2012; Meyer et al., 2012; Li et al., 2014).

RST (Rhetorical Structure Theory) (Mann and Thompson, 1987) is a linguistic theory that correlates macro and micro units of discourse in a coherent way. The correlation is made among EDUs (Elementary Discourse Units). EDUs are defined at sentence, phrase or paragraph-level. These correlations are represented in the form of a tree. Marcu et al. (2000) explore RST focusing on identifying the feasibility of building a discourse-based MT system. Guzmán et al. (2014) use RST trees comparison for MT evaluation.

Topic models capture word usage, although they are more robust than lexical cohesion structures because they can correlate words that are not repetitions or do not present any semantic relation. These methods can measure if a document follows a topic, is related to a genre or belongs to a specific domain. Work on improving MT that uses topic models include Zhengxian et al. (2010) and Eidelman et al. (2012).

3 Planned Work

In this paper, we describe the three main research questions that we aim to answer in this PhD work:

1. How to address document-level QE?
2. Are discourse models appropriate to be used for QE at document level? Are these models applicable for different languages?
3. How can we use the discourse information for the evaluation of Automatic Summarisation and Readability Assessment?

In this section, we summarise how we are addressing these research questions.

3.1 Document-level Quality Estimation

As mentioned previously, one aim of this PhD is to identify a suitable quality label for document-level QE. Our hypothesis is that document quality is more complex than a simple aggregation of sentence quality. In order to exemplify this assumption, consider document A and document B. Documents A and B have the same number of sentences (10 sentences) and score the same value when we access quality as an average of HTER at sentence level, 0.5. However, 5 sentences of document A score 1 and the other five sentences score 0. On the other hand, document B shows a more smooth distribution of scores among sentences (the majority of the sentences score a value close to 0.5). Are document A and B comparable just because the averaged HTERs are the same? Our assumption is that a real score at document level or a more clever combination of sentence-level scores are the more suitable ways to evaluate documents.

Another drawback of averaging sentence-level scores is that sentences have different importance inside a document, they contain different information across a document. Therefore, documents that have important sentences badly translated should be penalised more heavily. The way we propose to address this problem is by using summarisation or information retrieval techniques in order to identify the most important sentences (or even paragraphs) and assign different weights according to the relevance of the sentence.

Moreover, we studied several traditional evaluation metrics as quality labels for QE at document level and found out that, on average, all the documents seem to be similar. Part of this study is showed in Table 1 for 9 documents of WMT2013 QE shared task corpus (English-Spanish translations) and for 119 documents of LIG corpus (Potet et al., 2012) (French-English translations, with post-editions).[3] The quality metrics considered were BLEU, TER, METEOR (Banerjee and Lavie, 2005) and an average of HTER scores at sentence level.

All traditional MT evaluation metrics showed low standard deviation (STDEV) in both corpora. Also the HTER at sentence level averaged to obtain a document-score showed low variation. This means that all documents in the corpora seem similar in terms of quality. Our hypothesis is that this evaluation is wrong and other factors should be considered in order to achieve a suitable quality label for document-level prediction.

Besides quality scores, another issue in document-level QE is the features to be used. Thus far, the majority of features for QE are at word or sentence level. Since a document can be viewed as a combination of words and sentences one way to explore document-level features is to combine word- or sentence-level features (by averaging them, for example). Another way is to explore linguistic phenomena document-wide. This is discussed on the next subsection.

New features and prediction at document level can be included in existing frameworks, such as QuEst. This is the first step to integrate document-level and sentence-level prediction and features.

3.2 Modelling discourse for Quality Estimation

Discourse phenomena happen document-wide and, therefore, these can be considered a strong candidate for the extraction of document-level features. A document is not only a bag of words and sentences, although the words and sentences are in fact organised in a logical way by using linguistic clues. Discourse was already studied in the MT field, aiming to improve MT systems and/or MT outputs and also to automatically evaluate MT against human references. However, for QE, we should be able to deal with evaluation for several language pairs, considering features for source and target. Another issue is that QE features should correlate with the quality score used. Therefore, the use of discourse for QE purposes deserves further investigation.

We intend to model discourse for QE by applying linguistic and statistical knowledge. Two cases are being explored:

3.2.1 Linguistic-based models

Certain discourse theories could be used to model discourse for QE purposes, such as such as the Rhetorical Structure Theory (RST) (Mann and Thompson, 1987) and Entity-Grid models (Barzilay and Lapata, 2008; Elsner, 2011). We refer to these two theories mainly because they can be readily applied, for English language, given the existence of

[3]Both corpora were translated by only one SMT system.

	WMT		LIG	
	Average	STDEV	Average	STDEV
BLEU (↑)	0.26	0.046	0.27	0.052
TER (↓)	0.52	0.049	0.53	0.069
METEOR-ex (↑)	0.46	0.050	0.29	0.031
METEOR-st (↑)	0.43	0.050	0.30	0.030
Averaged HTER (↓)	0.25	0.071	0.21	0.032

Table 1: Average values of evaluation metrics in the WMT and LIG corpora

parsers (RST parser (Joty et al., 2013) and Entity Grid parser).[4] Although these resources are only available for English, it is important in this stage to study the impact of this information for document-level QE, considering English as source or target language. In this scenario, we intend to explore source and target features isolated (source features will be applied only when English is source language and target features only when English is target).

Moreover, other linguistic information could be used to model discourse for QE. Anaphoric information, co-reference resolution and discourse connectives classification could be used. (Scarton and Specia, 2014) explore lexical cohesion features for QE. These features are based on repetitions of words or lemmas. Looking at more complex structures, such as synonym in order to count repetitions beyond word matching can lead to improvements in the results.

We have also studied linguistic phenomena and their correlations with HTER values at document level on the LIG corpus. Results are shown in Figure 1. This figure shows four scenarios with different numbers of documents. The first scenario has ten documents: the five best documents and the five worst (in terms of averaged HTER). The second scenario considers the ten best and ten worst, the third the 20 best and 20 worst and the fourth the 40 best and 40 worst. The last scenario considers all the data. The bars are Pearson's r correlation values between a given feature and the real HTER value. Features were: number of connectives, number of pronouns, number of RST nucleus relations, number of RST satellite relations, number of elementary discourse units (EDUs) breaks, lexical cohesion (LC) features and LSA features from the work of (Scarton and Specia, 2014). The most successful features of QuEst framework were also considered: QuEst1 - number of tokens, QuEst2 - language model probability, QuEst3 - number of occurrences of the target word within the target hypothesis (averaged for all words in the hypothesis - type/token ratio) and QuEst4 - number of punctuation marks. Features were only applied for target (English) due to resources availability.

Mainly for scenarios with 10 and 20 documents, features considering discourse phenomena counts performed better than QuEst features. In the other scenarios LC and LSA features were the best. It is worth mentioning that this study is on-going and much more can be extracted from discourse information such as RST, than only simple counts.

3.2.2 Latent variable models

Latent variable models such as Latent Dirichlet Allocation (LDA) (Blei et al., 2003) and Latent Semantic Analysis (LSA) (Landauer et al., 1998) have been widely used to extract topic models from corpora. The idea behind these methods is that a matrix of words versus sentences is built and mathematical transformations are applied, in order to achieve correlations among the word vectors. However, as Graesser et al. (2004) suggests, they can also be used to find lexical cohesion information within documents. In fact, topic modelling approaches have already been used to improve MT and also for QE at sentence level. Their advantage is that they are fast, language independent and do not require robust resources (such as discourse parsers). Previous work has used LSA and LDA for QE purposes (Scarton and Specia, 2014; Rubino et al., 2013).

We could also use latent variable models to find how close a machine translated document is from original documents in the same language, genre and domain.

[4]https://bitbucket.org/melsner/browncoherence

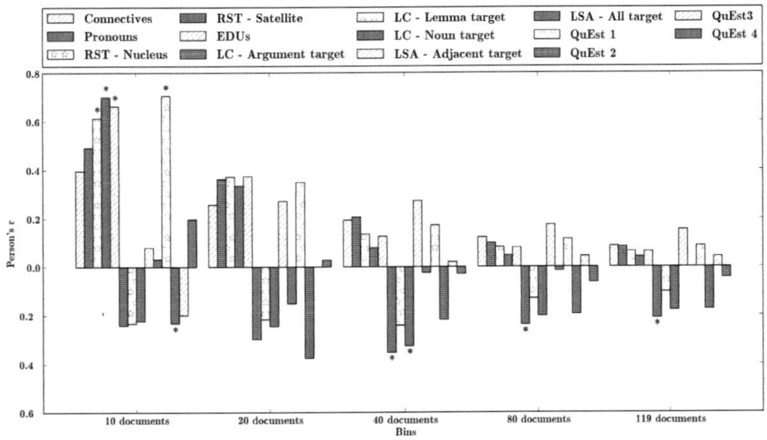

Figure 1: Impact of discourse features on document-level QE - '*' means *p-value* < 0.05

3.3 Using discourse models for other NLP tasks

One of our aims is to evaluate whether the discourse models built for QE can be used for the evaluation of other tasks in NLP. AS evaluation could benefit from QE: to an extent, AS outputs could be viewed as "translations" from "source language" into "source summarised language". Up to now, only (Louis and Nenkova, 2013) proposed an approach for evaluating summaries without references (by using pseudo-references). Moreover, discourse evaluation of AS outputs is expected to show more correlation with quality scores than MT because of the nature of the tasks. While MT outputs are dependent on the source language (and, as shown by Carpuat and Simard (2012), they tend to preserve discourse constituents of the source), AS outputs are built by choosing sentences from one or more documents trying to keep as much relevant information as possible. The combination of text from multiple documents can lead to loss of coherence of automatic summaries more than MT does to translated texts.

Another task in NLP that could benefit from advances in QE is **Readability Assessment (RA)**. This task consists in evaluating the complexity of documents for a given audience (therefore, the task is an evaluation per se). Several studies have already explored discourse information for RA (Graesser et al., 2004; Pitler and Nenkova, 2008; Todirascu et al., 2013). QE techniques can benefit RA in scenarios where we need to compare texts produced by or for native speakers or second language learners (SLL) or texts produced by or for mentally impaired patient compared to healthy subjects (in these scenarios, the documents produced by or for the "experts" could be considered as source documents and documents produced by or for "inexpert or mentally impaired" as target documents).

4 Conclusion

In this paper we presented a proposal to address to document-level quality estimation. This includes the study of quality labels for document-level prediction and also document-level features. We intend to focus on discourse features, because of the nature of discourse phenomena.

We showed that traditional MT evaluation metrics are not suitable for QE at document level because they cannot measure quality of documents according to relevance of sentences.

Discourse features were also evaluated for document-level QE showing higher correlation with HTER scores than the most successful features from QuEst framework. This is sign that discourse information can help in document-level prediction.

Finally, we discussed ways to use the discourse models developed for QE to improve evaluation of other NLP task: AS and RA.

Acknowledgments

This work was supported by the EXPERT (EU Marie Curie ITN No. 317471) project.

References

Hala Almaghout and Lucia Specia. 2013. A CCG-based Quality Estimation Metric for Statistical Machine Translation. In *The XIV Machine Translation Summit*, pages 223–230, Nice, France.

Eleftherios Avramidis, Maja Popovic, David Vilar Torres, and Aljoscha Burchardt. 2011. Evaluate with Confidence Estimation: Machine ranking of translation outputs using grammatical features. In *The Sixth Workshop on Statistical Machine Translation*, pages 65–70, Edinburgh, UK.

Satanjeev Banerjee and Alon Lavie. 2005. METEOR: An Automatic Metric for MT Evaluation with Improved Correlation with Human Judgments. In *The ACL 2005 Workshop on Intrinsic and Extrinsic Evaluation Measures for MT and/or Summarization*, pages 65–72, Ann Harbor, MI.

Regina Barzilay and Mirella Lapata. 2008. Modeling local coherence: An entity-based approach. *Computational Linguistics*, 34(1):1–34.

Gousheng Ben, Deyi Xiong, Zhiyang Teng, Yajuan Lu, and Qun Liu. 2013. Bilingual Lexical Cohesion Trigger Model for Document-Level Machine Translation. In *The 51st Annual Meeting of the Association for Computational Linguistics*, pages 382–386, Sofia, Bulgaria.

John Blatz, Erin Fitzgerald, George Foster, Simona Gandrabur, Cyril Goutte, Alex Kulesza, Alberto Sanchis, and Nicola Ueffing. 2004. Confidence Estimation for Machine Translation. In *The 20th International Conference on Computational Linguistics*, pages 315–321, Geneva, Switzerland.

David M. Blei, Andrew Y. Ng, and Michael I. Jordan. 2003. Latent Dirichlet Allocation. *The Journal of Machine Learning research*, 3:993–1022.

Ondřej Bojar, Christian Buck, Chris Callison-Burch, Christian Federmann, Barry Haddow, Philipp Koehn, Christof Monz, Matt Post, Radu Soricut, and Lucia Specia. 2013. Findings of the 2013 Workshop on Statistical Machine Translation. In *The Eighth Workshop on Statistical Machine Translation*, pages 1–44, Sofia, Bulgaria.

Marine Carpuat and Michel Simard. 2012. The Trouble with SMT Consistency. In *The Seventh Workshop on Statistical Machine Translation*, pages 442–449, Montréal, Quebec, Canada.

Vladimir Eidelman, Jordan Boyd-Graber, and Philip Resnik. 2012. Topic Models of Dynamic Translation Model Adaptation. In *The 50th Annual Meeting of the Association for Computational Linguistics*, pages 115–119, Jeju Island, Korea.

Micha Elsner. 2011. *Generalizing Local Coherence Modeling*. Ph.D. thesis, Department of Computer Science, Brown University, Providence, Rhode Island.

Mariano Felice and Lucia Specia. 2012. Linguistic Features for Quality Estimation. In *The Seventh Workshop on Statistical Machine Translation*, pages 96–103, Montréal, Quebec, Canada.

Jesús Giménez, Lluís Màrquez, Elisabet Comelles, Irene Catellón, and Victoria Arranz. 2010. Document-level Automatic MT Evaluation based on Discourse Representations. In *The Joint 5th Workshop on Statistical Machine Translation and MetricsMATR*, pages 333–338, Uppsala, Sweden.

Arthur C. Graesser, Danielle S. McNamara, Max M. Louwerse, and Zhiqiang Cai. 2004. Coh-Metrix: Analysis of text on cohesion and language. *Behavior Research Methods, Instruments, and Computers*, 36:193–202.

Francisco Guzmán, Shafiq Joty, Lluís Màrquez, and Preslav Nakov. 2014. Using Discourse Structure Improves Machine Translation Evaluation. In *The 52nd Annual Meeting of the Association for Computational Linguistics*, pages 687–698, Baltimore, MD.

Christian Hardmeier and Marcello Federico. 2010. Modelling Pronominal Anaphora in Statistical Machine Translation. In *The 7th International Workshop on Spoken Language Translation*, pages 283–289.

Christian Hardmeier. 2011. Improving machine translation quality prediction with syntatic tree kernels. In *Proceedings of the 15th conference of the European Assoaciation for Machine Translation (EAMT 2011)*, pages 233–240, Leuven, Belgium.

Christian Hardmeier. 2014. *Discourse in Statistical Machine Translation*. Ph.D. thesis, Department of Linguistics and Philology, Uppsala University, Sweden.

Shafiq Joty, Giuseppe Carenini, Raymond T. Ng, and Yashar Mehdad. 2013. Combining Intra- and Multi-sentential Rhetorical Parsing for Document-level Discourse Analysis. In *The 51st Annual Meeting of the Association for Computational Linguistics*, pages 486–496, Sofia, Bulgaria.

Thomas K. Landauer, Peter W. Foltz, and Darrell Laham. 1998. An Introduction to Latent Semantic Analysis. *Discourse Processes*, 25:259–284.

Ronan LeNagard and Philipp Kohen. 2010. Aiding Pronoun Translation with Co-Reference Resolution. In *The Joint 5th Workshop on Statistical Machine Translation and MetricsMATR*, pages 252–261, Uppasala, Sweden.

Junyi Jessy Li, Marine Carpuat, and Ani Nenkova. 2014. Assessing the Discourse Factors that Influence the Quality of Machine Translation. In *The 52nd Annual Meeting of the Association for Computational Linguistics*, pages 283–288, Baltimore, MD.

Chin-Yew Lin and Franz J. Och. 2004. Automatic Evaluation of Machine Translation Quality Using Longest

Common Subsequence and Skip-Bigram Statics. In *The 42nd Meeting of the Association for Computational Linguistics*, pages 605–612, Barcelona, Spain.

Annie Louis and Ani Nenkova. 2013. Automatically Assessing Machine Summary Content Without a Gold Standard. *Computational Linguistics*, 39(2):267–300, June.

Willian C. Mann and Sandra A. Thompson. 1987. *Rhetorical Structure Theory: A Theory of Text Organization*. Cambridge University Press, Cambridge, UK.

Daniel Marcu, Lynn Carlson, and Maki Watanabe. 2000. The automatic translation of discourse structures. In *The 1st North American chapter of the Association for Computational Linguistics conference*, pages 9–17. Association for Computational Linguistics, April.

Thomas Meyer and Andrei Popescu-Belis. 2012. Using Sense-labeled Discourse Connectives for Statistical Machine Translation. In *The Joint Workshop on Exploiting Synergies between Information Retrieval and Machine Translation (ESIRMT) and Hybrid Approaches to Machine Translation (HyTra)*, pages 129–138, Avignon, France.

Thomas Meyer, Andrei Popescu-Belis, Najeh Hajlaoui, and Andrea Gesmundo. 2012. Machine translation of labeled discourse connectives. In *The Tenth Biennial Conference of the Association for Machine Translation in the Americas*, San Diego, CA.

Kishore Papineni, Salim Roukos, Todd Ward, and Wei jing Zhu. 2002. BLEU: a Method for Automatic Evaluation of Machine Translation. In *The 40th Annual Meeting of the Association for Computational Linguistics*, pages 311–318, Philadelphia, PA.

Daniele Pighin and Lluís Màrquez. 2011. Automatic Projection of Semantic Structures: an Application to Pairwise Translation R anking. In *The Fifth Workshop on Syntax, Semantics and Structure in Statistical Translation*, pages 1–9, Portland, OR.

Emily Pitler and Ani Nenkova. 2008. Revisiting Readability: A Unified Framework for Predicting Text Quality. In *The Conference on Empirical Methods in Natural Language Processing*, pages 186–195, Waikiki, Honolulu, Hawaii.

Andrei Popescu-Belis, Thomas Meyer, Jeevanthi Liyanapathirana, Bruno Cartoni, and Sandrine Zufferey. 2012. Discourse-level Annotation over Europarl for Machine Translation: Connectives and Pronouns. In *The Eighth International Conference on Language Resources and Evaluation*, pages 2716–2720, Istanbul, Turkey.

Marion Potet, Emmanuelle Esperança-Rodier, Laurent Besacier, and Hervé Blanchon. 2012. Collection of a Large Database of French-English SMT Output Corrections. In *The 8th International Conference on Language Resources and Evaluation*, pages 23–25, Istanbul, Turkey.

Raphael Rubino, Jos G. C. de Souza, Jennifer Foster, and Lucia Specia. 2013. Topic Models for Translation Quality Estimation for Gisting Purposes. In *The XIV Machine Translation Summit*, pages 295–302, Nice, France.

Carolina Scarton and Lucia Specia. 2014. Document-level translation quality estimation: exploring discourse and pseudo-references. In *The 17th Annual Conference of the European Association for Machine Translation*, pages 101–108, Dubrovnik, Croatia.

Matthew Snover, Bonnie Dorr, Richard Schwartz, Linnea Micciulla, and John Makhoul. 2006. A Study of Translation Edit Rate with Targeted Human Annotation. In *The Seventh Biennial Conference of the Association for Machine Translation in the Americas*, pages 223–231, Cambridge, MA.

Radu Soricut and Abdessamad Echihabi. 2010. TrustRank: Inducing Trust in Automatic Translations via Ranking. In *The 48th Annual Meeting of the Association for Computational Linguistics*, pages 612–621, Uppsala, Sweden.

Lucia Specia, Kashif Shah, Jose G.C. de Souza, and Trevor Cohn. 2013. QuEst - A translation quality estimation framework. In *The 51st Annual Meeting of the Association for Computational Linguistics: System Demonstrations*, pages 79–84, Sofia, Bulgaria.

Amalia Todirascu, Thomas Françoí, Nuria Gala, Cédric Fairon, Anne-Laure Ligozat, and Delphine Bernhard. 2013. Coherence and Cohesion for the Assessment of Text Readability. In *The 10th International Workshop on Natural Language Processing and Cognitive Science*, pages 11–19, Marseille, France.

Ferhan Ture, Douglas W. Oard, and Philip Resnik. 2012. Encouraging Consistent Translation Choices. In *The 12th Annual Conference of the North American Chapter of the Association for Computational Linguistics*, pages 417–426, Montréal, Quebec, Canada.

Billy T. M. Wong and Chunyu Kit. 2012. Extending Machine Translation Evaluation Metrics with Lexical Cohesion to Document Level. In *The 2012 Joint Conference on Empirical Methods in Natural Language Processing and Computational Natural Language Learning*, pages 1060–1068, Jeju Island, Korea.

Tong Xiao, Jingbo Zhu, Shujie Yao, and Hao Zhang. 2011. Document-level Consistency Verification in Machine Translation. In *The XII Machine Translation Summit*, pages 131–138, Xiamen, China.

Gong Zhengxian, Zhang Yu, and Zhou Guodong. 2010. Statistical Machine Translation Based on LDA. In *The 4th International Universal Communication Symposium*, pages 279–283, Beijing, China.

Speeding Document Annotation with Topic Models

Forough Poursabzi-Sangdeh and Jordan Boyd-Graber
Computer Science
University of Colorado Boulder
{forough.poursabzisangdeh, Jordan.Boyd.Graber}@colorado.edu

Abstract

Document classification and topic models are useful tools for managing and understanding large corpora. Topic models are used to uncover underlying semantic and structure of document collections. Categorizing large collection of documents requires hand-labeled training data, which is time consuming and needs human expertise. We believe engaging user in the process of document labeling helps reduce annotation time and address user needs. We present an interactive tool for document labeling. We use topic models to help users in this procedure. Our preliminary results show that users can more effectively and efficiently apply labels to documents using topic model information.

1 Introduction

Many fields depend on texts labeled by human experts; computational linguistics uses such annotation to determine word senses and sentiment (Kelly and Stone, 1975; Kim and Hovy, 2004); social science uses "coding" to scale up and systemetize content analysis (Budge, 2001; Klingemann et al., 2006). In general text classification is a standard tool for managing large document collections.

However, these labeled data have to come from somewhere. The process for creating a broadly applicable, consistent, and generalizable label set and then applying them to the dataset is long and difficult, requiring expensive annotators to examine large swaths of the data.

We present a user interactive tool for document labeling that uses topic models to help users assign appropriate labels to documents (Section 2). In Section 3, we describe our user interface and experiments on Congressional Bills data set. We also explain an evaluation metric to assess the quality of assigned document labels. In preliminary results, we show that annotators can more quickly label a document collection given a topic modeling overview. While engaging user in the process of content-analysis has been studied before(as we discuss in Section 4), in Section 4 we describe how our new framework allows for more flexibility and interactivity. Finally, in Section 5, we discuss the limitation of our framework and how we plan to extend it in future.

2 Interactive Document Labeling

We propose an alternative framework for assigning labels to documents. We use topic models to give an overview of the document contents to the user. Users can create a label set incrementally, see the content of documents, assign labels to documents, and classify documents. They can go back and forth in these steps and edit label set or document labels and re-classify.

Having labeled documents is necessary for automatic text classification. With a large collection of unstructured documents, labeling can be excruciating since it is essential to label enough documents in different labels to obtain acceptable accuracy. Topic models are a solution to reduce this effort since they provide some information about the underlying theme of corpus. Given a fixed number of topics, topic models

Proceedings of NAACL-HLT 2015 Student Research Workshop (SRW), pages 126–132,
Denver, Colorado, June 1, 2015.

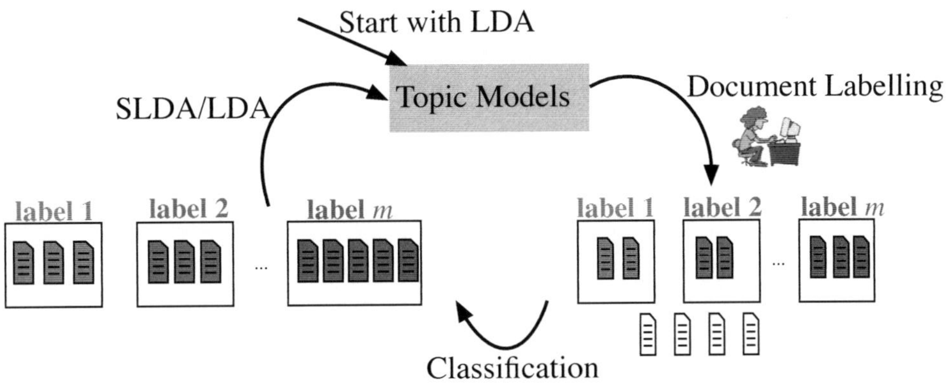

Figure 1: Interactive document labeling: Start with LDA topic modeling, show users relevant documents for each topic, get user labels, classify documents, and use SLDA to generate topics[1]. Repeat this until the user is satisfied with labels.

output (i) a set of words for each topic (*Topic words*) and (ii) a distribution over topics for each document (*Document's Topic Distribution*).

Topic words can be used to reveal the content of a topic and thus content of documents with a high probability of that topic. Therefore, assuming the number of topics is chosen carefully, top documents for each topic are similar in content and can be labeled appropriately.

Thus, rather than showing an unstructured collection of documents to the user, providing the topic words and highly relevant documents to that topic helps them in the process of document labeling, both in the step of choosing appropriate label names and choosing appropriate document to assign a label to. Another way to think about this is that if the topics are perfect (they are not too general or too detailed), all labels associated with the topic's high relevant documents can be viewed as subjects explaining the topic. Table 1 provides an example of how topic models can help a user craft document labels.

Having a set of user labeled documents, classification algorithms can be used to predict the label of unseen documents. Next, classification results are shown. Users can change document labels. They can also edit/delete label set and re-run the classifier. The explained procedure can be repeated iteratively until satisfaction is achieved with existing (*document,label*) pairs. Figure 1 shows the explained procedure.

3 Experiments with Interactive Labeling Interface

Data: In our experiments, we need a labeled corpus to be able to assess the quality of user-generated labels. We chose US Congressional Bills corpus (Adler and Wilkerson, 2006). GovTrack provides bill texts along with the discussed congressional issues as labels. Example of labels are "education", "agriculture", "health", and "defense". There are total of 19 unique labels. We use the 112th congress, which has 12274 documents. We remove bills with no assigned gold label or that are short. We end with 6528 documents.

Topic Modeling: To generate topics, we use Mallet (McCallum, 2002) to apply LDA on the data. A set of extra stop words are generated based on TF-IDF scores to avoid displaying non-informative words to the user.

Features and Classification: A crucial step for text classification is to extract useful features to represent documents. Some common features for text classification are n-grams, which makes the dimensionality very high and classification slower. Since response time is very important in user interactive systems, instead of n-grams, we

[1]Currently, we are not using SLDA. We just use the original topics generated by LDA. The idea behind SLDA is explained in Section 5.

Topic	Words	Document Title	Document Labels
16	dod, sbir, afghanistan, phase, sttr, missile, combat, capabilities, command, elements	HR 4243 IH 112th CONGRESS 2d Session H. R. 4243 To strengthen the North Atlantic Treaty Organization.	military
19	historic, conveyance, dated, monument, depicted, generally, boundary, creek, preservation, recreation	HR 4334 IH 112th CONGRESS 2d Session H. R. 4334 To establish a monument in Dona Ana County, New Mexico, and for other purposes.	wildlife
		S 617 IS 112th CONGRESS 1st Session S. 617 To require the Secretary of the Interior to convey certain Federal land to Elko County, Nevada, and to take land into trust for the Te-moak Tribe of Western Shoshone Indians of Nevada, and for other purposes.	nature

Table 1: An example of topic words and the labels user has assigned to top documents for that topic.

use topic probabilities as features, which reduces the dimensionality and classification time significantly. User can choose 10, 15, 25, or 50 topics. We want to show the label probabilities generated by classifier to users. We use Liblinear (Fan et al., 2008) to run L2 regularized logistic regression for classifying documents and generating label probabilities.

Interface: We start with the web-based interface of Hu et al. (2014) for interactive topic modeling. The existing interface starts with asking user information, corpus name, and number of topics they want to explore. Then it displays topic words and the most relevant documents for each topic. Also, the user can see the content of documents. Users can create new labels and/or edit/delete an existing label.

When seeing a document, user has 3 options:

1. Create a new label and assign that label to the document.
2. Choose an existing label for the document.
3. Skip the document.

At any point, the user can run the classifier. After classification is finished, the predicted labels along with the certainty is shown for each document. User can edit/delete document labels and re-run classifier as many times as they desire. We Refer to this task as *Topic Guided Annotation*(TGA).

Figure 2 shows a screenshot of the interface when choosing a label for a document.

3.1 Evaluation

We introduce an interactive framework for document labeling using topic models. In this section, we evaluate our system.

Our goal is to measure whether showing users a topic modeling overview of the corpus helps them apply labels to documents more effectively and efficiently. Thus, we compare user-generated labels (considering labels assigned by user and classifier altogether) with gold labels of US Congressional Bills provided by GovTrack. Since user labels can be more specific than gold labels, we want each user label to be "pure" in gold labels. Thus, we use the purity score (Zhao and Karypis, 2001) to measure how many gold labels are associated with each user label. Purity score is

$$\text{purity}(\mathscr{U},\mathscr{G}) = \frac{1}{N}\sum_k \max_j |U_k \cap G_j|, \qquad (1)$$

where $\mathscr{U} = \{U_1, U_2, ..., U_K\}$ is the user clustering of documents, $\mathscr{G} = \{G_1, G_2, ..., G_J\}$ is gold clustering of documents, and N is the total number of documents. Moreover, we interpret U_k and G_j as the set of documents in user cluster U_K or gold cluster G_j. Figure 3 shows an example of purity calculation for a clustering, given gold labels.

Purity is an external metric for cluster evaluation. A very bad labeling has a purity score close to 0 and a perfect labeling has purity score of 1.

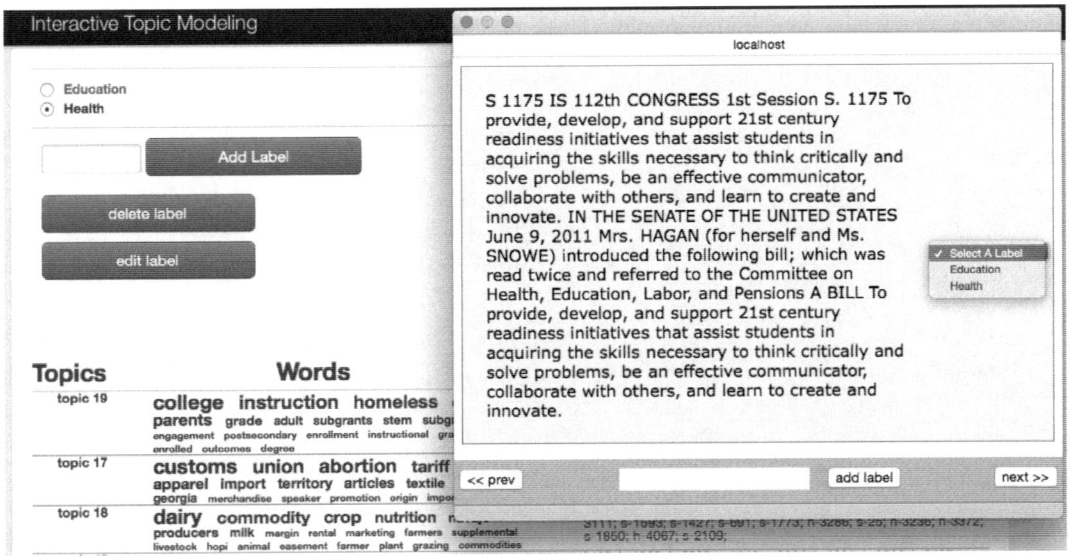

Figure 2: A screenshot of interactive document labeling interface. The user sees topic words and the most relevant documents for each topic. The user has created two labels: "Education" and "Health" and sees the content of a documents. The user can create a new label and assign the new label to the document, or choose one of the two existing labels to assign to the document, or skip the document and view the previous or next document.

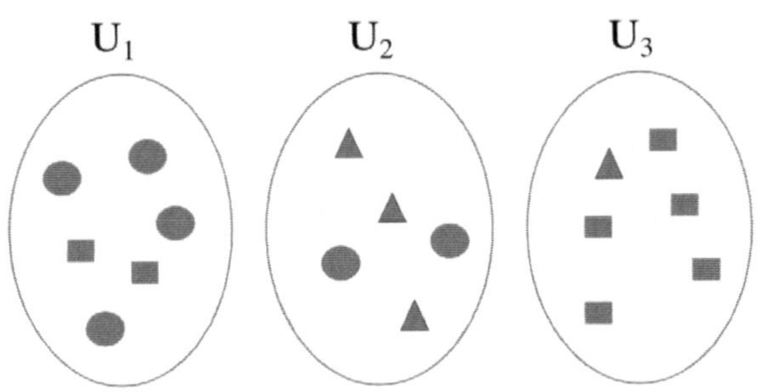

Figure 3: An example of computing purity: Clusters correspond to user labels and different shapes correspond to different associated gold labels. Majority gold label numbers for three clusters are $4(U_1)$, $3(U_2)$, and $5(U_3)$. Purity is $\frac{1}{17} \times (4+3+5) \approx 0.71$.

The higher this score, the higher the quality of user labels.

To evaluate TGA, We did a study on two different users. For User 1, we chose 15 topics and for User 2, we chose 25 topics. They were asked to stop labeling whenever they were satisfied with the predicted document labels.

We compare the user study results with a baseline. Our baseline ignores topic modeling information for choosing documents to labels. It considers the scenario when users are given a large document collection and are asked to categorize the documents without any other information. Thus, we show randomly chosen documents to users and want them to apply label to them. All users can go back and edit or delete document labels, or refuse to label a document if they find it confusing. After each single labeling, we use the same features and classifier that we used for user study with topic models to classify documents. Then we calculate purity for user labels with respect to gold labels. Figure 4 shows the purity score over different number of labeled documents for User 1, User 2, and baseline.

User 1 did the labeling in 6 rounds, whereas User 2 did total of 7 rounds. User 1 ended with 116 labeled documents and user 2 had 42 labeled documents in the end.

User 2 starts with a label set of size 9 and labels 11 documents. Two documents are labeled as "wildlife", other two are labeled as "tax", and all other documents have unique labels. This means that even if there are very few instance per label, baseline is outperformed. This is an evidence of

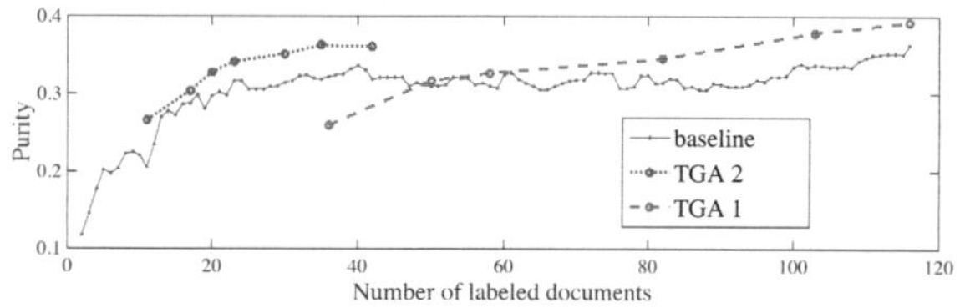

Figure 4: Purity score over number of labeled documents. TGA 1 and TGA 2 refer to results for User 1 and User 2.

User 1	Baseline
36	12
50	52
58	60
82	109
103	> 116
116	> 116

(a)

User 2	Baseline
11	12
17	18
20	38
23	40
30	112
35	116
42	115

(b)

Table 2: The number of required labeled documents for baseline to get the same purity score as (a) User 1 (b) User 2, in each round

choosing informative documents to assign labels with the help of topic models. On the other hand, User 1 starts with a label set of size 7 and labels 36 documents and is outperformed by baseline significantly. One reason for this is that assigning too many documents relevant to a topic, with the same label doesn't provide any new information to the classifier and thus the user could get the same purity score with a lower number of labeled documents, which would lead to outperforming baseline. User 1 outperforms the baseline in the second (8 labels and 50 labeled documents) and third round (9 labels and 58 labeled documents) slightly. In the fourth round, user creates more labels. With total of 13 labels and 82 labeled documents, the gap between user's purity score and baseline gets larger. Both users outperform baseline in the final round.

To see how topic models help speed up labeling process, we compare the number of user labeled documents with the approximate number of required labeled documents to get the same purity score in baseline. Table 2 shows the results for User 1 and User 2.

User 1 starts with man labeled documents and baseline can achieve the same performance with one third of the labeled documents. As the user keeps labeling more documents, the performance improves and baseline needs more labeled documents to get the same level of purity. For User 2, baseline on average needs over two times as many labeled documents to achieve the same purity score as user labels. These tables indicate that topic models help users choose documents to assign labels to and achieve an acceptable performance with fewer labeled documents.

4 Related Work

Topic Models such as Latent Dirichlet Allocation (Blei et al., 2003, LDA) are unsupervised learning algorithms and are a useful tool for understanding the content of large collection of documents. The topics found by these models are the set of words that are observed together in many documents and they introduce correlation among words. Top words in each topic explain the semantics of that topic. Moreover, each document is considered a mixture of topics. Top topics for each document explain the semantics of that document.

When all documents are assigned a label, supervised topic models can be used. SLDA (Mcauliffe and Blei, 2008) is a supervised topic model that generates topics that give an overview of both document contents and assigned labels. Perotte et al. (2011) extend SLDA and introduce HSLDA, which is a model for large-scale multiply-labeled documents and takes advantage of hierarchical structure in label space. HSLDA is used for label prediction. In general, supervised topic models help users understand labeled document collections.

Text classification predicts a label for documents and help manage document collections. There are known classifiers as well as feature extraction methods for this task. However, providing an initial set of labeled documents for both text classification and supervised topic models still requires lots of time and human effort.

Active learning (Settles, 2010), reduces the amount of required labeled data by having a learner which actively queries the label for specific documents and collects a labeled training set. In a user interactive system, the active learner queries document labels from users (Settles, 2010). In other words, the learner suggests some documents to the user and wants the user to assign a label to those. Settles (2011) discusses that having interactive users in annotation process along with active learning, reduces the amount of annotation time while still achieving acceptable performance. In more detail, they presents an interactive learning framework to get user annotations and produce accurate classifiers in less time. The shortcoming of active learning is that they don't provide any overview information of corpus, like topic model approaches do.

Nevertheless, new methods in both analysis and evaluation are needed. Classification algorithms restrict document labels to a predefined label set. Grimmer and Stewart (2013) show that to be able to use the output of automatic text analysis in political science, we need careful validation methods. There has been some work done on bringing user in this task for refining and evaluating existing methods. Hu et al. (2014) show that topic models are not perfect from the user view and introduce a framework to interactively get user feedback and refine topic models. Chuang et al. (2013) present an interactive visualization for exploring documents by topic models to address user needs.

We bring these tools together to speed up annotation process. We believe having users engaged in content analysis, not only reduces the amount of annotation time, but also helps to achieve user satisfaction. We propose an iterative and user interactive procedure for document annotation. We use topic models to provide some high-level information about the corpus and guid users in this task. We show top words and documents for each topic to the user and have them start labeling documents. Users can create/edit/delete labels. Then users can run a classifier to predict the labels for the unlabeled documents. They can change document labels and re-classify documents iteratively, until satisfaction is achieved.

5 Future Work

There are some obvious directions that will expand this ongoing research. First, we are planning to use active learning to better aid classification. We expect that active learning will reduce the number of required labeled documents while still getting a high purity score and user satisfaction.

Second, we will use supervised topic models (Mcauliffe and Blei, 2008, SLDA) instead of LDA after the first round to update topics based on document labels. SLDA uses labeled documents to find topics that explain both document content and their associated labels. We believe using SLDA instead of LDA after the first round will give users more information about the overview of documents and help them further for applying labels to documents.

Third, we want to allow the user to refine and correct labels further. Our existing interface allows the user to delete a label or edit a label. We believe it is also important for users to merge labels if they think the labels are too specific. In addition, we believe a crucially important step is to generate the label set. Giving the user some information about the range of documents can help them generate a better label set. One other option is to suggest labels to users based on topic models (Lau et al., 2010).

Fourth, we will explore other corpora such as European Parliament corpus (Koehn, 2005). To our knowledge, there are no true labels for Europarl corpus and using our interactive tool can help users find the categorized information they need.

Finally, for evaluating our method, in addition to using the correct labeling and purity score, we will conduct a user experiment with more users involved. Since the task of labeling congress data set requires some political knowledge, we will choose annotators who have some political science background.

Acknowledgments

We thank the anonymous reviewers for their insightful comments. We thank Dr. Niklas Elmqvist for his advice for revising the user interface. We also thank Alvin Grissom II for helping us in the user study. This work was supported by NSF Grant NCSE-1422492. Any opinions, findings, results, or recommendations expressed here are of the authors and do not necessarily reflect the view of the sponsor.

References

E Scott Adler and John Wilkerson. 2006. Congressional bills project. *NSF*, 880066:00880061.

David M. Blei, Andrew Ng, and Michael Jordan. 2003. Latent Dirichlet allocation. *Journal of Machine Learning Research*, 3.

Ian Budge. 2001. *Mapping policy preferences: estimates for parties, electors, and governments, 1945-1998*, volume 1. Oxford University Press.

Jason Chuang, Yuening Hu, Ashley Jin, John D Wilkerson, Daniel A McFarland, Christopher D Manning, and Jeffrey Heer. 2013. Document exploration with topic modeling: Designing interactive visualizations to support effective analysis workflows. In *NIPS Workshop on Topic Models: Computation, Application, and Evaluation.*

Rong-En Fan, Kai-Wei Chang, Cho-Jui Hsieh, Xiang-Rui Wang, and Chih-Jen Lin. 2008. Liblinear: A library for large linear classification. *The Journal of Machine Learning Research*, 9:1871–1874.

Justin Grimmer and Brandon M Stewart. 2013. Text as data: The promise and pitfalls of automatic content analysis methods for political texts. *Political Analysis*, page mps028.

Yuening Hu, Jordan Boyd-Graber, Brianna Satinoff, and Alison Smith. 2014. Interactive topic modeling. *Machine learning*, 95(3):423–469.

Edward F Kelly and Philip J Stone. 1975. *Computer recognition of English word senses*, volume 13. North-Holland.

Soo-Min Kim and Eduard Hovy. 2004. Determining the sentiment of opinions. In *Proceedings of the 20th international conference on Computational Linguistics*, page 1367. Association for Computational Linguistics.

Hans-Dieter Klingemann, Andrea Volkens, Judith Bara, Ian Budge, Michael D McDonald, et al. 2006. *Mapping policy preferences II: estimates for parties, electors, and governments in Eastern Europe, European Union, and OECD 1990-2003.* Oxford University Press Oxford.

Philipp Koehn. 2005. Europarl: A parallel corpus for statistical machine translation. In *MT summit*, volume 5, pages 79–86.

Jey Han Lau, David Newman, Sarvnaz Karimi, and Timothy Baldwin. 2010. Best topic word selection for topic labelling. In *Coling 2010: Posters*, pages 605–613, Beijing, China, August.

Jon D Mcauliffe and David M Blei. 2008. Supervised topic models. In *Advances in neural information processing systems*, pages 121–128.

Andrew Kachites McCallum. 2002. Mallet: A machine learning for language toolkit. http://www.cs.umass.edu/ mccallum/mallet.

Adler J. Perotte, Frank Wood, Noemie Elhadad, and Nicholas Bartlett. 2011. Hierarchically supervised latent Dirichlet allocation. In *Advances in Neural Information Processing Systems 24*, pages 2609–2617.

Burr Settles. 2010. Active learning literature survey. *University of Wisconsin, Madison*, 52(55-66):11.

Burr Settles. 2011. Closing the loop: Fast, interactive semi-supervised annotation with queries on features and instances. In *Proceedings of the Conference on Empirical Methods in Natural Language Processing*, pages 1467–1478. Association for Computational Linguistics.

Ying Zhao and George Karypis. 2001. Criterion functions for document clustering: Experiments and analysis. Technical report, Citeseer.

Lifelong Machine Learning for Topic Modeling and Beyond

Zhiyuan Chen
Department of Computer Science
University of Illinois at Chicago
czyuanacm@gmail.com

Abstract

Machine learning has been popularly used in numerous natural language processing tasks. However, most machine learning models are built using a single dataset. This is often referred to as one-shot learning. Although this one-shot learning paradigm is very useful, it will never make an NLP system understand the natural language because it does not accumulate knowledge learned in the past and make use of the knowledge in future learning and problem solving. In this thesis proposal, I first present a survey of *lifelong machine learning* (LML). I then narrow down to one specific NLP task, i.e., topic modeling. I propose several approaches to apply lifelong learning idea in topic modeling. Such capability is essential to make an NLP system versatile and holistic.

1 Introduction

Machine learning serves as a prevalent approach for research in many natural language processing tasks. However, most of existing machine learning approaches are built using a single dataset, which is often referred to as one-shot learning. This kind of one-shot approach is useful but it does not usually perform well to various datasets or tasks. The main shortcoming of such one-short approach is the lack of continuous learning ability, i.e., learning and accumulating knowledge from past tasks and leveraging the knowledge for future tasks and problem solving in a lifelong manner.

To overcome the above shortcoming, *lifelong machine learning* (LML) has attracted researchers' attention. The term was initially introduced in 1990s (Thrun, 1995, Caruana, 1997). LML aims to design and develop computational systems and algorithms that learn as humans do, i.e., retaining the results learned in the past, abstracting knowledge from them, and using the knowledge to help future learning. The motivation is that when faced with a new situation, we humans always use our previous experience and learned knowledge to help deal with and learn from the new situation, i.e., we learn and accumulate knowledge continuously. The same rationale can be applied to computational models. When a model is built using a single dataset for a task, its performance is limited. However, if the model sees more datasets from the same or similar tasks, it should be able to adjust its learning algorithm for better performance. There are four components in a LML framework: knowledge representation, knowledge extraction, knowledge transfer, and knowledge retention and maintenance. These components are closely connected. I will illustrate each component using examples from topic modeling in Section 3.

Compared to the significant progress of machine learning theory and algorithm, there is relatively little study on lifelong machine learning. One of the most notable works is Never-Ending Language Learner (NELL) (Carlson et al., 2010) which was proposed to extract or read information from the web to expand the knowledge base in an endless manner, aiming to achieve better performance in each day than the previous day. Recently, we proposed **lifelong Topic Modeling** (**LTM**) that extracts knowledge from topic modeling results of many domains and utilizes the knowledge to generate coherent topics in the new domains (Chen and Liu, 2014b). In (Ruvolo and Eaton, 2013), the authors proposed a method that tackles online multi-task learning in the lifelong learning setting. Some other LML related works include (Silver, 2013, Raina et al., 2007, Pentina and Lampert, 2014, Kamar et al., 2013, Kapoor and Horvitz, 2009). Note that LML is different from transfer learning which usually considers one single source domain where the knowledge is coming from and one target domain where the knowledge is applied on (Pan and Yang, 2010).

Proceedings of NAACL-HLT 2015 Student Research Workshop (SRW), pages 133–139,
Denver, Colorado, June 1, 2015.

In this thesis proposal, I narrow down the scope and focus on LML in topic modeling. Topic modeling has been successfully applied to extract semantic topics from text data. However, the majority of existing topic models (one exception is the LTM model mentioned before) belong to the one-shot approach, i.e., they are proposed to address a specific problem without any knowledge accumulation. To leverage the idea of LML, I propose several new approaches to advance topic modeling. I believe that the proposed approaches can significantly advance LML in topic modeling. More broadly, this thesis proposal aims to encourage the community to apply LML in a variety of NLP tasks.

This thesis proposal makes the following three contributions:

1. It studies and discusses lifelong machine learning (LML) in natural language processing. It identifies several important components in LML: knowledge representation, knowledge extraction, knowledge transfer, knowledge retention and maintenance. As there is relatively little study on LML compared to classic machine learning, I believe this thesis proposal will shed some light on the area and encourage the NLP community to advance the area of LML.
2. It reviews the LTM model and discusses the model in terms of LML components. In each component, the model mechanism as well as the shortcomings are discussed.
3. It proposes several new approaches to improve LML in the context of topic modeling. It proposes to enrich the knowledge representation, address knowledge conflicts, select domains and make the algorithm scalable. It further proposes new evaluation frameworks for LTM.

2 Background of Topic Modeling

Topic modeling, such as LDA (Blei et al., 2003) and pLSA (Hofmann, 1999), have been popularly used in many NLP tasks such as opinion mining (Chen et al., 2014), machine translation (Eidelman et al., 2012), word sense disambiguation (Boyd-Graber et al., 2007), phrase extraction (Fei et al., 2014) and information retrieval (Wei and Croft, 2006). In general, topic models assume that each document is a multinomial distribution over topics, where each topic is a multinomial distribution over words. The two types of distributions in topic modeling are document-topic distributions and topic-word distributions respectively. The intuition is that words are more or less likely to be present given the topics of a document. For example, "sport" and "player" will appear more often in documents about sports, "rain" and "cloud" will appear more frequently in documents about weather.

My work is mainly related to knowledge-based topic models (Chen and Liu, 2014a, Andrzejewski et al., 2009) which incorporate different types of prior knowledge into topic models. Supervised label information was considered in (Blei and McAuliffe, 2010, Ramage et al., 2009). Some works also enable the user to specify prior knowledge as seed words/terms for some topics (Mukherjee and Liu, 2012). Interactive topic modeling was proposed in (Hu et al., 2011) to improve topics with the interactive help from the user. However, these works require labeled data or user manual guidance while my proposed approaches do not.

3 Lifelong Topic Modeling

This section introduces the LTM model (Chen and Liu, 2014b). It first presents the overall algorithm of LTM. Then it reviews the model using the four components in the LML framework: knowledge representation, knowledge extraction, knowledge transfer, and knowledge retention and maintenance.

3.1 Overall Algorithm

The basic idea of LTM is that it extracts knowledge from the topic results obtained by topic models in the previous domains or tasks. The knowledge should reflect the correct semantic relationship by investigating different topic model results. By exploiting such knowledge, the LTM model can generate more coherent topics. It consists of 3 main steps:

1. Given a set of document corpora $D = \{D_1, \ldots, D_n\}$ from n domains, LTM runs a topic model (e.g., LDA) on each $D_i \in D$ to produce a set of topics S_i. Such topics are called the *prior topics* (or *p-topics* for short), forming the *topic base* in LTM.
2. A set of *pk-sets* (prior knowledge sets) K are mined from all the p-topics $S = \cup_i S_i$ in the topic

base. The *knowledge base* in LTM is composed of such pk-sets.

3. The knowledge, i.e., pk-sets K, is used in LTM to generate topics for a test document collection D^t (D^t may or may not be from D).

3.2 Knowledge Representation

The prior knowledge set (pk-sets) K for LTM is represented by *must-links*, i.e., if a pair of words form a must-link, they are more likely to belong to the same topic. For example, words "price" and "expensive" can form a must-link. Such knowledge representation is also used in other topic models such as (Andrzejewski et al., 2009). However, they did not model in the lifelong setting. The must-links indicate a positive semantic relationship while some other existing models (Chen and Liu, 2014a, Andrzejewski et al., 2009) also used the negative relationship called *cannot-links*. Cannot-links express that two words do not share the semantic meaning, e.g., words "price" and "beauty". Note that for topic modeling, semantics related knowledge is mostly beneficial as topic modeling tries to group words into topics with different semantics.

3.3 Knowledge Extraction

To extract pk-sets from all the prior topics (Step 2 in Section 3.1, LTM utilizes frequent itemset mining (FIM) (Agrawal and Srikant, 1994). The goal of FIM is to identify all itemsets (an itemset is a set of items) that satisfy some user-specified frequency threshold (also called minimum support) in a set of transactions. The identified itemsets are called frequent itemsets. In the context of LTM, an item is a word and an itemset is a set of words. Each transaction consists of the top words in a past topic. Note that top words ranked by the topic-word distribution from topic modeling are more likely to represent the true semantics embedded in the latent topic. The frequent itemsets of length 2 are used as pk-sets. The rationale for using frequency-based approach is that a piece of knowledge is more reliable when it appears frequent in the prior topics.

3.4 Knowledge Transfer

For topic modeling, Gibbs sampling is a popular inference technique (Griffiths and Steyvers, 2004). The Gibbs sampler for LDA corresponds to the *simple Pólya urn (SPU)* model (Mimno et al., 2011). In SPU, a ball of a color (each color denotes each word) is randomly drawn from an urn (each urn corresponds to each topic) and then two balls of the same color are put back into the urn. It increases the probability of seeing a ball of the drawn color in the future, which is known as "the rich get richer".

LTM instead uses the *generalized Pólya urn (GPU)* model (Mahmoud, 2008). The difference is that after sampling the ball of a certain color, two balls of that color are put back along with a certain number of balls of some other colors. This flexibility is able to change the probability of multiple colors in each sampling step. Based on the GPU model, LTM increases the probabilities of both words in a pk-set when seeing either of them. For example, given the pk-set {price, expensive}, seeing word "price" under topic t will increase the probability of seeing word "expensive" under topic t; and vice versa. In other words, word "price" promotes word "expensive" under topic t. The extent of promotion of words is determined by the promotion scale parameter μ. This mechanism can transfer the information from the knowledge to the topics generated by LTM.

Since the knowledge is automatically extracted, to ensure the knowledge quality, LTM proposes two additional mechanisms. First, for each topic in the current domain, it uses KL-Divergence to find the matched topics from the topic base. Note that in topic modeling, a topic is a distribution over words. In addition, LTM proposes to use Pointwise Mutual Information (PMI) to estimate the correctness of the knowledge towards the current task/domain. The intuition is that if a piece of knowledge, i.e., must-link, is appropriate, both words in the must-link should have reasonable occurrences in the corpus of the current domain, which means the PMI value of both words is positive. On the other hand, a non-positive PMI value indicates little or no semantic correlation, and thus making the knowledge unreliable.

3.5 Knowledge Retention and Maintenance

LTM simply retains knowledge by adding the topics of a new domain into the topic base which contains all prior topics (Step 1 in Section 3.1). Then, the knowledge is extracted from the new topic base by using FIM mentioned in Section 3.3. There is no knowledge maintenance.

4 Shortcomings of LTM

This section presents the shortcomings of LTM that corresponds to each of the four LML components.

4.1 Knowledge Representation

There are two shortcomings in terms of knowledge representations in LTM:

1. Since must-links only contain two words, the information contained is limited. The knowledge in the form of sets (containing multiple words) may be more informative.
2. The knowledge does not have a confidence value. The prior knowledge is represented and treated equally. Due to the different frequency of each piece of knowledge (i.e., each pk-set), there should be an additional value indicating confidence attached to each pk-set.

4.2 Knowledge Extraction

Knowledge extraction in LTM also has two main shortcomings:

1. The frequent itemset mining (FIM) used in LTM only extracts frequent itemsets that appear more than a uniformed support threshold. However, due to the power law distribution of natural language (Zipf, 1932), only a small portion of words in the vocabulary appears very frequently while the majority of words are relatively rare. Since the frequencies of words are different, the corresponding support threshold should also be distinct.
2. FIM cannot easily produce knowledge of richer forms. For example, as mentioned above, each piece of knowledge should contain an additional value, e.g., confidence. It is unclear how FIM generates such value, especially if the value needs to be a probability.

4.3 Knowledge Transfer

The shortcoming here is that depending on the promotion scale parameter μ set by the user (Section 3.4), the GPU model may over-promote or under-promote the words in the pk-sets. That means that if the promotion scale parameter μ is set too low, the knowledge may not influence the topics much. In contrast, if this parameter is set too high, the words in the knowledge may dominate the topics resulting inscrutable topics. So the manual setting of this parameter requires expertise from the user.

4.4 Knowledge Retention and Maintenance

Since LTM does not focus on this component, it has three main issues:

1. It is unclear how to retrieve knowledge efficiently when the number of prior topics is huge. This issue is ignored in the LTM model.
2. How a user interacts with the knowledge base (i.e., pk-sets) to improve the quality of knowledge base is also unknown. Since the knowledge is automatically extracted in LTM, the assistance from human beings should contribute to improving the quality of the knowledge base.
3. If the time factor is considered, the new added topics in the topic base may better represent emerging topics while old prior topics may not fit the new tendency anymore. In that case, the knowledge base should weight the new topics more than old topics.

5 Proposed Approaches

The previous section pointed out the shortcomings of LTM. In this section, I propose several approaches to address some of them. Additional strategies are proposed to deal with issues beyond the knowledge components.

5.1 Expanding Knowledge Base

As mentioned above, each piece of knowledge in the knowledge base (i.e., pk-set) is stored and treated equally. However, a piece of knowledge may be more reliable if it gets supports from a large number of domains or it is extracted from the domains or data of higher quality with less noise. In such case, it is more informative to assign a value to the knowledge to indicate its confidence. I propose to add this additional value to each piece of knowledge in the knowledge base. The value is obtained from the normalized support of the knowledge, i.e., the normalized frequency of the knowledge in multiple domains. This expansion can also benefit the knowledge estimation part because the confidence field can provide the prior information to the model for knowledge filtering and estimation.

Another useful expansion is to consider cannot-links with confidence value (Chen and Liu, 2014a, Andrzejewski et al., 2009). Cannot-links express the negative semantic relationship between words, which can lead the model to separate them in different topics. Same as for must-links, cannot-links can also be attached with a confidence value, indicating its prior reliability.

5.2 Knowledge Conflict

After expanding the knowledge base, knowledge retention and maintenance needs additional attention. As we know, must-links express positive semantic correlations while cannot-links express the negative correlations, which means must-links and cannot-links are completely exclusive. Apparently, two words can form a must-link or cannot-link, but not both. The extracted knowledge can contain noise due to 3 reasons below:

1. The corpora which topic models are built on contain noise. This becomes a more serious problem if the corpora are coming from social media with informal languages.
2. Topic modeling is an unsupervised learning method and thus it can generate illogical topics containing words without any semantic correlation. Such topics will then produce incorrect knowledge.
3. The knowledge extraction step is not perfect either. The knowledge extracted using frequency-based FIM approach may include noisy must-links as some words are very frequent that their pairs can also pass the support threshold and form must-links.

The noise in knowledge base means that the newly extracted knowledge may have conflict with the ones in knowledge base. For example, the knowledge base contains the must-link $\{A, B\}$. However, the new knowledge contains cannot-link $\{A, B\}$. In such a case, we should not simply merge such knowledge into the knowledge base as it will make the knowledge base nonsensical. It requires us to propose a new strategy when such conflict happens. I propose two approaches to deal with the above situations:

1. Leverage the confidence assigned to each piece of knowledge. Intuitively, when a must-link and a cannot-link forms a conflict, the knowledge base should remain the type of knowledge (must-link or cannot-link) if its confidence is significantly higher than the conflicted one. By doing so, I make sure that the knowledge base does not contain conflicted knowledge and the knowledge piece in the knowledge base has the highest confidence among its conflicted ones.
2. If the confidence is same or similar between two types of knowledge having conflicts, I use the words that share must-links to make the decision. Let us say the must-link is $\{A, B\}$, I denote the set of words in which each word shares a must-link with A (or B) as S_A (or S_B). Then I use the overlapping percentage of S_A and S_B as estimation that how likely words A and B share the positive semantic correlation. This is intuitive since if words A and B are truly semantically correlated, they should share a lot of words in their must-links. For instance, words "price" and "expensive" can form must-links with words such as "cheap", "cost", "pricy", etc.

5.3 Domain Selection

I also notice an important issue that LTM struggles with, i.e., LTM uses all the domains as the source from which the knowledge is extracted. In other words, LTM assumes all the domains are relevant and helpful to the current domain. However, this assumption may not always hold. For example, the topics from the domain "Politics" may not contribute much to the domain "Laundry" as they are very different in terms of both word usage and word semantics. Simply using all the domains as LTM has two major drawbacks:

1. The knowledge extracted from all the domains may contain some inappropriate knowledge towards a particular domain. Although LTM has a mechanism to estimate and filter knowledge, it is still not perfect. For a more effective knowledge transfer, a domain selection step is indispensable to make sure the knowledge is more relevant and beneficial.
2. Extracting knowledge from all the domains can be time-consuming given a huge number of domains. Many of the extracted knowledge is useless as a particular domain only contains a limited set of words. So domain selection can also improve the knowledge extraction efficiency.

To select domains, I propose to measure the domain distance by utilizing JS-Divergence. Given two distributions P and Q, JS-Divergence between them is defined as below:

$$JS(P,Q) = \frac{1}{2}KL(P,M) + \frac{1}{2}KL(Q,M) \quad (1)$$

$$M = \frac{1}{2}(P+Q) \quad (2)$$

$$KL(P,Q) = \sum_i ln\left(\frac{P(i)}{Q(i)}\right)P(i) \quad (3)$$

Since each topic produced by topic models is a distribution over words, I can use JS-Divergence to measure the distance between topics. The problem is defined as given two domains D_1 and D_2, the goal is to estimate the domain distance by estimating their corresponding topic distance. I propose the following algorithm: for each topic t in domain D_1, I find the most similar topic (say t') in domain D_2 that has the smallest JS-Divergence with t. I denote this smallest JS-Divergence by $e(t)$. Then, the distance between domain D_1 and domain D_2 is defined as below:

$$DIST(D_1, D_2) = \sum_{t \in D_1} e(t) + \sum_{t' \in D_2} e(t') \quad (4)$$

Note that to make the distance symmetric, I calculate function $e()$ for each topic in domain D_1 as well as domain D_2. After the domain distance is calculated, given a new domain D', I can rank all existing domains by Equation 4 and pick up top K most relevant domains.

5.4 Scalability

In this sub-section, I also consider the scalability issue. There are generally 2 bottlenecks in LTM.

The first one is frequent itemset mining (FIM). There are some proposed scalable versions of FIM such as (Chester et al., 2009, Moens et al., 2013).

The second one is Gibbs sampling in topic models. Gibbs sampling (Griffiths and Steyvers, 2004) is a popular inference technique for topic modeling. However, it is not scalable to large datasets as it needs to make pass over the corpus many times. Some promising frameworks have been proposed (Yao et al., 2009, Zhai et al., 2012, Hu et al., 2014) to solve this issue. Since the GPU model used in LTM is a natural extension to that in LDA, these proposed methods are also applicable to LTM.

6 Evaluation

This section proposes a new evaluation framework that suits our proposed approaches. In (Chen and Liu, 2014b), the evaluation measurements are Topic Coherence (Mimno et al., 2011) and Precision@n which asks annotators to label both topics and words. A more comprehensive evaluation framework can contain the following two measurements:

1. Knowledge Evaluation. In order to evaluate each piece of knowledge (must-link or cannot-link) in the knowledge base, PMI score of both words using a large standard text corpus (Newman et al., 2010) can be applied. Human annotation can also be used to label the correctness of each piece of knowledge. This is to evaluate the effectiveness of knowledge handling in the model.
2. Domain Evaluation. As mentioned in 5.3, not all the prior domains are suitable to a new domain. It is important to evaluate the model performance by providing different sets of prior domains. There could be three main sets of prior domains for an extensive evaluation: 1) all relevant; 2) all irrelevant; 3) a combination of both. The relevance of domains should be defined by experts that are familiar with these domains.

7 Conclusions

This thesis proposal studied lifelong machine learning in topic modeling. It first introduced lifelong machine learning and its important components. Then, it reviewed the LTM model and pointed out its drawbacks. The corresponding approaches were proposed to address the issues and further advance the problem. For future direction, I would like to further integrate lifelong machine learning in the context of other NLP tasks, such as word sense disambiguation. I believe that the lifelong machine learning capacity is essential to a robust NLP system to overcome the dynamics and complexity of natural language, and for the purpose of a deeper understanding of natural language.

Acknowledgments

This work was supported in part by grants from National Science Foundation (NSF) under grant no. IIS-1111092 and IIS-1407927.

References

Rakesh Agrawal and Ramakrishnan Srikant. 1994. Fast Algorithms for Mining Association Rules. In *VLDB*, pages 487–499.

David Andrzejewski, Xiaojin Zhu, and Mark Craven. 2009. Incorporating Domain Knowledge into Topic Modeling via Dirichlet Forest Priors. In *ICML*, pages 25–32.

David M. Blei and Jon D. McAuliffe. 2010. Supervised Topic Models. In *NIPS*, pages 121–128.

David M Blei, Andrew Y Ng, and Michael I Jordan. 2003. Latent Dirichlet Allocation. *Journal of Machine Learning Research*, 3:993–1022.

Jordan L Boyd-Graber, David M. Blei, and Xiaojin Zhu. 2007. A Topic Model for Word Sense Disambiguation. In *EMNLP-CoNLL*, pages 1024–1033.

Andrew Carlson, Justin Betteridge, and Bryan Kisiel. 2010. Toward an Architecture for Never-Ending Language Learning. In *AAAI*, pages 1306–1313.

Rich Caruana. 1997. Multitask Learning. *Machine learning*, 28(1):41–75.

Zhiyuan Chen and Bing Liu. 2014a. Mining Topics in Documents : Standing on the Shoulders of Big Data. In *KDD*, pages 1116–1125.

Zhiyuan Chen and Bing Liu. 2014b. Topic Modeling using Topics from Many Domains, Lifelong Learning and Big Data. In *ICML*, pages 703–711.

Zhiyuan Chen, Arjun Mukherjee, and Bing Liu. 2014. Aspect Extraction with Automated Prior Knowledge Learning. In *ACL*, pages 347–358.

Sean Chester, Ian Sandler, and Alex Thomo. 2009. Scalable apriori-based frequent pattern discovery. In *CSE*, pages 48–55.

Vladimir Eidelman, Jordan Boyd-Graber, and Philip Resnik. 2012. Topic Models for Dynamic Translation Model Adaptation. In *ACL*, pages 115–119.

Geli Fei, Zhiyuan Chen, and Bing Liu. 2014. Review Topic Discovery with Phrases using the Pólya Urn Model. In *COLING*, pages 667–676.

Thomas L Griffiths and Mark Steyvers. 2004. Finding scientific topics. *PNAS*, 101 Suppl:5228–5235.

Thomas Hofmann. 1999. Probabilistic Latent Semantic Analysis. In *UAI*, pages 289–296.

Yuening Hu, Jordan Boyd-Graber, and Brianna Satinoff. 2011. Interactive Topic Modeling. In *ACL*, pages 248–257.

Yuening Hu, Ke Zhai, Vladimir Edelman, and Jordan Boyd-Graber. 2014. Polylingual Tree-Based Topic Models for Translation Domain Adaptation. In *ACL*, pages 1166–1176.

Ece Kamar, Ashish Kapoor, and Eric Horvitz. 2013. Lifelong Learning for Acquiring the Wisdom of the Crowd. In *IJCAI*, pages 2313–2320.

Ashish Kapoor and Eric Horvitz. 2009. Principles of lifelong learning for predictive user modeling. In *User Modeling*, pages 37–46.

Hosam Mahmoud. 2008. *Polya Urn Models*. Chapman & Hall/CRC Texts in Statistical Science.

David Mimno, Hanna M. Wallach, Edmund Talley, Miriam Leenders, and Andrew McCallum. 2011. Optimizing semantic coherence in topic models. In *EMNLP*, pages 262–272.

Sandy Moens, Emin Aksehirli, and Bart Goethals. 2013. Frequent Itemset Mining for Big Data. In *IEEE International Conference on Big Data*, pages 111–118.

Arjun Mukherjee and Bing Liu. 2012. Aspect Extraction through Semi-Supervised Modeling. In *ACL*, pages 339–348.

David Newman, Jey Han Lau, Karl Grieser, and Timothy Baldwin. 2010. Automatic evaluation of topic coherence. In *HLT-NAACL*, pages 100–108.

Sinno Jialin Pan and Qiang Yang. 2010. A Survey on Transfer Learning. *IEEE Trans. Knowl. Data Eng.*, 22(10):1345–1359.

Anastasia Pentina and Christoph H Lampert. 2014. A PAC-Bayesian Bound for Lifelong Learning. In *ICML*, pages 991–999.

Rajat Raina, Alexis Battle, Honglak Lee, Benjamin Packer, and Andrew Y Ng. 2007. Self-taught Learning : Transfer Learning from Unlabeled Data. In *ICML*, pages 759–766.

Daniel Ramage, David Hall, Ramesh Nallapati, and Christopher D Manning. 2009. Labeled LDA : A supervised topic model for credit attribution in multi-labeled corpora. In *EMNLP*, pages 248–256.

Paul Ruvolo and Eric Eaton. 2013. ELLA: An efficient lifelong learning algorithm. In *ICML*, pages 507–515.

Daniel L Silver. 2013. On Common Ground: Neural-Symbolic Integration and Lifelong Machine Learning. In *9th International Workshop on Neural-Symbolic Learning and Reasoning NeSy13*, pages 41–46.

Sebastian Thrun. 1995. Lifelong Learning: A Case Study. Technical report.

Xing Wei and W Bruce Croft. 2006. LDA-based document models for ad-hoc retrieval. In *SIGIR*, pages 178–185.

Limin Yao, David Mimno, and Andrew McCallum. 2009. Efficient methods for topic model inference on streaming document collections. In *KDD*, pages 937–946.

Ke Zhai, Jordan Boyd-Graber, Nima Asadi, and Mohamad L. Alkhouja. 2012. Mr. LDA: a Flexible Large Scale Topic Modeling Package using Variational Inference in MapReduce. In *WWW*, pages 879–888.

George Kingsley Zipf. 1932. *Selected Papers of the Principle of Relative Frequency in Language*. Harvard University Press.

Semantics-based Graph Approach to Complex Question-Answering

Tomasz Jurczyk
Mathematics and Computer Science
Emory University
Atlanta, GA 30322, USA
tomasz.jurczyk@emory.edu

Jinho D. Choi
Mathematics and Computer Science
Emory University
Atlanta, GA 30322, USA
jinho.choi@emory.edu

Abstract

This paper suggests an architectural approach of representing knowledge graph for complex question-answering. There are four kinds of entity relations added to our knowledge graph: syntactic dependencies, semantic role labels, named entities, and coreference links, which can be effectively applied to answer complex questions. As a proof of concept, we demonstrate how our knowledge graph can be used to solve complex questions such as arithmetics. Our experiment shows a promising result on solving arithmetic questions, achieving the 3-folds cross-validation score of 71.75%.

1 Introduction

Question-answering has lately gained lots of interest from both academic and industrial research. Services such as Yahoo! Answers[1] or Quora[2] provide platforms for their users to ask questions to one another; however, answer accuracy or response rate of these services strongly depends on the users' willingness of sharing their knowledge, which is not always consistent. This kind of inconsistency has led many researchers to focus on developing question-answering systems that retrieve, analyze, and answer questions without much human engagement.

Although the task of question-answering has been been well-explored, several challenges still remain. One of such challenges concerns about architectural aspects of meaning representation. Thanks to years of research on statistical parsing, several tools are already available that provide rich syntactic and semantic structures from texts. Output of these tools, however, often needs to be post-processed into more complicated structures, such as graphs of knowledge, in order to retrieve answers for complex questions. These graphs consist of relations between entities found not only within a sentence, but also across sentences. Vertices and edges in these graphs represent linguistic units (e.g., words, phrases) and their syntactic or semantic relations, respectively.

Robustness of handling several types of questions is one of the key aspects about a question-answering system; yet most of previous work had focused on answering simple factoid questions (Yao et al., 2013; Yih et al., 2013). Recently, researchers started focusing on solving complex questions involving arithmetics or biological processes (Hosseini et al., 2014; Berant et al., 2014). A complex question can be described as a question requiring the collection and synthesis of information from multiple sentences (Chali and Joty, 2008). The more complex the questions become, the harder it is to build a structural model that is general enough to capture information for all different types of questions.

This paper suggests an architectural approach of representing entity relations as well as its application to complex question-answering. First, we present a systematic way of building a graph by merging four kinds of information: syntactic dependencies, semantic role labels, named entities, and coreference links, generated by existing tools (Section 3). We then demonstrate, how our graph can be coupled with statistical learning to solve complex questions such as arithmetic, which requires understanding of the entire

[1] https://answers.yahoo.com
[2] https://www.quora.com

Proceedings of NAACL-HLT 2015 Student Research Workshop (SRW), pages 140–146,
Denver, Colorado, June 1, 2015.

context (Section 4). Our experiments show that it is possible to retrieve document-level entity relations through our graph, providing enough information to handle such complex questions (Section 5).

2 Related Work

Punyakanok et al. (2004) presented a system using edit distance between question and potential answer pairs, measured by the number of required transformations of their dependency trees. Heilman and Smith (2010) presented a more sophisticated system finding the most efficient tree transformation using a greedy search. Cui et al. (2005) proposed a system utilizing fuzzy relation matching guided by statistical models. Yao et al. (2013) described an approach taking both an edit distance and sequence tagging for selecting finer-grained answers within answer candidates. All the work above leverages dependency tree matching similar to ours; however, our approach performs matching through semantic relations as well as coreference links, and also is designed for handling complex questions whereas the others mainly focused on factoid questions.

Kushman et al. (2014) described an approach for predicting sentence-to-equation alignments for solving arithmetic questions. Hosseini et al. (2014) presented a system predicting verb categories, and constructing equations from the context using these categories. Berant et al. (2014) proposed an approach that extracted structures from biological processes, and mapped each question to a query form. Our work is related to the first two work; however, it is distinguished in a way that our constructed graph is not designed to handle just arithmetic questions, but complex questions in general.

Our work is also related to research of aligning text into a set of entities and instances describing states of the world. Snyder and Barzilay (2007) presented an approach for solving text-to-database alignment as a structured multi-label classification. Vogel and Jurafsky (2010) presented a learning system that followed navigational paths based on natural language by utilizing apprenticeship from directions on the map paired with human language. Chambers and Jurafsky (2009) presented an unsupervised learning system for narrative schemas based on coreferent arguments in chains of verbs. Pourdamghani et al. (2014) and Pan et al. (2015) presented Abstract Meaning Representation (AMR) consisting of multi-layered relations for English sentences. Our semantics-based graph shares a similar idea with AMR; however, our graph is constructed from existing structures such as dependency trees and semantic roles, whereas AMR requires its won annotation, which could be manual intensive work for building statical parsing models.

3 Semantics-based Knowledge Approach

3.1 Motivation

Our motivation arises from both the complexity and the variety of questions and their relevant contexts. The complexity concerns with exploiting syntactic dependencies, semantic role labels, named entities, and coreference links all together for finding the best answers. For arithmetic questions, such complexity comes from the flow of entity relations across sentences and semantic polarities of verb predicates, which are required to transform the contexts in natural language into mathematical equations.

The variety concerns with robustly handling various types of questions. It is relatively easier to develop an architecture designated to handle just one type of questions (e.g., a system to extract answers for factoid questions) than many different types of questions (e.g., opinions, recommendations, commentaries). In this section, we present a semantic-based knowledge approach (constructed graph) that not only conveys relations from different layers or linguistic theories, but also is effective for finding answers for various types of questions.

3.2 Components

Given a *document*, our system first parses each sentences into a dependency tree, then finds predicate-argument structures on top of the dependency tree. Once sentences are parsed, coreference links are found for nodes across all trees. Finally, each dependency node gets turned into an *instance*, which can be linked to other related instances. Multiple instances can be grouped together as an *entity* if they are coreferent. Our graph is semantically driven because semantic predicate-argument relations take precedence over syntactic dependencies when both exist.

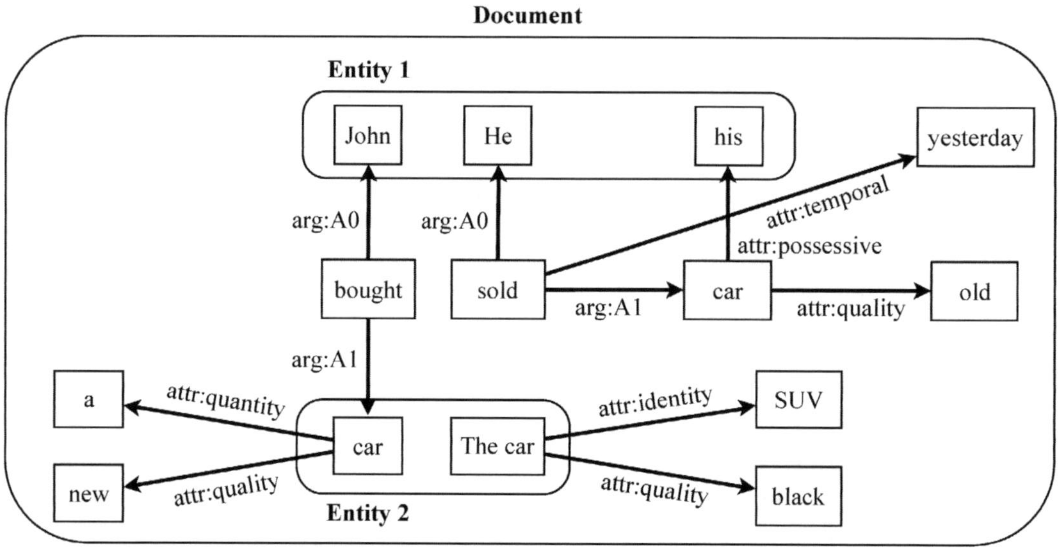

Figure 1: Example of our semantic-based graph given three sentences:
John bough a new car, *The car was black SUV*, and *He sold his old car yesterday*.

Document

A *document* contains a graph consisting of a set of entities, instances, and relations between the instances (Figure 1). A document can be small as a microblog or big as the entire Wikipedia articles.

Entity

An *entity* can be described as a set of instances referring to the same object mostly found through coreference resolution. In Figure 1, although *John*, *He*, and *his* are recognized as individual instances, they are grouped into one entity because they all refer to *John*. Maintaining these relations is crucial for answering complex questions.

Instance

An *instance* is the atomic-level object in our graph that usually represents a word-token, but can also represent compound words (e.g., *New York*), multi-word expressions, etc. The instance is linked to other instances as a predicate, an argument, or an attribute.

Predicate & Argument

An instance is a *predicate* of another instance if it forms any argument structure (Palmer et al., 2005). Currently, our graph takes non-auxiliary verbs and a few eventive nouns as predicates provided by a semantic role labeler. An instance is an *argument* of another if it is required to complete the meaning of the other instance. In Figure 1, *John* and *car* are arguments of *bought* because they are necessary to give an understanding of *bought*. We plan to improve these relations through semantic parsing in the future.

The *predicate* and *argument* relations represent both semantic and syntactic relations between instances in the document. Semantic role labels in (Palmer et al., 2005) and dependency labels in (Choi and Palmer, 2012) are used to represent semantic and syntactic relations in our graph. Our experiments show that these relations play a crucial role in answering arithmetic questions (Section 5).

Attribute

An instance is an *attribute* of another if it is not an argument but gives extra information about the other instance. While an argument completes the meaning of its predicate, an attribute augments the meaning with specific information. In Figure 1, *new* is not an argument but an attribute of *car* because this information is not required for understanding *car*, but provides finer-grained information about the car.

Attributes can be shared among instances within the same entity. In Figure 1, the attributes *new* and *black* are shared between instances *car* and *the car*. This is particularly useful for questions requiring information scattered across sentences. Table 1 shows the types of attributes that we have specified so far.

This list will be continuously updated as we add more question types to our system.

Type	Description
Locative	Geographical or relative location information (e.g., *New York*, *near my house*).
Temporal	Absolute or relative temporal information (e.g., *tomorrow noon*, *2 years ago*).
Possessive	Possessor of this instance (e.g., *his*, of *Mary*).
Quantity	Absolute or relative quantity information (e.g., *two* books, *few* books).
Quality	Every other kind of attributes.

Table 1: List of attributes used in our graph.

3.3 Graph construction

Algorithm 1 shows a pseudo-code for constructing our graph given a dependency tree, consisting of syntactic and semantic relations, and coreference links.

```
Input: D: a dependency tree,
       C: a set of coreference links.
Output: G: Graph.
foreach node N in D do
    if N.skip() then
        continue;
    else if N.isArgument() then
        P ← N.getPredicate();
        L ← N.getArgumentLabel();
        G.addArgument(P, N, L);
    else if N.isAttribute() then
        A ← N.getAttributeHead();
        L ← N.getAttributeType();
        G.addAttribute(A, N, L);
    else
        H ← N.getSyntacticHead();
        L ← N.getSyntacticLabel();
        G.addArgument(H, N, L);
    end
    if C.hasEntityFor(N) then
        E ← C.getEntityFor(N)
        G.addToEntity(E, N);

end
```

Algorithm 1: Graph constructing algorithm.

Every node in the dependency tree has exactly one syntactic head and can be a semantic argument of zero to many predicates. For each node, it first checks if this node should be added to the graph (i.e., auxiliary verbs are not added). If it should, it checks it is a semantic argument of some predicate. If not, it checks if it is an attribute of some instance. By default, it becomes an argument of its syntactic head. Finally, it gets added to an entity if it is coreferent to some other instance. Moreover, our graph is also designed to support weights of vertices and edges. Now, we assign a value of 1 as a weight for every element, but we plan to extend our work by determining the importance of different weights for specific semantic relations. We believe that an intelligent weighting system will improve the overall accuracy of the system by enhancing the matching process.

4 Case Study

4.1 Arithmetic questions

This section demonstrates our approach to the application of complex question-answering, targeted on arithmetic questions. The purpose of this section is to show a proof of concept that our graph can be effectively applied to answer such questions. For our experiments, we take a set of arithmetic questions used for elementary and middle school students. These questions consist of simple arithmetic operations such as addition and subtraction. Table 2 shows a sample of these questions.

The main challenge of this task is mostly related to the contiguous representation of state changes. The question at the end concerns about either the start state, the transitions, or the end state of a specific theme (e.g., *pizza*, *kitten*). Therefore, simplistic string matching approaches, which would have worked well on factoid questions, would not perform well on this type of questions. Another challenge is found by coreference mentions in these questions. Arithmetic questions generally consist of multiple sentences such that coreference resolution plays a crucial role for getting high accuracy. These issues are further discussed in Section 5.4.

4.2 Verb polarity sequence classification

We turn the task of arithmetic question-answering into a sequence classification of verb polarities. We

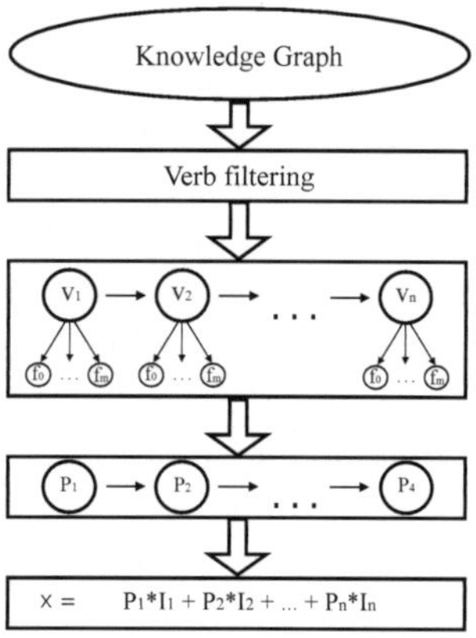

(a) Flow of execution in our system for solving arithmetic questions. First, the verb filtering process is applied to select verbs in all sentences (V_i), which share the same semantic argument with the question. Given the selected verbs, their features (f_i) are extracted and the polarities (P_i) are predicted by a statistical model. Finally, the equation X is formed, where polarities are multiplied by the quantities of the arguments.

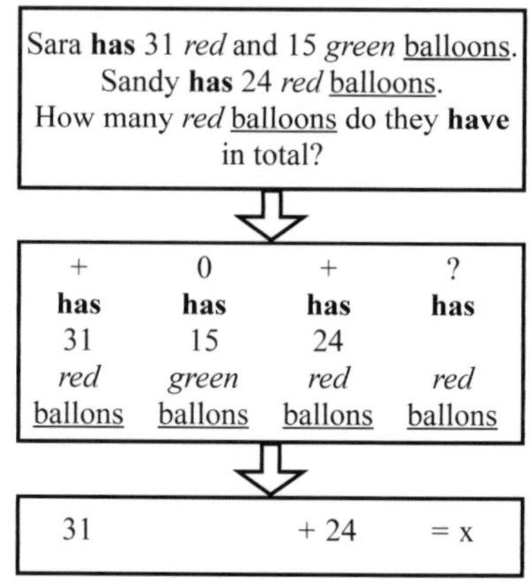

(b) Flow of execution for the example document. First, verbs are filtered and selected for the polarity selection. Next, all necessary information (numericals, themes etc.) is collected and organized into states. Finally, based on the verbs polarity, equation is being formed.

Figure 2: Flow of execution in general (a) and for an example document (b).

believe the verbs need to be classified in sequence because the same verb can convey different polarities in different contexts. Three types of verb polarities are used: `+`, `-`, and `0`. Given the list of sentences in each question and the equation associated with it (Table 2), we map each verb with its polarity by comparing their quantities. '+' and '−' are assigned to verbs whose arguments show a plus sign or a minus sign in the equation, respectively. '`0`' is assigned to verbs whose arguments do not appear in the equation. This information is used to build a statistical model, which is used for decoding.

Arithmetic questions often contain verbs whose arguments are not relevant to the final question. For instance, in "*Jason has 43 blue and 16 red marbles. Tom has 24 blue marbles. How many blue marbles do they have in all?*", "*16 red marbles*" is more like a noise to answer this question. Our approach classifies such verbs as `0` so that they do not participate into the final equation. Once the equation is form, it is trivial to solve the problem using simple algebra.

Our approach is distinguished from some of the previous work where each verb is categorized into multiple classes (Hosseini et al., 2014) in a sense that our verb classes are automatically derived from the equations (no extra annotation is needed). Furthermore, our approach can be extended to more complicated operations such as multiplication and division as long as the correct equations are provided. The dataset used in Kushman et al. (2014) contains this type of questions and we plan to apply our approach on this dataset as the future work.

Question	Equation
A restaurant served 9 pizzas during lunch and 6 during dinner today. How many pizzas were served today?	x = 9 + 6
Tim's cat had kittens. He gave 3 to Jessica and 6 to Sara. He now has 9 kittens. How many kittens did he have to start with?	x = 3 + 6 + 9

Table 2: Sample of arithmetic questions.

5 Experiments

5.1 Data

For our experiments, we use the arithmetic dataset provided by the Allen Institute.[3] The dataset consists of 395 arithmetic questions together with their

[3] `allenai.org/content/data/arithmeticquestions.pdf`

equations and answers. We parsed all data using the dependency parser, the semantic role labeler, the named entity tagger, and the coreference resolution in ClearNLP (Choi and McCallum, 2013; Choi, 2012).[4] We then split the dataset into 3-folds for cross validation in a way that the polarity distributions are similar across different sets (Table 3).

5.2 Features

The following features are used for our experiments:

- Semantic role labels; especially numbered arguments as in PropBank (Palmer et al., 2005).
- Sequence of verbs and arguments whose semantic roles are recognized as 'themes'.
- Frequency of verbs and theme arguments in the current context.
- Similarity between verbs and theme arguments across sentences.
- Distance of the verb to the final question.

Given our graph, it was trivial to extract all features.

5.3 Machine learning

To build statistical models, we use a stochastic adaptive subgradient algorithm called ADAGRAD that uses per-coordinate learning rates to exploit rarely seen features while remaining scalable (Duchi et al., 2011). This is suitable for NLP tasks where rarely seen features often play an important role and training data consists of a large number of instances with high dimensional features. We use the implementation of ADAGRAD in ClearNLP using the hinge-loss, and take their default hyper-parameters (learning rate: $a = 0.01$, termination criterion: $r = 0.1$).

5.4 Evaluation

Table 3 shows the distributions of each fold and the accuracy of our system in answering arithmetic questions. Our cross-validation score is 71.75%, which is promising given how complex these questions are. Hosseini et al. (2014) were able to achieve 77.7% accuracy on the same dataset, which is higher than our result. However, our main goal for these experiments remains as to prove that our graph can be utilized to answer complex questions.

We also analyzed errors found in our experiment. The majority of errors were caused by errors from dependency parsing, semantic role labeling, or coreference resolution. For instance, verbs are not recognized correctly in some dependency trees, which becomes a major factor of decreasing accuracy. Also, semantic role labels sometimes were incorrectly assigned, which extremely influenced the accuracy of our system. As mentioned earlier, coreference resolution remains as one of the main challenges in handling complex questions. We will explore ways of improving these NLP tools, hoping to achieve higher accuracy for answering complex questions.

	1st fold	**2nd fold**	**3rd fold**
# of questions	118	118	118
# of verbs	418	423	420
# of + verbs	326	330	328
# of − verbs	51	51	51
# of 0 verbs	41	42	41
Accuracy	67.80	76.27	71.19

Table 3: Distributions and accuracies of all folds.

6 Conclusion and future work

This paper presents semantics-based knowledge approach for answering different types of complex questions. As a proof of concept, we demonstrate the application of our graph for arithmetic question-answering. By using the grounded knowledge in our graph, our system was able to extract appropriate features and build a statistical model for recognizing verb polarities that effectively solved arithmetic questions. Our system shows a promising result for answering arithmetic questions. Although we view the problem of solving arithmetic questions as a significant step towards complex question-answering, numerous challenges still remain, not only in the sub-domain of arithmetic questions, but also in other types of complex questions.

In the future, we plan to extend our work by exploring new features for the statistical model. Also, we plan to make improvement in dependency parsing, semantic role labeling, and coreference resolution through error analysis of our question-answering system. Finally, we will try to apply our knowledge approach to other types of complex questions.

[4] http://www.clearnlp.com

References

Jonathan Berant, Vivek Srikumar, Pei-Chun Chen, Abby Vander Linden, Brittany Harding, Brad Huang, Peter Clark, and Christopher D. Manning. 2014. Modeling Biological Processes for Reading Comprehension. In *Proceedings of the 2014 Conference on Empirical Methods in Natural Language Processing*, EMNLP'14, pages 1499–1510, Doha, Qatar, October. Association for Computational Linguistics.

Yllias Chali and Shafiq Joty. 2008. Selecting Sentences for Answering Complex Questions. In *Proceedings of the 2008 Conference on Empirical Methods in Natural Language Processing*, EMNLP'08, pages 304–313, Honolulu, Hawaii, October.

Nathanael Chambers and Dan Jurafsky. 2009. Unsupervised Learning of Narrative Schemas and their Participants. In *Proceedings of the Joint Conference of the 47th Annual Meeting of the ACL and the 4th International Joint Conference on Natural Language Processing of the AFNLP*, ACL'09, pages 602–610, Suntec, Singapore, August.

Jinho D. Choi and Andrew McCallum. 2013. Transition-based Dependency Parsing with Selectional Branching. In *Proceedings of the 51st Annual Meeting of the Association for Computational Linguistics (Volume 1: Long Papers)*, ACL'13, pages 1052–1062, Sofia, Bulgaria, August.

Jinho D. Choi and Martha Palmer. 2012. Guidelines for the Clear Style Constituent to Dependency Conversion. Technical report, Technical Report 01-12, University of Colorado at Boulder.

Jinho D. Choi. 2012. *Optimization of Natural Language Processing Components for Robustness and Scalability*. Ph.D. thesis, University of Colorado Boulder.

Hang Cui, Renxu Sun, Keya Li, Min-Yen Kan, and Tat-Seng Chua. 2005. Question Answering Passage Retrieval Using Dependency Relations. In *Proceedings of the 28th annual international ACM SIGIR conference on Research and development in information retrieval*, pages 400–407. ACM.

John Duchi, Elad Hazan, and Yoram Singer. 2011. Adaptive Subgradient Methods for Online Learning and Stochastic Optimization. *The Journal of Machine Learning Research*, 12(39):2121–2159.

Michael Heilman and Noah A Smith. 2010. Tree Edit Models for Recognizing Textual Entailments, Paraphrases, and Answers to Questions. In *Human Language Technologies: The 2010 Annual Conference of the North American Chapter of the Association for Computational Linguistics*, NAACL'10, pages 1011–1019.

Mohammad Javad Hosseini, Hannaneh Hajishirzi, Oren Etzioni, and Nate Kushman. 2014. Learning to Solve Arithmetic Word Problems with Verb Categorization. In *Proceedings of the 2014 Conference on Empirical Methods in Natural Language Processing*, EMNLP'14, pages 523–533, Doha, Qatar, October.

Nate Kushman, Yoav Artzi, Luke Zettlemoyer, and Regina Barzilay. 2014. Learning to Automatically Solve Algebra Word Problems. In *Proceedings of the 52nd Annual Meeting of the Association for Computational Linguistics*, ACL'14, pages 271–281, Baltimore, Maryland, June.

Martha Palmer, Daniel Gildea, and Paul Kingsbury. 2005. The Proposition Bank: An Annotated Corpus of Semantic Roles. *Computational linguistics*, 31(1):71–106.

Xiaoman Pan, Taylor Cassidy, Ulf Hermjakob, Heng Ji, and Kevin Knight. 2015. Unsupervised Entity Linking with Abstract Meaning Representation. In *Proceedings of the 2015 Conference of the North American Chapter of the Association for Computational Linguistics - Human Language Technologies*, NAACL'15.

Nima Pourdamghani, Yang Gao, Ulf Hermjakob, and Kevin Knight. 2014. Aligning English Strings with Abstract Meaning Representation Graphs. In *Proceedings of the 2014 Conference on Empirical Methods in Natural Language Processing*, EMNLP'14, pages 425–429, Doha, Qatar, October.

Vasin Punyakanok, Dan Roth, and Wen-tau Yih. 2004. Mapping Dependencies Trees: An Application to Question Answering. In *Proceedings of AI&Math*, pages 1–10.

Benjamin Snyder and Regina Barzilay. 2007. Database-Text Alignment via Structured Multilabel Classification. In *IJCAI*, pages 1713–1718.

Adam Vogel and Daniel Jurafsky. 2010. Learning to Follow Navigational Directions. In *Proceedings of the 48th Annual Meeting of the Association for Computational Linguistics*, ACL'10, pages 806–814, Uppsala, Sweden, July.

Xuchen Yao, Benjamin Van Durme, Chris Callison-Burch, and Peter Clark. 2013. Answer Extraction as Sequence Tagging with Tree Edit Distance. In *Proceedings of the 2013 Conference of the North American Chapter of the Association for Computational Linguistics: Human Language Technologies*, NAACL'13, pages 858–867, Atlanta, Georgia, June.

Wen-tau Yih, Ming-Wei Chang, Christopher Meek, and Andrzej Pastusiak. 2013. Question Answering Using Enhanced Lexical Semantic Models. In *Proceedings of the 51st Annual Meeting of the Association for Computational Linguistics (Volume 1: Long Papers)*, EMNLP'13, pages 1744–1753, Sofia, Bulgaria, August.

Recognizing Textual Entailment using Dependency Analysis and Machine Learning

Nidhi Sharma
cs5080219@cse.iitd.ac.in

Richa Sharma
anz087535@cse.iitd.ac.in

Kanad K. Biswas
kkb@cse.iitd.ac.in

Indian Institute of Technology Delhi
Hauz Khas, New Delhi, India - 110016

Abstract

This paper presents a machine learning system that uses dependency-based features and lexical features for recognizing textual entailment. The proposed system evaluates the feature values automatically. The performance of the proposed system is evaluated by conducting experiments on RTE1, RTE2 and RTE3 datasets. Further, a comparative study of the current system with other ML-based systems for RTE to check the performance of the proposed system is also presented. The dependency-based heuristics and lexical features from the current system have resulted in significant improvement in accuracy over existing state-of-art ML-based solutions for RTE.

1 Introduction

Recognizing textual entailment (RTE) has aroused lot of interest in natural language research community with recent Pascal RTE challenges. RTE provides a generic evaluation framework and is useful across various applications like question-answering, information-extraction, machine translation etc.

Textual Entailment is a directional relation between text fragments (Dagan et al., 2005) which holds true when the truth of one text fragment, referred to as 'hypothesis', follows from another, referred to as 'text'. The task of recognizing textual entailment can be thought of as a classification problem to classify a given pair of sentences, text (T) and hypothesis (H), as true or false entailment as suggested by Bos and Markert (2005). Machine Learning approaches to RTE challenges have used combination of features like syntactic, semantic or lexical features. However, in most of the cases, the features used for the purpose are either large in number which makes the evaluation time consuming or are not very intuitive which makes them difficult to comprehend. In our work, we have attempted to address these two concerns.

Our approach uses a combination of dependency and lexical features to train Machine Learning (ML) classifiers. We use only 8 features that are simple and intuitive. The process of evaluating feature values is automated, thereby reducing any manual effort and intervention. The system performance has been tested over RTE1, RTE2 and RTE3 datasets. Our system shows significant improvement in accuracy over the state-of-the-art ML solutions to RTE challenges.

The paper is organized as follows. Section 2 gives a brief of the earlier work of ML based approaches for RTE. Section 3 describes our solution approach for RTE, including details on the features used and the experimental setup. We present the results and observations in Section 4, followed by conclusion in Section 5.

2 Related Work

There have been various solution approaches proposed to RTE challenges like rule-based, logical-inference based, graph-based and ML-based. Of these, applying ML algorithms to automatically learn models from training examples is an effective way to approach RTE challenges like other NLP problems.

ML-based systems often use lexical matching features (Inkpen et al. 2006, Kozareva and Motoyo 2006 and Pakray et al. 2011) such as word overlap count, word similarity, n-gram, etc, and semantic

Proceedings of NAACL-HLT 2015 Student Research Workshop (SRW), pages 147–153,
Denver, Colorado, June 1, 2015.

features such as WordNet similarity measures (Kozareva and Motoyo 2006). Inkpen et al. (2006) have achieved an accuracy of 52.85% on RTE2 dataset using lexical match and mismatch features. Bos and Markert (2005) use a combination of shallow and deep semantic features using logical inference to build a hybrid model that achieves an accuracy of 57.7 % on RTE1 dataset. They also show that using task label as feature in their model increases the overall accuracy to 61.2%. Pazienza et al. (2009) have defined a measure for textual entailment based on graph matching theory applied to syntactic dependency graphs. They perform comparison of rule-based and SVM-based approach with rule-based approach giving an accuracy of 52.45% and SVM-based approach giving an accuracy of 51.82%. Pakray et al. (2011) describe a two-way textual entailment recognition system that uses lexical features such as n-gram match, stemming etc. and syntactic features like subject comparison, subject-verb comparison, etc.

Our approach builds mainly on the works of Inkpen et al. (2006) and Pakray et al. (2011) and, improves accuracy over their work as presented in the following section.

3 Our Approach

We have developed an RTE system that takes as input sentence pairs, text (T) and hypothesis (H), and outputs an entailment decision (True/False) for each pair. The system evaluates a set of 8 different dependency and lexical features for the input sentence pairs. One of these features is a mismatch feature while the other seven are match features. For evaluating the dependency features, we have used Stanford Dependency parser (Marneffe et al., 2006) to obtain the dependency relations present in the sentences. We generate a structured representation for both text and hypothesis using their respective dependency relations. This structured representation is used to evaluate six of the eight lexical and the syntactic features. Structured representation proves to be an effective representation of the sentence for calculating feature values.

We first present a brief overview of the structured representation of the sentences before discussing the features used in the feature vector to develop classifiers using ML algorithms.

3.1 Structured Representation

The Stanford dependencies describe the grammatical relationships in a sentence. Each dependency is a tuple consisting of a pair of words in a sentence and the relation that links them. A dependency is represented as follows:

reln(govVal,depVal)

where,

reln is the dependency relation
depVal is the dependent value
govVal is the governing value

The structured representation is generated by using the dependency tags and converting them to a slot-filler frame-based structure. The entities extracted from the dependency relations are:

a) Subject: The dependencies tagged as *nsubj* (Nominal Subject), *nsubjpass* (passive nominal subject), *csubj* (clausal subject), *csubjpass* (passive clausal subject) and *xsubj* (controlling subject) are used to extract the words acting as subject in the sentence.

b) Subject Modifier: The dependency tags *advmod* (adverbial modifier), *amod* (adjectival modifier), *appos* (appositional modifier), *nn* (noun compound modifier) and *npadvmod* (noun phrase as adverbial modifier) are used to identify modifiers. Each dependency relation is returned as a pair of (governing value, dependent value). If for a given modifier relation, the governing value is a subject in the sentence, then the dependent value acts as the subject modifier.

c) Object: The Stanford parser returns *dobj* (direct object), *iobj* (indirect object) and *pobj* (prepositional object) as tags for different objects. We include all these in the frame entity 'object'.

d) Object Modifier: The process to extract object modifier is similar to the one used for Subject Modifier except that if the governing value in the modifier relation is an object in the sentence, the dependent value acts as the object modifier.

e) Verb: The dependency tagged as root is generally the main verb of the sentence. The tags *cop* (copula), *ccomp* (clausal complement) and *xcomp* (open clausal complement) also list the verbs in the sentence.

f) Verb Complements: In some cases, the dependencies tagged as *root*, *xcomp* or *ccomp* (clausal complement) contain noun instead of verb. The dependent value is then listed as a verb complement. The tags *acomp* (adjectival complement), *pcomp* (prepositional complement), *advcl* (adverberial clause modifier) and *vmod* (verbal modifier) also contains dependency values that complement the verb.

g) Negation: The parser uses the tag *neg* (negation modifier) to identify negation words (such as, not, don't, etc.) in the sentence. The governing value of this dependency contains the word (usually verb) it negates. We store this value with the negation word for negation frame entity.

h) Number: The dependency tagged as *num* (numeric modifier) contains a numeric value and the noun-phrase that it modifies. We store both the number and the entity it modifies under this label.

The generation of the frame-based structured representation is illustrated using statement S1 and this structured representation is shown in Table 1.

S1: *A two-day auction of property belonging to actress Katharine Hepburn brought in 3.2 million pounds.*

Label	Value
Subject	Auction
Subject Modifier	two-day
Object	property, Hepburn, pounds
Object Modifier	Actress
Verb	Brought
Verb Complements	Belonging
Negation	-
Number	3.2 million (pounds)

Table 1: Structured Representation for S1

3.2 Features

After obtaining a structured representation, we evaluate the following features (i) to (viii). While features (i) and (ii) have been borrowed from previous work (Inkpen et al. 2006, Kozareva and Motoyo 2006, Pakray et al. 2011), the features (iii), (iv) and (iv), present significant modifications to features used by researchers (Inkpen et al. 2006, Molla 2003 and Pakray et al. 2011) in the past. The features (vi), (vii) and (viii) are new features contributing to our feature set. The *dependency overlap* and *word overlap* features do not require structured representation for evaluation.

(i) Word Overlap

This feature is a ratio of the count of directly overlapping words between text and hypothesis to the count of words in hypothesis, after removal of stop words. A direct word count also takes care of the overlapping named entities. This feature is a significant contributor to entailment. The overlap is evaluated as follows:

$$wordOverlap = \frac{countTnH}{countH}$$

where,
countTnH = number of common words in text and hypothesis after stop word removal
countH = total number of words in hypothesis after stop word removal

(ii) Negation Check

This feature checks if a verb in hypothesis has been negated in text or vice-versa. Negation can be explicit in the form of keywords, such as 'not', 'can't', 'don't', etc. or it can be implicit in the form of antonym or negative sense of the verb. We capture explicit as well as implicit negation check through the structured representation of the sentence. In order to identify if the antonym of a verb (non-negated) in hypothesis is present in text or vice-versa, we first identify the root form of the verbs present in text as well as hypothesis using Wordnet[1]. The root form of the verbs is then checked for antonym (or negative sense) relationship by using VerbOcean[2].

This is a binary feature assuming a value of 1 for the presence of negation, either explicit or implicit and, it remains 0 otherwise. For example, consider the following text-hypothesis pair:

T: *The Philippine Stock Exchange Composite Index rose 0.1 percent to 1573.65*

H: *The Philippine Stock Exchange Composite Index dropped.*

In this example, the verbs 'rose' and 'dropped' are converted to their root forms 'rise' and 'drop' respectively and found to have an antonym relation (rise [opposite-of] drop) in VerbOcean.

(iii) Number Agreement

This is a binary feature to check if the numeric modifiers of the same governing entities are in agreement in text-hypothesis pair. We use structured representation to evaluate this feature. The feature takes a value of 1 for number agreement and 0 otherwise. We illustrate number agreement

[1]http://projects.csail.mit.edu/jwi/
[2] http://demo.patrickpantel.com/demos/verbocean/

using the pair T1-H1 and number disagreement with the help of pair T2-H2 as follows:

T1: *The twin buildings are 88 stories each, compared with the Sears Tower's 110 stories.*

H1: *The Sears Tower has 110 stories.*

T2: *A small bronze bust of Spencer Tracy sold for £174,000.*

H2: *A small bronze bust of Spencer Tracy made £180,447.*

(iv) Dependency Overlap

Dependency overlap has been considered as a good approximation to sentence meaning in context of question-answering problem by Molla (2003). We have borrowed the same idea to approximate the entailment relationship between text and hypothesis. The dependency relations returned by the Stanford parser consist of a pair of words from the sentence that are related. We count such similar pairs irrespective of the relation binding them. The value of the feature is computed as:

$$depOverlap = \frac{countTnH}{countH}$$

where,
countTnH = number of overlapping dependency pairs in text and hypothesis and,
countH = total number of dependencies in hypothesis

Considering an example:

T: *His family has steadfastly denied the charges*

H: *The charges were denied by his family*

Dependency list for T is:

[*poss(family-2, His-1), nsubj(denied-5, family-2), aux(denied-5, has-3), advmod(denied-5, steadfastly-4), root(ROOT-0, denied-5), det(charges-7, the-6), dobj(denied-5, charges-7)*]

Dependency list for H is:

[*det(charges-2, The-1), nsubjpass(denied-4, charges-2), auxpass(denied-4, were-3), root(ROOT-0, denied-4), poss(family-7, his-6), agent(denied-4, family-7)*]

This example has five overlapping dependency pairs, namely: *the-charges, denied-charges, ROOT-denied, his-family* and *denied-family*. We evaluate dependency overlap for this example as follows:

$$depOverlap = \frac{countTnH}{countH} = \frac{5}{6} = 0.833$$

(v) Syntactic Role Match

This feature is set to 1 if the (subject, object, verb) tuple in text matches the (subject, object, verb) tuple in hypothesis. The subject and object are matched directly whereas the verbs are matched after extracting their root forms from Wordnet and using the 'similar' relation from VerbOcean.

Similar feature has been used in Pakray et al.'s (2011) approach, wherein they have considered matching pairs of subject-verb, verb-object, subject-subject and object-object. However, the semantics of any sentence are governed by subject, verb and the object, if present. Our feature differs in the sense that a value of 1 is assigned for matching of the subject, object and the verb altogether; else its value remains 0. For example:

T: *Israeli Prime Minister Ariel Sharon threatened to dismiss Cabinet ministers who don't support his plan to withdraw from the Gaza Strip.*

H: *Israeli Prime Minister Ariel Sharon warned to fire cabinet opponents of his Gaza withdrawal plan.*

In this example, the subject in both T and H is *Ariel Sharon*, the direct object in T is *plan* whereas the direct object in H, is *opponents* but H has *plan* as the prepositional object and so we consider it as an object agreement. The verbs 'threaten' in T and 'warn' in H are similar as inferred from VerbOcean. Therefore, the value of syntactic-role match feature for the above-mentioned text-hypothesis pair is 1. In contrast, following Pakray et al.'s (2011) approach, the value of Wordnet-based subject-verb feature is 0.5 instead of 1 and the value of Wordnet-based verb-object feature is 0 due to mismatch in direct object.

(vi) Complement Verb Match

The sentences are not always simple and apart from main action-verbs, there can be entailment relationship due to complementing verb or clausal components. This feature performs a semantic match of root form (derived from Wordnet) of such verbs of text and hypothesis using VerbOcean. In addition, it also checks if the acting verb of hypothesis matches the acting verb or verb complement of the text and vice-versa. Let us consider an example to understand such pairs:

T: *Officials said Michael Hamilton was killed when gunmen opened fire and exchanged shots with Saudi security forces yesterday.*

H: *Michael Hamilton died yesterday.*

The main verb in T is 'said' while the main verb in H is 'died' and these verbs do not match. However, 'killed' is a clausal complement in T which is similar to the verb 'died' in H. Thus, a match results in this case assigning a value of 1 to the feature else the value of the feature would be 0.

(vii) Modifier Relation

In this feature, we check if the subject-object pair of hypothesis appears as subject-subject modifier or object-object modifier pair in the text. It is also a binary feature assuming a value of 1 for match and 0 for mismatch. For example:

T: *Antonio Fazio, the Bank of Italy governor, engulfed in controversy.*

H: *Antonio Fazio works for the Bank of Italy.*

In T, '*Antonio Fazio'* is the subject and '*Bank of Italy governor'* is the appositional modifier of the subject. In H, '*Antonio Fazio*' is the subject and '*Bank of Italy*' is the object. Therefore, a match occurs and the value of feature assigned is 1.

(viii) Nominalization

This features checks for nominal forms of the verbs as there can be correspondence between text and hypothesis owing to nominal verbs. We check if the nominal form of a verb in hypothesis acts as object in the text or the nominal form of verb in text acts as object in hypothesis. If a match is found, then we assign 1 to this feature else we assign 0. Following pair presents one such example:

T: *Satomi Mitarai died of blood loss.*

H: *Satomi Mitarai bled to death.*

In this example, the verb 'bled' in H has its noun-form 'blood' in T and the verb 'died' in T has its noun-form 'death' in H.

3.3 Experimental Setup

The system performance is evaluated by conducting experiments on RTE1, RTE2 and RTE3 datasets. The RTE1 dataset consists of 567 sentences pairs (T and H) in the development set and 800 sentence pairs in the test set. These sets are further divided into seven subsets, namely: Information Retrieval (IR), Comparable Documents (CD), Question Answering (QA), Information Extraction (IE), Machine Translation (MT) and Paraphrase Acquisition (PP). The RTE2 and RTE3 datasets contain 800 sentence pairs each in their development as well as test sets. Both the development and test sets of RTE2 and RTE3 are subdivided into four tasks, namely: IE, IR, QA and SUM (summarization).

We have conducted experiments with different ML algorithms including Support Vector Machines (SVM), Naïve Bayes and Decision Trees (DT) using Weka[3] tool. For each of the RTE datasets, respective training set has been used while experimenting with corresponding test-set. We have also performed task based analysis for RTE1 dataset. Following section summarizes the observations of our experiments.

4 Results

Table 2 presents the results achieved with 67% split evaluation of the classifiers on each of the development (training) datasets:

Classifier	Accuracy	Precision	Recall
	RTE - 1		
NB	59.28	57.8	68.6
SVM	**67.02**	63.3	80.9
DT	66.07	64	73.6
	RTE - 2		
NB	60.62	62.2	54.3
SVM	**65.75**	67	62
DT	63.0	60.7	73.8
	RTE - 3		
NB	64.75	68.2	59.2
SVM	66.62	66.4	71.4
DT	**67.87**	67	74

Table 2: Validation of system on development sets

As evident from table 2, highest accuracy is achieved with DT algorithm and SVM with RBF kernel. DT learns very fast and identifies strong relationship between input and target values (Ville, 2006). In our case, DT turned out to be efficient and fast learners to identify relationship between the feature vectors and the expected entailment results. For SVM, though it is not guaranteed which kernel performs better in a situation, RBF kernel is generally more flexible than the linear or polynomial kernels as it can model a high dimensional feature space with minimum error. The observations with these algorithms are strengthened by the test-set results as presented in table 3.

We have also experimented by using task label as a feature in our system as Bos and Markert

[3] http://www.cs.waikato.ac.nz/ml/weka/

(2005) experimented with their system. Like Bos and Markert's (2005) observation, we also found that the system performance increases with DT algorithms in contrast to other ML classifiers. Table 4 shows our system's performance on RTE1, RTE2 and RTE3 datasets using DT algorithm.

Classifier	Accuracy	Precision	Recall
RTE – 1			
NB	57.62	56.4	67.5
SVM	57.25	57.6	55.3
DT	**60.12**	60.3	68.7
RTE – 2			
NB	59.12	60.9	60
SVM	59.62	60	61
DT	**59.87**	57.5	73.2
RTE – 3			
NB	60.62	62.1	63.9
SVM	62.12	61.5	69.75
DT	**62.75**	62	71

Table3: Performance of system on test sets

DataSet	Accuracy	Precision	Recall
RTE1	**61.25**	61.7	57.7
RTE2	**60.41**	62.8	60.3
RTE3	**64.38**	62	78

Table 4: System Performance - Task label as Feature

For task-based analysis, we experimented with the tasks of RTE1 dataset separately. We present the comparative study of the accuracy achieved by our system with the SVM-based solution of Pazienza et al. (2005) and DT-based solution of Bos and Markert (2005) in table 5. The improvement in accuracy by our system is reflected in table 5.

Task	Pazienza et al. (2005)	Our System (SVM)	Bos & Markert (2005)	Our System (DT)
IE	49.17	**59.16**	54.2	**55.83**
IR	48.89	**71.33**	62.2	**67.51**
QA	45.74	**63.84**	56.9	**60.76**
MT	47.9	**62.5**	52.5	**58.33**
RC	52.14	**62.0**	50.7	**61.3**
CD	64.43	**83.46**	70.0	**81.04**
PP	50.0	**78.03**	56	**75.75**

Table 5: Task-based performance comparison for RTE1 test set

We carried out a comparative study of our system with other ML-based systems for RTE to check the performance of our system. The observations from this comparative analysis of our system with relevant related systems for RTE along with the feature counts (FC) used by the respective systems in presented in table 6. The comparative study indicates significant improvement in accuracy of our system over most of the existing state-of-art ML-based solutions for RTE except for few solutions only.

Accuracy	FC	RTE 1	RTE 2	RTE 3
(Bos&Markert, 2005)[4]	> 8	57.7	-	-
(Inkpen et al., 2006)	26	-	58.25	-
(Kozareva & Montoyo, 2006)	17	-	55.8	-
(Pakray et al., 2011)	16	53.7	59.2	61
(MacCartney et al., 2006)	28	59.1	-	-
(Hickl et al., 2006)	12	-	**65.25**	-
(Adams et al., 2006)	13	-	-	**67**
Ours	**8**	**60.12**	**59.87**	**62.75**

Table 6: Comparison of accuracy of our system with other systems

5 Conclusion

As the results indicate, our dependency-based heuristics and lexical features have resulted in significant improvement in accuracy of RTE1, RTE2 and RTE3 datasets. DT outperforms other classifiers with only 8 features that are syntactic and lexical in nature. SVM classifier shows comparable performance with the RBF kernel. The features are simple and intuitive; easy to comprehend and evaluate. The task-based performance for RTE1 dataset shows improved performance as compared to the similar study by Pazienza et al. (2005) and by Bos and Markert (2005). We intend to identify more syntactic and semantic features in future and improve upon and, experiment with them to refine the results further.

[4]Authors have used 8 deep semantic feature and some shallow lexical features, count of which is not clear from the paper. Therefore, we are considering their feature-count to be more than 8

References

Andrew Hickl, Jeremy Bensley, John Williams, Kirk Roberts, Bryan Rink and Ying Shi. 2006. Recognizing Textual Entailment with LCC's Groundhog System. In *Proceedings of the Second PASCAL Challenges Workshop on Recognizing Textual Entailment.*

Barry de Ville. 2006. *Decision Trees for Business Intelligence and Data Mining.* SAS Enterprise Miner.

Bill MacCartney, Trond Grenager, Marie-Catherine de Marneffe, Daniel Cer and Christopher D. Manning. 2006. Learning to recognize features of valid textual entailments. In *Proceedings of North American Chapter of ACL (NAACL-2006.*

Diana Inkpen, Darren Kipp, and Vivi Nastase. 2006. Machine Learning Experiments for Textual Entailment. In *Proceedings of the Second Challenge Workshop Recognizing Textual Entailment*: 10-15, Italy.

Diego Molla. 2003. Towards semantic-based overlap measures for question answering. In *Proceedings of the Australasian Language Technology Workshop 2003,* Australia.

Fabio M. Zanzotto, Marco Pennacchiotti and Alessandro Moschitti. 2009. A machine learning approach to textual entailment recognition. *Natural Language Engineering*, 15(4): 551-582.

Ido Dagan, Oren Glickman and Bernardo Magnini. 2005. The PASCAL Recognizing Textual Entailment Challenge, In *Proceedings of the First PASCAL Recognizing Textual Entailment Workshop.*

Johan Bos and Katja Markert. 2005. Recognising textual entailment with logical inference, In *Proceedings of the conference on Human Language Technology and Empirical Methods in Natural Language Processing*: 628-635.

Maria T. Pazienza, Marco Pennacchiotti and Fabio M. Zanzotto. 2005. Textual Entailment as Syntactic Graph Distance: a Rule Based and a SVM Based Approach. In *Proceedings of first PASCAL RTE challenge*:528—535.

Marie-Catherine de Marneffe, Bill MacCartney and Christopher D. Manning. 2006. Generating Typed Dependency Parses from Phrase Structure Parses. In *LREC 2006.*

Partha Pakray, Alexander Gelbukh and Sivaji Bandyopadhyay. 2011. Textual Entailment using Lexical and Syntactic Similarity. *International Journal of Artificial Intelligence & Applications (IJAIA)*, 2(1): 43-58.

Rod Adams, Gabriel Nicolae, Cristina Nicolae and Sanda Harabagiu. 2007. Textual Entailment through Extended Lexical Overlap and Lexico-Semantic Matching. In *Proceedings of the Third PASCAL Challenges Workshop on Recognizing Textual Entailment.*

Zornitsa Kozareva and Andrés Montoyo. 2006. MLEnt: The Machine Learning Entailment System of the University of Alicante. In *Proceedings of the Second Challenge Workshop Recognizing Textual Entailment*: 17-20.

Bilingual lexicon extraction for a distant language pair using a small parallel corpus

Ximena Gutierrez-Vasques
GIL IINGEN
UNAM
Mexico City, Mexico
xim@unam.mx

Abstract

The aim of this thesis proposal is to perform bilingual lexicon extraction for cases in which small parallel corpora are available and it is not easy to obtain monolingual corpus for at least one of the languages. Moreover, the languages are typologically distant and there is no bilingual seed lexicon available. We focus on the language pair Spanish-Nahuatl, we propose to work with morpheme based representations in order to reduce the sparseness and to facilitate the task of finding lexical correspondences between a highly agglutinative language and a fusional one. We take into account contextual information but instead of using a precompiled seed dictionary, we use the distribution and dispersion of the positions of the morphological units as cues to compare the contextual vectors and obtaining the translation candidates.

1 Introduction

Parallel corpora are a rich source of bilingual lexical information, they are a valuable resource that allows the development of several language technologies such as automatic construction of bilingual lexicons and statistical machine translation systems (SMT). Automatic construction of bilingual lexicons is useful since bilingual dictionaries are expensive resources and not many are available when one of the languages is resource-poor.

One way to perform bilingual lexical extraction from a parallel corpus is through word alignment. However, most of the methods to perform word-alignment, and in general the approaches to SMT, require huge amounts of parallel data. The task of extracting bilingual lexicon becomes even harder when we are dealing with very different languages, i.e., languages from different linguistic families that do not share orthographic, morphological or syntactic similarity.

The goal of this thesis is to propose a method for bilingual lexicon extraction that could be suitable for low-resource settings like the mentioned above. We work with the language pair Spanish-Nahuatl which are languages distant from each other (Indo-European and Uto-Aztecan language families) with different morphological phenomena. Nahuatl is an agglutinative language with polysynthetic tendency, this means that it can agglutinate many different morphemes to build highly complex words. On the other hand, Spanish can be classified as a fusional language where the words don't contain many different morphemes since several morphemes can be fused or overlaid into one encoding several meanings.

Although both languages are spoken in the same country, there is scarcity of parallel and monolingual corpora for Nahuatl. It is not easy to find general standard dictionaries due to the big dialectal variation and the lack of orthographical normalization of Nahuatl. Automatic extraction of a bilingual lexicon could be useful for contributing with machine-readable resources for the language pair that we are studying. Spanish is one of the most widely spoken languages in the world but, in the case of Nahuatl, few digital resources are available even though there exist around two million speakers of this language.

Our proposal aims to explore which information

Proceedings of NAACL-HLT 2015 Student Research Workshop (SRW), pages 154–160,
Denver, Colorado, June 1, 2015.

can be combined in order to estimate the bilingual correspondences and therefore building a bilingual lexicon. We plan to take into account correlation measures, positional cues and contextual information. Many of the methods that exploit contextual information require a precompiled digital seed dictionary or lexicon. We would like to propose a way to leave aside this language dependent requirement since many language pairs can face the same situation in which it is not easy to obtain a precompiled digital dictionary.

Unlike other approaches, we plan to take into account morphological information for building the word representations. The motivation behind is that morpheme-based representations can be useful to overcome the sparseness problem when building semantic vectors for morphologically rich languages with small corpus available.

The structure of the paper is as follows: Section 2 contains a general overview of the existing methods that tackle the bilingual extraction task and a description of our particular problem. In section 3, we describe the dataset and our proposal to address the bilingual lexical extraction for our low-resource setting. Finally, section 4 contains the conclusions.

2 Research Problem

2.1 Bilingual Lexicon Extraction

Bilingual lexicon extraction is the task of obtaining a list of word pairs deemed to be word-level translations (Haghighi et al., 2008). This has been an active area of research for several years, especially with the availability of big amounts of parallel corpuora that allow to model the relations between lexical units of the translated texts. One direct way to perform bilingual lexicon extraction is through word alignment from a parallel corpus. Word alignment is a fundamental part of SMT systems which build probabilistic translation models, based on several millions of parallel sentences, in order to estimate word and phrase level alignments (Brown et al., 1993).

However, the quality of word alignment methods used in SMT are heavily dependant on the amount of data and they require even more parallel data if we are dealing with very different languages. Since most of the language pairs do not have large amounts of clean parallel corpora readily available, there are alternative approaches for extracting multilingual information. Some methods rely on association and similarity measures to estimate the lexical correspondences, e.g., log-likelihood measures (Tufiş and Barbu, 2002), t-scores (Ahrenberg et al., 1998), positional difference between two successive occurrences of a word (Fung, 2000), just to mention some.

2.2 The low-resource setting

If there is not enough parallel corpora for a language pair, another alternative is to assume that there is enough comparable corpora or monolingual corpora for each of the languages. In these approaches bilingual lexicons are induced by taking into account several features, e.g, orthographic similarity, temporal similarity (Schafer and Yarowsky, 2002), association measures, topical information (Mimno et al., 2009) and contextual features. There are many works focused on the latter, they are based on the distributional notion (Harris, 1954) that a word that occurs in a given context in a language should have a translation that occurs in a similar context in the other language.

The general approach for using contextual information includes: 1. building a context vector for each lexical unit in both languages 2. Translating or projecting these context vectors to a common space using a seed dictionary or lexicon 3. Computing the similarity between the source and target words to find the translation candidates. There are several works that use contextual information, they vary in the way they represent the contexts and how they measure the similarity of the contextual vectors to extract translation candidates. (Rapp, 1995; Fung and Yee, 1998; Rapp, 1999; Diab and Finch, 2000; Déjean et al., 2002; Gaussier et al., 2004; Haghighi et al., 2008; Shezaf and Rappoport, 2010; Laroche and Langlais, 2010)

Another alternative is to use pivot languages as an intermediary language to extract bilingual lexicon (Tanaka and Umemura, 1994; Wu and Wang, 2007; Tsunakawa et al., 2008; Seo and Kim, 2013).

Lately there has been interest in multilingual distributed representation learning (Klementiev et al., 2012; Zou et al., 2013). These approaches are related with the ones that transfer information between languages using distributed representations and deep learning techniques (Lauly et al., 2014; Hermann and Blunsom, 2014). These approaches have the potential of semantic transfer into low-resource languages.

2.3 Our case of study

We focus on the language pair Spanish-Nahuatl, this represents a setting in which there is a small parallel corpus available, the two languages are very distant from each other and it is not easy to obtain comparable corpora or monolingual corpora for one of the languages.

These two languages are spoken in same country but Nahuatl does not have a web presence or text production comparable to Spanish. Most of the documents that can be easily found in Nahuatl are translations, that is why it is easier to obtain parallel corpora than monolingual. Although there are existing dictionaries for this language pair, not all of them are machine readable, the most extensive ones were made several centuries ago causing that some Spanish entries do not correspond anymore to the language spoken nowadays. Moreover, there is a big dialectal variation that complicates having one standard dictionary.

Under these conditions traditional statistical methods for word alignment are not the most suitable, in fact, to our knowledge it does not exist a SMT system yet for this language pair. We cannot rely either on orthographic similarity and there is no a pivot language that could be useful. On the other hand, practically all the methods based on contextual information require at some point a seed bilingual dictionary. This represents a chicken-egg problem (Koehn and Knight, 2002): If we have a bilingual lexicon we can translate the context vectors but we can only generate a bilingual lexicon with these methods if we are able to translate the context vectors.

The transfer based approaches have the potential of transferring semantic knowledge to low resource languages, e.g., alignment between sentences or phrases. However, they need to be trained with resource fortunate languages, usually requiring some supervised signal like word alignments to learn the bilingual embeddings.

We aim to address our low resource setting by combining several sources of information, mainly contextual features and association measures. In order to counteract the sparseness derived from working with a small parallel corpus of morphologically rich languages, we aim to use to morpheme representations instead of words. For the contextual approach, we prefer not to use the available noisy dictionaries as seed lexicon. Instead, we would like to explore features like the distribution and the dispersion of the positions of a morpheme in a text in order to be able to compare two contextual vectors representing lexical units in different languages.

Our conjecture is that the combination of several features, some of them usually applied for extracting lexicon from comparable corpora, could be suitable for a small, noisy parallel corpus of a distant language pair. Unlike other methods, our proposal aims to prescind from prior knowledge, e.g., a precompiled seed lexicon.

3 Methodology

3.1 The parallel corpus

To our knowledge, it did not exist a digital Spanish-Nahuatl parallel corpus publicly available. We had to build one, most of the sources were non digital books. As we have mentioned before, for some languages is not easy to extract parallel content from the typical web sources. Working with a low resource language sometimes implies difficulties that are not common when working with other languages, e.g., we had to perform a manual correction of the texts after being digitized since the OCR software confused several character patterns (it was probably assuming that it was processing a different language).

The documents of the parallel corpus are not quite homogeneous in the sense that there is dialectal, diachronic and orthographical variation. This variation can represent noise for many of the statistical methods, as an attempt to reduce it we performed an orthographic normalization. It does not exist a general agreement regarding to the appropriate way to write nahuatl language. We chose a set of normalization rules (around 270) proposed by linguists to normalize classical nahuatl (Thouvenot and Maynez, 2008) in order to obtain a more systematic writing. We implement them in FOMA (Hulden, 2009) a finite state toolkit used mainly for computational morphology. The set of rules that we used reduces the variation of many of the texts but unfortunately not from all them.

The total size of the corpus is around 1 million tokens (included both languages) which is still very small for the SMT approaches. To this scarcity, we have to add the fact that we will only work with a subset of documents, those that do not have a big dialectal or orthographical variation

3.2 Morphology

In order to perform the bilingual lexicon extraction, we would like to take into account the morphology of the language pair since the alignment complexity between typologically different languages is far away from the alignment complexity between similar languages (Cakmak et al., 2012).

Nahuatl is a polysynthetic language that allows compact nominal and verbal constructions where the complements, adjectives and adverbs can agglutinate with the verbal or nominal roots. This language also has incorporation and some other morphological phenomena. In contrast, Spanish is a fusional language in which a single morpheme can simultaneously encode several meanings. Regarding to the word order, Nahuatl and Spanish are relativetely flexible, specially Nahuatl.

Dealing with the morphology could be important to reduce the negative impact of sparseness and therefore having better representations of the lexical units. Specially in cases like ours where the corpus is small and the languages are morphologically rich, this may cause many different word types but few repetitions of them in the documents. If we have few contexts characterizing a word, then the contextuals vectors will not have a good quality, affecting the performance of the methods that exploit contextual features. Building morpheme based representations could be also useful for pairing the bilingual lexical units, since in agglutinative languages a single word can correspond to many in another language. The next example shows a morphologically segmented word in nahuatl and its correspondence to Spanish:

ti- nech - maca- z - nequi
2SG.S-1S.O-'give'-FUT-'want'
"Tu me quieres dar" (Spanish)
"You want to give me"

Recent approaches take into account morphology and investigate how compositional morphological distributed representations can improve word representations (Lazaridou et al., 2013) and language models (Botha and Blunsom, 2014; El-Desoky Mousa et al., 2013; Luong et al., 2013).

We aim to use, already implemented, unsupervised methods to perform morphological segmentation. Software like Morfessor (Creutz and Lagus, 2005) that seems to work well for agglutinative languages could be useful as well for languages like Nahuatl. Additionally, there is a morphological analysis tool based on rules for classical nahuatl (Thouvenot, 2011) that could be used to improve the unsupervised morphological segmentation. As for the Spanish case, there are unsupervised approaches that have proven to be successful in discovering Spanish affixes (Urrea, 2000; Medina-Urrea, 2008).

Once we have the segmented morphemes, we can build morpheme-based representations to extract the bilingual correspondences. Initially we plan to focus in extracting bilingual lexicon only for words with lexical meaning and not the grammatical ones.

At this moment, we have not still decided if we will work only with vector representations of each morpheme or with a composed representation of the words based on the morphemes.

3.3 Bilingual lexicon extraction without using a seed dictionary

For the bilingual lexical extraction we aim to combine several cues including correlation measures and contextual information. As we have mentioned before, most of the contextual methods have in common a need for a seed lexicon of translations to efficiently bridge the gap between languages. We would like to prescind from this requirement.

Seed lexicons are necessary to compare the contexts between the word representations in different languages. Few works have tried to circumvent this requirement, e.g., building a seed lexicon based on spelling and cognate cues (Koehn and Knight, 2002), using punctuation marks as a small seed lexicon and find alignments by measuring intralingual association between words (Diab and Finch, 2000). Lately some works have explored training a cross-language topic model on comparable corpora in order to obtain a seed lexicon without prior knowledge (Vulić and Moens, 2012).

We would like to explore the positions in which a word occurs in a text and the dispersion of these positions as cues for finding similar words in both languages and being able to compare the context vectors that characterize the words in both languages. The hypothesis is that words that are translations of each other tend to occur in similar positions of a parallel text and the distributions have similar dispersions. It is noteworthy that in our case we attempt to work at the morpheme level instead of the word level.

For each type in the text, in our case morphemes, we can store a vector of offsets, i.e. the positions in which the type occurs relative to the size of corpus. After recollecting all the positions for a lexical unit we can also measure the dispersion by calculating the variance or the standard deviation.

We conjecture that those lexical units between languages that obtain high similarity in their position distributions and their dispersion, are useful to compare the context vectors. They can be seen as a sort of initial seed lexicon constructed in a language independent way. The similarity can be calculated in terms of measurements like cosine similarity or measurements that take into account correlations or divergence between distributions.

Regarding to the construction of vectors encoding contextual information of the lexical units, we plan to try different experimental setups, examining different representations of word contexts, i.e., different association measures and weighting schemes for building the semantic vectors, different sizes of context windows and other important parameters that must be taken into account when working with distributional semantic representations.

Once we have the contextual vectors that represent the lexical units (in our case representations based on morphology) translation candidates can be obtained. Based on the contexts that are similar between the two vectors we can compare a source and a target contextual vector using different techniques or projecting them into a joint space and calculate the distance between them.

Taking into account the contexts and positions of the words in the whole document could be useful for noisy parallel corpora where there is not always a one to one correspondence between sentences. This is the case of some of the texts of our parallel corpus.

3.4 Combination of features and evaluation

It is very common for bilingual extraction methods to use a diverse set of cues and then combine them in order to obtain better translation candidates (Koehn and Knight, 2002; Tiedemann, 2003; Irvine, 2013). We will not use some of the typical cues like orthographic similarity or temporal, but we would like to combine the contextual information explained in the above section with some association measures between words or morphemes. Our intention is to propose a weighting scheme that allows to combine the several criteria and to obtain a rank of the translation candidates.

Once the translation candidates are extracted, we can establish a baseline by using some of the methods suitable for parallel corpora, e.g., the typical word alignment methods used in SMT. Additionally, it would be interesting to try different language pairs with more resources, in order to evaluate if our method can be competitive to more downstream approaches that rely on more data. For instance, we can evaluate in resource fortunate distant pairs like Spanish-German, since German is also morphologically rich with extensive use of compounds.

4 Conclusions

In this work we have presented a thesis proposal where the goal is to extract a bilingual lexicon under a particular low-resource setting in which is difficult to obtain big amounts of parallel or monolingual corpora and also is not easy to have an extensive standard electronical dictionary. The particularities of the methods are not completely defined since the work is in progress, we propose to combine morpheme based representations with contextual and association features in order to obtain translation candidates for the lexical units.

In our proposal we try to circumvent the need of a bilingual electronic dictionary which can be hard to obtain when working with low-resource languages. Although we focus in a particular language pair, the proposed methods are language independent and they could be used for languages with similar settings or even for comparable corpora.

Some of the aspects that are missing to tackle are

the problems that may arise when dealing with synonyms and polysemic words.

5 Acknowledgements

This work is supported by the Mexican Council of Science and Technology (CONACYT), funds 370713 and CB-2012/178248. Thanks to the reviewers for their valuable comments.

References

Lars Ahrenberg, Mikael Andersson, and Magnus Merkel. 1998. A simple hybrid aligner for generating lexical correspondences in parallel texts. In *Proceedings of the 17th international conference on Computational linguistics-Volume 1*, pages 29–35. Association for Computational Linguistics.

Jan A Botha and Phil Blunsom. 2014. Compositional morphology for word representations and language modelling. *arXiv preprint arXiv:1405.4273*.

Peter F Brown, Vincent J Della Pietra, Stephen A Della Pietra, and Robert L Mercer. 1993. The mathematics of statistical machine translation: Parameter estimation. *Computational linguistics*, 19(2):263–311.

Mehmet Talha Cakmak, Süleyman Acar, and Gülsen Eryigit. 2012. Word alignment for english-turkish language pair. In *LREC*, pages 2177–2180.

Mathias Creutz and Krista Lagus. 2005. *Unsupervised morpheme segmentation and morphology induction from text corpora using Morfessor 1.0*. Helsinki University of Technology.

Hervé Déjean, Éric Gaussier, and Fatia Sadat. 2002. An approach based on multilingual thesauri and model combination for bilingual lexicon extraction. In *Proceedings of the 19th international conference on Computational linguistics-Volume 1*, pages 1–7. Association for Computational Linguistics.

Mona Diab and Steve Finch. 2000. A statistical word-level translation model for comparable corpora. Technical report, DTIC Document.

A El-Desoky Mousa, H-KJ Kuo, Lidia Mangu, and Hagen Soltau. 2013. Morpheme-based feature-rich language models using deep neural networks for lvcsr of egyptian arabic. In *Acoustics, Speech and Signal Processing (ICASSP), 2013 IEEE International Conference on*, pages 8435–8439. IEEE.

Pascale Fung and Lo Yuen Yee. 1998. An ir approach for translating new words from nonparallel, comparable texts. In *Proceedings of the 36th Annual Meeting of the Association for Computational Linguistics and 17th International Conference on Computational Linguistics-Volume 1*, pages 414–420. Association for Computational Linguistics.

Pascale Fung. 2000. A statistical view on bilingual lexicon extraction. In *Parallel Text Processing*, pages 219–236. Springer.

Eric Gaussier, J-M Renders, Irina Matveeva, Cyril Goutte, and Hervé Déjean. 2004. A geometric view on bilingual lexicon extraction from comparable corpora. In *Proceedings of the 42nd Annual Meeting on Association for Computational Linguistics*, page 526. Association for Computational Linguistics.

Aria Haghighi, Percy Liang, Taylor Berg-Kirkpatrick, and Dan Klein. 2008. Learning bilingual lexicons from monolingual corpora. In *ACL*, volume 2008, pages 771–779.

Zellig S Harris. 1954. Distributional structure. *Word*.

Karl Moritz Hermann and Phil Blunsom. 2014. Multilingual models for compositional distributed semantics. *arXiv preprint arXiv:1404.4641*.

Mans Hulden. 2009. Foma: a finite-state compiler and library. In *Proceedings of the 12th Conference of the European Chapter of the Association for Computational Linguistics: Demonstrations Session*, pages 29–32. Association for Computational Linguistics.

Ann Irvine. 2013. Statistical machine translation in low resource settings. In *HLT-NAACL*, pages 54–61.

Alexandre Klementiev, Ivan Titov, and Binod Bhattarai. 2012. Inducing crosslingual distributed representations of words.

Philipp Koehn and Kevin Knight. 2002. Learning a translation lexicon from monolingual corpora. In *Proceedings of the ACL-02 workshop on Unsupervised lexical acquisition-Volume 9*, pages 9–16. Association for Computational Linguistics.

Audrey Laroche and Philippe Langlais. 2010. Revisiting context-based projection methods for term-translation spotting in comparable corpora. In *Proceedings of the 23rd international conference on computational linguistics*, pages 617–625. Association for Computational Linguistics.

Stanislas Lauly, Alex Boulanger, and Hugo Larochelle. 2014. Learning multilingual word representations using a bag-of-words autoencoder. *arXiv preprint arXiv:1401.1803*.

Angeliki Lazaridou, Marco Marelli, Roberto Zamparelli, and Marco Baroni. 2013. Compositional-ly derived representations of morphologically complex words in distributional semantics. In *ACL (1)*, pages 1517–1526. Citeseer.

Minh-Thang Luong, Richard Socher, and Christopher D Manning. 2013. Better word representations with recursive neural networks for morphology. *CoNLL-2013*, 104.

Alfonso Medina-Urrea. 2008. Affix discovery based on entropy and economy measurements. *Computational Linguistics for Less-Studied Languages*, 10:99–112.

David Mimno, Hanna M Wallach, Jason Naradowsky, David A Smith, and Andrew McCallum. 2009. Polylingual topic models. In *Proceedings of the 2009 Conference on Empirical Methods in Natural Language Processing: Volume 2-Volume 2*, pages 880–889. Association for Computational Linguistics.

Reinhard Rapp. 1995. Identifying word translations in non-parallel texts. In *Proceedings of the 33rd annual meeting on Association for Computational Linguistics*, pages 320–322. Association for Computational Linguistics.

Reinhard Rapp. 1999. Automatic identification of word translations from unrelated english and german corpora. In *Proceedings of the 37th annual meeting of the Association for Computational Linguistics on Computational Linguistics*, pages 519–526. Association for Computational Linguistics.

Charles Schafer and David Yarowsky. 2002. Inducing translation lexicons via diverse similarity measures and bridge languages. In *proceedings of the 6th conference on Natural language learning-Volume 20*, pages 1–7. Association for Computational Linguistics.

Hong-Seok Kwon Hyeong-Won Seo and Jae-Hoon Kim. 2013. Bilingual lexicon extraction via pivot language and word alignment tool. *ACL 2013*, page 11.

Daphna Shezaf and Ari Rappoport. 2010. Bilingual lexicon generation using non-aligned signatures. In *Proceedings of the 48th annual meeting of the association for computational linguistics*, pages 98–107. Association for Computational Linguistics.

Kumiko Tanaka and Kyoji Umemura. 1994. Construction of a bilingual dictionary intermediated by a third language. In *Proceedings of the 15th conference on Computational linguistics-Volume 1*, pages 297–303. Association for Computational Linguistics.

Marc Thouvenot and Romero-Galvan Ruben Maynez, Pilar. 2008. La normalizacion grafica del codice florentino. In *El universo de Sahagun pasado y presente*. UNAM.

Marc Thouvenot. 2011. Chachalaca en cen, juntamente. In *Compendio Enciclopedico del Nahuatl, DVD*. INAH.

Jörg Tiedemann. 2003. Combining clues for word alignment. In *Proceedings of the tenth conference on European chapter of the Association for Computational Linguistics-Volume 1*, pages 339–346. Association for Computational Linguistics.

Takashi Tsunakawa, Naoaki Okazaki, and Jun'ichi Tsujii. 2008. Building a bilingual lexicon using phrase-based statistical machine translation via a pivot language. In *COLING (Posters)*, pages 127–130.

Dan Tufiş and Ana-Maria Barbu. 2002. Lexical token alignment: Experiments, results and applications. In *Proceedings from The Third International Conference on Language Resources anrd Evaluation (LREC-2002), Las Palmas, Spain*, pages 458–465.

Alfonso Medina Urrea. 2000. Automatic discovery of affixes by means of a corpus: A catalog of spanish affixes. *Journal of quantitative linguistics*, 7(2):97–114.

Ivan Vulić and Marie-Francine Moens. 2012. Detecting highly confident word translations from comparable corpora without any prior knowledge. In *Proceedings of the 13th Conference of the European Chapter of the Association for Computational Linguistics*, pages 449–459. Association for Computational Linguistics.

Hua Wu and Haifeng Wang. 2007. Pivot language approach for phrase-based statistical machine translation. *Machine Translation*, 21(3):165–181.

Will Y Zou, Richard Socher, Daniel M Cer, and Christopher D Manning. 2013. Bilingual word embeddings for phrase-based machine translation. In *EMNLP*, pages 1393–1398.

Morphological Paradigms: Computational Structure and Unsupervised Learning

Jackson L. Lee
University of Chicago
jsllee@uchicago.edu

Abstract

This thesis explores the computational structure of morphological paradigms from the perspective of unsupervised learning. Three topics are studied: (i) stem identification, (ii) paradigmatic similarity, and (iii) paradigm induction. All the three topics progress in terms of the scope of data in question. The first and second topics explore structure when morphological paradigms are given, first within a paradigm and then across paradigms. The third topic asks where morphological paradigms come from in the first place, and explores strategies of paradigm induction from child-directed speech. This research is of interest to linguists and natural language processing researchers, for both theoretical questions and applied areas.

1 Introduction

Morphological paradigms (e.g., *walk-walks-walked-walking*) are of central interest to both linguists and natural language processing researchers for the connectedness (e.g., *jumps, jumping* sharing the lexeme JUMP) and predictability across words (e.g., inducing *googles* for *google* based on *jump-jumps* etc). This thesis explores the computational structure of morphological paradigms, particularly from the perspective of unsupervised learning for modeling how such structure can be induced from unstructured data. Three topics under study are as follows:

- **Stem identification:** The first part of the thesis concerns the structure *within* a morphological paradigm, focusing on stem identification. The goal is to devise general and language-independent strategies for stem extraction applicable for different types of morphology across languages, and goes beyond the common substring-based approaches.

- **Paradigmatic similarity:** The second part of the thesis asks what structure there is *across* morphological paradigms. Paradigms often do not inflect in the exact same pattern, which leads to inflection classes, e.g., Spanish verbs in distinct conjugation groups. At the same time, paradigms inflect in remarkably similar ways, e.g., Spanish verbs in the second plural all end with *-mos* regardless the inflection classes. This part of the thesis develops a string-based hierarchical clustering algorithm that computationally characterizes the similarity and differences across morphological paradigms.

- **Induction of morphological paradigms from unstructured data**: The third part of the thesis seeks to induce paradigms from unstructured data. The kind of unstructured data of interest here is child-directed speech. Building on previous work on unsupervised learning of morphological paradigms from raw text, this thesis develops an approach of paradigm induction that incorporates results from the previous two parts of this thesis and has a version taking child-directed speech data incrementally.

These three topics on morphological paradigms progress in terms of the scope of data in question. The first and second parts explore structure when paradigms are given – one paradigm at a time, and

Proceedings of NAACL-HLT 2015 Student Research Workshop (SRW), pages 161–167,
Denver, Colorado, June 1, 2015. ©2015 Association for Computational Linguistics

then a list of paradigms together. The third part asks where morphological paradigms come from in the first place. This research will be of interest to both linguistics (the nature of strings, morphemes, and paradigms) and natural language processing (information retrieval, machine translation).

2 Stem identification

Given a morphological paradigm with inflected word forms, what is the stem of the paradigm? This question on stem identification is part of the morpheme segmentation problem, important for both theoretical linguistics (Spencer 2012) and computational linguistics (Goldsmith 2010, Hammarström and Borin 2011); once the stem is identified, what is not the stem in each word form can be subject to further segmentation and morphological analysis for potential affixes. Stem identification is far from being a trivial problem. Strictly concatenative morphology, as exemplified by English *jump-jumps-jumped-jumping* with "jump" as the stem, appears intuitively simple. In contrast, non-concatenative morphology, a well-known case being Arabic root-and-pattern morphology (e.g., *kataba* 'he wrote', *yaktubu* 'he writes/will write' with "k-t-b" as the stem) has been treated as something fundamentally different. The first part of this thesis seeks to develop language-independent, algorithmic approaches to stem identification which are sufficiently general to work with both concatenative and non-concatenative morphology.

2.1 Linearity and contiguity

The problem of stem identification begins with the definition of "stem" in a morphological paradigm. A common and language-independent assumption is that the stem (broadly construed, encompassing "root" and "base") is the maximal common material across all word forms in the paradigm. This thesis explores different definitions of "maximal common material" in search of general algorithms of stem identification for languages of different morphological types. In particular, we examine ways of characterizing strings in terms of linearity and contiguity.

As a point of departure, we take the maximal common material to mean the maximal common *substring*, a very intuitive and common assumption in morpheme segmentation. To illustrate the idea of a substring with respect to linearity and contiguity, consider the string "abcde". "a", "bc", and "cde" are its substrings. "ac" is not a possible substring, because "a" and "c" are not contiguous. "ba" is not a substring either, because "a" does not linearly come after "b" in the string "abcde". Because substrings embody both linearity and contiguity, if a stem in a morphological paradigm is the longest common substring across the word forms, then this approach of stem identification works well only for strictly concatenative morphology but not for anything that deviates from it. To solve this problem, this thesis explores various ways of defining the maximal common material with regard to linearity and contiguity.

2.2 Substrings, multisets, and subsequences

The definition of maximal common material may depend on whether linearity and contiguity are respected. Three major definitions along these two parameters are of interest; see Table 1:

	Substring	Multiset	Subsequence
Linearity	✓	✗	✓
Contiguity	✓	✗	✗

Table 1: Three definitions of maximal common material for stem identification in terms of linearity and contiguity

(The possibility of maintaining contiguity but abandoning linearity results in pairs of symbols which appear to be less informative for stem identification.)

As noted above, defining the stem as the maximal common *substring* is suboptimal for non-concatenative morphology. The two other strategies consider the stem as the maximal common *multiset* or *subsequence*, illustrated in Table 2 by the Spanish verb PODER 'to be able' conjugated in present indicative. Taking the stem to be the maximal common *multiset* yields the set {p,d,e} as the stem for the PODER paradigm. Table 2 highlights the stem material for each word form. Certain word forms have multiple stem analyses because of the multiple occurrences of "e" in the words concerned; these can be resolved by cross-paradigmatic comparison in section 3 below or paradigm-internal heuristics (e.g., choosing the stem that is the most congruent with non-stem material compared to other words in the paradigm, as in Ahlberg et al. 2014). In contrast, if the stem is the maximal common *subsequence*, then there are two competing stems for the PODER paradigm: p-d and p-e (using '-' to denote linear order without committing to contiguity). These two stems are tied because they each contain two symbols and are the longest possible common subsequences in the paradigms.

	Multiset {p,d,e}	Subsequence p-d	p-e
puedo	**pued**o	**pued**o	**pue**do
puedes	**pued**es **pu**e**de**s	**pued**es	**pue**des **pu**ed**e**s
puede	**pued**e **pu**e**de**	**pued**e	**pue**de **pu**ed**e**
podemos	**pode**mos	**pod**emos	**po**d**e**mos
podéis	**pode**is	**pod**eis	**po**d**e**is
pueden	**pued**en **pu**e**de**n	**pued**en	**pue**den **pu**ed**e**n

Table 2: Stem as maximal common multiset or subsequence for the Spanish PODER paradigm conjugated for present indicative

The subsequence approach has clear merits. Recent work—both directly and indirectly on stem identification—appears to converge on the use of the subsequence approach (Fullwood and O'Donnell 2013, Ahlberg et al. 2014). This is because it can handle Arabic-type non-concatenative morphology, infixation, circumfixation (as in German *ge*-X-*t*), and (trivially) the *jump*-type strictly concatenative morphology. In general, linearity appears to be more important than contiguity in stem identification. It must be noted, however, that probably for the more familiar properties of substrings, linguists are accustomed to using multi-tier substrings to handle surface non-contiguity, e.g., McCarthy (1985) on templatic morphology and Heinz and Lai (2013) on vowel harmony.

This part of the thesis serves as the foundational work for the later parts. For this first part, languages of interest include those with morphology diverging from simple concatenation, e.g., English with weak suppletion, Spanish with stem allomorphy, Arabic with templatic morphology, and German with circumfixation. Datasets come from standard sources such as Wiktionary (cf. Durrett and DeNero 2013). In terms of evaluation, a particular stem identification algorithm can be tested for whether it provides the correct stems for paradigm generation, an evaluation method connected to the clustering of paradigms in section 3.

Apart from stems, stem identification necessarily identifies the residual, non-stem material in each word form in the paradigm. The non-stem material is analogous to the affixes and stem allomorphs (e.g., the *o*∼*ue* alternation in PODER). It plays an important role in terms of structure across morphological paradigms, the subject of the next section.

3 Paradigmatic similarity

The second part of the thesis asks what structure there is *across* morphological paradigms. Word forms across paradigms do not alternate in the same pattern. Linguists discuss this in terms of inflection classes, which introduce differences across morphological paradigms. At the same time, however, morphological patterns are also systematically similar. This part of the thesis focuses on the modeling of *paradigm similarity* and develops a string-based hierarchical clustering algorithm that computationally characterizes the similarity and differences across morphological paradigms, with both theoretical and practical values.

3.1 Inflection classes

Morphological paradigms often do not inflect in the same way, which leads to inflection classes. For example, Spanish verbs are classified into three conjugation groups (commonly referred to as -AR, -ER, and -IR verbs), illustrated in Table 3 for the inflectional suffixes (all person and number combinations) in present indicative.

	-AR	-ER	-IR
1.SG	-o	-o	-o
2.SG	-as	-es	-es
3.SG	-a	-e	-e
1.PL	-amos	-emos	-imos
2.PL	-áis	-éis	-ís
3.PL	-an	-en	-en

Table 3: Suffixes for the three Spanish conjugation groups in present indicative

The Spanish conjugation classes show what is common across languages that this part of the thesis models: *partial* similarity across morphological paradigms. Spanish is described as having three conjugation classes for the three distinct overall suffixing patterns. For example, they are completely different for first-person plurals (*-amos, -emos*, and *-imos*). At the same time, they share a great deal in common. Across all three classes, the first-person singular suffixes are *-o*, the second-person singular suffixes end with *-s*, and so forth. Some classes share properties to the exclusion of others: the second and third conjugation groups share *-es, -e, -en* for 2.SG, 3.SG, 3.PL respectively, but the first conjugation group have *-as, -a, -an* instead.

The similarities and differences which morphological paradigms exhibit as inflection classes are of interest to both linguistics and natural language processing. In linguistics, the partial similarities across inflection classes prompt theoretical questions on the extent to which paradigms can differ from one another (Carstairs 1987, Müller 2007). Computationally, inflection classes introduce non-uniformity across paradigms and must be handled in one way or another in an automatic morphology learning system. Previous work has opted to explicitly learn inflection classes (Goldsmith and O'Brien 2006) or collapse them in some way (Chan 2006, Hammarström 2009, Monson 2009, Zeman 2009).

3.2 Clustering for paradigm similarity

This thesis aims to characterize paradigm similarity in a way that is amenable to a linguistic analysis and a formal model of paradigm similarity useful for computational tasks related to paradigms. As discussed above, similarities and differences crisscross one another in morphological paradigms and result in inflection classes. It is therefore reasonable to think of morphological paradigms as having a string-based hierarchical structure, where paradigms more similar to one another by the inflectional patterns cluster together. Haspelmath and Sims (2010) explore just this idea using data from Greek nouns and demonstrate how inflection classes can be modeled as a problem of clustering, though their work appears to be based purely on the human linguist's intuition and is not computationally implemented. This thesis proposes a string-based hierarchical clustering algorithm (with morphological paradigms as the objects of interest to cluster) for modeling paradigm similarity, which is (i) built on results of stem identification from section 2 and (ii) useful for further computational tasks such as paradigm generation.

There are multiple advantages of proposing a clustering algorithm for morphological paradigms. To the linguist, results of clustering paradigms can be visualized, which will be helpful for the study of inflectional structure of the morphology of less familiar languages (such as those based on fieldwork data). For computational linguistics and natural language processing, clustering provides a similarity measure that is useful for inducing unobserved word forms of incomplete morphological paradigms.

The proposed algorithm performs agglomerative hierarchical clustering on a given list of morphological paradigms. It involves stem identification (section 2) that determines the non-stem material in the word forms of each paradigm. The distance metric measures similarity among the paradigms by comparing non-stem material, which forms the basis of the distance matrix for hierarchical clustering.

Preliminary work (Lee 2014) suggests that clustering morphological paradigms gives desirable results. To illustrate, Figure 1 shows the clustering results of our algorithm under development for several English verbal paradigms (by orthography). For reasons of space, the results of only ten English verbs are discussed here; see Lee (2014) for details.

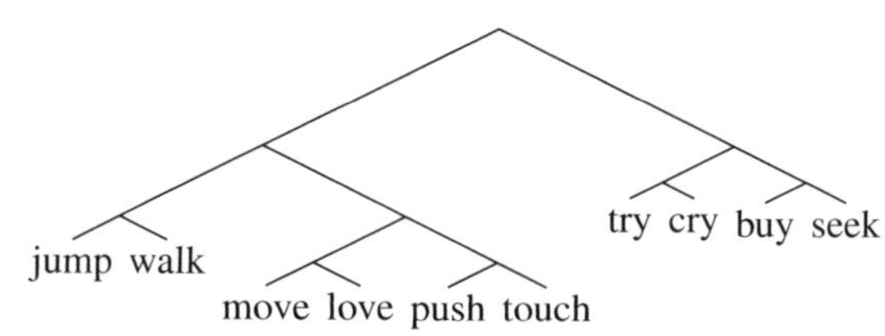

Figure 1: Simplified clustering results for a few English verbal paradigms, each represented by the infinitive form

In Figure 1, the two largest clusters of verbs are the one with more regular morphology on the left (JUMP, WALK, MOVE, LOVE, PUSH, TOUCH) and the other on the right with verbs of more drastic inflectional/orthographic alternations (TRY, CRY with the $i{\sim}y$ alternation, and BUY, SEEK with *-ght* in past tense). The smaller clusters among the regular verbs are due to the form for third person singular in present tense (PUSH, TOUCH with an additional ‘e’) and the verb-final ‘e’ (MOVE, LOVE with ‘e’ dropped for the *-ing* form). This example shows that clustering morphological paradigms provides a much more fine-grained characterization of inflection classes, which are usually described in non-hierarchical terms in linguistics.

An open question here is how to evaluate the results of clustering morphological paradigms. The major issue is that morphological paradigms are usually not hierarchically represented in standard descriptions, thereby making it unclear what the gold standard could be. One possibility is that the learned inflection classes (based on clusters of paradigms) be compared to those in standard grammatical descriptions of the language in question. Alternatively, the results can be evaluated indirectly by what the induced structure should facilitate, namely paradigm generation; this also evaluates stem identification in section 2. Datasets of paradigm tables for languages with inflection classes (English, Greek, Spanish, etc) come from standard sources such as Wiktionary. Paradigm generation takes a paradigm table with held-out words for some paradigms, and the goal is to recover the missing words using (i) stems computed based on the available words in the respective paradigms (section 2) and (ii) non-stem material as predicted based on the cross-paradigmatic cluster information (this section).

4 Induction of morphological paradigms from unstructured data

The discussion so far has assumed that a list of morphological paradigms are available for the study of structure within (section 2) and across (section 3) paradigms. While this is a common practice in the cognitive and computational modeling of morphological paradigms (Albright and Hayes 2002, Durrett and DeNero 2013), it is legitimate to ask where a list of morphological paradigms come from in the first place. This part of the thesis attempts to provide an answer to this question. Building on previous work on unsupervised paradigm induction, this thesis will propose a language-independent, incremental paradigm learning system that induces paradigms with child-directed speech data as the input.

4.1 Incremental paradigm induction

The unsupervised learning of morphological paradigms has attracted a lot of interest in computational linguistics and natural language processing (Goldsmith 2001, Schone and Jurafsky 2001, Chan 2006, Creutz and Lagus 2005, Monson 2009, Dreyer and Eisner 2011, Ahlberg et al. 2014). Virtually all previous work proposes a batch algorithm of paradigm induction, rather than an online and incremental learner, that takes some raw text as the input data. This is probably cognitively implausible, because a human child does not have access to all input data at once. This thesis proposes an incremental paradigm induction system to fill this gap of the relative lack of work on the incremental and unsupervised learning of morphological paradigms.

As a starting point, the proposed paradigm induction system will use one akin to Linguistica (Goldsmith 2001) and adapt it as an incremental version. The choice of a system like Linguistica as the point of departure is justified, because the goal here is to induce morphological paradigms from unstructured data but not necessarily morpheme segmentation (accomplished by other systems such as Morfessor (Creutz and Lagus 2005) that focus strongly on morphologically rich languages such as Finnish and Turkish). Linguistica induces paradigms by finding the optimal cut between a stem and an affix across words that could enter into paradigmatic relations, and does not perform further morpheme segmentation. A characteristic of Linguistica that will be modified in this thesis is that of stem identification: as it currently stands, it assumes (i) strictly concatenative morphology (i.e., stem as maximal common *substring*), and (ii) knowledge of whether the language under investigation is suffixing or prefixing. In line with the general goal of coming up with language-independent algorithms to handle natural language morphology, we will make use of the results from section 2 on stem identification for languages of diverse morphological types.

The input data will child-directed speech from CHILDES (MacWhinney 2000) for North American English. Specifically, we will be using a dataset of four million word tokens compiled from child-directed speech data of age range from a few months old to 12 years old. The proposed algorithm will make use of the temporal information of the child-directed speech and read the data in small and chronologically ordered chunks. As such, this incremental version of Linguistica models child language acquisition, and the results will be of much interest to linguists. For evaluation, research on the child acquisition of English morphology (Cazden 1968, Brown 1973) provides the gold standard information on the order of acquisition of major morphological patterns (plurals acquired before possessives, present progressives acquired before pasts, etc).

4.2 Collapsing paradigms of different inflection classes

A recurrent problem in unsupervised learning of morphological paradigms is that certain induced morphological paradigmatic patterns may appear incomplete (due to unobserved word forms) or distinct on the surface (due to inflection classes), but should intuitively be collapsed in some way (Goldsmith 2009). For inflection classes, for instance, English verbs display a regular morphological pattern as in *Ø-s-ed-ing* (e.g., for JUMP), but there is also a very similar—but distinct—pattern, with *e-es-ed-ing* (e.g., for MOVE with the silent 'e'); this English example is by orthography, but is analogous to Spanish verbs with inflection classes discussed above. Ideally, it would be desirable to collapse morphological patterns, e.g., the two English morphological patterns just mentioned as belonging to the verbal category and with the correct morphosyntactic alignment for the suffixes across the two patterns. Previous work either ignores this issue and treats the distinct surface patterns as is (e.g., Goldsmith 2001) or attempts to collapse morphological patterns (e.g., Chan 2006, with the assumption of part-of-speech tags being available).

This thesis will explore the possibility of collapsing paradigms of different inflection classes with no annotations (e.g., part-of-speech tags) in the input data. Some sort of syntactic information will have to be induced and combined with the induced morphological knowledge, in the spirit of previous work such as Higgins (2002) and Clark (2003). We are currently using graph-theoretical approaches to the unsupervised learning of syntactic categories. Based on Goldsmith and Wang's (2012) proposal of the word manifold, a given corpus is modeled as a graph, where the nodes are the words and the edges connect words that are distributionally similar based on n-grams from the corpus. The resulting graph has distributionally (and therefore syntactically) similar words densely connected together, e.g., modal verbs and infinitives in Figure 2. Various graph clustering algorithms are being explored for the purposes of word category induction.

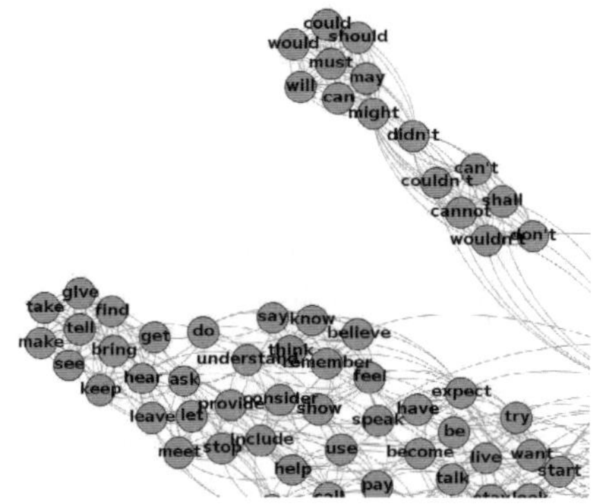

Figure 2: A zoomed-in image of clusters of modal verbs and infinitives in a 1,000-word graph

5 Contributions

This thesis will contribute to both the unsupervised learning of natural language morphology as well as bringing theoretical linguistics and computational linguistics closer together.

On the unsupervised learning of natural language morphology, this thesis explores structure within and across morphological paradigms and proposes algorithms for adducing such structure given a list of morphological paradigms. Furthermore, we also ask how an unsupervised learning system can induce morphological paradigms from child-directed speech, an area much less researched than previous work on non-incremental and batch algorithms for paradigm induction.

As for bridging theoretical linguistics and computational linguistics, this thesis represents a serious attempt to do linguistics that is theoretically informed from the linguist's perspective and is computationally rigorous for implementation. Using natural language morphology as an example, this thesis shows the value of reproducible, accessible, and extensible research from the computational community that will benefit theoretical linguistics.

References

Malin Ahlberg, Markus Forsberg, and Mans Hulden. 2014. Semi-supervised learning of morphological paradigms and lexicons. In *Proceedings of the 14th Conference of the European Chapter of the Association for Computational Linguistics*, 569-578. Gothenburg, Sweden.

Adam Albright and Bruce Hayes. 2002. Modeling English past tense intuitions with minimal generalization. In *Proceedings of the 6th meeting of the ACL Special Interest Group in Computational Phonology*.

Roger Brown. 1973. *A First Language: The Early Stages*. Cambridge, MA: Harvard University Press.

Andrew Carstairs. 1987. *Allomorphy in Inflexion*. London: Croom Helm.

Courtney Cazden. 1968. The acquisition of noun and verb inflections. *Child Development* 39: 433-448.

Erwin Chan. 2006. Learning probabilistic paradigms for morphology in a latent class model. In *Proceedings of the Eighth Meeting of the ACL Special Interest Group on Computational Phonology at HLT-NAACL 2006*, 69-78. New York City.

Alexander Clark. 2003. Combining distributional and morphological information for part of speech induction. In *Proceedings of the Tenth Conference on European Chapter of the Association for Computational Linguistics* (volume 1), 59-66.

Mathias Creutz and Krista Lagus. 2005. Inducing the morphological lexicon of a natural language from unannotated text. In *Proceedings of AKRR'05, International and Interdisciplinary Conference on Adaptive Knowledge Representation and Reasoning*, 106-113.

Markus Dreyer and Jason Eisner. 2011. Discovering morphological paradigms from palin text using a dirichlet process mixture model. In *Proceedings of Empirical Methods in Natural Language Processing*, 616-627.

Greg Durrett and John DeNero. 2013. Supervised learning of complete morphological paradigms. In *Proceedings of the North American Chapter of the Association for Computational Linguistics*.

Michelle A. Fullwood and Timothy J. O'Donnell. 2013. Learning Non-concatenative Morphology. In *Proceedings of the Fourth Annual Workshop on Cognitive Modeling and Computational Linguistics* (CMCL).

John A. Goldsmith. 2001. Unsupervised learning of the morphology of a natural language. *Computational Linguistics* 27(2): 153-198.

John A. Goldsmith. 2009. Morphological analogy: Only a beginning. In James P. Blevins and Juliette Blevins (eds.), *Analogy in Grammar: Form and Acquisition*, 138-164. Oxford: Oxford University Press.

John A. Goldsmith. 2010. Segmentation and morphology. In Alexander Clark, Chris Fox, and Shalom Lappin (eds.), *Handbook of Computational Linguistics and Natural Language Processing*, 364-393. Oxford: Wiley-Blackwell.

John A. Goldsmith and Jeremy O'Brien. 2006. Learning inflectional classes. *Language Learning and Development* 2(4): 219-250.

John A. Goldsmith and Xiuli Wang. 2012. Word manifolds. University of Chicago, ms.

Harald Hammarström. 2009. Unsupervised Learning of Morphology and the Languages of the World. Ph.D. thesis, Chalmers University of Technology and University of Gothenburg.

Harald Hammarström and Lars Borin. 2011. Unsupervised learning of morphology. *Computational Linguistics* 37(2): 309-350.

Jeffrey Heinz and Regine Lai. 2013. Vowel Harmony and Subsequentiality. In Andras Kornai and Marco Kuhlmann (eds.) *Proceedings of the 13th Meeting on the Mathematics of Language (MoL 13)*, 52-63.

Jackson L. Lee. 2014. Automatic morphological alignment and clustering. Technical report TR-2014-07, Department of Computer Science, University of Chicago.

Martin Haspelmath and Andrea D. Sims. 2010. *Understanding Morphology*. London: Hodder Education, 2nd ed.

Derrick Higgins. 2002. A Multi-modular Approach to Model Selection in Statistical NLP. University of Chicago Ph.D. thesis.

Brian MacWhinney. 2000. *The CHILDES Project*. New Jersey: Lawrence Erlbaum Associates.

John J. McCarthy. 1985. Formal Problems in Semitic Phonology and Morphology. New York: Garland.

Christian Monson. 2009. ParaMor: From Paradigm Structure to Natural Language Morphology Induction. Ph.D. thesis, Carnegie Mellon University.

Gereon Müller. 2007. Notes on paradigm economy. *Morphology* 17: 1-38.

Patrick Schone and Daniel Jurafsky. 2001. Knowledge-free induction of inflectional morphologies. In *Proceedings of the second meeting of the North American Chapter of the Association for Computational Linguistics on Language Technologies*, 1-9. Association for Computational Linguistics.

Andrew Spencer. 2012. Identifying stems. *Word Structure* 5(1): 88-108.

Daniel Zeman. 2009. Using unsupervised paradigm acquisition for prefixes. In *Evaluating Systems for Multilingual and Multimodal Information Access*, 9th Workshop of the Cross-Language Evaluation Forum, CLEF 2008, Aarthus, Denmark, September 17-19, 2008, Revised Selected Papers, 983-990. Springer-Verlag, Berlin.

Computational Exploration of the Linguistic Structures of Future-Oriented Expression: Classification and Categorization

Aiming Nie[1,2], Jason Shepard[2], Jinho Choi[1], Bridget Copley[3], Phillip Wolff[2]
[1]Dept. of Computer Science, Emory University, [2]Dept. of Psychology, Emory University
[3]Structures Formelles du Language, 4CNRS / Universite Paris 8, Paris, France 30322
{anie, jason.s.shepard, jinho.choi, pwolff}@emory.edu, bridget.copley@sfl.cnrs.fr

Abstract

English, like many languages, uses a wide variety of ways to talk about the future, which makes the automatic identification of future reference a challenge. In this research we extend Latent Dirichlet allocation (LDA) for use in the identification of future-referring sentences. Building off a set of hand-designed rules, we trained a ADAGRAD classifier to be able to automatically detect sentences referring to the future. Uni-bi-trigram and syntactic rule mixed feature was found to provide the highest accuracy. Latent Dirichlet Allocation (LDA) indicated the existence of four major categories of future orientation. Lastly, the results of these analyses were found to correlate with a range of behavioral measures, offering evidence in support of the psychological reality of the categories.

1 Introduction

Early formal work on tense such as (Prior, 1967) treated tenses as logical operators; this approach, however, could not correctly account for complex tenses, and was superseded by relational accounts (Reichenbach, 1947; Hornstein, 1990; Klein, 1997). However, these frameworks too fall short to the extent that they only posit three times (corresponding to the speech time, a reference time, and a time at which an event happens (Reichenbach's S, R, and T respectively). Natural language, however, can accommodate more than three times, as in *Before yesterday, Mary had been going to go to Paris on Friday*. In a Reichenbachian system, the reference time referred to by this sentence, would be *yesterday*, but then not only is there the event time of her going to Paris, but a time before yesterday is needed for Mary's plan as well. The future orientation (that is, the future relationship between reference time and event time) of such a sentence cannot be modeled in Reichenbach's system. Such examples indicate that a analysis with greater sensitivity to linguistic structure is needed if reference to the future is to be identified and modeled.

In this paper we use the syntactic properties of a sentence to identify references to the future. We also examine how references to the future might be diagnostic of a person's psychological wellbeing. In particular, we hypothesize that references to the future reflect, in part, a person's future-orientation, that is the proportion of time a person's thoughts concern the future.

Apparently, reference to future has sparked the interests of many Psychologists. Recent researches suggest that future-oriented thinking is linked to physical and mental health, academic achievement, increased social involvement, and lower distress (Kahana et al., 2005; Aspinwall, 2005; Simons et al., 2004).

While future-oriented thought appears to play a central role in cognition, it's identification in languages such as English is not easily accomplished. As pointed out earlier, the absence of explicit and necessary morphology for the encoding of future reference often makes distinguish references to the future or present difficult to determine.

The goal of this research is to develop procedures for the automated detection of references to the future, even in the context of a mix of verbs with differ-

Proceedings of NAACL-HLT 2015 Student Research Workshop (SRW), pages 168–173,
Denver, Colorado, June 1, 2015.

ent tenses. Such procedures will allow linguists and psychologists to more effectively mine text from social media to better extract chains and causation, as well as, potentially determine a person's or group's state of wellbeing. To the best of our knowledge, this is the first time that a project of this kind has been done in English, though similar research has been conducted in Japanese (Nakajima et al., 2014).

2 Related work

Document classification has been a long researched topic. Tools and algorithms have been developed to enable people to classify pre-labeled documents. The approach in this paper is single-label text classification using ADAGRAD (Duchi et al., 2011a).

Later on, we explored Latent Dirichlet Modeling (Blei et al., 2003) on the basis of induced subtrees, which are commonly used in data mining, but not frequently seen in Natural Language Processing. Frequent Subtree Mining is a common data mining topic. Related algorithms such as TreeMiner, FreeQT have been developed to find most frequent structure in a given tree bank (Chi et al., 2005).

Similar approaches have been explored in Moschitti (2006)'s work on using subtrees as features for Support Vector Machine. We did not use his approach because were were not interested in the similarity between tree structures, but rather in the linguistic regularities implicit in the text. For this reason, we chose to use Varro algorithm developed by Martens (2010), to exhaustively generate subtrees.

3 Data

We used data collected through Amazon Mechanical Turk (MTurk). Participants were asked to write down their mind wanderings as follows:

> *Please think back to the last time you were thinking about something other than what you were currently doing. Please share with us what you were thinking about. If you found yourself thinking about many different things, please share with us as many of these things that you can remember.*

In addition to writing down their mind wanderings, participants (N = 795) also answered a series of behavioral survey questions related to anxiety, health, happiness, life and financial satisfaction. The task resulted in a total of 2007 sentences. Table 1 describes the distribution of our data.

The sentences were rated by three human raters. For each sentence, raters indicated whether the expression referred to the future and their level of confidence of their decision.

	Sentence	**Subtree**	**Token**
Future	867	164,772	11,910
Not Future	1140	196,049	15,228

Table 1: Total number of sentences, subtrees and tokens

We used the Stanford factored parser (Klein and Manning, 2002) to parse sentences into constituency grammar tree representations. Tokens were generated by a uni-bi-trigram mixed model. Subtree structures were generated using the Varro algorithm (Martens, 2010) with threshold k = 1 to include lexicons. For the future corpus, 2,529,040 subtrees were processed while for the non-future corpus 2,792,875 were processed. A subset of the subtrees were selected as *words* for the LDA analysis, as described in Martens (2009).

4 Examples

While there are many cases of grammatical future marking (i.e., *will*, *be going to*) and lexical future meaning (e.g., *plan*, *want*, *need*, *tomorrow*, *goal*, *ambition*), many of the ways people use to refer to the future do not fall into one of these two types of linguistic categories.

For example, as we have seen, it's possible to have future reference without an obvious grammatical or lexical way of referring to the future. One way of doing this is with so-called *futurate* sentences (Copley, 2009; Kaufmann, 2005), such as *Mary is going to Paris*, which can refer to a contextually-provided future time (e.g., *tomorrow*). Another way to refer to the future without grammatical or lexial means is to use a *wh*-question word with an infinitive, such as in *I'm thinking about what to eat*. Such cases will be missed by ngram approaches.

Secondly, relying purely on lexical targets will not work well when sense disambiguation is required. Modals in English can have multiple meanings (Palmer, 1986):

I was thinking about the local news because they were showing what the weather would be like.

I was thinking about my life and marriage and how much money or lack of plays a role in my obligations, and what my husband would do if I died.

Both sentences have the modal word *would*. Many cases of *would* are "sequence-of-tense" *woulds*, as in the first sentence above. That is, they should really be seen as *will* in the past; the past-tense marking inherent to *would* is functioning as a kind of tense agreement with the main clause past. The future orientation provided by *would* is future with respect to the past reference time. However, the *would* in the second sentence is not a *will* of a past reference time, but picks out a "less-vivid" future relative to the present reference time (Iatridou, 2000).

5 Classification

5.1 Syntactic structural rules

We used the constituency grammar rules generated by Wolff and Copley. Rules were generated on the basis of linguistic theory, and then later refined on the basis of analyses of the false positives and misses.

The rules were instantiated in the Tregex pattern language (Levy and Andrew, 2006), which could then be used to find matching structures in the parsed sentences. There were 39 future-related rules, 16 past-related rules, and 3 present-related rules. The rules varied from the purely syntactic to the lexical, with a number of rules containing of mix of both. Syntactic information helped to disambiguate the senses of the modal verbs. Fourteen of the future-related rules emphasized the modal verbs. Rules are released online at `https://github.com/clir/time-perception`.

5.2 Adaptive sub-gradient descent

To build statistical models, we used a stochastic adaptive subgradient algorithm called ADAGRAD that uses per-coordinate learning rates to exploit rarely seen features while remaining scalable (Duchi et al., 2011b). This is suitable for NLP tasks where rarely seen features often play an important role and training data consists of a large number of instances with high dimensional features. We use the implementation of ADAGRAD in ClearNLP (Choi, 2013) using the hinge-loss, and the default hyperparameters (learning rate: $a = 0.01$, termination criterion: $r = 0.1$).

5.3 Experiments

Our experiment consists of four parts. First, we used the Tregex-based rule discussed in section 5.1 to determine whether the sentences referred to the future. Each sentence was matched against all rules, and an odd ratio score was calculated on the basis of the equation in (1).

$$\frac{Future}{Future + Past + Present} \tag{1}$$

We used this as our baseline classifier. In the second part of the experiment, we converted the rule matches into vector: matches were coded as 1's, absences as 0's.

In the third part of the experiment, we used a more traditional uni-bi-trigram mixed model as features for ADAGRAD. The extracted number of tokens from the corpus are represented in Table 1. Finally, we mixed the ngram features with rule-based features to train the final classifier. All classifiers were trained through a 5-fold cross-validation process. In the case of the human raters, we selected the label that was selected by 2 of the 3 raters. Table 3 shows the results of our classification.

	odd-ratio	human
accuracy	70.75	87.38[1]

Table 2: Simple Rule and Human Performance

6 Categorization

6.1 Induced subtree

Three types of subtrees are generally researched in subtree mining: bottom-up subtrees, induced subtrees, and embedded subtrees. They are ranked in order from the most restrictive to the most free

[1] Due to the fact that the corpus was slowly built over a year, and confidence rating task was later added to the rating task, thus only tested over 1034 sentences.

rules	ngram	ngram + rules
75.12	77.61	83.33
71.14	81.09	78.86
75.56	83.54	83.29
74.81	79.30	82.04
74.81	80.55	84.79
74.29	80.42	82.46

Table 3: 5-fold Cross-Validation: ADAGRAD Classifier Performance in Accuracy

form. Bottom-up subtree mining does not capture the transformations of a sentence, while embedded tree mining breaks a sentence structure down into units that are often unhelpful. Given these limitations, we used induced subtree mining, as recomended in (Martens, 2009).

After the initial extraction, we combined subtrees from the future, past, and present corpora to produce 322,691 subtrees. Each subtree's weights were calculated using the frequency of the subtree appearing in the future corpus divided by total number of sentence in future corpus minus the same subtree appearing in non-future corpora divided by total number of sentences in non-future corpus.

Linguists have long argued that syntactic constructions encode meaning (Grimshaw, 1990; Levin and Hovav, 1995). We argue that by using the subtree structures to represent a sentence, the components of meaning associated with a syntactic construction can be teased apart. The components of meaning associated with these subtrees can then be inferred using procedures such as latent dirichlet allocation (LDA).

6.2 Recursive LDA

We implemented a procedure called recursive LDA in which LDA was performed iteratively within new topics. One of the obstacles of modelling data using LDA is that the number of topics must be chosen in advance. Therefore it is very necessary to understand the properties of the data being modelled and choose a number of categories appropriately. Variations and extensions of LDA should also be modelled to reflect the characteristics of the space and the categories being modelled. With this in mind, we hypothesize that the total future-oriented reference space could be divided into a small number of categories and within each semantic category, future-oriented reference relate to each other will form more specific categories. In comparison to a similar extension: hLDA (Griffiths and Tenenbaum, 2004), rLDA provides better control to researchers, and is more suitable to discover categories on well-studied problems.

To run rLDA, we selected subtrees with weights larger than 0 (N = 21,156; 6.56% of the total generated subtree structures) as our features (words) and sentences identified as referring to the future as our collections (N = 867)(documents). Specifically, LDA was run on all of the subtrees with the goal of discovering 2 topics. The solution from this analysis was then used to divide the subtrees into two groups, and LDA was subsequently run again on each set of subtrees.

6.3 Experiments

We obtained 4 topics through two recursive run with LDA. All of which have significant statistical correlations with behavioral data. Two topics on the first level are labeled as topic A and topic B.

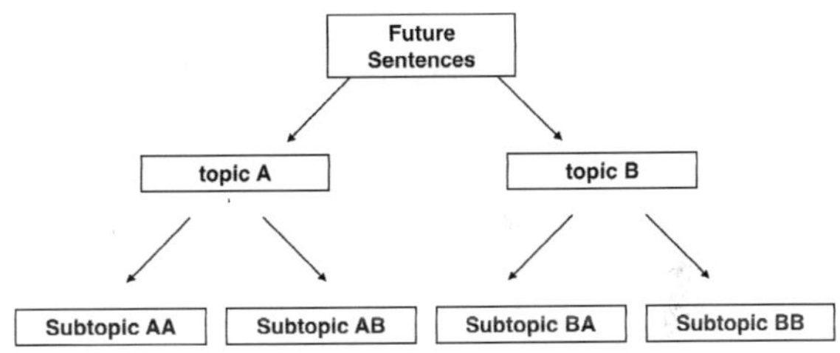

Figure 1: Recursive LDA Topic Hierarchy

The main semantic difference between A and B seemed to concern the distinction between open and fixed futures. Sentences in topic A indicate far fewer or more fixed choices, normally between just two choices. Sentences in topic B tend to include open-ended questions. Example sentences from these two sub-types are shown below:

> Topic A - Fixed future:
>
> *I was thinking that I should not be playing Hay Day and I should do my work.*
>
> *Last night I decided that I should travel to meet my aunt in Rhode Island as I haven't*

	Topic AA	Topic AB	Topic BA	Topic BB
Age	.055	.397**	-.286**	-.167
Vividness	.157	.199	-.266*	-.100
Anxiety-State	.105	-.383**	.260	-.041
Anxiety-Trait	.050	-.342*	.247	-.008
Financial Satisfaction	.114	.326*	-.364**	-.032
Control over Life	.107	-.299**	.149	.039

Table 4: Correlation Table Between LDA Topics and Behavioral Data. Due to the iterative design of our survey, we did not have a complete behavioral question section till the end of our data collection. 146 people accounting for 18.36% of the total sample participated in the behavioral question research, and a subset of 81 people had future sentences in their response. Only content items that correlated with at least one category reported. $*p < .01$, $**p < .002$

seen her in a long time.

Topic B - Open Future:

At the same time I was thinking about what I was going to have for breakfast.

I was thinking about what I would cook for dinner tonight.

From the second level, more fine-grained topics emerged. Descending from topic A (fixed future), the two sub-types seemed to differ with respect to level of certainty: Topic AA tended to involve sentences conveying the notion of uncertainty, while Topic AB tended to involve sentences implying certainty. From Table 4 People, who construct future sentences with high certainty, have less control over life, scored lower on the trait and state anxiety inventory (Spielberger, 2010).

Topic AA - Uncertainty:

I was thinking about a trip that I may take at the end of the summer.

I was wondering if we would end up together and thinking about the fact that something that can seem so certain now may not be in the future.

Topic AB - Certainty:

I was making my wife 's lunch to take to work , and I was thinking about playing golf this weekend .

I am getting married in April , and there is a bunch of stuff left to be done .

Topic B appeared to be mostly about an open future. Its sub-types seemed to differ with respect to the notion of constraint: Topic BA seemed to consist of sentences about an unconstrained future while Topic BB seemed to concern sentences implying a constrained future. Our categorization matches with behavioral data in Table 4. People using unconstrained future sentence constructs rated their future as less vivid. They also were younger and had lower financial satisfaction.

Topic BA - Unconstrained:

I was thinking about what I should do for the rest of the day.

I was thinking about what I should animate for my next cartoon.

Topic BB - Constrained:

Two hours ago I was debating what I should have for lunch and what I should watch while I was eating.

I was thinking about a girl I would like to meet , what we would do , and how long we would do it.

7 Conclusion

In this research we leveraged recent developments in linguistic theory (Iatridou, 2000; Condoravdi, 2002; Copley and Martin, 2014) to build an automated system capable of discovering different ways of expressing the future. Specifically, we trained a ADAGRAD classifier to a relatively high level of accuracy and examined the number of topics associated with references to the future through the use of recursive

LDA. Finally, we established the psychological reality of our topics via comparisons to behavioral measures.

8 Acknowledgements

This research was supported by a grant from the U Penn / John Templeton Foundation to B. Copley and P. Wolff.

References

L. G. Aspinwall. 2005. The psychology of future-oriented thinking: From achievement to proactive coping, adaptation, and aging. *Motivation and Emotion*, 29(4):203–235.

David M Blei, Andrew Y Ng, and Michael I Jordan. 2003. Latent dirichlet allocation. *the Journal of machine Learning research*, 3:993–1022.

Yun Chi, Richard R Muntz, Siegfried Nijssen, and Joost N Kok. 2005. Frequent subtree mining-an overview. *Fundamenta Informaticae*, 66(1):161–198.

Jinho D Choi. 2013. Clearnlp.

Cleo Condoravdi. 2002. Temporal interpretation of modals. In David Beaver, Stefan Kaufmann, Brady Clark, and Luis Casillas, editors, *Stanford Papers on Semantics*. CSLI Publications, Palo Alto.

Bridget Copley and Fabienne Martin, editors. 2014. *Causation in Grammatical Structures*. Oxford University Press.

Bridget Copley. 2009. *The semantics of the future*. Routledge.

John Duchi, Elad Hazan, and Yoram Singer. 2011a. Adaptive subgradient methods for online learning and stochastic optimization. *The Journal of Machine Learning Research*, 12:2121–2159.

John Duchi, Elad Hazan, and Yoram Singer. 2011b. Adaptive Subgradient Methods for Online Learning and Stochastic Optimization. *The Journal of Machine Learning Research*, 12(39):2121–2159.

DMBTL Griffiths and MIJJB Tenenbaum. 2004. Hierarchical topic models and the nested chinese restaurant process. *Advances in neural information processing systems*, 16:17.

Jane Grimshaw. 1990. *Argument structure*. the MIT Press.

Norbert Hornstein. 1990. *As Time Goes By*. MIT Press.

Sabine Iatridou. 2000. The grammatical ingredients of counterfactuality. *LI*, 31:231–270.

E. Kahana, B. Kahana, and J. Zhang. 2005. Motivational antecedents of preventive proactivity in late life: Linking future orientation and exercise. *Motivation and emotion*, 29(4):438–459.

Stefan Kaufmann. 2005. Conditional truth and future reference. *Journal of Semantics*, 22(3):231–280, August.

Dan Klein and Christopher D Manning. 2002. Fast exact inference with a factored model for natural language parsing. In *Advances in neural information processing systems*, pages 3–10.

Wolfgang Klein. 1997. *Time in Language*. Routledge, New York.

Beth Levin and Malka Rappaport Hovav. 1995. *Unaccusativity: At the syntax-lexical semantics interface*, volume 26. MIT press.

Roger Levy and Galen Andrew. 2006. Tregex and tsurgeon: tools for querying and manipulating tree data structures. In *Proceedings of the fifth international conference on Language Resources and Evaluation*, pages 2231–2234. Citeseer.

Scott Martens. 2009. Quantitative analysis of treebanks using frequent subtree mining methods. In *Proceedings of the 2009 Workshop on Graph-based Methods for Natural Language Processing*, pages 84–92. Association for Computational Linguistics.

Scott Martens. 2010. Varro: an algorithm and toolkit for regular structure discovery in treebanks. In *Proceedings of the 23rd International Conference on Computational Linguistics: Posters*, pages 810–818. Association for Computational Linguistics.

Alessandro Moschitti. 2006. Making tree kernels practical for natural language learning. In *EACL*, volume 113, page 24.

Yoko Nakajima, Michal Ptaszynski, Hirotoshi Honma, and Fumito Masui. 2014. Investigation of future reference expressions in trend information. In *Proceedings of the 2014 AAAI Spring Symposium Series,Big data becomes personal: knowledge into meaning–For better health, wellness and well-being*, pages 31–38.

F. R. Palmer. 1986. *Mood and modality*. Cambridge University Press, Cambridge.

Arthur Prior. 1967. *Past, Present, and Future*. Oxford University Press, Oxford.

Hans Reichenbach. 1947. *The tenses of verbs*. na.

J. Simons, M. Vansteenkiste, W. Lens, and M. Lacante. 2004. Placing motivation and future time perspective theory in a temporal perspective. *Educational Psychology Review*, 16(2):121–139.

Charles D Spielberger. 2010. *State-Trait Anxiety Inventory*. Wiley Online Library.

Author Index